NATIONAL
GEOGRAPHIC

ALMANAC
2021

Photographer Marc Stone hangs in a hammock over alligator-infested waters in central Florida.

NATIONAL GEOGRAPHIC

ALMANAC

2021

| TREN
| BIG IDEA
| PHOTOS, MAPS, F.

NATIONAL GEOGRAPHIC
WASHINGTON, D.C.

CONTENTS

FOREWORD 8

By Susan Tyler Hitchcock

TRENDING 2021 10

QUIZMASTER

Biodiversity
The Ways of Water
Human Migration
Infectious Agents
Space Telescope

EXPLORATION & ADVENTURE 34

QUIZMASTER

EXPLORATION

Exploration Time Line
Nat Geo Explorers
Kris Tompkins, Conservationist
Diving Antarctica
Get Out Into Your Country
Best of @NatGeo: Adventure

EXTREMES

A History of Climbing Everest
Earth's Extremes
Underwater Museum
The Speed of Innovation
Miho Aida, Activist
Extreme Abilities

CLASSIC TRAVEL

Transportation Time Line
Iconic Destinations
Savor the World's Best Cities
A Taste of Italy
Greatest Expeditions
U.S. National Parks
Australia's Barrier Reef

TRAVEL TRENDS

Best of @NatGeo: Travel
Galway Makes Waves
Into India's Wild
Marvels of the Maya
Off the Beaten Path
Tokyo
Iceland's Hot Springs

FURTHER

Giant clams cluster at Kingman Reef.

Camels walk amid sand dunes in the Arabian Desert.

Cape ground squirrel in Namibia's Kalahari Desert

THIS PLANET & BEYOND 92

QUIZMASTER
PLANET EARTH
Earth Science Time Line
Clarifying Climate
Reading the Clouds
Combating a Blaze
Hurricanes
Volcanoes
Lithium
Best of @NatGeo: Weather
EARTH, SEA & SKY
Minerals Revealed
Enric Sala, Marine Ecologist
Volcanic Islands
Winter Sky
Summer Sky
Shapes in the Stars
Best of @NatGeo: Aerial Views
THE SOLAR SYSTEM
Our Neighborhood
Dwarf Planets
Earth's Moon
On to Mars
Asteroids
Moons Beyond Ours
Space Science Time Line

THE UNIVERSE & BEYOND
Birth of the Universe
Jennifer W. Lopez, Data Scientist
When a Star Explodes
Space Radiation
Exoplanets: Is There Life?
Dark Matter
FURTHER

LIFE ON EARTH 154

QUIZMASTER
ALL LIVING THINGS
Life Science Time Line
Domains of Life
Fossils: Past Lives
Nodosaur
Plants Up Close
Wild Flowers
Talking Trees
OF THE EARTH
Best of @NatGeo: Life on Land
Rae Wynn-Grant, Ecologist
Telltale Tracks
Domestication Transformation
Meet the Quoll
Primate Family Tree
Jane Goodall, Primatologist

Callanish Stones on Scotland's Isle of Lewis

THE SCIENCE OF US 218

QUIZMASTER
ORIGINS
   Human Evolution Time Line
   Meet Our Human Ancestors
   Our New Ancestor
   Our Deep Ancestry
   Neanderthals Join the Family
THE HUMAN JOURNEY
   Intangible Culture
   Play Carnival
   Best of @NatGeo: World Traditions
   Disappearing Languages
   Wade Davis, Anthropologist
   Urbanization
   Urban Nature
   Religion Around the World
   Religious Holidays
   Best of @NatGeo: People
BODY & BRAIN
   The Science of Sleep
   Eating Insects
   Internal Clock
   Understanding Gender
   Inside Your Brain
   Steve Ramirez, Neuroscientist
HEALTH & MEDICINE
   Medicine Time Line
   Inside Cheese
   Antibiotic Resistance
   The Story of a Face
   Psychobiome
   Herbs & Spices for Health
   Mindfulness
FURTHER

OF THE SEA
   Best of @NatGeo: Sea Life
   Whales
   Spineless Swimmers
   Sea Shells
   The Amazing Octopus
OF THE SKY
   Best of @NatGeo: Life on the Wing
   Backyard Birds
   Hummingbirds: Winged Wonders
   Parrots
   J. Drew Lanham, Ornithologist
   Whose Caterpillar?
   Plight of the Honeybee
CARE FOR ALL LIFE
   Conservation Time Line
   Photo Ark
   Plastic in Our World
FURTHER

A boat traces the curves of Utah's Reflection Canyon.

YESTERDAY TO TOMORROW 280

QUIZMASTER
WORLD HISTORY
Prehistory to 1600 Time Line
Tales Older Than the Hills
Semiramis, Queen of Babylon
Mapping History
1600 to Recent Past Time Line
A History of Democracy
Pearce Paul Creasman, Archaeologist
Best of @NatGeo: Historic Places
Terra-Cotta Warriors
Genome Clues in Egypt
Innovations Time Line
Clotilda's Painful Past
Amelia Earhart, Aviator
U.S. HISTORY
United States Time Line
Woman Suffrage
Phoenix at Ground Zero
Stars & Stripes Through the Centuries
Flags of the United States
Territories of the United States
FURTHER

OUR WORLD 326

QUIZMASTER
WORLD VIEWS
Our Physical World
Our Political World
Best of @NatGeo: Landscapes
CONTINENTS & OCEANS
The Continents
North America
South America
Europe
Asia
Africa
Australia & Oceania
Antarctica
Oceans of the World
Atlantic Ocean
Pacific Ocean
Indian Ocean
Arctic Ocean
Ocean Around Antarctica
Best of @NatGeo: Oceanscapes
COUNTRIES OF THE WORLD
Flags of the World
United Nations
More of the World
THE FUTURE
Future of the Planet
Future of the Wild on Earth
Future of Humans on Earth
FURTHER

CREDITS 382
INDEX 386

Horsfield's tarsier, an Indonesian primate

OPENING UP
TO THE WORLD

Like a sunflower field in bloom, our minds open as we gain new knowledge and experience.

More than a century ago, National Geographic's founding father Alexander Graham Bell defined geography broadly as "The world and all that is in it." It's a phrase that could describe this fact-filled, colorful, and far-reaching almanac as well. From the depths of the ocean under Antarctica to the heights of Patagonia and Everest; from volcanoes that have shaped islands to the moons of planets billions of miles away; from bacteria to butterflies, dinosaurs to whales; from our hominid ancestors to the cities of tomorrow: Roam through these pages and you will travel the world—and beyond, as far as our knowledge and imagination can take us.

Each year, as we create the National Geographic Almanac, the editorial team scans the horizon for the big ideas of the coming year. We've hit on five trends sure to be in the news in 2021. Every warning about species extinction can be better understood against the backdrop of **biodiversity** and why it matters to us and to the planet. We learn **the ways of water** in today's changing climate, paradoxically overwhelming—torrential rains, floods, sea level rise—and dwindling—droughts and freshwater crises—and show innovative responses to these planet-wide problems.

Fascinating maps and data tell us how **human migration** has influenced history and shapes the future. We watch with respect and concern as laboratory scientists and public health researchers seek to understand and control the **coronavirus**. Finally, we look to the revolutionary **James Webb Space Telescope,** soon to gather signals from far beyond our solar system, far back in time, telling us more about the birth of stars, galaxies, and the universe itself.

As we explore these big new ideas, we recognize people past, present, and future whom we call "geniuses": women and men who embody the spirit of curiosity and care for the planet at the heart of National Geographic's mission. Some are familiar names, such as Jane Goodall and Amelia Earhart. Others may be new to you—athlete and women's advocate Miho Aida or ornithologist Drew Lanham, for example. All push boundaries, driven by the passion to know more and share their knowledge. We also have many unnamed geniuses to thank for the treasures you will find on these pages: explorers and scientists, writers and editors, designers and illustrators, cartographers and photographers, all of whose contributions make every page of this book an adventure.

This is our third annual National Geographic Almanac, and as the senior editor of the project, I can tell you that we work hard and have a lot of fun as we pull it all together. I think you'll have fun, too, using the Quizmaster pages that begin each chapter as jumping-off points for the ideas and information within. Some may call this trivia, but it's also valuable knowledge, an essential step toward caring more deeply.

Every chapter ends with pages titled "Further," National Geographic's motto, expressing the momentum we hope to fuel toward a better world. Here we invite you to step off the page and into a future full of promise and new ideas. While we cannot turn away from today's crises and challenges, intelligence and imagination will carry us further: deep into the ocean, far out into the heavens, and all around this planet we cherish, honoring one another, all living things, and planet Earth, the home we all share.

TRENDING 2021

BIODIVERSITY | **THE WAYS OF WATER** | **HUMAN MIGRATION**

Meltwater gushes from an ice cap on the island of Nordaustlandet, located in Norway's Svalbard archipelago.

INFECTIOUS AGENTS | SPACE TELESCOPE

QUIZ MASTER

Tomorrow's Ideas Today Today In the news and on your mind, here are topics we predict will be foremost in our conversations this year. Challenges or accomplishments, threats or triumphs? Knowledge helps us shape the future.

—SUSAN TYLER HITCHCOCK, *Nat Geo Quizmaster*

WHAT HEAVENLY BODY WILL THE **JAMES WEBB SPACE** TELESCOPE **ORBIT?**
p30

p27
FROM **WHAT TYPE OF ANIMAL** DO SCIENTISTS BELIEVE **THE SARS VIRUS** ORIGINATED?

ABOUT **HOW MANY** NEW **SPECIES ARE** DISCOVERED **EVERY YEAR?**

p33
WHAT IS THE DIAMETER OF **THE MIRROR** INSTALLED **ON THE JAMES WEBB SPACE** TELESCOPE?

p17
NAME THE FIVE COUNTRIES WHERE THE MOST **REFUGEES CAME** FROM IN **2018.**
p25

WHO PROPOSED A SYSTEM FOR **MAKING SEAWATER** DRINKABLE IN THE **1600S?**

p20

p20
WHAT IS THE LONGEST RIVER IN **ASIA?**

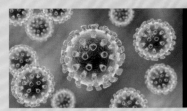

IN WHAT YEAR DID RESEARCHERS BEGIN TO USE THE WORD "CORONAVIRUS": **1968, 1998, OR 2018?**

p26

ABOUT HOW MANY **INCHES** HAS THE **WORLD'S** SEA LEVEL **RISEN** SINCE **1900?**

p21

WHAT YEAR IS THE **JAMES WEBB** SPACE TELESCOPE **EXPECTED TO BE** LAUNCHED?

p30

WHAT TYPE OF **INFECTIOUS DISEASE** IS **RINGWORM:** A **VIRUS,** A **PARASITE,** OR A **FUNGUS?**

p29

WHERE DO MORE **PEOPLE** IN THE **WORLD** LIVE: IN THE **CITY** OR IN THE **COUNTRY?**

p22

CHINA'S YANGTZE FLOWS THROUGH HOW MANY PROVINCES?

p20

OF THESE COUNTRIES, WHICH ONE WAS AMONG THE TOP FIVE OFFERING ASYLUM TO REFUGEES IN THE YEAR 2018: MEXICO, THE UNITED STATES, OR TURKEY?

p24

BOOSTING
BIODIVERSITY

ALL CREATURES GREAT & SMALL

Bounded by the Andes Mountains to the east and the Pacific Ocean to the west, the Chocó-Darién forests are a lush green landscape, home to jaguars, macaws, and spider monkeys. They are part of the Tumbes-Chocó-Magdalena region, one of the planet's 36 biodiversity hot spots: fragile locales that are rich in species yet facing an uncertain future. From microscopic bacteria to flowering plants to apex predators, biodiversity is a key driver of any ecosystem's health—and a vital element in the health of the planet. Protecting biodiversity is in our best interests: Healthy and diverse ecosystems clean the air, protect freshwater, stabilize climate, provide vital resources—and bring us joy. To preserve the biodiversity of the planet is, in short, to sustain the life of all species, including our own.

A jaguar on the hunt trips a camera trap in Ecuador's Yasuni National Park—an ecologically and culturally rich area at risk because of oil demand.

BIODIVERSITY HOT SPOTS MAKE UP 2.4% OF EARTH'S LAND SURFACE, BUT SUPPORT NEARLY 43% OF BIRD, MAMMAL, REPTILE, AND AMPHIBIAN SPECIES AS ENDEMICS.

VARIETIES OF LIFE

HONORING THE PLANTS & ANIMALS THAT SHARE THIS PLANET

Madagascar's ring-tailed lemur is on the IUCN Red List.

THE RED LIST

ASSESSING ENDANGERED SPECIES

The International Union for Conservation of Nature's (IUCN) Red List of Threatened Species stands as an indicator of the world's biodiversity. Pooling observations over decades, scientists assess species according to population size, habitat, ecology, and threats, and then categorize them on a scale from "least concern" to "extinct."

Since 1964, the IUCN has assessed more than 100,000 species, with thousands more evaluated every year. Governments and conservation groups use the Red List to inform further research, policy changes, and actions needed to preserve natural resources.

PROTECTING DIVERSITY

COUNTRIES PRACTICE CONSERVATION

Biodiversity is a shared human concern, and the United Nations Convention on Biological Diversity works with countries to fight extinction. These protections are especially important for a country like the Philippines, where a variety of ecosystems support many endemic species—species found only there. Building on a 1997 action plan, the Philippines has increased forest cover, expanded protected park lands, and launched initiatives to protect watersheds and coastlines—all measures intended to protect the country's biodiversity. At the same time, a vigorous campaign against wildlife trafficking protects many species—pangolins, hawksbill turtles, cockatoos and parrots, orchids and pitcher plants, for example—from leaving the country and entering the international wildlife market.

Chocolate Hills, protected area in the Philippines

Trans-Canada Highway wildlife crossing

MORE THAN 28,000 SPECIES ARE NOW THREATENED WITH EXTINCTION— THAT'S 40% OF ALL AMPHIBIAN SPECIES, 25% OF ALL MAMMAL SPECIES, AND 33% OF REEF-BUILDING CORAL SPECIES.

EVER NEW SPECIES

NEW BUDS ON THE TREE OF LIFE

Estimates of how many species exist on Earth vary wildly—between 3 million and a trillion! Of those, some 2.3 million have been scientifically logged so far. Each year, some 14,000 new plants and animals are added to that list. Taxonomists distinguish a new species through details of anatomy, physiology, behavior, genetics, and evolution.

Gathering that information can take decades. For instance, it took until 2019 to collect samples of a possible new species of orca that was first recorded in 1955. And it will be more time yet while scientists do the DNA analysis, measurements, and observations required to make a formal argument for distinguishing this orca from others.

WILD CROSSINGS

SAFER ROADS FOR ANIMALS & PEOPLE

We humans build roads through areas that were once vast wildernesses, dividing up habitats and introducing threats to native wildlife: fast-moving vehicles, engine exhaust, and sound pollution. One way we are reducing these threats is through wildlife crossings—bridges and tunnels built for animals, allowing them to cross roads and highways without encountering traffic.

In Canada's Banff National Park, six overpasses and 38 underpasses make it easier for animals to coexist with the busy Trans-Canada Highway. Large animals with wide ranges such as cougars, black bears, and moose tend to be early adopters of these crossings, creating paths that other animals have learned to follow. In just one two-mile (3.2 km) stretch, the average annual number of wildlife-vehicle crashes fell from 12 to 2.5.

Newfound katydid species in Borneo

THE WAYS
OF WATER

RECKONING WITH THE RISING TIDE

In our warming world, some locales struggle with the strain of drought while others are drowning. In 2019, parts of the United States spent the first months of the year underwater as they dealt with record-breaking floods and rainfall—and scientists project that heavy rainfall events will continue to increase as global temperature rises. Warmer temperatures worldwide are increasing the rate at which snowpack and glaciers melt, and a warmer atmosphere is capable of holding—and dropping—more water.

Floodwater from the Mississippi River engulfs a home on June 1, 2019, in West Alton, Missouri.

IN ONE LOUISIANA TOWN, THE MISSISSIPPI RIVER REMAINED ABOVE FLOOD LEVELS FOR 214 DAYS STRAIGHT FROM LATE DECEMBER 2018 TO LATE JULY 2019.

NARY A DROP
TO DRINK

RETHINKING OUR WATER RESOURCES

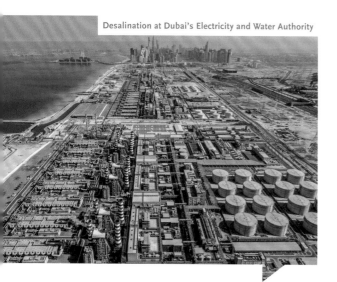

Desalination at Dubai's Electricity and Water Authority

DRINK SEAWATER

THE DESALINATION SOLUTION

In 1627, Sir Francis Bacon theorized that by filtering seawater through sand, it could be turned into drinkable water. Though that system did not work, technology has recently made desalination—removing the salt from saltwater—a reality.

In some parts of the world, freshwater is scarce, but saltwater is abundant. For these regions, desalination offers a solution to drinking water shortages. Most modern plants use reverse osmosis technology, pressing water through semipermeable membranes, but these systems are expensive, energy-intensive, and wasteful. The search is on to make desalination more sustainable and available to those who need it the most.

CHINA'S RIVER

TRACKING POLLUTION TO ITS SOURCE

China's Yangtze is Asia's longest river and one of the world's most polluted. It flows through 10 provinces, touching the lives of some 400 million people. Determined to help people understand the safety of their water—and hold polluters accountable—Chinese environmentalist Ma Jun founded the Institute of Public and Environmental Affairs (IPE) in 2006.

IPE was responsible for China's first public database of water pollution information. IPE researchers worked with the government to share data on pollutants and created an app that allows users to check the air and water quality all over China and report issues as they see them. IPE has also helped more than 8,000 factories resolve wastewater issues so far, and more are making changes to clean up their acts every day.

China's Mekong River

A polar bear and cub peer out from an iceberg.

NEARLY ONE-THIRD OF THE MUNICIPAL WATER PROVIDED IN MELBOURNE, AUSTRALIA, IS DESALINATED— SEAWATER MADE DRINKABLE.

SAVE THE CURRENTS

THE OCEAN'S ROLE AS REGULATOR

Ocean currents cool, warm, and water the planet's terrestrial surfaces—and transfer heat from the Equator to the poles; it's called thermohaline ("heat" + "salt") circulation. Warm, salty water flows from the tropics north, losing heat as it goes. The colder, saltier, denser water sinks deep and flows back south, eventually mixing with warmer water and rising back to the surface.

A warming Arctic delivers long-frozen freshwater into the system, reducing the salt content of seawater. Too much change in ocean temperature and salinity could disrupt the North Atlantic thermohaline circulation, causing drastic climate changes in time spans as short as a decade—a disturbing, but thankfully still remote, possibility.

A WORD FROM

Cleaner Water in China The challenges are big, but we've seen a historic progress in China in terms of enforcement and especially transparency. There's an increasing need for us to try to look for more innovative solutions that can help balance growth and protection. By leveling the playing field, we hope that we can have the market reward those who want to be responsible.

—MA JUN, *environmentalist*

SEA LEVEL RISE

CAN YOU TASTE IT?

We use the concept of sea level as a constant in our world: Elevations are measured in feet, meters, or miles above sea level. But that constant isn't so constant anymore: Our oceans meet land 7 to 8 inches (18 to 20 cm) higher than they did in 1900, and sea level may rise 23 inches (58 cm) in the next 100 years.

Coastline communities can see the change, but if the trend continues, they may taste the change as well. According to recent United Nations statistics, nearly 2.4 billion people—40 percent of the world—live 60 miles (97 km) or less from a coast. Depending on the character of the soil along a given coastline, rising seawater could penetrate the water table and turn drinking water brackish.

Bangladeshi villagers fishing in a flooded rice field

PERPETUAL
MOTION

HUMAN MIGRATION HAS ALWAYS SHAPED OUR WORLD

From our earliest ancestors moving out of Africa to modern immigration and refugee escape, our history has been a story of movement. Today, more than a billion people are on the move within or between countries, many by choice but others forcibly displaced. The factors that drive human migration—labor markets, economics, visa policies, war and conflict, climate and agricultural conditions—are constantly fluctuating, shaping human pathways. Right now, much of this movement is into cities. In 2014, the world reached a tipping point, with more than half of all people living in cities. The UN estimates that figure will reach 68 percent by 2050.

Refugees crowded into a boat north of Libya were rescued by the Italian navy thanks to its "Mare Nostrum" campaign, no longer in operation.

IN 2017, MORE THAN 60% OF PEOPLE FORCED TO MIGRATE WITHIN THEIR OWN COUNTRIES DID SO AS A RESULT OF NATURAL DISASTERS.

FINDING HOME

MAPPING THE IMPACT OF IMMIGRATION WORLDWIDE

Today, some 258 million international migrants have moved from their homelands to other locales. Of those, 25.9 million are considered refugees, fleeing untenable conditions in their homelands. In 2018, an estimated 13.6 million fled due to conflict or persecution.

In 2018, asylum-seekers submitted 1.7 million new claims. The top recipients of those claims were:

1. United States (254,300)
2. Peru (192,500)
3. Germany (161,900)
4. France (114,500)
5. Turkey (83,800)

In 2018, the top countries offering asylum to refugees were:

1. Turkey (3.7 million)
2. Pakistan (1.4 million)
3. Uganda (1.2 million)
4. Sudan (1.1 million)
5. Germany (1.1 million)

Migrant Population
(percent of total population)
- More than 25
- 15.1–25
- 5.5–15
- 2.5–5.4
- 1–2.4
- Less than 1
- No Data

NORTH AMERICA

SOUTH AMERICA

IN 2019, 70.8 MILLION PEOPLE WERE FORCIBLY DISPLACED FROM THEIR HOMELANDS, MORE THAN HALF OF THEM UNDER THE AGE OF 18.

In 2018, more than two-thirds of refugees worldwide came from just five countries:

1. Syria (Syrian Arab Republic) (6.7 million)
2. Afghanistan (2.7 million)
3. South Sudan (2.3 million)
4. Myanmar (1.1 million)
5. Somalia (0.9 million)

EUROPE

ASIA

AFRICA

AUSTRALIA

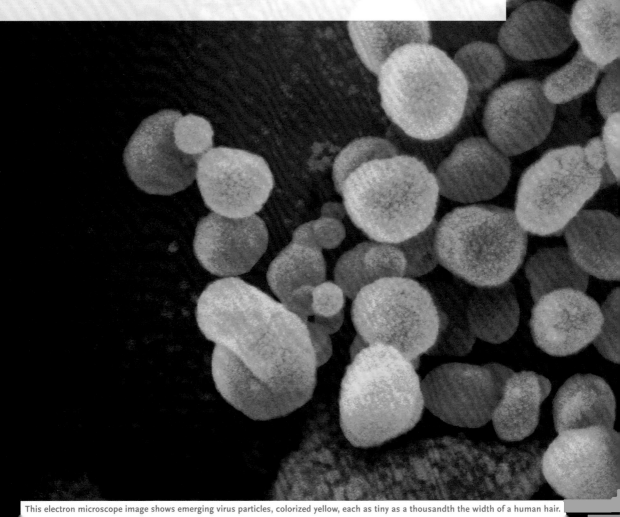

CORONAVIRUS
DISEASE

PLAGUE OF THE 21ST CENTURY

The word "coronavirus" originated in 1968 when researchers recognized that a large family of viruses, viewed with an electron microscope, looked like spheres encircled by crown-like projections, like coronas around the sun. Some coronaviruses cause minor illnesses, such as the common cold, but others prove to have far more devastating impacts—particularly Middle East respiratory syndrome (MERS-CoV), severe acute respiratory syndrome (SARS-CoV), and now coronavirus disease (COVID-19), discovered in 2019.

This electron microscope image shows emerging virus particles, colorized yellow, each as tiny as a thousandth the width of a human hair.

CORONAVIRUSES ARE ZOONOTIC: THEY SPILL OVER FROM ANIMALS TO HUMANS. SARS LIKELY ORIGINATED IN A SPECIES OF BAT, AS DETERMINED BY COMPARING THE GENETICS OF THE ANIMALBORNE AND HUMANBORNE VIRUSES.

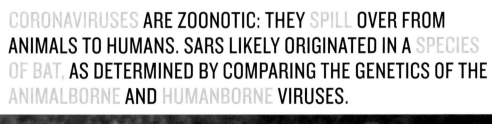

DISTINCTIVE SHAPE

Each coronavirus virion, or viral unit, is covered with club-shaped projections called peplomers, shown in this CDC illustration, which attach to the cells of the host during infection. Researchers seek knowledge by culturing viruses in the lab, using specimens from patients who have contracted the COVID-19 disease. Their findings, combined with public health data, help us understand this and other viral onslaughts.

INFECTIOUS AGENTS

HOW THEY MAKE US SICK

There are many types of infectious agents that pose serious health risks to humans, causing a variety of diseases affecting various parts of the body. They can enter the body through the mouth, nose, eyes, or in some cases through bites or wounds. They can be transmitted through direct contact, ingestion, via the air, or via a vector, like a tick or mosquito. The five main types of infectious agents are bacteria, protozoa, viruses, parasitic worms, and fungi.

BACTERIA

Bacteria are unicellular and prokaryotic organisms— that is, cells that lack nuclei. They exist all over the planet, and many are benign or beneficial.

How they infect: Bacteria enter the body through a wound, ingestion, or inhalation. Harmful bacteria can invade cells, damage tissues, and produce toxins. An imbalance of bacteria already present in the body can lead to illness as well.

Examples: Pneumonia, meningitis, food poisoning

Prevention & treatment: Improved sanitation can fend off bacterial infection. Antibiotics are typically used as treatment.

PROTOZOA

Protozoa are single-celled, animal-like organisms, but, unlike bacteria, they are eukaryotic—each cell has a nucleus and organelles enclosed in a membrane.

How they infect: Protozoa enter the body through ingestion, sexual transmission, or introduction by insects. They can infect the digestive tract, blood, and other parts of the body, depriving it of nutrients.

Examples: Malaria, giardia, toxoplasmosis

Prevention & treatment: Improved hygiene and avoiding contamination through direct contact fends off these infections. Some can be treated with medication.

VIRUSES

Viruses are extremely small bits of living tissue made up of an outer protein shell containing DNA or RNA and sometimes lipids, or fatty molecules. They cannot reproduce on their own but use the host's cellular resources to replicate and infect other cells.

How they infect: Different viruses enter the body in different ways: through mucous membranes, sexual transmission, or insect vectors, for example.

Examples: Common cold, influenza, measles, herpes, COVID-19

Prevention & treatment: Sanitation, hygiene, and avoidance of infected people and areas help prevent viral transmission. Prescription antivirals can sometimes reduce symptoms and severity. Vaccines are synthesized to combat specific viruses.

PARASITIC WORMS

Parasitic worms are multicellular animals, in adult form usually visible to the naked eye, capable at various life stages—from egg, to larva, to adult—of entering the human body and affecting health.

How they infect: Humans can be infected with worms, including eggs or larvae, through contaminated food or soil or unhygienic conditions. When parasites latch onto host tissues, they can steal nutrients or cause intestinal blockage, nausea, vomiting, or diarrhea.

Examples: Tapeworms, hookworms, pinworms

Prevention & treatment: Hygiene and sanitation help; washing produce, thoroughly cooking meat, and being vigilant about drinking water sources are important. Deworming medications are available, prescribed based on identification of the invading species.

FUNGI

Fungi are multicellular, eukaryotic organisms; this kingdom includes not only familiar mushrooms but also yeasts, molds, and mildews.

How they infect: Some fungi reproduce by spores, which can infect humans when they land on the skin or are inhaled. Moist environments especially support them.

Examples: Athlete's foot, jock itch, yeast infections, ringworm

Prevention & treatment: Fungal infections are best prevented by avoiding contact with an infected person or animal, minimizing contact with fungus in the environment, and maintaining good hygiene, especially keeping the skin clean and dry. Over-the-counter treatments are readily available.

GAZING OUT
EVEN FARTHER

THE JAMES WEBB, NEXT-GENERATION TELESCOPE

After more than two decades of development, the James Webb Space Telescope (JWST) is set to launch in 2021. As successor to the Hubble Space Telescope, it will probe even deeper. Unlike Hubble, which orbits Earth, JWST will orbit the sun along with Earth, at the same time revolving around L2, a point a million miles from Earth. Once it reaches its permanent home in space—a journey that will take about a month—JWST will begin collecting infrared signals from very distant objects, data that will enhance our knowledge about the formation of the universe, from the earliest appearance of light to the birth of galaxies, stars, and planetary systems.

A full-scale model of the James Webb Space Telescope—long as a tennis court and four stories tall—glows against the skyline of Austin, Texas.

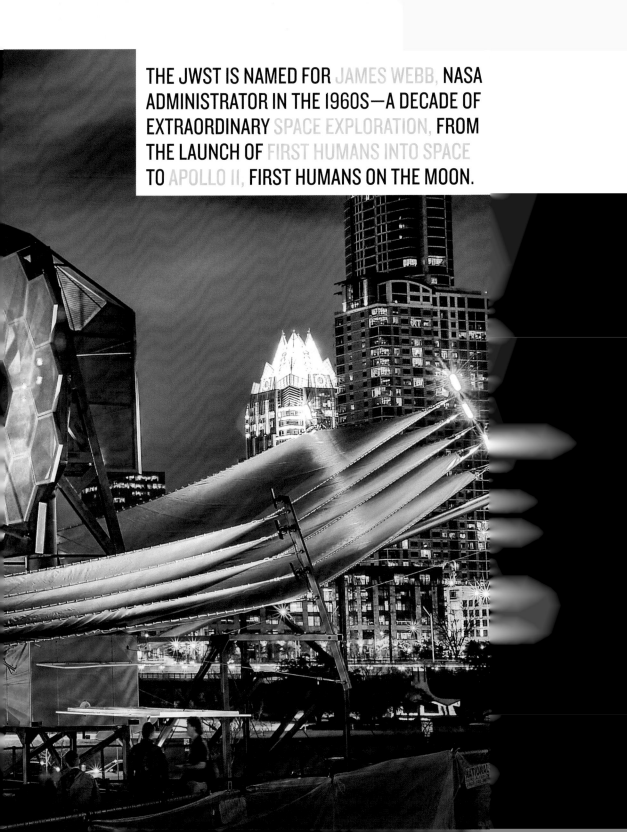

THE JWST IS NAMED FOR JAMES WEBB, NASA ADMINISTRATOR IN THE 1960S—A DECADE OF EXTRAORDINARY SPACE EXPLORATION, FROM THE LAUNCH OF FIRST HUMANS INTO SPACE TO APOLLO 11, FIRST HUMANS ON THE MOON.

HOW THE JAMES WEBB
TELESCOPE WORKS

VIEWING OUTER SPACE A NEW & DIFFERENT WAY

The Andromeda galaxy as seen by Hubble (left) and James Webb

MICROSHUTTERS

WINDOWS INTO THE UNKNOWN

It took more than six years to develop the microshutters on the JWST's Near InfraRed Spectrograph (NIRSpec). These miniscule windows are about the size of a few human hairs bundled together and need to be capable of opening and closing repeatedly at temperatures near absolute zero.

There are some 250,000 of them on the telescope, designed to open and shut in patterns that allow NIRSpec to simultaneously observe up to 100 deep-space objects. Even with thousands of these microshutters and the Webb's giant mirror, it will take hundreds of hours to collect the faint light of one of these systems.

INFRARED SPECTRUM

A NEW WAY OF SEEING

While the Hubble Space Telescope observed objects in the visible and ultraviolet spectrum, Webb's instruments rely on infrared light. Light's wavelength becomes longer as it travels, shifting toward red and ultimately infrared, which is essentially heat. If you put your hand in a box, a standard camera sees the box, while an infrared camera can "see past" the box by picking up on the heat and take a picture of your hand.

Therefore, with the Webb, we will be able to see inside nebulas and galaxies—the gorgeous, colorful swirls that the Hubble has shown us—and capture light from stars so far away they are only visible on the infrared spectrum.

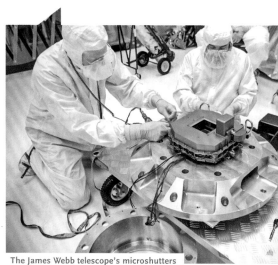

The James Webb telescope's microshutters

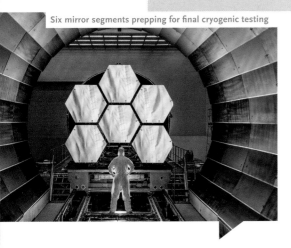
Six mirror segments prepping for final cryogenic testing

FOLDING MIRRORS

OUTER SPACE ORIGAMI

To photograph an object more than 13 billion light-years away, JWST needed a mirror tremendously large and yet light and compact enough to make the million-mile (1.6 million km) journey from Earth. The solution: Webb's primary mirror is made of 18 hexagonal segments that fold up to fit into a rocket but once in space unfold out to about 21 feet (6.5 m) in diameter, thanks to tiny motors. The mirror is made of beryllium, a strong but lightweight metal that can handle extremely cold temperatures. It is covered in a thin layer of gold that helps reflect infrared light. When assembled, JWST's mirror will be more than six times larger than Hubble's primary mirror, and about 100 times more powerful.

A WORD FROM

Lots Still to Learn There are many huge questions . . . how do black holes work; what the big bang was really like; . . . was Einstein really right; and are there gravity waves coming from the deaths of stars and black holes spiraling together to meet each other . . . and that is not even thinking about "Let's go visit a planet and see if there is life here in the solar system."

—**JOHN C. MATHER,** *senior project scientist, JWST*

BIRTH OF STARS & SYSTEMS

PEERING INTO ANCIENT SPACE

One of the JWST mission objectives is to gather data on the formation of galaxies, stars, and planetary systems, using infrared cameras sensitive enough to collect the faint light traveling from so far away. These cameras can also see inside the dusty gas of stellar nurseries like the Eagle Nebula's iconic Pillars of Creation.

We are just beginning to understand how clouds of gas and dust collapse to form stars, why most stars form in groups, and what the building blocks of planetary systems might be. Studying young stars gives scientists a front-row seat to the process, offering insight into the evolution of not only our own solar system but also similar planetary systems elsewhere in space.

The Carina Nebula, home to many young stars

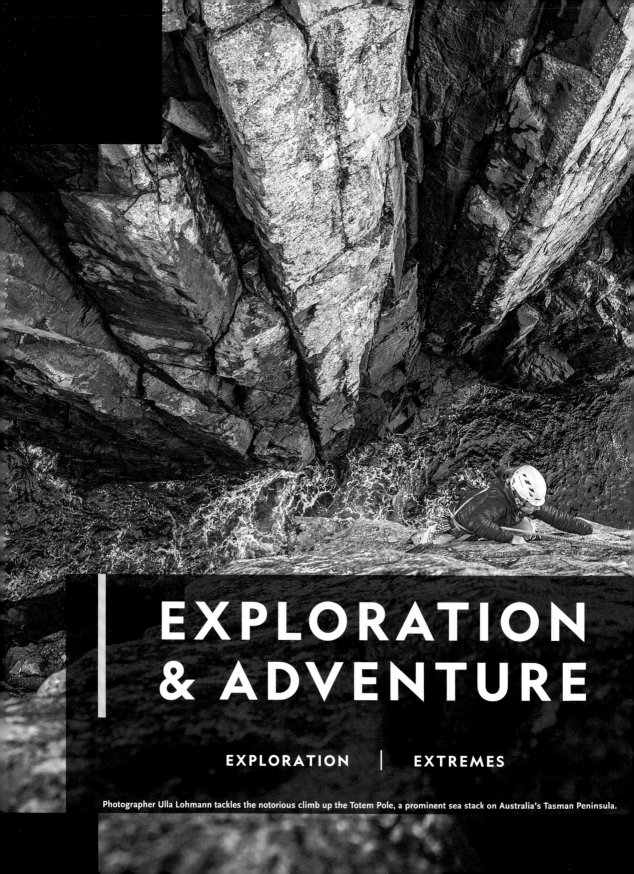

EXPLORATION & ADVENTURE

EXPLORATION | EXTREMES

Photographer Ulla Lohmann tackles the notorious climb up the Totem Pole, a prominent sea stack on Australia's Tasman Peninsula.

Up for Adventure? From daring athletics to round-the-world journeys, let's trek the world of travel and discovery. Test how much you know with these questions, then follow the path to answers in this chapter.

—SUSAN TYLER HITCHCOCK, *Nat Geo Quizmaster*

p69

p57
IN WHAT SPORT HAS FLORENCE GRIFFITH-JOYNER HELD THE WORLD WOMEN'S RECORD SINCE 1988?

WHAT DO **CHEFS** **IN ROME** USE TO MAKE **GNOCCHI:** SEMOLINA, POTATOES, OR CORN?

p81
IN WHAT YEAR WAS THE SUEZ CANAL COMPLETED: 1869, 1919, OR 1969?

p63
WHAT ENDANGERED MAMMAL, NATIVE TO THE HIMALAYA, IS NICKNAMED THE GRAY GHOST?

p53
NAME THE TWO MEN WHO MADE THE FIRST RECORDED SUMMIT OF MOUNT EVEREST.

WHERE IS THE WORLD'S LONGEST CAVE SYSTEM?

WHAT IRISH CITY WAS EUROPE'S CAPITAL OF CULTURE IN 2020?

p51

p78

THE RUINS OF WHAT ANCIENT CIVILIZATION CAN BE SEEN BY VISITING **MEXICO'S YUCATÁN PENINSULA?**

p75

p82

THE BOLSHOI EXPRESS **TRAVELS** BETWEEN WHAT TWO **RUSSIAN** CITIES?

p65

HOW MANY DIFFERENT TYPES OF MOLLUSKS LIVE ON **AUSTRALIA'S** **BARRIER REEF:** 50, 500, OR **5,000?**

HOW DID **SURFING** CHAMPION BETHANY HAMILTON LOSE HER **LEFT** ARM?

p60

IN WHAT CENTURY WAS THE FIRST COMPASS **USED:** 3rd, 7th, OR 12th?

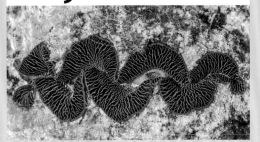

p86

WHAT'S THE WORLD'S **LARGEST** CITY BY POPULATION?

HOW DEEP A HOLE DO YOU NEED TO DRILL THROUGH THE ICE **IN ORDER TO** REACH THE **WATER** TO GO DIVING IN **ANTARCTICA?**

EXPLORATION
TIME LINE

PREHISTORY

■ 80,000 ya*
Homo sapiens moves
out of Africa.

■ ca 75,000 ya
Modern humans reach
Southeast Asia.

■ ca 65,000 ya
Humans reach Australia.

■ ca 15,000 BC
First settlements appear
in North America.

■ ca 8000 BC
Dogs help pull sleds
over snow.

■ ca 6300 BC
Earliest known
boat is made.

■ ca 2300 BC
The earliest known
maps are produced
in Mesopotamia.

* years ago

2000 to 1 BC

■ ca 2000 BC
Austronesians settle
on various islands
in the South Pacific.

■ ca 700 BC
Celts are introducing Iron
Age technology to
Europe.

■ 240 BC
Greek mathematician
Eratosthenes calculates
the circumference
of the Earth.

■ ca 115 BC
Early trade agreements
form between Chinese
and European powers.

AD 1 to 1000

■ 150
Ptolemy maps
the world in
his *Geography*.

■ 271
A compass is first
used in China.

■ ca 400
Polynesian seafarers
settle the Hawaiian
Islands.

■ ca 600
Silk Road is in full use,
with China absorbing
influences from the West.

■ 1000
Viking longships under
the command of Leif
Eriksson cross the Atlantic
and reach North America.

1000 to 1500

■ 1050
Arab astronomers
and navigators introduce
the astrolabe to Europe.

■ 1271
Marco Polo sets off
on a four-year, 7,500-mile
journey from Venice, Italy,
to Shangdu, China.

■ 1331
Arab traveler Ibn Battuta
visits East Africa as
part of a long voyage
through the Islamic
world.

■ 1492
Christopher Columbus
lands on a Caribbean
island that he names
Hispaniola.

■ 1499
Italian navigator
Amerigo Vespucci
explores the northeast
coastline of
South America.

1500 to 1750	1750 to 1900	1900 to 1950	1950 to PRESENT

1513
Ponce de León arrives in today's Florida, first of the Spanish conquistadors in the Americas.

1519
Ferdinand Magellan begins his circumnavigation of the globe.

1535
Jacques Cartier travels up St. Lawrence River to site of today's Montreal.

1595
Gerardus Mercator's first atlas is published.

1607
The English establish Jamestown on the James River in North America.

1722
The Dutch land on Easter Island.

1768
Britain's Capt. James Cook begins exploring the Pacific Ocean.

1799
The Rosetta Stone is discovered in Egypt.

1804–1806
Lewis and Clark run an expedition across the western territory of what is now the United States.

1841
The first wagon trains to cross the Rocky Mountains arrive in California.

1891
Construction begins on the Trans-Siberian Railroad.

1901
The city of Fairbanks is settled on the Alaskan frontier.

1904
Much of Chichén Itzá is discovered in Mexico.

1909
Cmdr. Robert E. Peary and Matthew Henson lead the first expedition to the North Pole.

1937
Amelia Earhart disappears during an attempt at a flight around the world.

1946
Richard E. Byrd leads an expedition to the South Pole.

1953
Edmund Hillary and Tenzing Norgay reach Mount Everest's summit.

1957
The U.S.S.R. launches Sputnik 1, setting off a space race with America.

1960
Jacques Piccard becomes the first human to visit the Challenger Deep, the deepest point in the ocean.

1969
Apollo 11 lands men on the moon.

1990
The Hubble Space Telescope is put into operation.

2004
NASA's Spirit and Opportunity rovers land on Mars.

NAT GEO
EXPLORERS

THE NEXT GENERATION

These explorers are using conservation, photography, science, and innovation to better understand our world and work toward improving it.

LESLIE DEWAN
UNITED STATES
CEO of Transatomic Power, nuclear engineer Dewan is spearheading the development of sustainable nuclear power plants.

KAKANI KATIJA
UNITED STATES
In the Monterey Bay Aquarium's Bioinspiration Lab, Katija carries design concepts from ocean life-forms into new technologies.

GUILLERMO DE ANDA
MEXICO
An underwater archaeologist, de Anda is part of a team working to preserve the Great Maya aquifer, which includes Chichén Itzá.

LEONARDO LANNA
BRAZIL
Through his Projeto Mantis, biologist and photographer Lanna shares his fascination with the insects of the Atlantic Forest.

GIOVANNI CHIMIENTI
ITALY
A marine biologist, Chimienti specializes in corals and their role in deep-sea environments. He discovered one of the Mediterranean's largest black coral forests.

TOMAS DIAGNE
SENEGAL
Dedicated to protectin freshwater turtles and tortoises, Diagne co-founded a sanctuar and breeding facility now caring for hundreds of these animals

NORTH AMERICA

SOUTH AMERICA

PACIFIC OCEAN

ATLANTIC OCEAN

ALTON BYERS
NEPAL
Glaciologist Byers spends up to six months a year in remote mountain regions, supporting community conservation and awareness in the Himalaya.

ARCTIC OCEAN

EUROPE

ASIA

AFRICA

PACIFIC OCEAN

INDIAN OCEAN

AUSTRALIA

66 BELIEVE IN YOURSELF, AND STRIVE TO MAKE A DIFFERENCE. PUSH BOUNDARIES, MEET PEOPLE, TRAVEL, AND UNDERSTAND THE WORLD AROUND YOU."

—TASHI DHENDUP, CONSERVATION BIOLOGIST

WASFIA NAZREEN
BANGLADESH
An accomplished climber, Nazreen founded the Ösel Foundation to empower girls in Bangladesh and Nepal through mindful outdoor adventure.

ONKURI MAJUMDAR
SOUTH ASIA
Working for Freeland India, Majumdar combats wildlife trafficking by strengthening government protections and law enforcement.

GLADYS KALEMA-ZIKUSOKA
UGANDA
A wildlife veterinarian, Kalema-Zikusoka works with endangered mountain gorillas and communities that intersect with gorilla habitats.

INTAN SUCI NURHATI
INDONESIA
Nurhati combines history with science in her work as a paleooceanographer, projecting her findings about the past of tropical oceans into our future.

KRIS TOMPKINS
CONSERVATIONIST

PROTECTING PATAGONIA

Kristine McDivitt Tompkins spent 25 years at Patagonia, Inc., helping build the brand's reputation as an environmentally responsible "anti-corporation." In the 1990s, she and husband Doug Tompkins began buying large swaths of land in Chile and Argentina to restore it to a wild state and return it to public control. Their work has led to the largest private conservation project in history.

Kris Tompkins overlooks land that Tompkins Conservation donated to the Chilean government.

Tompkins grew up in southern California. She was a competitive ski racer when she met rock climber Yvon Chouinard, who invited her to work at his outdoor apparel company. That was the start of her more than two decades with Patagonia, which she helped turn into one of the largest and most influential outdoor gear companies in the world.

LOVE FOR THE LAND

In the early 1990s, she met Doug Tompkins, a co-founder of The North Face, who shared her love for the outdoors. They married, retired, and moved to a remote farmhouse in southern Chile when she was 43 years old.

The next decade saw the Tompkinses put their fortunes to work buying and restoring millions of acres (or hectares) of land. Pumalín Park, an 800,000-acre (323,749 ha) public-access nature reserve in Chile's Lakes Region, was their first project. Their efforts soon expanded. In 2000, Kris founded Conservación Patagónica to create national parks in the southernmost region of Chile and Argentina. "Both countries now see national parks as a source of tourism," she says, and "that is an area of huge growth."

Tragedy interrupted their plans in 2015, when Doug died as his boat capsized during a kayaking trip in Chile. Still, Kris continues their work. In addition to the 3.4 million acres (1,375,931 ha) already secured, Tompkins Conservation is in the process of donating another million acres (404,686 ha) of land to Chile's national parks.

She is also working to reintroduce native species—"rewilding" the landscape by returning giant anteaters, green-shouldered macaws, tapirs, and jaguars to their native habitats, another way in which Kris Tompkins's vision and generosity is helping to heal the land.

> " WILD PLACES AND CREATURES HAVE A RIGHT TO EXIST FOR THEIR OWN SAKE, TO FLOURISH IN THEIR OWN WAY REGARDLESS OF THEIR USEFULNESS TO PEOPLE."

The national park system in Patagonia, Chile, encompasses 10 million acres.

KEY DATES

Some of the Tompkinses'
ACHIEVEMENTS

1992
Doug endows foundation to acquire land for Pumalín Park.

1997
Kris and Doug start the Iberá Project, eventually including nearly 350,000 acres (141,640 ha) in northeastern Argentina.

2000
Kris founds Conservación Patagónica to support the creation of national parks in Patagonia.

2005
Kris and Doug donate land for Corcovado National Park, sixth largest in Chile.

2016
Chile approves the Tompkins team's proposal for five more national parks, including the 200,000-acre (80,937 ha) Patagonia Park.

DIVING ANTARCTICA

SUIT UP FOR SUBFREEZING WATER & BRAVE THE COLD

It takes more than thick skin and a steel will to explore the underwater world of Antarctica. Guides drill a hole in ice some 10 feet (3 m) thick to create a portal into this frigid marine experience. Divers suit up with extra protection—neoprene dry suit, tight hood, special gloves, and thermal underwear—since the water temperature hovers just below freezing. The sights are like nowhere else on Earth: sea stars 15 inches (38 cm) across, sea spiders with legs 7 inches (18 cm) long. Chunky Weddell seals swim in and out of view. Translucent sea anemones and iridescent jellyfish, life-forms almost unimaginable, pulsate with the icy currents.

A WORD FROM

The Way Back Up Seals, when they need air, somehow find their way back to their hole; our greatest dread is getting lost and trapped under the ice. So we drop a luminescent yellow rope into the hole and pull it along with us during the dive. At the end we follow it back up.

—**LAURENT BALLESTA,** *biologist and photographer*

These ephemeral tendrils form when trapped, supercooled brine escapes from the ice and freezes less salty seawater.

ANTARCTIC ICEFISH HAVE NO RED BLOOD CELLS—BUT THEY DO HAVE ANTIFREEZE PROTEINS IN THEIR BLOOD AND CAN THEREFORE SURVIVE IN SUBFREEZING WATERS.

GET OUT INTO
YOUR COUNTRY

WONDERS & THRILLS BOTH NEAR & FAR

Adventure enthusiasts from all over the world travel to the United States to explore stunning national parks, trek iconic trails, and immerse themselves in America's vast wilderness. Each state has its own unique landscape, packed with outdoor activities for every skill level. Don't overlook some obvious choices, for the changing seasons can bring new displays of beauty even to well-known locales.

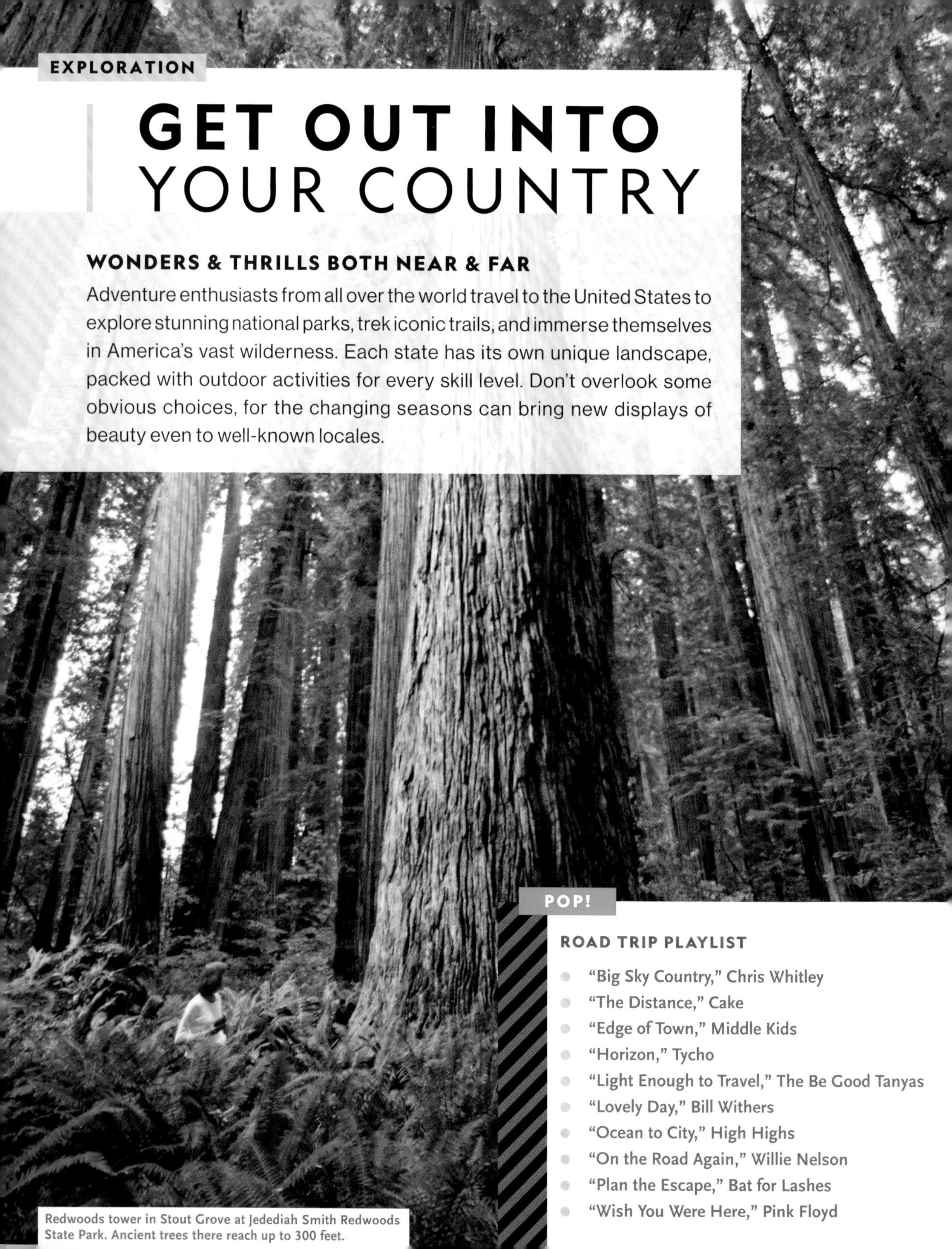

POP!

ROAD TRIP PLAYLIST

- "Big Sky Country," Chris Whitley
- "The Distance," Cake
- "Edge of Town," Middle Kids
- "Horizon," Tycho
- "Light Enough to Travel," The Be Good Tanyas
- "Lovely Day," Bill Withers
- "Ocean to City," High Highs
- "On the Road Again," Willie Nelson
- "Plan the Escape," Bat for Lashes
- "Wish You Were Here," Pink Floyd

Redwoods tower in Stout Grove at Jedediah Smith Redwoods State Park. Ancient trees there reach up to 300 feet.

CALIFORNIA

Jedediah Smith Redwoods State Park in Northern California is home to trees that date back thousands of years and are only able to thrive in the state's North Coast. Take a scenic drive, snorkel in the Smith River, or camp among the majestic trees.

COLORADO

Adventurers can bike, hike, or four-wheel-drive to Bridal Veil Falls, a 365-foot free-falling waterfall, before continuing on to the Colorado Basin for expansive mountain vistas or ascending cliffs along Telluride's Via Ferrata, a route with metal ladder rungs.

FLORIDA

Large schools of fish flurry throughout the Snapper Ledge dive site in the Florida Keys National Marine Sanctuary. One of 15 marine protected areas of the National Marine Sanctuary System, this sanctuary protects 2,900 square nautical miles of water—including shipwrecks.

KANSAS

The native habitats and ecosystems of Konza Prairie in the Flint Hills of Kansas remain largely untouched for research and conservation, though bison are present. Close to 80 percent of the world's remaining unplowed tallgrass prairie is within this four-million-acre terrain.

MARYLAND

Maryland's Blackwater National Wildlife Refuge is home to three major habitats—forest, marsh, and shallow water—visible from walking trails, water trails, and an auto tour route. Originally a waterfowl sanctuary, it now hosts more than 85 species of birds, including bald eagles.

NEW HAMPSHIRE

Frankenstein Cliff (not as scary as it sounds) in New Hampshire's Crawford Notch State Park is a popular destination for ice climbers. Stunning icefalls, with routes to

A sea kayaker paddles around the Apostle Islands National Lakeshore in Wisconsin.

match every visitor's skill level, are usually found here from December to March.

PENNSYLVANIA

Hyner View State Park has one of the most scenic overlooks in Pennsylvania, with a glorious view of the Susquehanna River. The six-acre park is also popular with hang gliders, who sail over the river's west branch.

RHODE ISLAND

Junior sailors train on Narragansett Bay, which covers 150 square miles and sits at the geographic center of Rhode Island. Sunset sails and fishing cruises promise exciting wildlife viewing, including harbor seals in winter, and uninterrupted sea views.

SOUTH CAROLINA

Table Rock Mountain stands tall above South Carolina's Pinnacle Lake, a popular draw for kayakers. Serious hikers will find access to the 77-mile Foothills Trail that connects Table Rock State Park and Oconee State Park.

TENNESSEE

Churning white-water rapids draw professional and recreational kayakers to the Caney Fork River Gorge in Tennessee's Rock Island State Park. Highlights are the ruins of an old mill and an unusual waterfall—created by the nearby dam—that comes through the walls of a gorge.

TEXAS

The dynamic desert dunes of Monahans Sandhills State Park in Texas grow and change each season, making each trip different from the previous one. Visitors rent sand disks on-site to surf the dunes or bring horses for a different encounter.

WASHINGTON

Climbers are drawn to the steep slopes found in Washington's Icicle Creek Canyon, a beloved spot in the Okanogan-Wenatchee National Forest. Hikers, families, birders, and runners can take in views of Icicle River and Tumwater Canyon along trails to the mountain summit.

WISCONSIN

The Apostle Islands National Lakeshore—a 21-island archipelago in Wisconsin known as the Jewels of Lake Superior—is home to thousands-year-old ice caves open to visitors for winter exploration.

BEST OF @NATGEO

TOP PHOTOS OF ADVENTURE

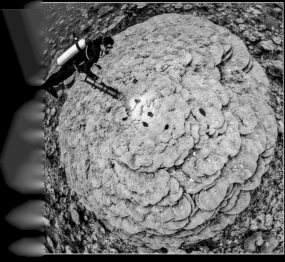

@brianskerry | **BRIAN SKERRY**
Researcher Enric Sala hovers over a newly discovered coral colony at Kingman Reef in the Pacific Ocean.

@geosteinmetz | **GEORGE STEINMETZ**
Paragliding the megadunes of the Dasht-e Lut in Iran, the hottest place on Earth according to NASA

@shonephoto | **ROBBIE SHONE**
An explorer ascends a rope through a narrow slot in the sculpted ice inside Switzerland's Gorner Glacier.

@coryrichards | **CORY RICHARDS**
Explorers trudge through glacial ice and wind-sculpted snow dunes in the untouched Antarctic wilderness.

" ADVENTURE IS WORTHWHILE IN ITSELF."

—AMELIA EARHART, AVIATOR

@jimmy_chin | JIMMY CHIN
Alex Honnold free soloes one of the upper pitches of Freerider on El Capitan in Yosemite, California.

@renan_ozturk | RENAN OZTURK
Climbers trek the receding Vatnajökull glacier, largest in Europe, at Iceland's popular Jökulsárlón ice lagoon.

@salvarezphoto | STEPHEN ALVAREZ
Examples of Cherokee syllabary, a writing system developed in the 1810s, can be found in Alabama's Manitou Cave.

@paulnicklen | PAUL NICKLEN
Surfers dive below the crashing waves of Hawaii's Makaha Beach, while waiting to ride the perfect wave.

A HISTORY OF
CLIMBING EVEREST

PROPELLED BY AMBITION & AWE

For generations, the mountain we know as Everest was a presence to be honored, not conquered. But once British mountaineers attempted to reach its summit in 1922, Everest became an irresistible challenge to climbers from all over the world, forever altering the lives of people living around it. Small teams of 20th-century climbers tackled the mountain, but today trekking companies and Sherpa guides lead hundreds up during May's narrow weather window. A crowd of climbers lines up on the final stretch. In 2019, some 800 summitted Everest, and at least 11 climbers died.

A WORD FROM

Working Together To be successful, you have to trust the other people you're climbing with, and be inherently playing on the same team, pardon the cliché. From a climbing standpoint, gravity is the adversary. You and your fellow humans are striving together to get to the same place at the same time. And I think that's a really good way for humans to interact.

—**CONRAD ANKER,** *mountaineer*

In 1963, the first American Everest expedition, shown here, approached the stretch alone; today, a crowd lines up to ascend.

AMID CONCERNS OVER COVID-19, BOTH CHINA AND NEPAL CANCELED THE 2020 CLIMBING SEASON ON EVEREST.

Setting Records on EVEREST

■ **MAY 1953 (SOUTH FACE)**
Edmund Hillary (New Zealand) and Tenzing Norgay (Nepal) accomplish the first recorded summit of Everest.

■ **MAY 1963 (WEST RIDGE AND NORTH FACE)**
First successful American expedition: Team members Thomas Hornbein and Willi Unsoeld traverse Everest via West Ridge.

■ **MAY 1975 (SOUTH FACE)**
Junko Tabei (Japan) becomes first woman to reach summit—just 12 days after being injured in an avalanche.

■ **AUG. 1980 (NORTH FACE)**
Reinhold Messner (Italy) makes first solo ascent—notably without supplementary oxygen, as on his previous summit in May 1978.

■ **SEPT. 1988 (SOUTH RIDGE)**
Jean-Marc Boivin (France) accomplishes the first paraglider descent from the summit, thus also clocking the fastest descent ever.

■ **MAY 2010 (NORTH FACE)**
Jordan Romero (U.S.) becomes the youngest person to summit, at 13 years and 10 months old.

■ **MAY 2012 (NORTH FACE)**
Tamae Watanabe (Japan) becomes the oldest female to summit, at age 73 years and 180 days—breaking her own record.

■ **MAY 2013**
Yuichiro Miura (Japan) reclaims title of oldest man to summit, at age 80.

■ **MAY 2013**
Dave Hahn (U.S.) sets a new record, 15, for number of ascents by a non-Sherpa.

■ **MAY 2019**
Kami Rita Sherpa, age 49, summits twice in the same week to beat his own record and reach the peak 24 times, a world record.

EARTH'S EXTREMES

PUTTING THE AWE BACK IN AWESOME

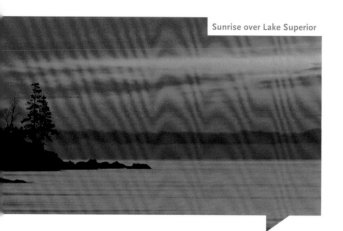
Sunrise over Lake Superior

WATER RECORDS

LARGEST FRESHWATER LAKE
Lake Superior stretches across 31,700 square miles of the United States and Canada, making it the largest lake by surface area. It was formed about 10,000 years ago.

LOWEST POINT
The Challenger Deep in the Pacific is the lowest point on Earth: 36,037 feet below sea level. Mount Everest could be sunk into its depths and still be covered by more than one mile of water.

DEEPEST LAKE
Russia's Lake Baikal is both the deepest lake, at 5,387 feet, and the oldest, at 25–30 million years old. It is part of a rift valley, where tectonic plates are breaking apart.

LARGEST RIVER
There is no competition here: The Amazon River and its tributaries flow through Peru, Bolivia, Venezuela, Colombia, Ecuador, and Brazil before emptying into the Atlantic Ocean. The next largest, India's "Mother Ganges," discharges a significantly lower volume of water than the Amazon does.

LONGEST RIVER
Calculating the length of rivers is a complicated and controversial process. Freshwater scientists often cannot agree on a river's precise source or on how far to extend its watershed boundaries. But most agree that the Nile, stretching through northeast Africa, is the longest in the world at 4,160 miles. The Amazon is a close second at 4,150 miles and the Yangtze clocks in at 3,880 miles long.

The Nile in Sudan

The Valle de la Luna in Chile's Atacama Desert

SCIENTISTS THINK THE DRY VALLEYS OF ANTARCTICA MAY BE THE CLOSEST OF ANY ENVIRONMENT ON EARTH TO THE PLANET MARS.

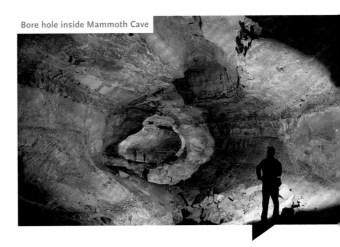
Bore hole inside Mammoth Cave

LAND RECORDS

DRIEST PLACE
Parts of the high plateau of the Atacama Desert in Chile and the Dry Valleys of Antarctica have never recorded a drop of rain. They are ringed by high mountains that prevent moisture from reaching the dry basins.

HIGHEST POINT
Mount Everest is the world's highest elevation, 29,035 feet above sea level—a figure that increases as the Indian subcontinent crashes into Asia. Hawaii's Mauna Kea is the world's tallest mountain, 33,000 feet from seafloor to summit.

WETTEST PLACE
Asian monsoons make the Indian state of Meghalaya the rainiest place in the world. The town of Mawsynram received about 83 feet of rain in 1985. In 1861, nearby Cherrapunji received 86.6 feet.

FARTHEST FROM THE OCEAN
About 200 miles north of Urumqi, a city in Xinjiang, China, is a "pole of inaccessibility"—a location that is "challenging to reach owing to its remoteness from geographical features that could provide access." The most remote pole of inaccessibility—the place farthest from the ocean—is also in Xinjiang, about 1,644 miles from the coast.

LONGEST CAVE SYSTEM
The Mammoth-Flint Ridge cave system in Kentucky stretches about 400 miles, nearly twice the length of the next longest cave system, Mexico's Sac Actun underwater cave.

HOTTEST PLACE
The temperature at Furnace Creek Station in Death Valley National Park, which straddles California and Nevada, reached 134°F (56.7°C) on July 10, 1913. However, the Danakil Depression—which reaches into Eritrea, Djibouti, and Ethiopia—has the highest average year-round temperature—93.92°F (34.4°C).

COLDEST PLACE
A region near Vostok Station, a Russian research station in Antarctica atop ice almost two and a half miles thick, set the world record on August 10, 2010, when the temperature dipped to minus 135.8°F (−93.2°C).

UNDERWATER MUSEUM

SWIMMING WITH SCULPTURE

A barren sand flat does not typically inspire creativity, but it happens to be a perfect setting for the first Underwater Museum of Art (UMA) in the United States. Located just off the Florida Panhandle, near Walton County's Grayton Beach State Park, the UMA installed its first seven sculptures in 2018. Over time, the collection will become a marine habitat. As at similar projects near Cancún and the Canary Islands, the experience is best suited for scuba divers. On clear days, snorkelers will also be able to enjoy the submerged journey, which sits at a depth of around 60 feet.

POP!

MOVIES WITH UNDERWATER WORLDS

- *The Little Mermaid* (1989)
- *Sphere* (1998)
- *Atlantis: The Lost Empire* (2001)
- *Finding Nemo* (2003)
- *Deepsea Challenge* (2014)
- *Aquaman* (2018)
- *Avatar 2 and 3* (in production)

A school of gray snappers swims among the sculptures at the Underwater Museum of Art in Cancún, Mexico, precursor to the new one in Florida.

Inaugural Class of
SUBMERGED ART

◼ ANAMORPHOUS OCTOPUS
This perforated steel sculpture was created by artist Allison Wickey, who first proposed the museum. Her painter's eye is evident in the textured, shaded surface of her piece.

◼ CONCRETE ROPE REEF SPHERES
With a goal of supporting oyster colonies, architecture professor and artist Evelyn Tickle developed a concrete formula that matches the constitution of oyster shells and used it to make the nooks and crannies of her creature-friendly tangled sculpture.

◼ THE GRAYT PINEAPPLE
In the American colonies, rare and expensive pineapples symbolized hospitality. Artist Rachel Herring's steel sculpture is welcoming to small fish in particular. Its name refers to Grayton Beach.

◼ JYC'S DREAM
In a nod to explorer Jacques Cousteau's Aqua-Lung, designer Kevin Reilly created this oversize stainless-steel depiction of a diver's head gear with rising bubbles—some containing children's art.

◼ PROPELLER IN MOTION
Furniture designer Marek Anthony based his stainless-steel sculpture on a ship's propeller to elicit thoughts of motion and of nature reclaiming what humans have discarded. Swimming creatures can easily move through the hollow blades.

◼ SELF PORTRAIT
Justin Gaffrey's eight-foot-tall stag evokes the stillness of an encounter on land. Its steely presence invites parallels between the underwater setting and a forest scene—with dashing fish instead of scurrying forest animals.

◼ SWARA SKULL
The steel, cement, and limestone hollow skull created by film designer (and divemaster) Vince Tatum aims to attract corals and reclusive marine life. (SWARA stands for South Walton Artificial Reef Association.)

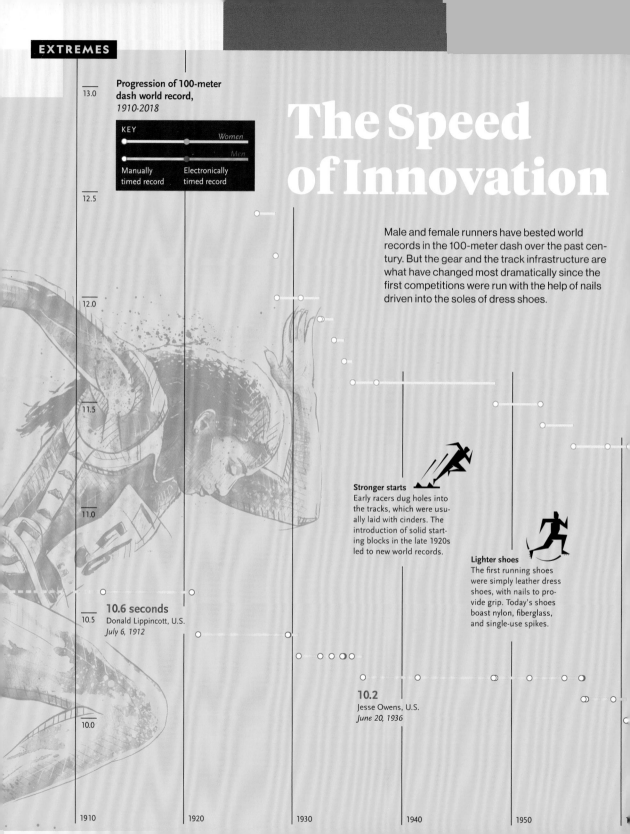

Progression of 100-meter dash world record,
1910-2018

KEY

Women

Men

Manually timed record

Electronically timed record

The Speed of Innovation

Male and female runners have bested world records in the 100-meter dash over the past century. But the gear and the track infrastructure are what have changed most dramatically since the first competitions were run with the help of nails driven into the soles of dress shoes.

Stronger starts
Early racers dug holes into the tracks, which were usually laid with cinders. The introduction of solid starting blocks in the late 1920s led to new world records.

Lighter shoes
The first running shoes were simply leather dress shoes, with nails to provide grip. Today's shoes boast nylon, fiberglass, and single-use spikes.

10.6 seconds
Donald Lippincott, U.S.
July 6, 1912

10.2
Jesse Owens, U.S.
June 20, 1936

13.0

12.5

12.0

11.5

11.0

10.5

10.0

1910   1920   1930   1940   1950

ATHLETIC ACHIEVEMENTS IMPROVED FOR DECADES,
IN PART BECAUSE OF NEW TECHNOLOGY AND THE USE
OF PERFORMANCE-ENHANCING STEROIDS.
WITH ATHLETES UNDER INCREASED SCRUTINY,
WORLD RECORDS ARE STILL GETTING BROKEN—BUT
NOT INCREMENTALLY, SUGGESTING THAT WE ARE
PUSHING THE LIMITS OF OUR ATHLETIC POTENTIAL.

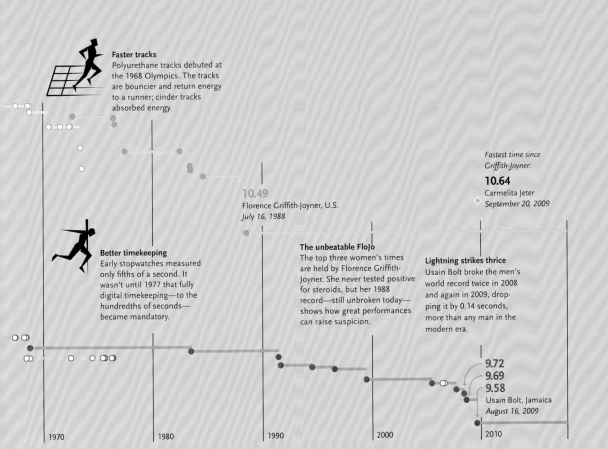

Faster tracks
Polyurethane tracks debuted at
the 1968 Olympics. The tracks
are bouncier and return energy
to a runner; cinder tracks
absorbed energy.

*Fastest time since
Griffith-Joyner:*
10.64
Carmelita Jeter
September 20, 2009

10.49
Florence Griffith-Joyner, U.S.
July 16, 1988

Better timekeeping
Early stopwatches measured
only fifths of a second. It
wasn't until 1977 that fully
digital timekeeping—to the
hundredths of seconds—
became mandatory.

The unbeatable FloJo
The top three women's times
are held by Florence Griffith-
Joyner. She never tested positive
for steroids, but her 1988
record—still unbroken today—
shows how great performances
can raise suspicion.

Lightning strikes thrice
Usain Bolt broke the men's
world record twice in 2008
and again in 2009, drop-
ping it by 0.14 seconds,
more than any man in the
modern era.

9.72
9.69
9.58
Usain Bolt, Jamaica
August 16, 2009

1970   1980   1990   2000   2010

MIHO AIDA
ACTIVIST

OUTSPOKEN ATHLETE

Translated from Japanese, Miho Aida's name means "a creator of greater democracy and protector of people, culture, and environment." Born and raised in Tokyo, she saw a television special on the U.S. national parks and fell in love with them. She studied environmental science, eventually moved to the United States, and has since become an activist dedicated to promoting women of color in conservation and adventure sports.

Miho Aida rode more than 3,000 miles (4,828 km) across the United States, promoting the message of outdoor engagement, especially to women of col

Aida left Japan in 1999 to begin a master's program in Wyoming. She became an environmental educator and a certified Wilderness First Responder and backpacking and rock climbing instructor. Since 2014, she has biked more than 3,000 miles (4,828 km) across the United States, raising awareness and building communities, focused on the goal of protecting the Arctic.

RESILIENT COMMUNITIES

In 2008, Aida created "If She Can Do It, You Can Too"—a campaign dedicated to documenting the diversity of women active in environmental protection. She felt a calling to increase "the visibility and access of people who had little, if any, voice and access to our public lands, environmental education careers and outdoor adventures." She supports everyone working to eliminate the barriers to women in the outdoors.

Traveling to the southern edge of the Arctic National Wildlife Refuge, she came to know women from the Gwich'in Nation who have spent decades fighting against oil and gas drilling. To them, the coastal plain is a sacred place—and a critical habitat for the Porcupine Caribou Herd, on which the Gwich'in rely for their physical, cultural, and spiritual livelihoods. Aida produced *The Sacred Place Where Life Begins,* a short documentary amplifying the voices of the Gwich'in women she met.

Now partnering with outdoors retailers, Aida's goal is to support communities of color and promote environmentalism rooted in social justice.

> ❝ TRAVELING AND WORKING WITH WOMEN I MET HELPED ME TO RECOGNIZE MY OWN PRIVILEGE AND PERSONAL POWER. I HAVE A RESPONSIBILITY TO TAKE ACTIONS SUPPORTING GLOBAL EQUITY. ❞

Aida (right) with two Gwich'in women (middle) and a Sierra Club coordinator

KEY DATES

Miho Aida's
JOURNEY

■ **1999**
Moves from Tokyo to Jackson Hole, Wyoming, to study environmental education at Teton Science School.

■ **2008**
Launches "If She Can Do It, You Can Too" to elevate stories of women of color in the outdoors.

■ **2013**
Releases the award-winning short film *The Sacred Place Where Life Begins: Gwich'in Women Speak.*

■ **2017**
Named 2017 Adventure Athlete of the Year by SHIFT—Shaping How we Invest For Tomorrow, a festival run by the Center for Jackson Hole—for best promoting conservation leadership.

EXTREME ABILITIES

SPORTS ARE HARD ENOUGH, BUT THESE ATHLETES PUSH EVEN FURTHER

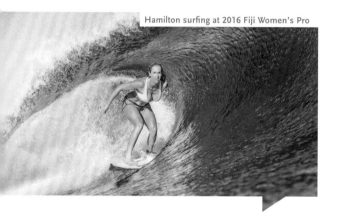

Hamilton surfing at 2016 Fiji Women's Pro

BETHANY HAMILTON

SHARKS WON'T STOP HER

At 13, Bethany Hamilton was already a star when a 14-foot (4.3 m) tiger shark attacked her. She lost her left arm—but less than two years later, she won a national surfing competition. The documentary film *Bethany Hamilton: Unstoppable* shows her maneuvering Maui's legendary 60-foot (18.2 m) wave called Jaws. Now she's got her sights set on an even taller wave in Namibia.

"Taking off on that wave," she says about Jaws, "it felt like the most exhilarating, beautiful, powerful kind of moment experiencing nature." The Friends of Bethany Foundation now helps amputees find healing and strength in the success that Bethany Hamilton represents.

MARTYN ASHTON

ROAD BIKE PARTY ON

He'd been biking for more than 20 years, winning world competitions and posting "Road Bike Party" videos viewed by millions, when Martyn Ashton fell backward during a stunt and landed head first, snapping his spine mid-torso. An hour later he was asking, "So how are we going to do it now?"

The answer: with friends, a custom-made bike, and the same spirit of adventure that drove him in the first place. He shared his comeback through the gleeful "Back on Track" video, in which he and three friends cycle through Wales's Snowdonia National Park. As much as anything, Ashton says, he endures thanks to his friends, which is the point of any sport: camaraderie.

Ashton mountain-biking in Canada

Beck calculating her next climbing move

THE PARALYMPICS GAMES STARTED IN ROME IN 1960, WITH 400 ATHLETES. MORE THAN 10 TIMES THAT MANY PARTICIPATE TODAY.

OZ SANCHEZ

HE KNOWS NO LIMITS

It has been a long journey for Oz Sanchez. He pulled himself out of a difficult Los Angeles child-hood by joining the Marines at 21. The military suited him, and he was on his way to becoming a Navy SEAL when a hit-and-run accident in 2001 left him with a spinal cord injury, paralyzed from the thighs down.

But his motto is "Know No Limits"—because despite all that, Sanchez is now recognized as an elite hand cyclist and triathlete, winning two gold medals and many other honors internationally. He is "a warrior at heart," says Greg Strom, producer of the documen-tary *Unbeaten,* which features Sanchez and 30 other para-athletes. Sanchez now contributes time and passion to causes including Wounded Warriors and the Challenged Athletes Foundation, encouraging others, no matter what their abilities, to live by the motto that serves him so well.

MAUREEN BECK

HAND OVER STRENGTH & WILLPOWER

Maureen Beck was born with what she calls a "stump" below her left elbow—no forearm, no hand. But from the beginning, she says, her par-ents never treated her as different. She went canoeing, played baseball and soccer, and ulti-mately found her dream sport: rock climbing. "It gets you outside, it gets you pushing yourself, and it's a sport where everyone fails a lot before those brief, amazing moments of success," she says. Early on, Beck used a climbing pick attached to a prosthetic, but she found she did better just by wrapping the limb she had. She learned about Paradox Sports, a nonprofit that develops adap-tive climbing opportunities. She began entering competitions run by IFSC (International Federa-tion of Sport Climbing), winning medals in para-climbing again and again—second place internationally in 2019.

Sanchez cycling on the Paralympic team

TRANSPORTATION
TIME LINE

PREHISTORY	1700 to 1 BC	AD 1 to 1000	1000 to 1700

PREHISTORY

■ **ca 65,000 ya***
Modern humans reach New Guinea and Australia by b...

■ **ca 14,700 ya**
Humans are present in the Americas.

■ **ca 10,000 ya**
Dugout canoes are in use in Europe.

■ **ca 5500 BC**
Humans use bits and reins to manage horses for riding.

■ **ca 3500 BC**
The wheel is invented in Mesopotamia.

■ **ca 2500 BC**
Mesopotamians waterproof boats and buildings with tar.

1700 to 1 BC

■ **ca 1700 BC**
Horses and chariots are introduced to Egypt.

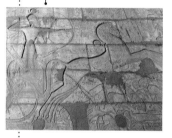

■ **691 BC**
Assyrians build an aqueduct to carry water to their capital, Nineveh.

■ **312 BC**
Rome builds its first major road, the Appian Way.

■ **110 BC**
Romans use rudimentary horseshoes.

AD 1 to 1000

■ **415**
In India, suspension bridges are built using iron chains.

■ **ca 660**
Camel herds support a nomadic way of life among people living in the Sahara.

■ **ca 700**
Europeans begin to adopt the use of stirrups for riding horses.

■ **ca 800**
Roads in Baghdad, Iraq, are paved with tar extracted from nearby oil fields.

■ **ca 860**
Viking longships venture as far west as Iceland.

1000 to 1700

■ **ca 1088**
Shen Kuo first describes a magnetic compass used for navigation.

■ **ca 1450**
The Inca construct a road system 20,000 miles long to unite their empire.

■ **1457**
The first four-wheel passenger coach is built in Hungary.

■ **1500**
Chinese scientist Wan Hu attempts to make a flying machine out of rockets tied to a chair.

■ **1692**
In France, the 32-mile Canal du Midi, linking the Mediterranean Sea with the Atlantic Ocean, is completed.

* years ago

| 1700 to 1900 | 1900 to 1930 | 1930 to 1960 | 1960 to PRESENT |

1769

James Watt patents the modern steam engine.

1783

French brothers Joseph and Jacques Montgolfier first demonstrate the hot air balloon.

1869

The Suez Canal is completed in Egypt.

1869

The U.S. Transcontinental Railroad is completed.

1879

Karl Benz runs the first gas-powered automobile.

1891

Construction begins on the Trans-Siberian Railroad.

1903

Orville and Wilbur Wright fly a powered airplane at Kitty Hawk, North Carolina.

1904

The first portion of the New York City subway opens.

1908

The first Model T Ford comes off the assembly line.

1909

French aviator Louis Blériot flies across the English Channel.

1927

Charles Lindbergh flies the *Spirit of St. Louis* nonstop from New York to Paris.

1933

The first modern airliner, the Boeing 247, enters service.

1937

The *Hindenburg* dirigible bursts into flames when attempting to dock after a transatlantic flight.

1939

Inventor Igor Sikorsky builds the first helicopter.

1945

James Martin designs the ejector seat.

1947

American airman Charles "Chuck" Yeager makes the first supersonic flight.

1958

Australian engineer David Warren invents the "black box" flight data recorder.

1961

Soviet cosmonaut Yuri Gagarin becomes the first man in space.

1969

The British-French supersonic airliner Concorde takes its maiden flight.

1969

NASA's Apollo 11 makes the first piloted moon landing.

1998

English inventor David Baker patents the Land Shark, a high-speed amphibious car.

2010

Self-driving cars make their first test drives on public streets.

ICONIC
DESTINATIONS

JOURNEYS THAT SHOULD BE ON EVERY BUCKET LIST

NASHVILLE
U.S.
Immerse yourself in Americana at the Country Music Hall of Fame and Hatch Show Print. Then make a pilgrimage to the Ryman Auditorium and Music Row.

DUTCH BULBFIELDS
Netherlands
In spring the famed bulbfields in South Holland become a blaze of color. Cycle around fields of brilliant hues, and then visit world-famous gardens.

PACIFIC COAST HIGHWAY
U.S.
Savor the sweeping Pacific vistas and hairpin bends of the highway that clings to America's western edge. Cruise north from Hearst Castle to historic Monterey.

HANA HIGHWAY
U.S.
A restorative for mind and body, Maui's Hana coast—with black-sand beaches, plunging waterfalls, limpid pools, and rainbow eucalyptus— unspools for 52 miles.

NORTH AMERICA

ATLANTIC

OCEAN

PACIFIC

OCEAN

TAHITI & BORA BORA
French Polynesia
A stroll along a black-sand beach, a dive into a translucent lagoon, or a visit to palm-shaded coral atolls will show you why these islands are considered paradise.

GALÁPAGOS
Ecuador
Visit for a day or more to see the lava fields, white-sand strands, and giant cliffs that are home to the abundant wildlife that inspired Charles Darwin.

SOUTH AMERICA

PYRAMIDS OF GIZA
Egypt
The lone survivor of the original Seven Wonders of the World, these tombs have been astonishing visitors since they were first erected in the 26th century BC.

"TRAVEL IS MORE THAN THE SEEING OF SIGHTS; IT IS A CHANGE THAT GOES ON, DEEP AND PERMANENT, IN THE IDEAS OF LIVING."

—MIRIAM BEARD, HISTORIAN & ACTIVIST

GREEK ISLANDS
Greece
Azure Aegean waters, terraced hillsides, olive groves, blue-domed churches, and whitewashed villages overlooked by windmills bring visitors unfailing delight.

BOLSHOI EXPRESS
Russia
Get a taste of Russian extravagance aboard the overnight *Bolshoi (Grand) Express* between Moscow and St. Petersburg. Service starts at first class.

GREAT WALL
China
This is the world's largest human-made military structure and one of its oldest. Climb the Mutianyu section of wall and take in views of far-off misty green hills.

MOUNT FUJI
Japan
Contemplate the sacred volcano and its serene setting while soaking in the hot springs or taking a leisurely bike ride at Lake Kawaguchi, one of the Fuji Five Lakes.

TAJ MAHAL
India
The shimmering Taj Mahal is a monument to human skill as well as to an emperor's love. Visit it at sunrise to watch the white marble change color with the light.

KILIMANJARO
Tanzania
The trek up Africa's highest mountain passes through five distinct temperate zones, from rainforest to tundra. Uhuru Peak affords an infinite horizon line.

SYDNEY OPERA HOUSE
Australia
A masterful feat of architecture, the building's profile resembles pearly billowing sails, an illusion achieved with multiple interlocking shells set on a pedestal.

ARCTIC
OCEAN

EUROPE

ASIA

AFRICA

PACIFIC

OCEAN

INDIAN

OCEAN

AUSTRALIA

SAVOR THE WORLD'S
BEST CITIES

Puerto Madero, Buenos Aires

BUENOS AIRES

LIKE A LOCAL
Calle Florida in downtown Buenos Aires has been at least partly pedestrianized since 1913. Now totally off-limits for vehicles, it's one of the city's biggest tourist attractions, with shops and arcades selling leather, jewelry, and souvenirs.

READ AHEAD
The translated short stories of Argentina's most important writer, Jorge Luis Borges, are a great way to learn about the city, especially the tumultuous dark underworld of the *compadritos,* gangsters, of the 1920s and 1930s. Pick up his *Collected Fictions* (1999).

MARRAKECH

GREEN OASES
Marrakech is known for its gardens, particularly the Jardin Majorelle (Rue Yves Saint Laurent), a breathtaking landscape of exotic plants, trees, pools, and fountains. But few realize its haute couture legacy. Fashion legends Yves Saint Laurent and Pierre Berg bought and restored the garden in 1980, saving it from becoming part of a hotel complex.

READ AHEAD
Lords of the Atlas by Gavin Maxwell (1966), an account of the ruling Glaoua clan, who maintained a near-medieval fiefdom in southern Morocco from 1893 to 1956, is a must-read.

Jardin Majorelle in Marrakech

Aerial view of Paris at night

Yu Garden in Shanghai

PARIS

LA TOUR MAGNIFIQUE

The Eiffel Tower—built as the centerpiece for the 1889 World's Fair—is France at its best: confident, brilliant, putting on a show for the world. Glass-roofed shopping arcades are another Paris invention, also from the 19th century. The ones that survive, mostly around the old Bibliothèque Nationale, are utterly charming; some are packed with old bookstores and curiosity shops, others with chic galleries and boutiques.

FLEA MARKETS

No trip to Paris is complete without a day at the 17-acre, 3,000-stall Marché aux Puces de Saint-Ouen on the city limits. You might score vintage French cookery or antique tomes at the centrally located Marché aux Puces d'Aligre. A visit to the intimate and friendly Marché aux Puces de Vanves is like rummaging through the attic of the French grandparents you never had.

READ AHEAD

All of Georges Simenon's Maigret detective stories are great for evoking Parisian life, both high and low. *Maigret at the Crossroads* (1931) is regarded as one of the best.

SHANGHAI

VISIT THE PAST

Take a break from the busy streets and glitzy sky-scrapers and lose yourself in ancient China at the 400-year-old Yu Garden in the Huangpu District. The complex was a private garden in the Ming dynasty and has become one of Shanghai's most famous sites. See exquisite Chinese sculptures, carvings, garden pavilions, pagodas, and pools. Outside you'll find the bustling Yuyuan Bazaar with souvenir shops, teahouses, and restaurants.

READ AHEAD

Man's Fate (1933), which many consider to be André Malraux's best novel, follows two communist conspirators and two foreigners during the violent crackdown of the communist insurrection in 1927 Shanghai.

A TASTE OF ITALY

ABBONDANZA DELIZIOSA

Central Italy—its mountains, plains, valleys, and merry coastline—is both civilized and down to earth. Home of the Renaissance, this most visited part of Italy, along with its celebrated culture and cuisine, is what most travelers think of as "Italian." Indeed, the central Italian kitchen, which takes simplicity to a high level, characterizes much of what generally makes Italian food so special. That finesse is derived from two things: an ancient cosmopolitan heritage and a fidelity to high-quality ingredients that are locally grown or produced.

A WORD FROM

Traveling via Flavors The real Italy is so much more multifaceted, and so much more remarkable, than the Italy that lives on in popular imagination. For the traveler to Italy, this diversity means an incredible range of experiences and tastes, from heavenly white truffles in Alba to musky blood oranges in Sicily. These locally produced ingredients . . . shape the local cooking and produce the wide variety of regional cuisines . . . And 21st-century transport means these artisanal ingredients are likely available at your local market.

—**JACK BISHOP,** *chief creative officer of America's Test Kitchen*

Parmesan cheese and Bolognese sauce top homemade fettucine.

Traditional Dishes From
CENTRAL ITALY

CHICKEN UNDER A BRICK
(POLLO AL MATTONE)
This Tuscan technique ensures even cooking, speeds up the process, and maximizes contact with the cooking grate for perfectly crisp skin.

FRIED STUFFED OLIVES
(OLIVE ALL'ASCOLANA)
Crisp-coated, salty fried olives with a rich meat filling are a culinary marvel from the town of Ascoli Piceno in Le Marche.

ORECCHIETTE WITH
SAUSAGE AND CREAM
(ORECCHIETTE ALLA NORCINA)
The black pigs of Umbria are prized for their superlative flavor, owing to their diet of plants, herbs, and truffles.

ROMAN GNOCCHI
(GNOCCHI ALLA ROMANA)
Semolina gnocchi—no potatoes here—is appealingly creamy and slightly dense, similar to polenta.

SEAFOOD SOUP
(BRODETTO ALL'ANCONETANA)
Ancona's trademark dish has long served as a way for fishermen to use the bycatch remaining after selling the day's haul.

SPRING VEGETABLE STEW
(VIGNOLE)
Spring vegetables abound in Abruzzo's inland, and *vignole* is a vibrant (and speedy) braise that celebrates them.

TUSCAN TOMATO AND BREAD SOUP
(PAPPA AL POMODORO)
This is a tomato-bread soup finished with basil. In the pot, the ingredients meld to form a fragrant porridge-like stew that's downright luxurious.

VEGETABLE AND FARRO SOUP
(MINESTRA DI FARRO)
Umbrians use coarsely ground farro, a staple of Umbria that predates common wheat, to thicken and flavor soups.

GREATEST EXPEDITIONS

FOLLOW HISTORY'S PATHWAYS AROUND THE WORLD

Passengers traverse Switzerland's Landwasser viaduct.

BY TRAIN

SWISS ALPS & ITALIAN LAKE DISTRICT
Climb aboard the unhurried *Glacier Express* and savor the panorama of snowcapped peaks, dense forests, rushing rivers, Alpine meadows, and mountain villages near Switzerland's southern borders.

CANADIAN ROCKIES
Take the *Rocky Mountaineer's* dramatic route through the Canadian Rockies—rocky gradients, soaring pine trees, spiraling tunnels—from Vancouver to Banff.

SHINKANSEN TRANS-SIBERIAN RAILWAY
A weeklong Moscow-Beijing route via Mongolia weaves through the Russian hinterlands of Siberia, the wilderness of Mongolia, and the wastes of the Gobi, within sight of Lake Baikal and the Great Wall.

ACROSS LAND

MOROCCO'S CITIES OF LEGEND
A journey along age-old trade routes—from Ceuta (officially part of Spain) to the tiny fishing port of Tarfaya—immerses you in ancient cultures, exotic markets, and imposing mountain and desert scenery.

NEW ZEALAND NORTH TO SOUTH
The unspoiled (but accessible) landscape between Karamea and Jackson Bay includes two glaciers, exceptional ocean vistas, and alpine scenery.

PILGRIMAGE TO BHUTAN
One enchanted tour includes a trek into Trashi-yangtse, a stunning "lost" valley, with a monastery, a wildlife sanctuary, a shrine, and welcoming locals.

Prayer flags frame Bhutan's mythic Taktsang Monastery.

Sea Cloud II approaches St. Lucia's Pitons.

TOGETHER, TOURISTS FROM CHINA AND THE UNITED STATES SPEND ALMOST $400 BILLION A YEAR ON TRAVEL.

Zebras and wildebeests graze in Tanzania's Serengeti National Park.

BY SEA

CARIBBEAN DREAMING

These legendary islands are synonymous with paradise: idyllic beaches, water sports, and rum cocktails. A cruise through the breathtaking waters offers luxury, shopping, and outdoor fun.

EPIC POLYNESIA

During one seven-day excursion around Tahiti and nearby islands, guests can kayak, dive, snorkel, hike, or sunbathe. Inland spots to visit include an archaeological site and a vanilla plantation.

ANTARCTIC CRUISING

You'll be comfortable aboard an ice-reinforced vessel as icebergs float past, some of them as large as ships themselves. Time your trip right to catch sight of seals, whales, and penguins.

A WORD FROM

Overtourism According to figures from the United Nations World Tourism Organization, international tourism has grown 60-fold since commercial jet traffic began some six decades ago. The places that these people visit, however—the museums, the archaeological ruins, the natural attractions, the narrow medieval streets of historic cities—are still the same physical size.

—**JONATHAN TOURTELLOT,**
sustainable tourism expert

ON SAFARI

TANZANIA'S GREAT MIGRATION

On the ground, in the trees, along rivers, and in the sky—more than 1,000 bird species can be found here, and it's possible to see 100 species in a day. Birding is good year-round, but fall migration is spectacular.

BOTSWANA GAME RESERVE

On a guided safari, guests of the national parks shoot the "big five" of African wildlife—lion, leopard, buffalo, rhino, and elephant—with cameras rather than guns.

VICTORIA FALLS

On a microlight aircraft, there's not much between you and the tree-covered islands that dot the Zambezi River as it approaches Victoria Falls. Want to see wildlife? Book a flight over the nearby national park.

U.S. NATIONAL PARKS

START PLANNING YOUR NEXT BIG OUTDOOR ADVENTURE

KEY DESTINATIONS

Secret Gems Among the
U.S. PARKS

SHENANDOAH
Skyline Drive winds for 105 miles through this narrow park. Visitors can stroll to lookouts or hike to craggy summits, playful waterfalls, and watercolor vistas.

WIND CAVE
Above is a globally significant expanse of mixed-grass prairie; below is one of the world's most complex and unusual caves, sacred to indigenous peoples.

BIG BEND
This unusual habitat—the Chihuahuan Desert, the Rio Grande, and the Chisos Mountains—is home to more bird species than any other national park.

SAGUARO
This park, named for an iconic cactus, offers hikers, cyclists, mountain bike riders, and horseback riders desert, grassland, oak scrub, pine forest, and riparian zones.

ROCKY MOUNTAIN
Few other places make it so easy to traverse a true alpine environment, where rugged peaks rise above glacier-carved valleys, forested foothills, and the Continental Divide.

JOSHUA TREE
These wide-open desert spaces are rich with arid mountain ranges and fantastic boulder formations. Desert flora is surprisingly diverse and varies with season and elevation.

CRATER LAKE
This stunning sapphire lake, the country's deepest, is fed only by snowmelt. Many of the Cascade Range's neighboring volcanic mountains are visible from Rim Drive.

KATMAI
Accessible only by floatplane, this four-million-acre park offers opportunities for observing bears and experiencing the Valley of Ten Thousand Smokes, created after a 1912 eruption.

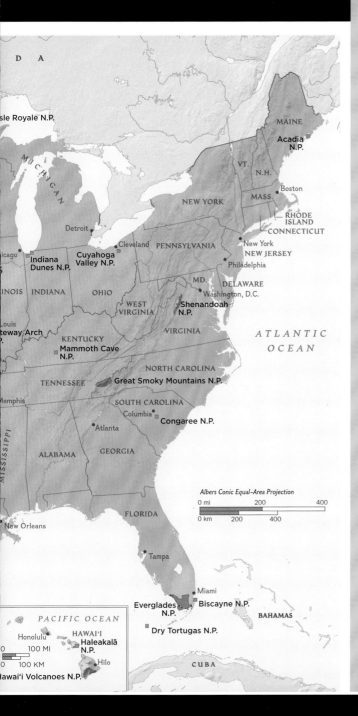

AUSTRALIA'S BARRIER REEF

UNDERWATER WONDERS

You can spend a lifetime exploring the Great Barrier Reef and still not see it all. Sprawling off the east coast of Queensland, Australia, it stretches over 1,250 miles and covers some 135,000 square miles in total. The magnificent structures we see today—the largest structure on Earth built by living organisms—were produced by a slow process played out over millions of years. Home to a staggering diversity of plant and lower animal life, this colorful aquatic ecosystem is also frequented by larger species like dugongs, sea turtles, sharks, and dolphins.

A transparent, jewel-like shrimp hovers within an anemone at Australia's Great Barrier Reef.

THE GREAT BARRIER REEF MARINE PARK HOSTS 5,000 TYPES OF MOLLUSKS, 1,800 SPECIES OF FISH, 125 KINDS OF SHARKS, AND INNUMERABLE MINIATURE ORGANISMS.

Varieties of
REEF LIFE

DUGONG
These enormous vegetarians are related to manatees, yet with a tail fluked like a whale's. They graze on underwater grasses and can stay underwater as long as six minutes.

CLOWNFISH
Bright orange with three white bars, just over four inches long, these are real-life Nemos. They nestle into color-ful sea anemones, immune from their lethal sting.

GREEN SEA TURTLE
Among the largest sea turtles in the world, these can weigh up to 700 pounds. Herbivorous as adults, the juveniles may also eat crabs, jellyfish, and sponges.

SALTWATER CROCODILE
Opportunistic predators, these creatures can weigh as much as a ton. They lurk under the water, seeking prey at the water's edge, but also swim into open water.

WHITE-BELLIED SEA EAGLE
One of the largest raptors in Australia, this bright white and ash-gray bird's wing-span may measure six feet as it soars over the coastline and inland as well.

HUMPBACK WHALE
These legendary singers feed on krill, plankton, and small fish. Found near the poles in summer, they migrate toward the Equator in winter.

BLACKTIP REEF SHARK
These small sharks glide through lagoons and in and out of coral reefs, their iconic black dorsal fin sticking up above the water.

SMOOTH CAULIFLOWER CORAL
With colors ranging from cream and pink to yellow and green, this coral grows short branches from which tentacles extend at night.

BEST OF @NATGEO

TOP PHOTOS OF TRAVEL

@lucalocatelliphoto | LUCA LOCATELLI
A view on an automated Metro train in Dubai, which aims to have the tiniest ecological footprint by 2050

@ivankphoto | IVAN KASHINSKY
Karla Gachet and her dog explore sand dunes in Mexico for a story about El Camino Real de Baja California.

@dguttenfelder | DAVID GUTTENFELDER
A summer Saturday draws families to Yoyogi Park, one of Tokyo's green spaces amid its urban landscape.

@hannahreyesmorales | HANNAH REYES MORALES
Kids in Manila, Philippines, play in a water fountain by Binondo Church, a relic of Spanish colonization.

> **"THE** MORE PLACES **I SEE AND** EXPERIENCE, **THE BIGGER I REALIZE THE WORLD TO BE."** —ANTHONY BOURDAIN

@mmuheisen | **MUHAMMED MUHEISEN**
A colorful and floral alley in downtown Athens, Greece, which has struggled with overtourism for years

@renaeffendiphoto | **RENA EFFENDI**
People in Seoul pose in the cloud-like ambience of "Shinseon Play," a sculpture based on Korean mythology.

@johnstanmeyer | **JOHN STANMEYER**
A couple floats in a boat along the Teesta River outside Siliguri, West Bengal, India, for a pre-wedding photo.

@dzalcman | **DANIELLA ZALCMAN**
Magd Ahmad and new wife Nisrine at their wedding in Tunisia. Magd's family, separated during war in Syria, traveled to Tunis to celebrate the day.

GALWAY
MAKES WAVES

IRELAND'S CREATIVE WESTERN HUB

Named Europe's 2020 Capital of Culture, Galway is imbued with character that arises from centuries of synthesis. As a seaport and trading town, the city has long absorbed currents from outsiders—Normans, Spaniards, Sri Lankans, North Africans. The stony, windswept wilderness surrounding the city, County Galway and Connemara, has sent its sons and daughters abroad and welcomed them and their broadened worldviews back home again.

Closed to traffic, Shop Street—here decorated for Christmas—is Galway's spirited city center.

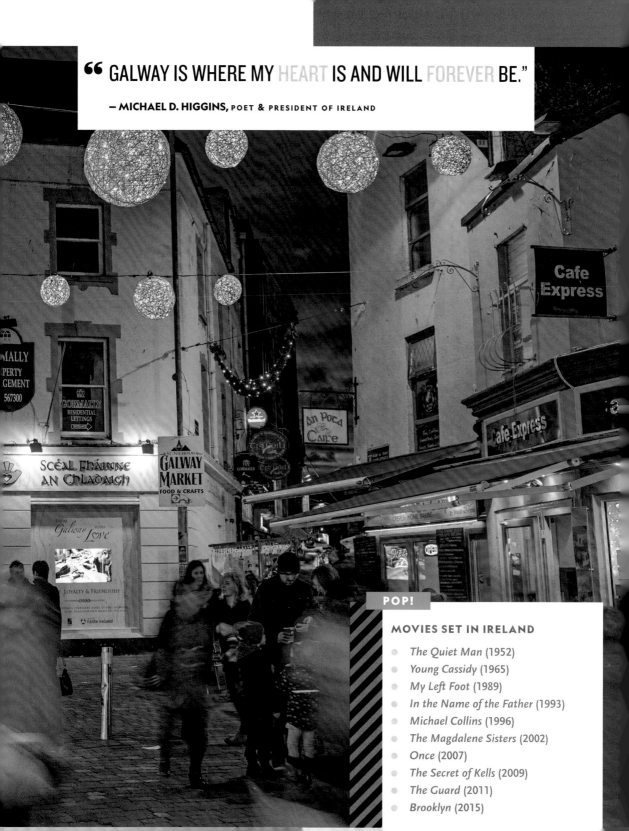

" GALWAY IS WHERE MY HEART **IS AND WILL** FOREVER **BE."**

— MICHAEL D. HIGGINS, POET & PRESIDENT OF IRELAND

POP!

MOVIES SET IN IRELAND

- *The Quiet Man* (1952)
- *Young Cassidy* (1965)
- *My Left Foot* (1989)
- *In the Name of the Father* (1993)
- *Michael Collins* (1996)
- *The Magdalene Sisters* (2002)
- *Once* (2007)
- *The Secret of Kells* (2009)
- *The Guard* (2011)
- *Brooklyn* (2015)

INTO INDIA'S WILD

INDIA HOSTS MORE THAN 100 NATIONAL PARKS

A tiger and her cub

KEOLADEO PARK

MIGRATORY FLYWAY

In centuries past, maharajas conducted royal duck-hunting expeditions on the land now part of the Keoladeo National Park, in Rajasthan, located along the Central Asian Flyway, where many bird species migrate between Siberia and the Indian Ocean. Declared a UNESCO World Heritage site in 1985, it provides wintering grounds for more than 350 species of birds, from storks to songbirds, including endangered eagles and cranes.

Best visited in the winter, the park is a two-hour drive from Agra, where you can also visit the Agra Fort, a Mughal stronghold dating back to the 16th century.

NAGARAHOLE PARK

SPOTTING TIGERS

Nagarahole National Park, located in Karnataka in southwestern India, is one of India's premier tiger destinations. Backed by the hills of the Western Ghats, the park is filled with fragrant sandalwood and teak trees, thick groves of bamboo, and dozens of winding streams. A jeep safari is the best option to spot big cats, while a slow drift in a coracle—a small, round boat—along the Kabini River offers prime viewing opportunities for aquatic birds, crocodiles, and Indian elephants.

The park is open year-round but can close due to flooding during monsoon season, July and August. Begin your visit in the city of Mysore, with its palace and ancient temples.

Painted stork juveniles

Ladakh's Stok Valley from 14,000 feet (4,267 m)

MAHATMA GANDHI PARK

ISLAND LIFE

Fifteen rocky islands, green with mangroves and tropical forest growth, compose Mahatma Gandhi Marine National Park in the Bay of Bengal. Some 3,000 people are known to live here, but only two of the islands are open to visitors: Jolly Buoy and Red Skin. From them, snorkel or scuba dive the fringing reefs to see fish including grouper, leatherback turtles, sea fans and sea stars, and an exquisite wall of coral.

The park is part of the Andaman and Nicobar Islands, which were devastated by the 2004 tsunami. Uprooted trees may be the most obvious sign of that history today, as nature restores itself and the white sand beaches glisten once again.

HEMIS PARK

GRAY GHOSTS

High in the Himalaya, Hemis National Park envelops snow-covered peaks and alpine tundra in the far northern reaches of India. Most visitors come in summer when Buddhist prayer flags flutter in the sun, but sightings of the endangered snow leopard—the elusive "gray ghost," rarely seen—will only occur in the stark winter landscape of Ladakh. One of India's largest nature preserves, Hemis is also home to several rare species of mountain sheep.

If you fly from Delhi to Leh, the gateway city to Hemis, be sure to plan for a day or two of acclimation to the altitude. Hemis Monastery, nearly 400 years old and the site of an annual Buddhist festival in June, is located inside the park.

Coral reef in the Andaman Sea

MARVELS
OF THE MAYA

SATISFYING AN EXPLORER'S SPIRIT

The tip of the Yucatán Peninsula is best known for the resort city of Cancún. But the region has a wealth of natural and historic attractions away from the tourist traps, including two UNESCO World Heritage sites: Chichén Itzá and the Sian Ka'an Biosphere Reserve. Come for the picturesque beaches and the turquoise cenotes (pools formed by inland sinkholes) but stay for the history—grand ruins of the sprawling Maya Empire, which thrived here for centuries.

Built facing east, Tulum may have originally been called Zama, meaning "dawn."

LIDAR SCANNING TECHNOLOGY RECENTLY DISCOVERED MORE THAN 60,000 MAYA STRUCTURES, BEFORE UNKNOWN, SUGGESTING A CIVILIZATION AS COMPLEX AS ANCIENT GREECE.

Exploring the RIVIERA MAYA

CHICHÉN ITZÁ
Vibrant urban center of the Maya Empire, with the Temple of Kukulkan

COBÁ
Largely unexcavated archaeological site with several Maya pyramids, including Nohoch Mul, the Yucatán Peninsula's tallest

DOS OJOS CENOTES
Part of the world's longest surveyed underwater cave system, irresistible for snorkeling and diving

EK BALAM
Sculpture-filled ruins (some from ca 100 BC) just a short bike ride from the tranquil Cenote Xcanche, a limestone sinkhole

ISLA BLANCA
Narrow peninsula north of Cancún, a favorite of kitesurfers, with quiet, pristine beaches and shallow lagoons

ISLA MUJERES
Island reached by ferry; popular for intimate snorkeling with whale sharks

PUNTA ALLEN
Quiet village on a remote peninsula, with a reef just offshore and opportunities for dolphin watching and lobster fishing

RIO SECRETO
Dramatic underground cave system with stalactites and stalagmites, accessible by hiking, biking, or swimming in a subterranean river

TULUM
Ruins of a 13th-century Maya walled seaport, including the Castillo and the Temple of the Frescoes

SIAN KA'AN
Biosphere Reserve Tropical forests, marshlands, mangroves, and a turquoise lagoon full of wildlife

VALLADOLID
Colorful town with colonial architecture, including the Convent de San Bernardino de Siena

OFF THE BEATEN PATH

PUT ADVENTURE BACK IN YOUR TRAVEL PLANS

CANADA
British Columbia
In British Columbia's Yoho National Park, you can hike, snowshoe, spot wildlife and wild orchids, kayak on Emerald Lake, and explore the Burgess Shale fossil beds without bumping into busloads of tourists.

NORTH AMERICA

GREECE
Lousios Gorge
Traverse rugged hiking trails in th region of the Peloponnese penins amid towering cypress trees, olive groves, terra-cotta-rooftop towns, medieval villages, and mountaint monasteries—like the Prodromos Monastery, built precariously into the rock face.

PACIFIC

ATLANTIC

OCEAN

OCEAN

SOUTH AMERICA

NICARAGUA
Lake Nicaragua
On a lake ringed by three volcanic peaks, the islets and lakeshores are shrouded in lush tropical forests that harbor myriad colorful bird and butterfly species. Nearby cities are awash with Spanish colonial splendor.

BRAZIL
Amazon Rainforest
Most of the action here takes place overhead. Ec tourism companies will take you climbing and pr vide the ropes, harnesse and hammocks you'll ne in the canopy, where you observe diverse, thriving flora and fauna.

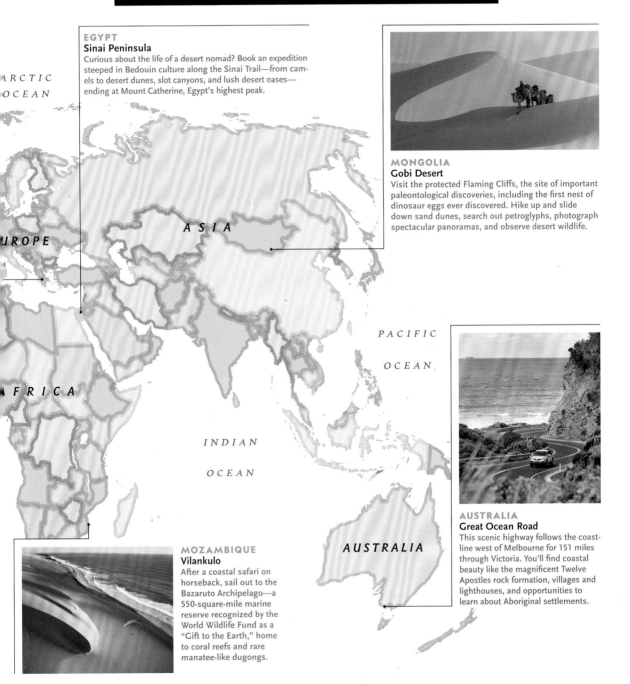

> ## "YOU THINK YOU ARE MAKING A TRIP, BUT SOON IT IS MAKING YOU—OR UNMAKING YOU."
> —NICOLAS BOUVIER, AUTHOR

EGYPT
Sinai Peninsula
Curious about the life of a desert nomad? Book an expedition steeped in Bedouin culture along the Sinai Trail—from camels to desert dunes, slot canyons, and lush desert oases—ending at Mount Catherine, Egypt's highest peak.

MONGOLIA
Gobi Desert
Visit the protected Flaming Cliffs, the site of important paleontological discoveries, including the first nest of dinosaur eggs ever discovered. Hike up and slide down sand dunes, search out petroglyphs, photograph spectacular panoramas, and observe desert wildlife.

AUSTRALIA
Great Ocean Road
This scenic highway follows the coastline west of Melbourne for 151 miles through Victoria. You'll find coastal beauty like the magnificent Twelve Apostles rock formation, villages and lighthouses, and opportunities to learn about Aboriginal settlements.

MOZAMBIQUE
Vilankulo
After a coastal safari on horseback, sail out to the Bazaruto Archipelago—a 550-square-mile marine reserve recognized by the World Wildlife Fund as a "Gift to the Earth," home to coral reefs and rare manatee-like dugongs.

ARCTIC OCEAN

EUROPE

ASIA

AFRICA

PACIFIC OCEAN

INDIAN OCEAN

AUSTRALIA

TOKYO

WHERE OLD MEETS NEW

Japan's capital—the world's largest city, population 37 million—can feel energetic one moment and calm the next, and that kind of mishmash is one of the city's endearing qualities. Plan to see some of the old and some of the new, some urban and some rural, and leave room in your itinerary for spontaneity so you can take part in a festival, sample street food, and explore alleyways.

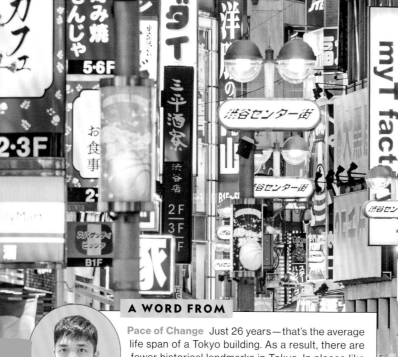

A WORD FROM

Pace of Change Just 26 years—that's the average life span of a Tokyo building. As a result, there are fewer historical landmarks in Tokyo. In places like Kyoto, there are more traditional buildings, but everything that is really vital in Tokyo is so because of its newness and its sense of change. The environment here transforms constantly to make way for the future.

—**DARRYL JINGWEN WEE,** *lead consultant, Tokyo Tomo*

Pedestrians flood the streets of Tokyo's Shibuya shopping district.

What to Do in
TOKYO

1 **WILDLIFE** Off the Izu Islands, teeming with birds, you might see dolphins, humpback whales, and sperm whales.

2 **OFFBEAT** Trails wind through mountain scenery in Tanzawa-Oyama Quasi-National Park. Historical treasures await at the foot of Mount Oyama.

3 **HISTORY** The Edo-Tokyo Museum brings to life Edo-era Tokyo (1603–1868) with reconstructions of Edo housing and dioramas of the city.

4 **MOST ICONIC PLACE** Nothing else encapsulates modern Tokyo like the Shibuya Crossing at night: Crowds cross from six directions against a neon-lit high-rise backdrop.

5 **LATE NIGHT** Unleash your inner diva at karaoke. Rent a booth at a karaoke chain for a private space and order from the long menu of party food and drinks.

6 **NATURAL BEAUTY** Take the 26-hour ferry to the Ogasawara Islands, designated for their rich ecosystems, with 195 endangered bird species and over 400 native plant taxa.

7 **HIP NEIGHBORHOOD** Kichijoji has used clothing stores, record shops, craft breweries, street performers, and the acclaimed anime-themed Ghibli Museum.

8 **TIMELESS GARDEN** Founded in the 1600s, the Koishikawa Korakuen garden is an example of traditional landscaping, with paths, ponds, and gorgeous seasonal foliage.

9 **ART** The Tokyo Metropolitan Art Museum brings art from Japan and the rest of the world together in the heart of the capital.

10 **VIEWS** The Tokyo Skytree is the second tallest structure in the world, with a 360-degree view of the sprawling city from its upper observation deck.

ICELAND'S
HOT SPRINGS

IMMERSIONS IN ICELAND

Escape the throngs of tourists and enjoy aquamarine-colored water at Mývatn Nature Baths in northern Iceland. Traveling farther afield means fewer people in the pools and increases your chances of witnessing the aurora borealis. More adventurous travelers will enjoy the challenge of reaching the geothermal pools inside the caves of Grjótagjá—a setting so magical it's appeared in *Game of Thrones*—or the hot stream at Reykjadalur, just an hour outside Reykjavík.

Bathers soak in the hot springs at Mývatn Nature Baths, where sulfur gives the water its blue tint.

ICELAND USES ITS GEOTHERMAL FEATURES FOR HEAT AND POWER GENERATION. IN REYKJAVÍK, 90% OF HOMES CONNECT DIRECTLY TO A GEOTHERMAL DISTRICT HEATING SYSTEM.

More of the World's Best
HOT SPRINGS

1   **BEPPU, JAPAN** The ultimate *onsen*—Japanese for "hot springs"; here you'll find eight bathhouses.

2   **DECEPTION ISLAND, ANTARCTICA** An active underwater volcano offers a steamy caldera with penguins nearby.

3   **PUCÓN, CHILE** Waterfalls, plunge pools, and a red boardwalk distinguish the Termas Geometricas in the Villarrica National Park.

4   **HOT SPRINGS, ARKANSAS, U.S.A.** Bathe your way into history on Bathhouse Row, the 19th-century main street now a national park.

5   **DUNTON, COLORADO, U.S.A.** Hot springs steam up this luxury destination, a reconstructed ghost town in the Colorado Rockies.

6   **BANFF, BRITISH COLUMBIA, CANADA** Gaze at the Canadian Rockies from the historic bathhouse, established in 1886.

7   **ROTORUA, NEW ZEALAND** The smell of sulfur infuses this region of the North Island, long deemed sacred by the Maori.

8   **PAMUKKALE, TURKEY** Naturally heated water cascades through 17 white limestone terraces, closed to bathers but still magnificent to view.

9   **MAREMMA, ITALY** Soak in mineral springs that once comforted Roman generals in Tuscany's Terme di Saturnia.

10   **BANJAR, BALI** Mineral-rich water spews from the mouths of intricately carved *naga*, mythical serpent demigods.

FURTHER

SKY-HIGH DUNES

It feels otherworldly, trekking the knife-edge ridge of a massive sand dune of Sossusvlei, part of the Namib-Naukluft National Park, Africa's largest conservation area. Here in the midst of what many call the world's oldest desert, the sand glows red because of its high iron oxide content. The slopes seem eternal, but these are shape-shifting dunes, caught in the crossfire of winds from many directions: hot, dry gusts from the Kalahari to the east; fog-bearing currents from the Atlantic to the southwest. Tomorrow's trek atop the dunes may lead in another direction.

Hikers trek the megadunes of Sossusvlei in Namibia's Namib-Naukluft National Park.

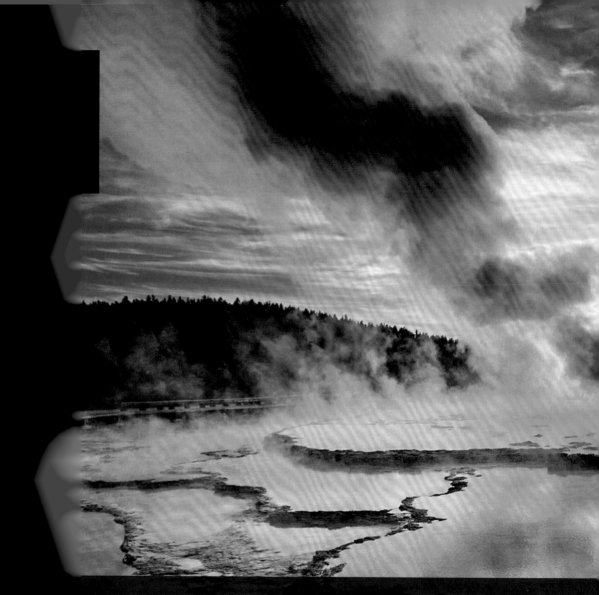

THIS PLANET
& BEYOND

The Great Fountain Geyser in Wyoming is fueled by vast magma stores below Yellowstone National Park.

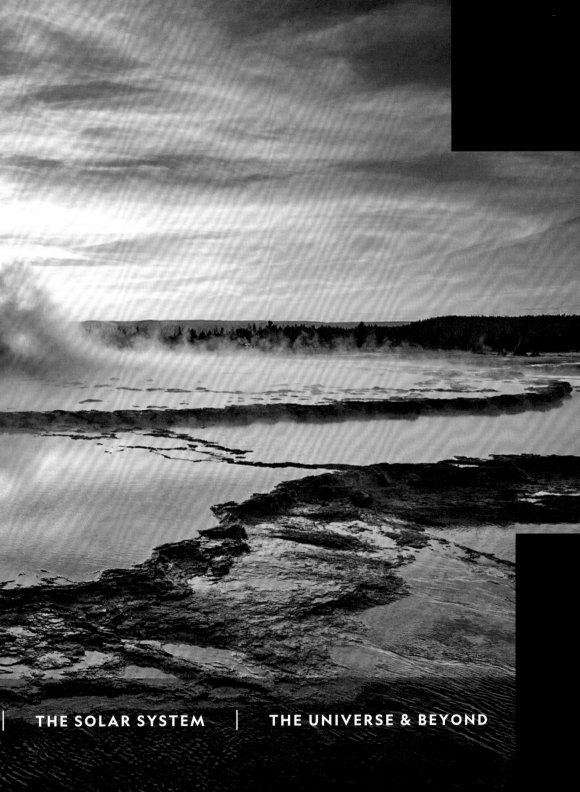

THE SOLAR SYSTEM | THE UNIVERSE & BEYOND

QUIZ MASTER

From Groundwater to Galaxies Our home planet spins amid a universe of wonder. Check out a few of the many facts in this chapter, which stretches from the soil under our feet to the planets and stars above.

—**SUSAN TYLER HITCHCOCK**, *Nat Geo Quizmaster*

p101

WHERE IN THE WORLD CAN **YOU** SEE **LIGHTNING** ALMOST EVERY NIGHT OF THE YEAR?

INTO WHICH **PLANET DID** NASA'S CASSINI SPACECRAFT DELIBERATELY **CRASH IN 2017?**

p127

NAME THE **ASTEROID** ON WHICH A **JAPANESE SPACECRAFT** RECENTLY **LANDED.**

p118

IN WHAT **CONSTELLATION** WILL YOU FIND THE TWO BRIGHT STARS BETELGEUSE AND RIGEL?

p135

IN WHAT COUNTRY DID THE WORLD'S TWO **DEADLIEST VOLCANO** ERUPTIONS OCCUR?

p140

HOW LONG AGO WAS THE BIG BANG?

WHAT COUNTRY IS THE WORLD'S TOP **PRODUCER** OF LITHIUM?

NAME THE LARGEST MOON IN OUR SOLAR SYSTEM. HINT: IT ORBITS JUPITER.

IS MARBLE AN IGNEOUS, SEDIMENTARY, OR META-MORPHIC ROCK?

p113

p131

GAGARIN CRATER IS A FEATURE ON THE FAR SIDE OF THE MOON. WHO IS IT NAMED FOR?

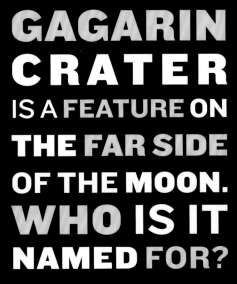

p136

WHAT 18TH-CENTURY SCIENTIST CREATED A CATALOG OF STARS, GALAXIES, AND OTHER SKY OBJECTS STILL IN USE TODAY?

p138

WHO INVENTED THE SCALE FOR MEASURING EARTHQUAKE INTENSITY? HINT: IT'S NAMED FOR HIM.

p97

p123

HOW MANY SUPERMOONS WILL THERE BE IN 2021?

WHAT WAS THE KEPLER SPACE MISSION DESIGNED TO STUDY: BIRTH OF STARS, EARTHLIKE PLANETS, OR SOLAR WIND?

p149

EARTH SCIENCE
TIME LINE

| 4.6 to 2.3 BYA | 2.3 BYA to 400 MYA | 400 to 200 MYA | 200 MYA to 20,000 YA |

■ 4.6 bya*
Planet Earth forms from the material that built the rest of the solar system.

■ 4.5 bya
Earth's moon forms out of space debris.

■ 4.3 bya
Liquid water appears on Earth.

■ 3.8 bya
Single-celled life emerges on Earth.

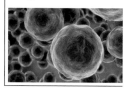

■ 3 bya
Earth's continental masses form.

■ 2.5–2.3 bya
Oxygen levels in the Earth's atmosphere rise.

* billion years ago

■ 2.1 bya
More complex multicellular organisms evolve.

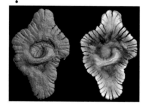

■ 720–635 mya*
The temperature on Earth falls, and the entire planet is covered in ice.

■ 541 mya
Most major animal groups evolve in an event known as the Cambrian explosion.

■ 520 mya
Animals with bilateral symmetry first flourish on Earth.

■ 470 mya
Plant life first appears on land.

* million years ago

■ 360 mya
Amphibious life emerges from the water to live on land.

■ 251 mya
Massive numbers of marine and land species die off in the Permian extinction, the largest mass extinction in history.

■ 250 mya
A single supercontinent called Pangaea emerges.

■ 240 mya
The first dinosaurs appear on Earth.

■ 200 mya
The supercontinent Pangaea breaks up into separate landmasses.

■ 130 mya
Flowering plants, the most diverse group of land plants, emerge.

■ 65 mya
Dinosaurs go extinct in the aftermath of the Chicxulub asteroid impact.

■ 2.6 mya
Continents arrive at roughly their modern positions and a pattern of glacial and interglacial periods emerges.

■ 200,000 ya*
Homo sapiens first appear, and modern humans emerge.

* years ago

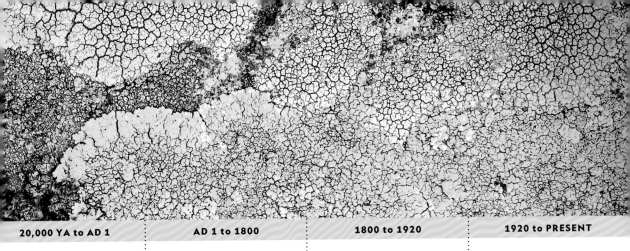

| 20,000 YA to AD 1 | AD 1 to 1800 | 1800 to 1920 | 1920 to PRESENT |

■ 11,700 ya
The Holocene,
the current geological
age, begins.

■ 10,000 ya
The last major
ice age ends.

■ ca 499 BC
Indian scientist Aryabhata
proposes that Earth
rotates on its axis.

■ 240 BC
Eratosthenes calculates
the circumference
of the Earth.

■ ca 1088
Chinese scientist
Shen Kuo first describes
a magnetic compass
used for navigation.

■ 1490s
Leonardo da Vinci begins
filling notebooks with
theories on astronomy,
Earth, physics, and more.

■ 1543
Copernicus publishes
ideas on heliocentrism.

■ 1595
Gerardus Mercator's
atlas of the world
is first published.

■ 1815
Explosion of Mount
Tambora temporarily
changes Earth's climate.

■ 1831
English explorer
James Ross locates
the position of the
north magnetic pole.

■ 1851
Léon Foucault constructs
Foucault's pendulum
to show Earth's rotation.

■ 1912
Alfred Wegener first
describes the theory
of continental drift.

■ 1913
Charles Fabry and Henri
Buisson discover
the ozone layer.

■ 1935
Charles Richter invents
the Richter scale
to measure earthquake
intensity.

■ 1960s
Scientists first describe
plate tectonics.

■ 1960
Jacques Piccard and Don
Walsh are first to visit
the deepest point in the
ocean, Challenger Deep.

■ 1970
The inaugural Earth Day
is held on April 22.

■ 2017
One of the largest
icebergs on record breaks
off from Antarctica's
Larsen C ice shelf.

CLARIFYING CLIMATE

TO UNDERSTAND CLIMATE CHANGE, WE MUST UNDERSTAND CLIMATE

The climate of any location on Earth depends on latitude, elevation above sea level, proximity to the ocean, and the circulation patterns in the atmosphere and ocean. This map displays the Köppen-Geiger system of climate zones based on seasonal temperatures and precipitation.

WARMING ALPS
Climate change is expected to transform much of the European Alps from a snow to a warm temperate climate by the end of the 21st century.

AR

NORTH

AMERICA

TREES AT RISK
In the northern Rocky Mountains as summers get longer and hotter, trees at high altitudes will be especially vulnerable to drought, wildfire, and destructive insects.

CARIBBEAN HURRICANES
The Gulf Stream's warm ocean water intensifies the hurricanes that pass over it, often tracking the storms toward mainland North America.

ATLANTIC

OCEAN

PACIFIC

OCEAN

RAIN SHADOWS
The Rocky Mountains and Andes form the spine of the Americas, influencing climate by stopping moist ocean air from reaching the interior.

SOUTH
AMERICA

EXPANDING DESERT
In Algeria, the desert has gradually expanded and displaced much of the warm temperate region where most people live.

DISAPPEARING ICE
Scientists expect the largest shifts in climate zones in the 21st century to replace about 1% of polar zones with warmer snow zones.

SOUTHERN AFRICA
The position of the island of Madagascar reduces the impact of wet trade winds on the mainland coast and lessens the chance of tropical cyclones landing there.

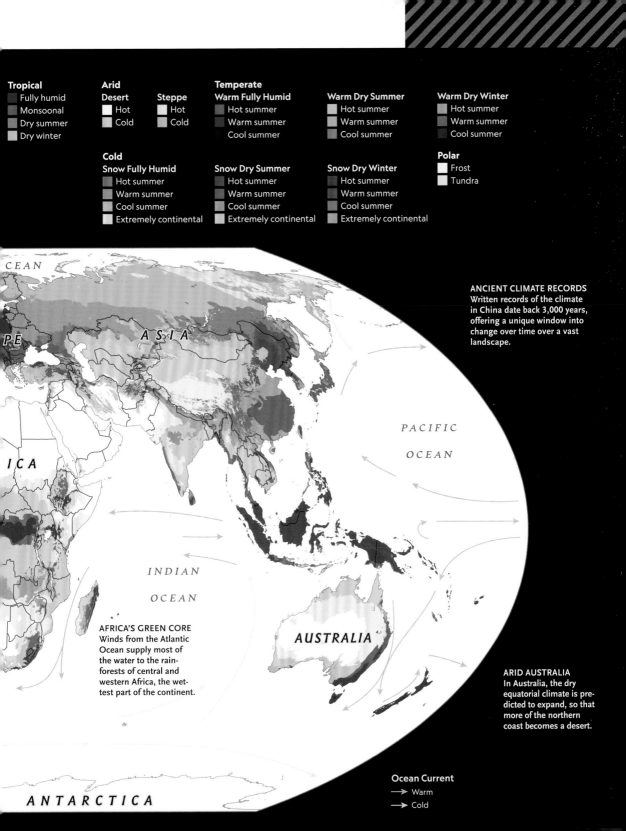

Tropical
- Fully humid
- Monsoonal
- Dry summer
- Dry winter

Arid
Desert
- Hot
- Cold

Steppe
- Hot
- Cold

Temperate
Warm Fully Humid
- Hot summer
- Warm summer
- Cool summer

Warm Dry Summer
- Hot summer
- Warm summer
- Cool summer

Warm Dry Winter
- Hot summer
- Warm summer
- Cool summer

Cold
Snow Fully Humid
- Hot summer
- Warm summer
- Cool summer
- Extremely continental

Snow Dry Summer
- Hot summer
- Warm summer
- Cool summer
- Extremely continental

Snow Dry Winter
- Hot summer
- Warm summer
- Cool summer
- Extremely continental

Polar
- Frost
- Tundra

CEAN

PE

ASIA

ICA

PACIFIC

OCEAN

INDIAN

OCEAN

AUSTRALIA

ANTARCTICA

ANCIENT CLIMATE RECORDS
Written records of the climate in China date back 3,000 years, offering a unique window into change over time over a vast landscape.

AFRICA'S GREEN CORE
Winds from the Atlantic Ocean supply most of the water to the rainforests of central and western Africa, the wettest part of the continent.

ARID AUSTRALIA
In Australia, the dry equatorial climate is predicted to expand, so that more of the northern coast becomes a desert.

Ocean Current
→ Warm
→ Cold

READING THE CLOUDS

Looking Up Though we've always had clouds above, we are still coming up with new ways to categorize and name them. Changes in technology, especially the sharing of photos, is also leading to new identifications.

FAIR-WEATHER CUMULUS
Small, puffy, white

CUMULIFORM
Puffy, humid air condensing

ORTHOGRAPHIC
Precipitation near mountains

CIRRUS
Thin and transparent

CIRROCUMULUS
White patches of high clouds

CIRROSTRATUS
High and thin, hazy

ALTOCUMULUS
Puffy clouds with darker patches

LENTICULAR
Lens-shaped, over mountains

ALTOCUMULUS CASTELLANUS
Tall, narrow

STRATOCUMULUS
Spread across large areas

STRATUS
Featureless gray layers

ALTOSTRATUS
Thin, gray, highest sheet-type

NIMBOSTRATUS
Low, dark, gloomy

CUMULUS CONGESTUS
Cauliflower-like

CUMULONIMBUS
Anvil shape, brings thunderstorms

ALTOCUMULUS MAMMATUS
Hanging pouches

THE INTERNATIONAL CLOUD ATLAS RECOGNIZED A NEW CLOUD TYPE IN 2017: THE ASPERITAS, DAPPLED LIKE THE SEA SEEN FROM UNDERWATER.

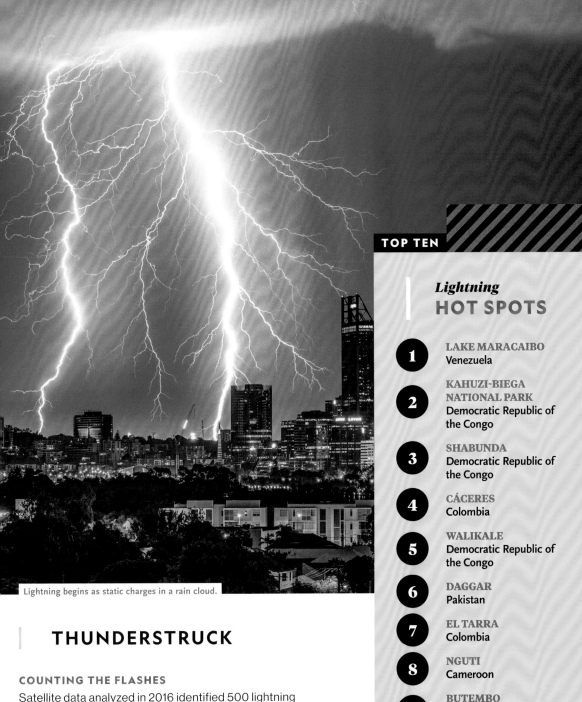

Lightning begins as static charges in a rain cloud.

TOP TEN

Lightning HOT SPOTS

1. **LAKE MARACAIBO** Venezuela
2. **KAHUZI-BIEGA NATIONAL PARK** Democratic Republic of the Congo
3. **SHABUNDA** Democratic Republic of the Congo
4. **CÁCERES** Colombia
5. **WALIKALE** Democratic Republic of the Congo
6. **DAGGAR** Pakistan
7. **EL TARRA** Colombia
8. **NGUTI** Cameroon
9. **BUTEMBO** Democratic Republic of the Congo
10. **BOENDE** Democratic Republic of the Congo

THUNDERSTRUCK

COUNTING THE FLASHES

Satellite data analyzed in 2016 identified 500 lightning "hot spots" around the world: the places where lightning flashes and strikes most often. Of those 500, more than half are in Africa, but the place that sees the most lightning—almost every night of the year—is Lake Maracaibo in Venezuela, South America's largest lake by area.

COMBATING
A BLAZE

THE COMPLICATED BATTLE AGAINST WILDFIRES

Fighting wildfire is often likened to a military campaign, with personnel deployed strategically on the ground and air support striking from above. Planning an attack, as here in the northern Rockies, firefighters weigh three factors that drive the course of any blaze: topography, weather, and the type of fuel in the line of fire.

1 Fires can spread especially rapidly up slopes and suddenly explode up canyons, which act as natural chimneys. Southern slopes, sunnier and drier, are more likely to burn than northern exposures.

2 Dramatic winds brought on by cold fronts and storms can shift a fire's direction or cause flare-ups. Low humidity and high temperatures make fuel, especially grass and accumulated underbrush, drier and quicker to burn.

3 Air tankers and helicopters, called in by coordinators on the ground, drop water or chemical fire retardant.

4 A fire crew's priority is to find a man-made or natural barrier to the fire's advance—a road or a stream—and from that anchor point dig a perimeter fire line to contain the blaze.

5 Long days are spent digging a fire line down to bare earth, even if a bulldozer is available to help. The line is banked to catch rolling debris.

6 Drip torches are used to burn out fuel between the fire line and the fire, halting its advance.

7 Felling dead trees prevents them from collapsing across the fire line or on firefighters and helps keep flames from climbing into the canopy.

8 Homes that have edged into forest fire territory can't be guaranteed protection. And even if fire is stopped before reaching a house, airborne embers can drift through vents and burn it down from the inside out.

A WORD FROM

Devastating Embers A fire acts like a living organism. The same way a plant spreads its seeds, a fire creates wind to spread its embers. A fire causes hot air and smoke to rise rapidly, pulling in air along the ground to replace it. This creates a wind that will push the fire along, which creates a self-perpetuating cycle of fire that is impossible to stop.

—**MARK THIESSEN,** *photographer and wildland firefighter*

HURRICANES

SWIRLING STORMS OF DESTRUCTION

Hurricanes are massive storm systems, sometimes broadening to more than a hundred miles across and packing damaging winds and intense amounts of water. In 2018, it was estimated that Hurricane Florence was carrying 18 trillion gallons of water in its rain bands, enough water to fill the Chesapeake Bay, and several North Carolina towns reported more than 30 inches of rain. Hurricane Harvey in 2017 held 25 trillion gallons. Like the ocean currents, hurricanes move heat from the warm tropics up toward the poles. They wreak chaos and can leave utter destruction in their wakes, but they also help maintain the thermal balance in tropical oceans.

ANTI-CYCLONE
High above the eye of the storm, an atmospheric anti-cyclone rotates in opposition to the hurricane below. This acts as an exhaust pipe for the warm winds spiraling up inside the eye wall.

EYE WALL
The eye wall is the strongest part of the storm; winds here can reach over 200 miles per hour.

NEGATIVE SURGE
Just as the winds push the ocean higher in a storm surge, they can also "blow away the ocean" in a negative surge, lowering tides when the winds aim seaward.

Tropical Storm Lowell strengthens into a hurricane in the Pacific Ocean.

HURRICANE WILMA IN 2005 IS THE MOST INTENSE ATLANTIC HURRICANE RECORDED SO FAR, WITH WIND SPEEDS REACHING 185 MILES AN HOUR. IT CAUSED AN ESTIMATED $34.4 BILLION IN DAMAGES.

SPIN
Hurricane spin depends on the Coriolis effect caused by Earth's rotation. Northern Hemisphere hurricanes rotate counterclockwise, and Southern Hemisphere hurricanes rotate clockwise.

EYE
The calm eye is the center of the storm, a central core of warm air that draws heat from the ocean to create intense low pressure that powers the devastating winds.

STORM SURGE
A hurricane's powerful winds can push the ocean over 10 feet higher than the highest tide, leading to devastating flooding, erosion, and property damage.

VOLCANOES

WHEN EARTH ERUPTS

When we talk about volcanoes in the continental U.S., we probably think of Mount St. Helens, the "Mount Fuji of America," which erupted spectacularly in May 1980. We are less likely to think of Yellowstone, even with its geysers and hot mud, because although it is surrounded by mountains, it is not one itself. But our most famous national park sits squarely atop one of Earth's biggest volcanoes—a supervolcano—and it is not extinct. Volcanoes, as we tend to imagine them, form mountains. Supervolcanoes erase them.

Sleeping Giants

Beneath Yellowstone is a hellish column of superheated rock—mostly solid, some viscous, some molten. Experts say three major blasts, bigger than most known prehistoric eruptions, have shaken Yellowstone in its two million years atop the plume. The smallest of these ejected 280 times the volume of what Mount St. Helens projected.

The U.S. Geological Survey's Yellowstone Volcano Observatory monitors sensors and satellites, looking for changes in activity. Despite rumors, a supereruption like the one illustrated on the facing page is not imminent. For its part, the USGS puts the rough yearly odds of another massive Yellowstone blast at one in 730,000.

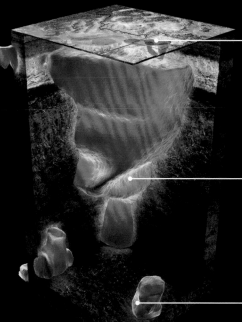

CALDERA
Buoyed by an expanding magma chamber, the caldera, formed by the last major eruption, has risen as much as 2.8 inches a year over the past decade.

PLUME
Beneath the caldera, a vast rocky zone of primordial heat emanates from the mantle. This plume feeds a magma chamber brimming with volcanic fuel just a few miles below the surface.

HOT POCKETS
Current seismic data and geological conditions suggest there may be smaller pockets of hot rock associated with the Yellowstone plume.

POP!

MOVIES STARRING VOLCANOES

- *The Last Days of Pompeii* (1935)
- *Stromboli* (1950)
- *Krakatoa: East of Java* (1969)
- *St. Helens* (1981)
- *Joe Versus the Volcano* (1990)
- *Dante's Peak* (1997)
- *Volcano* (1997)
- *Supervolcano* (2005)
- *Disaster Zone: Volcano in New York* (2006)
- *Volcano Zombies* (2014)
- *Pompeii* (2014)
- *Ixcanul* (2015)

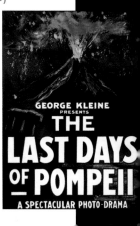

GEORGE KLEINE
PRESENTS
THE
LAST DAYS
OF POMPEII
A SPECTACULAR PHOTO-DRAMA

HOW DOES IT HAPPEN?

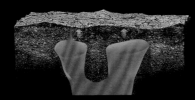

BEFORE THE ERUPTION Warning signs may appear years in advance. Pressure builds from below, driving seismic activity and doming of the land over the hot spot.

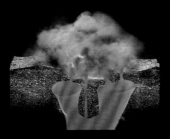

THE EARTH FRACTURES Gas-filled magma explodes upward; ash and debris soon rain down across hundreds of miles. Fiery ash flows clog rivers and carpet landscapes near and far.

ERUPTIONS CONTINUE Periodic blasts go on for weeks or even months, emitting pollutants and causing acid rain. Eventually, the land collapses and a new caldera is born.

World's Deadliest ERUPTIONS

1 **TAMBORA, INDONESIA**
Apr. 10, 1815: 92,000 killed
Largest in recorded history, with ejecta volume of 12 mi^3

2 **KRAKATAU, INDONESIA**
Aug. 26, 1883: 36,417 killed
Ash layer lowered temperatures and affected global climate.

3 **PELÉE, MARTINIQUE**
May 8, 1902: 29,025 killed
Most deaths direct result of eruption and not tsunami, etc.

4 **RUIZ, COLOMBIA**
Nov. 13, 1985: 25,000 killed
Mudflows caused by melting snow and ice buried thousands.

5 **UNZEN, JAPAN**
May 21, 1792: 14,300 killed
Eruption followed by earth-quake, landslide, and tsunami

6 **LAKI, ICELAND**
June 8, 1783: 9,350 killed
Lava flows and explosions continued for eight months.

7 **KELUD, INDONESIA**
May 19, 1919: 5,110 killed
Still active with hundreds killed in 1951, 1966, 1990, and 2014

8 **GALUNGGUNG, INDONESIA**
Oct. 8, 1882: 4,011 killed
Crater lake ejected boiling water and mud during eruptions.

9 **VESUVIUS, ITALY**
Dec. 16, 1631: 3,500 killed
Fatal pyroclastic flows followed a 30-mile-high cloud.

10 **VESUVIUS, ITALY**
79: 3,360 killed
Ash-covered Pompeii is famous for perfectly preserved victims.

LITHIUM

POWERING THE FUTURE

Lightweight, heat-resistant, and capable of storing lots of energy, lithium is the element of tomorrow. I in your smartphone, your camera, your hybrid vehicle; it has properties that make it ideal for use in all t rechargeable batteries we depend on today. Lithium-ion batteries entered the commercial market 1991, and since then advances in engineering and manufacturing mean their cost has dropped and the energy density has steadily increased.

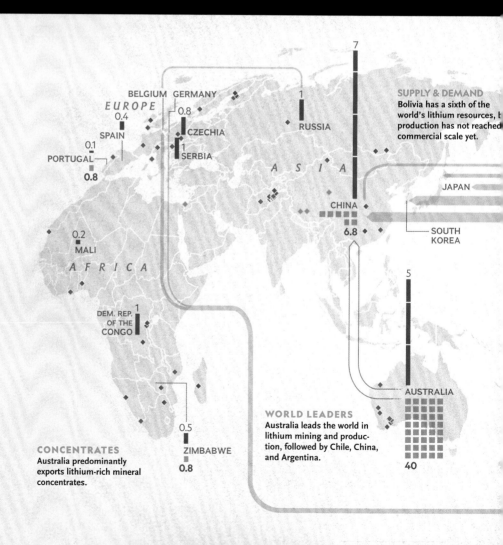

EUROPE

BELGIUM GERMANY
0.4   0.8

SPAIN

CZECHIA

0.1
PORTUGAL
0.8

1
SERBIA

1
RUSSIA

A S I A

7

SUPPLY & DEMAND
Bolivia has a sixth of the world's lithium resources, l production has not reached commercial scale yet.

JAPAN

CHINA
6.8

SOUTH KOREA

0.2
MALI

A F R I C A

DEM. REP.
OF THE
CONGO   1

5

AUSTRALIA

0.5
ZIMBABWE
0.8

CONCENTRATES
Australia predominantly exports lithium-rich mineral concentrates.

WORLD LEADERS
Australia leads the world in lithium mining and production, followed by Chile, China, and Argentina.

40

LITHIUM CAN BE EXTRACTED EITHER FROM ROCK (FROM PEGMATITES—COARSE-GRAINED IGNEOUS ROCK, FOR EXAMPLE) OR FROM BRINE (SALTWATER FOUND UNDERGROUND).

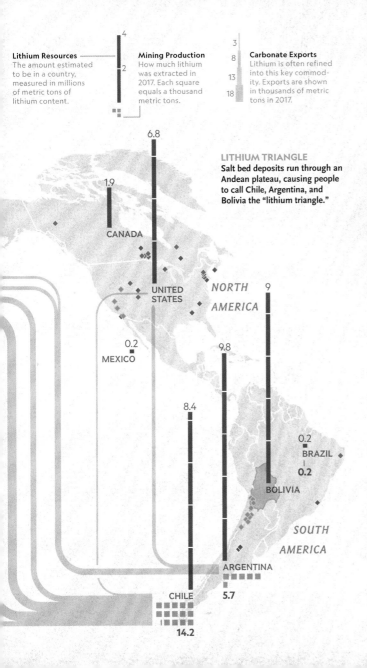

Lithium Resources The amount estimated to be in a country, measured in millions of metric tons of lithium content.

Mining Production How much lithium was extracted in 2017. Each square equals a thousand metric tons.

Carbonate Exports Lithium is often refined into this key commodity. Exports are shown in thousands of metric tons in 2017.

3
8
13
18

4
2

LITHIUM TRIANGLE
Salt bed deposits run through an Andean plateau, causing people to call Chile, Argentina, and Bolivia the "lithium triangle."

6.8

1.9

CANADA

0.2
MEXICO

UNITED
STATES

*NORTH
AMERICA*

9

9.8

8.4

0.2
BRAZIL
0.2

BOLIVIA

*SOUTH
AMERICA*

ARGENTINA

CHILE
5.7

14.2

KEY FACTS

All About LITHIUM

ATOMIC NUMBER 3 The world's lightest metal, lithium is the third element in the periodic table, after hydrogen and helium.

FROM THE START Astrophysicists believe that lithium, hydrogen, and helium were the first and only elements created at the big bang.

DISCOVERED & ISOLATED Swedish scientist John August Arfvedson discovered lithium in 1812. In 1818, it was isolated by English scientists Sir Humphry Davy and William Thomas Brande.

ROCKET'S RED GLARE Lithium burns red and, combined with another element, strontium, creates the red in fireworks.

LEVELING AGENT Lithium has long been used pharmaceutically as a treatment for bipolar disorder.

ROCKS & STREAMS Lithium does not occur free in nature but is a component of most igneous rocks and many mineral springs.

STAR ATTRACTION In 2018, Chinese astronomers announced discovery of a giant star containing 3,000 times the lithium in our sun—perhaps a clue to understanding the evolution of stars.

UP & AWAY Alloyed with aluminum, copper, manganese, and cadmium, lithium is used to manufacture aircraft.

BEST OF @NATGEO

TOP PHOTOS OF THE WEATHER

@babaktafreshi | BABAK TAFRESHI
A flashing thunderstorm coexists in the sky with stars above
he Haleakala volcanic crater in Maui, Hawaii.

@franslanting | FRANS LANTING
A howling blizzard forces these emperor penguins to hunke
down at their colony on Antarctic sea ice.

@sandracattaneoadorno | SANDRA CATTANEO ADORNO
Bathers on Ipanema beach in Rio de Janeiro appear hesitant
o plunge into the unusually rough and strong sea.

@salvarezphoto | STEPHEN ALVAREZ
A brief opening in the clouds creates a refraction of light
during a rainstorm near Volcán Cotopaxi, Ecuador.

@chancellordavid | DAVID CHANCELLOR
Bright light and mist stream through clouds during a storm in a rural area of South Africa's Eastern Cape.

@gabrielegalimbertiphoto | GABRIELE GALIMBERTI
An intense beam of lightning cuts through the cloudy, rural landscape of Siena, Tuscany, in central Italy.

@markthiessen | MARK THIESSEN
A firefighter faces a powerful wildfire, one of nature's fiercest forces, during wildfire season in America's West.

@ladzinski | KEITH LADZINSKI
Snowmelt pouring into lakes and a prolonged rain season cause swirling floods in Port Clinton, Ohio.

MINERALS
REVEALED

How Hard Is It? More than 4,000 naturally occurring minerals have been found on Earth. Geologists classify them according to hardness, using the Mohs' scale (opposite). All rocks are made of mixtures of minerals.

JASPER
Hardness: 6–7

FELDSPAR
Hardness: 6–7

OLIVINE
Hardness: 6.5–7

GARNET
Hardness: 6.5–7.5

EPIDOTE
Hardness: 6–7

STAUROLITE
Hardness: 7–7.5

TOURMALINE
Hardness: 7–7.5

PYROXENE
Hardness: 5–6.5

TALC
Hardness: 1

HORNBLENDE
Hardness: 5–6

BIOTITE
Hardness: 2.5–3

MUSCOVITE
Hardness: 2–2.5

KAOLINITE
Hardness: 2–2.5

SERPENTINE
Hardness: 3–6

DOLOMITE
Hardness: 3.5–4

CALCITE
Hardness: 3

GYPSUM & ANHYDRITE
Hardness: 2 & 3–3.5

MALACHITE
Hardness: 3.5–4

CHALCOPYRITE
Hardness: 3.5–4

GALENA
Hardness: 2.5–3

PYRITE
Hardness: 6–6.5

FLUORITE
Hardness: 4

MAGNETITE
Hardness: 5.5

HEMATITE
Hardness: 5–6

QUARTZ
Hardness: 7

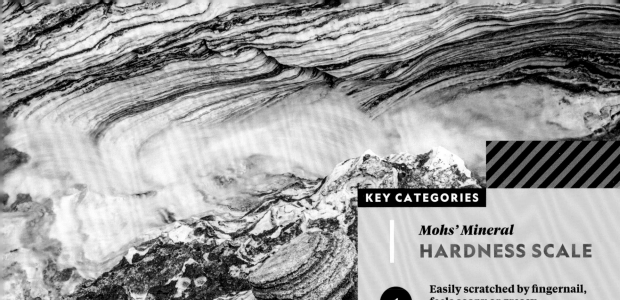

Marble rates between 3 and 5 on the Mohs' scale.

MARBLE

FROM ANCIENT SEAS TO KITCHEN COUNTERS
Marble countertops, statues, and columns dot the land-scapes, filling our homes and museums. Every piece of the iconic stone, so common today, began in the fires and fissures of Earth's molten seams, or volcanic hot spots. Marble is a metamorphic rock. It begins as the crystallized calcium remnants of deep sea corals or other creatures. In the fiery seams of Earth's tectonic plates, or volcanic magma chambers, new crystals begin to form, and the metamorphosis begins. The more this crystallization spreads, the larger and stronger the marble becomes. Eventually vast marble beds form, containing millions of tons of the soft stone ready to be shaped. It comes in colors from pure white to pink, yellow, and black, depending on the mineral content.

IN ADDITION TO ITS FAMILIAR USES IN SCULPTING AND ARCHITECTURE, GROUND MARBLE IS SOMETIMES ADDED TO ANIMAL FEED AS A SOURCE OF CALCIUM.

ENRIC SALA
MARINE ECOLOGIST

MAN ON A MISSION

For more than a decade, National Geographic Explorer-in-Residence Enric Sala has been doing everything in his power to save the world's oceans. Growing up on the east coast of Spain, Sala would snorkel in the Mediterranean and wonder at its marine life. He pursued a career in oceanography, but after years in academia, instead of continuing to write "the obituary of the ocean," as Sala puts it, he reshaped his mission and founded Pristine Seas.

Since starting Pristine Seas, Sala has completed more than 30 expeditions and inspired more than 21 marine reserves.

Through National Geographic's Pristine Seas program, Sala has helped protect nearly two million square miles (5 million sq km) of the ocean, by working with governments to create some of the largest marine reserves on Earth. Now, with 22 marine reserves created globally and more under way, he intends to get world leaders to commit to protecting 30 percent of the planet—land and sea—by 2030.

WILD SEAS

Pristine Seas combines exploration, research, media, and diplomacy to safeguard the last wild places in the ocean. Sala started the project in 2008 to support the United Nations' target of 10 percent of the ocean protected by 2020. Since then, Pristine Seas has carried out dozens of expeditions, often in remote, inhospitable regions—isolated islands in the Pacific, uninhabited stretches north of the Arctic Circle—collecting data to ascertain which waters can be called "pristine."

These unique places show what the ocean looked like before overfishing and pollution took their toll. Sala and his teammates have found, for example, that the more sharks in a region, the healthier it is. "Most people shoot out of the water when anyone claims that sharks are sighted," he says. "Our Pristine Seas team does the opposite. When we hear 'Sharks!' we jump into the sea as fast as we can. We have learned that an abundance of sharks indicates a healthy ocean area, possibly pristine waters."

> " IF 20 YEARS FROM NOW, OUR CHILDREN WERE TO JUMP INTO ANY RANDOM SPOT IN THE OCEAN, WHAT WOULD THEY SEE? A BARREN LANDSCAPE, LIKE MUCH OF OUR SEAS TODAY, OR AN ABUNDANCE OF LIFE, OUR LEGACY TO THE FUTURE?"

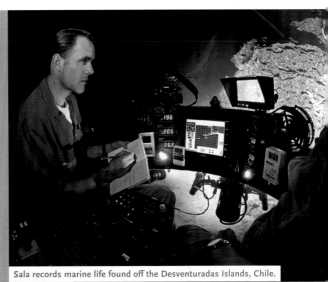

Sala records marine life found off the Desventuradas Islands, Chile.

KEY FACTS

Pristine Seas
SUCCESSES

ASCENSION ISLAND Marine reserve founded in 2019, largest in the Atlantic

NIUE A 49,000-square-mile (127,000 sq km) South Pacific marine park, founded in 2017

PATAGONIA World's largest protected ocean area, in Tierra del Fuego, some 30 million acres (12 million ha)

GABON 20 marine parks and aquatic reserves, protecting 26 percent of Gabon's territorial waters

FRANZ JOSEF LAND Russian Arctic archipelago, 34,000 square miles (88,000 sq km)

VOLCANIC
ISLANDS

BORN FROM LAVA

Earth is constantly changing. Volcanic eruptions can reshape shorelines and create new islands, while ocean waves can erode and strip them away. In 2018, Hawaii briefly gained a new island as lava from the Kilauea volcano filled in over 700 acres of what used to be open ocean. Across the Pacific, the Polynesian island of Hunga Tonga-Hunga Ha'ipi, which erupted into existence in 2014, fought the slow erosion of the tides. NASA originally gave the island just six months to live before erosion stripped it below the waves, but new research estimates it may survive as long as 30 years.

The Kilauea eruption briefly formed a tiny islet in Hawaii.

The World's VOLCANIC ISLANDS

■ **HAWAII**
Deep below the Pacific Ocean, submarine vents grew into volcanoes, building up the Hawaiian Islands over millions of years through continuous eruptions of lava. Today, the islands rise more than 10,000 feet above sea level.

■ **TRISTAN DA CUNHA**
This small island in the southern Atlantic Ocean measures just under 80 square miles; it may well be the most remote inhabited island in the world. The island is home to Queen Mary's Peak, which last erupted in 1961.

■ **KRAKATAU**
This massive volcano in Indonesia was the site of one of the largest and deadliest eruptions in recorded history in 1883. The sound of the eruption could be heard more than 2,800 miles away, and more than 34,000 people were killed.

■ **SANTORINI**
This well-known travel destination in the Aegean Sea is a volcanic lagoon, its rocky cliffs encircling a powerful shield volcano. The island's geological history is apparent in these cliffs, which show the layers of solidified lava built up over the course of many eruptions.

■ **ICELAND**
Located along a tectonic plate boundary, Iceland is one of the most active volcanic regions in the world. The island formed as the North American and Eurasian plates moved apart, and lava filled the gaps left between. The plates are still in motion, which means earthquakes and eruptions are common in Iceland today.

WINTER SKY

FINDING ORION

The winter sky hosts some of the brightest stars in the night sky, including the recognizable and popular constellation of Orion.

Orion: Hunter, Shepherd, Farmer

In the Northern Hemisphere, Orion is lord of the winter sky, his distinctive shape filled with bright stars and other astronomical sights. The constellation is named for a famed hunter of Greek mythology, but it is not the only story associated with this star pattern. Other cultures have seen the constellation as representing a shepherd or a harvesting scythe, because it first appears in the northern sky during harvest times.

Orion features two of the brightest stars in the sky. To the north, at the hunter's shoulder, is Betelgeuse, the ninth brightest star, with a diameter larger than the orbit of Earth and a mass of 20 suns. To the south Rigel, the sixth brightest, is also quite large (17 solar masses) and, thanks to its proximity to the Equator, was one of the "nautical stars" that sailors would use to locate themselves on the ocean. But the real action, astronomically speaking, is in Orion's belt and the "sword" that hangs from it. There you will find the Orion Nebula, one of the few easily seen with the naked eye.

> ## " IT OFTEN SEEMS TO ME THAT THE NIGHT IS MUCH MORE ALIVE AND RICHLY COLORED THAN THE DAY
>
> —VINCENT VAN GOGH, POST-IMPRESSIONIST PAINTER

STELLAR MAGNITUDES

- −0.5 and brighter
- −0.4 to 0.0
- 0.1 to 0.5
- 0.6 to 1.0
- 1.1 to 1.5
- 1.6 to 2.0
- 2.1 to 2.5
- 2.6 to 3.0
- 3.1 to 3.5
- 3.6 to 4.0
- 4.1 to 4.5
- 4.6 to 5.0
- Variable star

DEEP SKY OBJECTS

- Open star cluster
- Globular star cluster
- Bright nebula
- Planetary nebula
- Galaxy

A WORD FROM

Stars Being Born   Dangling below Orion's belt, there is a line of fainter stars just visible to the naked eye. This special "gleam" in the sword is a colossal stellar nursery more than 1,200 light-years distant called the Great Orion Nebula . . . a glowing cloud in the shape of a blooming flower made of dust and gas, mostly hydrogen. It's amazing to think that you see it glowing from the light of dozens of newborn stars inside.

—**ANDREW FAZEKAS,** *"The Night Sky Guy"*

SUMMER SKY

WARM WEATHER SKIES

When you're outside enjoying a pleasant summer evening, see how easy it is to find the Summer Triangle overhead.

The Bright Summer Triangle

Just because all of the officially recognized constellations were in place by the 18th century doesn't mean that people aren't finding new pictures and patterns in the sky. The Summer Triangle—an asterism (or group of stars) featuring three bright stars in three separate constellations—is an example of this: Although the asterism itself was first noted in the 19th century, the name Summer Triangle was not popularized until the 1950s, when British broadcaster and astronomer Sir Patrick Moore used it and astronomer H. A. Rey (creator of Curious George) included it in his guidebook, *Find the Constellations.*

The stars that create the Summer Triangle are three of the brightest in the northern sky: Vega, in Lyra, is the second brightest star in the summer sky and the first (apart from the sun) to be photographed: Deneb, in Cygnus, is estimated to be 60,000 times more luminous than the sun. Altair, in Aquila, is just 16.7 light-years away. The grouping is visible to most in the Northern Hemisphere.

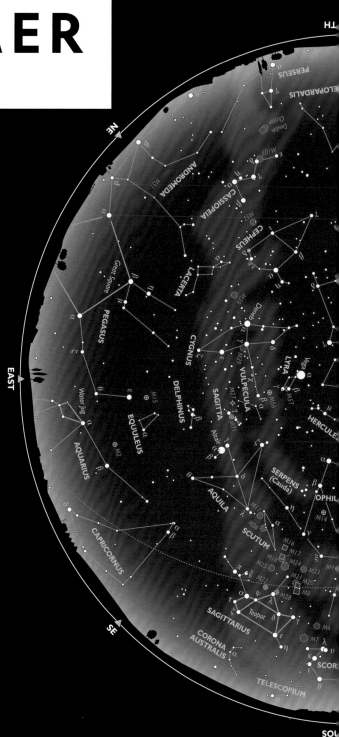

STELLAR MAGNITUDES

- −0.5 and brighter
- −0.4 to 0.0
- 0.1 to 0.5
- 0.6 to 1.0
- 1.1 to 1.5
- 1.6 to 2.0
- 2.1 to 2.5
- 2.6 to 3.0
- 3.1 to 3.5
- 3.6 to 4.0
- 4.1 to 4.5
- 4.6 to 5.0
- ⊛ Variable star

DEEP SKY OBJECTS

- Open star cluster
- ⊕ Globular star cluster
- ☐ Bright nebula
- ◇ Planetary nebula
- Galaxy

NW

WEST

SW

AURIGA

LYNX

LYNX

LEO MINOR

URSA MAJOR

Big Dipper

M81
M82
M108
M97
M106
M101
M63
M94
M51

CANES VENATICI

COMA BERENICES

Sickle

LEO

M64
M85 M100 M99
M90 M91 M88
Arcturus ⊕ M3
M53 M89 M98
M60 M59 M86 M84
M58 M87 M49

BOÖTES

CORONA BOREALIS

SERPENS (Caput)

M5

VIRGO

Spica

CORVUS

Ecliptic

LIBRA

LIBRA

HYDRA

M107
M80
M4

LUPUS

CENTAURUS

LUPUS

WIL TIRION

EARTH DAY EVERY DAY

For Better Viewing
LIGHTS OUT

More than 80 percent of the planet's land areas—and 99 percent of the population of the United States and Europe—live under skies so blotted with man-made light that the Milky Way has become virtually invisible.

SHAPES IN THE STARS

Connecting the Dots Humans have an urge to order the heavens—whether for tracking seasons, navigating travel, or conveying history and myth. Here are 16 easily distinguished constellations in the Northern Hemisphere.

ANDROMEDA, the Chained Maiden
View in Oct.–Nov.;
contains galaxy visible to naked eye

AQUARIUS, the Water Bearer
Large constellation visible
in the SW U.S. during autumn

CANIS MAJOR, the Dog
Just southeast of Orion; contains
Sirius, brightest star in the night sky

CAPRICORNUS, the Sea Goat
Distinctive triangle of 12 faint stars;
visible in southern sky in late summer

CASSIOPEIA, the Queen
W-shape visible year-round
near North Pole

CYGNUS, the Swan
Shaped as if a bird, wings out, flying
south; also called the Northern Cross

DRACO, the Dragon
A long tail visible year-round
between Ursa Major and Ursa Minor

GEMINI, the Twins
From the twins originate
December's Geminid meteor showers

HYDRA, the Sea Serpent
Largest constellation of all; a serpentine
series of 17 stars visible in spring

ORION, the Hunter
Huge stars; famous Orion Nebula
easy to spot under belt

PERSEUS, the Hero
Double star cluster atop head; source
of August's Perseid meteor shower

SAGITTARIUS, the Archer
Prominent in midsummer; contains
eight high-magnitude stars

SCORPIO, the Scorpion
Bright star Antares known to the
Romans as the "heart of the scorpion"

URSA MAJOR, the Great Bear
Includes the well-known Big Dipper;
points to the North Star

URSA MINOR, the Little Bear
Also called the Little Dipper;
includes Polaris, the North Star

VIRGO, the Virgin
Second largest constellation in the
sky; visible in the SE in late spring

> **" THE COSMOS IS ALSO WITHIN US. WE ARE MADE OF STAR STUFF. WE ARE A WAY FOR THE COSMOS TO KNOW ITSELF."**
>
> **—CARL SAGAN,** AUTHOR AND COSMOLOGIST

The annual Perseid meteor shower

Skywatching Checklist
IN 2021

1   **SUPERMOON, APRIL 27** First of this year's three supermoons, when the moon is closest to Earth and looks bigger and brighter.

2   **SUPERMOON & TOTAL LUNAR ECLIPSE, MAY 26** Full eclipse visible from Australia across Pacific to California and western Alaska.

3   **ANNULAR SOLAR ECLIPSE, JUNE 10** Light encircles darkened moon. Seen in Canada; partial in NE U.S., Europe, and Russia.

4   **SUPERMOON, JUNE 24** Last of 2021's three supermoons.

5   **DELTA AQUARIDS METEOR SHOWER, JULY 28–29** Up to 20 meteors per hour visible at peak, although full moon interferes.

6   **SATURN VISIBLE, AUGUST 2** Closest to Earth and illuminated by the sun; visible all night long.

7   **PERSEID METEOR SHOWER, AUGUST 12–13** Up to 60 meteors per hour at peak. Waxing crescent moon sets early, leaving skies dark.

8   **JUPITER VISIBLE, AUGUST 19** Four moons may be visible through strong binoculars.

9   **PARTIAL LUNAR ECLIPSE, NOVEMBER 19** Darkened moon visible in most of North America.

10   **GEMINIDS METEOR SHOWER, DECEMBER 7–17** Up to 120 meteors per hour at peak, although gibbous moon may outshine fainter meteors.

PLANETARY CONJUNCTIONS

At the dawn of our solar system, a massive proto-planetary disk of gas and dust formed along the celestial equator. Virtually all the planets in our solar system formed along this invisible plane. As the planets orbit the sun, they will fall into natural alignments and oppositions along this plane. A planetary conjunction occurs when Earth, the sun, and a planet or planets occur in a straight line. Astrologers and mystics have often ascribed great importance to these alignments, because from Earth, the planets seem to group together in the sky. While the grouping is amazing to witness, it is an illusion, belying the immense distance between them.

BEST OF @NATGEO

TOP PHOTOS OF AERIAL VIEWS

@katieorlinsky | KATIE ORLINSKY
The Alatna River flows for roughly 184 river miles (296 km) through the Gates of the Arctic National Park in Alaska.

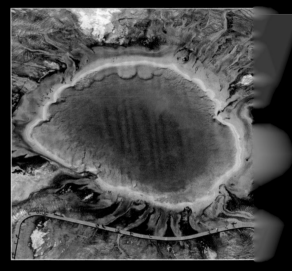

@yamashitaphoto | MICHAEL YAMASHITA
The largest hot spring in the United States can be seen from a helicopter over Yellowstone National Park.

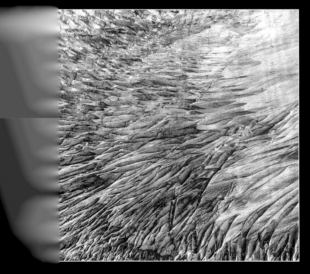

@stephenwilkes | STEPHEN WILKES
Glacial ice patterns reveal the physics of freezing in the Bella Coola Valley of British Columbia, Canada.

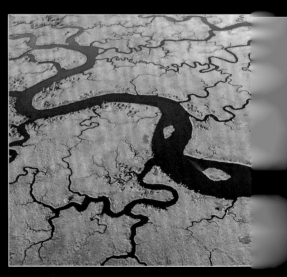

@carltonward | CARLTON WARD
The Suwannee River, about 240 miles (386 km) long, spreads like a tree into the Gulf of Mexico by Cedar Key, Florida.

WHEN WE LOOK DOWN AT THE EARTH . . . IT LOOKS LIKE A LIVING, BREATHING ORGANISM. BUT IT ALSO . . . LOOKS EXTREMELY FRAGILE.

—RON GARAN, ASTRONAUT

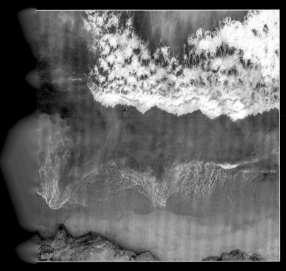

@pedromcbride | PETE MCBRIDE
Seen from above, the colors in this Mexican ocean edge seem like shades of blue in an abstract painting.

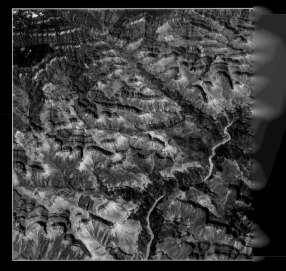

@dzalcman | DANIELLA ZALCMAN
An aerial view of the Grand Canyon takes in the cliffs, buttes and twists and turns of the Colorado River.

@ladzinski | KEITH LADZINSKI
This volcanic mountain, sacred to the local Aymara people, sits in Argentina's Salar De Arizaro salt flat.

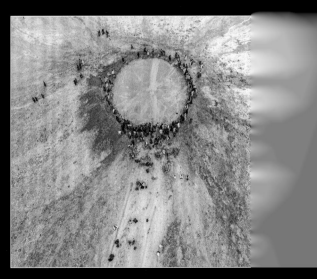

@paleyphoto | MATTHIEU PALEY
After a steep trek up, Hindu pilgrims gather around a mud volcano crater in Pakistan's Baluchistan desert.

OUR NEIGHBORHOOD

ONCE UPON A TIME

Many of us grew up with the idea of a static solar system, with well-behaved planets i
reliable orbits. But a more complicated view has arisen among some scientists. Not only c
solar system go through a dramatic birth, but it also experienced a raucous adolescence
dreds of millions of years after they formed, the biggest planets were swept into new
casting large rocks and comets every which way. The scarred surface of the moon is lin
testimony to a period of epic mayhem and gravitational instability.

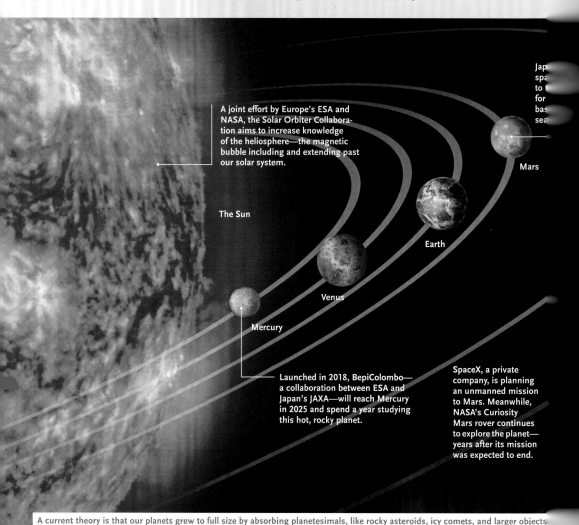

A joint effort by Europe's ESA and NASA, the Solar Orbiter Collaboration aims to increase knowledge of the heliosphere—the magnetic bubble including and extending past our solar system.

The Sun

Mars

Earth

Venus

Mercury

Ja
spa
to
for
bas
sea

Launched in 2018, BepiColombo—a collaboration between ESA and Japan's JAXA—will reach Mercury in 2025 and spend a year studying this hot, rocky planet.

SpaceX, a private company, is planning an unmanned mission to Mars. Meanwhile, NASA's Curiosity Mars rover continues to explore the planet—years after its mission was expected to end.

A current theory is that our planets grew to full size by absorbing planetesimals, like rocky asteroids, icy comets, and larger objects

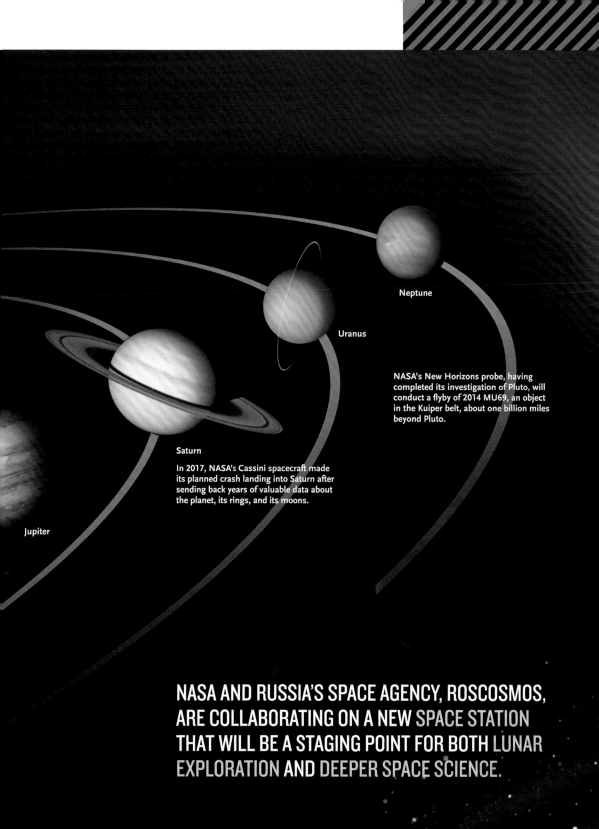

Neptune

Uranus

NASA's New Horizons probe, having completed its investigation of Pluto, will conduct a flyby of 2014 MU69, an object in the Kuiper belt, about one billion miles beyond Pluto.

Saturn

In 2017, NASA's Cassini spacecraft made its planned crash landing into Saturn after sending back years of valuable data about the planet, its rings, and its moons.

Jupiter

NASA AND RUSSIA'S SPACE AGENCY, ROSCOSMOS, ARE COLLABORATING ON A NEW SPACE STATION THAT WILL BE A STAGING POINT FOR BOTH LUNAR EXPLORATION AND DEEPER SPACE SCIENCE.

DWARF PLANETS

MEET THE NEW NEIGHBORS

An artist's rendering of Pluto

PLUTO

THE FORMER PLANET

Pluto may be the ninth largest body in our solar system, but it's not a planet. It sits in the crowded asteroid field known as the Kuiper belt, violating the rules of planethood. While it is only one and a half times the size of Earth's moon, Pluto has five smaller moons of its own. The rocky world was visited by NASA's New Horizons probe in 2015 and found to have blue skies and red snow.

ERIS

THE HIDDEN GIANT

Pluto once marked the edge of our solar system, but today that honor belongs to Eris. The dwarf planet's orbit is three times as far out as Pluto's, nearly 9.5 billion miles from the sun. Eris has an unusual orbit: It doesn't follow the parallel rings of the inner planets but instead follows its own path at a nearly 45-degree angle to the others.

PLANETARY RULES

PLANET OR DWARF?

In 2006, scientists at the International Astronomers Union conference created three rules for a planet: It orbits the sun, has enough mass that gravitational forces shape it nearly round, and has cleared its orbit of all other material. If a heavenly body meets only the first two categories, it is called a dwarf planet. It was a great advance for science but the death knell for Pluto, which was demoted to a dwarf. Our solar system lost one planet but gained dozens or even hundreds of dwarf planets in the exchange.

IN 2016, ASTRONOMERS DISCOVERED THAT DWARF PLANET MAKEMAKE HAS A MOON ABOUT 100 MILES (160 KM) IN DIAMETER.

An illustration of Makemake

CERES

A ONCE WATERY WORLD

Although most dwarf planets lie beyond Pluto in the vast Kuiper belt, Ceres can be found in the asteroid belt between Mars and Jupiter. It used to have vast oceans, but today all that remain are salts such as sodium carbonate. How Ceres got to the asteroid belt is perhaps one of its most intriguing mysteries. Some scientists think Ceres may have been a planetary wanderer, moving into the inner asteroid belt from beyond the solar system.

MAKEMAKE

MINIATURE WORLD

Makemake (pronounced MAH-keh MAH-keh) is the second brightest object in the Kuiper belt after Pluto. It's a small world, just 888 miles across, with the same red-brown shading as Pluto. But this is an airless place, with no atmosphere at all. Little is known about its makeup and structure, but its discovery changed history. The discovery of Eris in 2003 and Makemake in 2005 led astronomers to redefine what makes a planet.

HAUMEA

BATTERED PLANET

At some point in its distant past, the dwarf planet Haumea slammed into another world at 7,000 miles per hour. The collision blasted huge chunks of Haumea into space and sent the celestial body spinning. Haumea spins so rapidly that a day there is equivalent to four hours on Earth. This super-speed of its rotation has even shaped the dwarf planet into an elongated football. Two moons and faint rings, also remnants of ancient disaster, circle the planet.

KEY FACTS

Other Features of Our
SOLAR SYSTEM

■ **ASTEROID BELT**
In between Mars and Jupiter lies a region packed with asteroids that range in size from minuscule to hundreds of miles across.

■ **KUIPER BELT**
Farther out past the orbit of Neptune, the Kuiper belt is a doughnut-shaped area filled with icy objects. It is thought to be a source of many comets.

■ **COMETS**
These small, icy bodies are left over from the earliest days of the solar system. Some regularly pass close to Earth, creating a spectacular show as ice and dust blowing off their surfaces create glowing tails.

■ **OORT CLOUD**
At the edges of our solar system lies the mysterious Oort Cloud. Instead of orbiting in a flat plane, this region is believed to encompass the entire solar system and may contain massive icy objects.

EARTH'S MOON

MAGNIFICENT DESOLATION

The topography of the moon is varied. Collisions with meteors over its 4.5-billion-year life have created a surface of pulverized rock, called regolith. Craters are as wide as 1,600 miles across, with mountainous walls as high as 4.8 miles. Its distinctive "seas" are actually areas given a smooth sheen by molten lava brought to the surface after major impacts that occurred around 3.8 to 3.9 billion years ago.

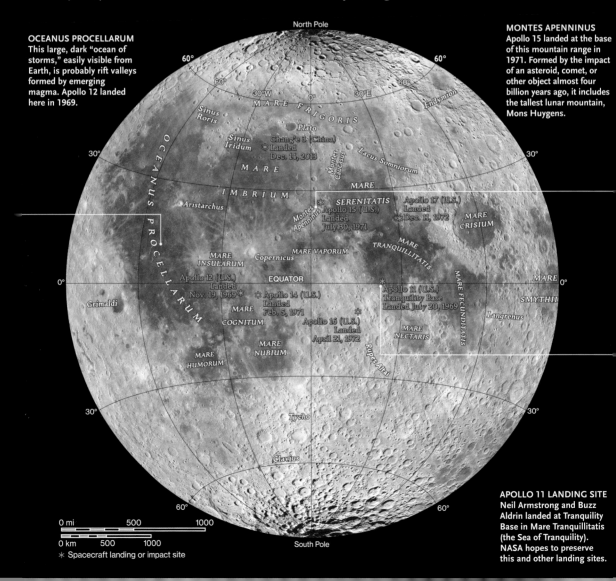

OCEANUS PROCELLARUM
This large, dark "ocean of storms," easily visible from Earth, is probably rift valleys formed by emerging magma. Apollo 12 landed here in 1969.

MONTES APENNINUS
Apollo 15 landed at the base of this mountain range in 1971. Formed by the impact of an asteroid, comet, or other object almost four billion years ago, it includes the tallest lunar mountain, Mons Huygens.

APOLLO 11 LANDING SITE
Neil Armstrong and Buzz Aldrin landed at Tranquility Base in Mare Tranquillitatis (the Sea of Tranquility). NASA hopes to preserve this and other landing sites.

North Pole

South Pole

* Spacecraft landing or impact site

0 mi 500 1000
0 km 500 1000

IN 2019, CHINA'S CHANG'E 4 BECAME THE FIRST CRAFT EVER TO LAND ON THE MOON'S FAR SIDE. IT BOUNCED IMAGES BACK TO EARTH VIA THE RELAY SATELLITE NAMED QUEQIAO.

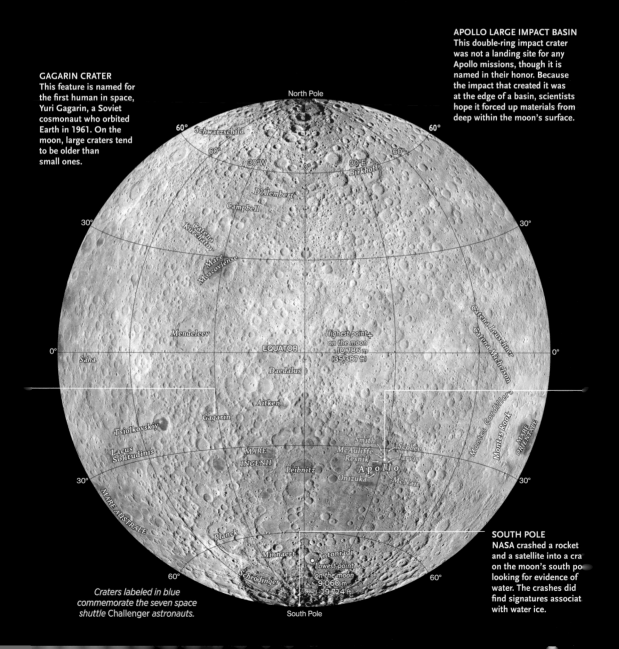

APOLLO LARGE IMPACT BASIN
This double-ring impact crater was not a landing site for any Apollo missions, though it is named in their honor. Because the impact that created it was at the edge of a basin, scientists hope it forced up materials from deep within the moon's surface.

GAGARIN CRATER
This feature is named for the first human in space, Yuri Gagarin, a Soviet cosmonaut who orbited Earth in 1961. On the moon, large craters tend to be older than small ones.

North Pole

60°
Schwarzschild
60°

60°
30°W
0°
30°E
60°
Birkhoff

D'Alembert

Campbell

30°
30°

Catena
Kurchatov

Mare
Moscoviense

Catena Lucretius

Mendeleev

Highest point
on the moon
10,786 m
(35,387 ft)

EQUATOR

Catena Michelson

0°
0°
Saha

Daedalus

Aitken

Gagarin

Tsiolkovskiy

Lacus
Solitudinis

Smith

McAuliffe
Resnik

Scobee
Jarvis

Montes Cordillera

Montes Rook

MARE
ORIENTALE

MARE
INGENII

Leibnitz

Apollo

Onizuka

McNair

30°
30°

MARE AUSTRALE

Planck

Minnaert

Antoniadi
Lowest point
on the moon
9,060 m
(29,724 ft)

Schrödinger

60°
60°

Craters labeled in blue commemorate the seven space shuttle Challenger *astronauts.*

South Pole

SOUTH POLE
NASA crashed a rocket and a satellite into a cra[ter] on the moon's south po[le] looking for evidence of water. The crashes did find signatures associat[ed] with water ice.

ON TO MARS

WATER ON THE FOURTH PLANET

Astronomers using some of the world's most powerful telescopes have determined that an ocean at least a mile deep covered a significant fraction of the Martian surface four billion years ago. The research reinforces earlier evidence that water once existed on the surface of the red planet, leaving traces such as stream pebbles, ancient shorelines, river deltas, minerals that must have formed in a watery environment, and more.

OLYMPUS MONS
This enormous shield volcano, the tallest mountain on Mars, is nearly three times as high as Mount Everest. Its base is as wide as Arizona.

CHRYSE PLANITIA
Scientists debate the origin of this plain—the landing site for both the Viking 1 lander, the first American spacecraft to reach the planet's surface, and the Mars Pathfinder probe. Was it formed by lava or by large bodies of water?

VALLES MARINERIS
Largest known canyon in the solar system—almost four times longer, 20 times wider, and four times deeper than our Grand Canyon—this may have formed as the planet cooled.

North Pole

PLANUM
BOREUM

VASTITAS BOREALIS

60° 60°

Scandia Colles

ARCADIA
PLANITIA

Alba Fossae
Tantalus Fossae

Extent of seasonal frost

ACIDALIA
PLANITIA

Phoenix (U.S.)
Landed
May 25, 2008

Erebus Montes

30°

Alba
Mons

Ascuris
TEMPE
Planum

CHRYSE
PLANITIA

Cydonia
Mensae

30°

AMAZONIS
PLANITIA

Lycus Sulci

Olympus Mons
Highest point on Mars
69,715 ft
21,249 m

Uranius
Mons

TERRA

Viking 1 (U.S.)
Landed
July 20, 1976 ✳

Sacra
Mensa

Mars Pathfinder
(U.S.) Landed
July 4, 1997
✳

ARABIA TERRA

210°

Jovis
Tholus

Ceraunius
Tholus

270°

300°

330°

ExoMars Schiaparelli
(ESA) Crashed
Oct. 19, 2016

240°

Ascraeus
Mons

Tharsis
Tholus

Echus
Montes

XANTHE

Ulysses
Tholus

LUNAE PLANUM

Biblis Tholus

Pavonis Mons EQUATOR

TERRA

0°

Amazonis
Mensae

TERRA

Arsia
Mons

Ophir
Planum

Meridiani

0°

Syria
Planum

Sinai

VALLES MARINERIS

Planum

Planum

Mars Exploration
Rover-B,
Opportunity
(U.S.) Landed
Jan. 25, 2004

DAEDALIA

Planum

Thaumasia

MARGARITIFER TERRA

Mars 6 ✳
(U.S.S.R.)
Crashed
Mar. 12, 1974

PLANUM

SOLIS PLANUM

Planum

Mars 3
(U.S.S.R.)
Landed, contact lost
Dec. 2, 1971

Icaria Planum

Bosporos Planum

Nereidum Montes

30°

Extent of seasonal frost

30°

✳

SIRENUM

AONIA

ARGYRE
PLANITIA

Aonia
Planum

Charitum Montes

ACHISTERRA

TERRA

ARGENTEA PLANUM

VALLES MARINERIS
Largest known canyon in the solar system—almost four times longer, 20 times wider, and four times deeper than our Grand Canyon—this may have formed as the planet cooled.

0 mi   750   1500   60°
0 km   750   1500

Parva Planum

NO

60°

✳ Spacecraft landing or impact site

South Pole

NASA'S MARS 2020 MISSION, A NEW ROVER DUE TO ARRIVE ON THE RED PLANET IN EARLY 2021, WILL COLLECT CORE SAMPLES TO BRING BACK TO EARTH SOME DAY.

VASTITAS BOREALIS
This region, which surrounds and includes Mars's north pole, had a visitor in 2008: NASA's Phoenix lander, which processed samples of soil and ice for evidence of life or indications that it could support life.

SYRTIS MAJOR PLANUM
Visible from Earth, this feature was included in depictions of Mars as far back as 1659. Its appearance has some variability, once thought to be caused by vegetation or a body of water.

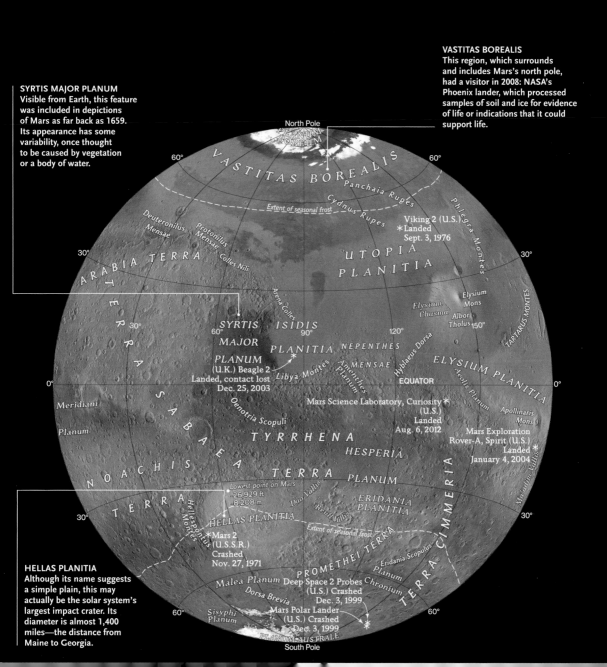

HELLAS PLANITIA
Although its name suggests a simple plain, this may actually be the solar system's largest impact crater. Its diameter is almost 1,400 miles—the distance from Maine to Georgia.

ASTEROIDS

REMNANTS OF THE EARLY SOLAR SYSTEM

In the 4.6 billion years since our solar system formed, the planets and their moons have gone through many changes. Asteroids, the rubble left behind by planetary formation, serve as a sort of fossil record of interstellar evolution. The majority of these rocky, irregular worlds lie within an area between Mars and Jupiter called the main asteroid belt. But thousands are much closer to Earth, crossing our own orbital path, sometimes visible with a telescope, and running the risk of collision. It's likely that asteroid impacts brought some of the chemical components necessary for life to our planet.

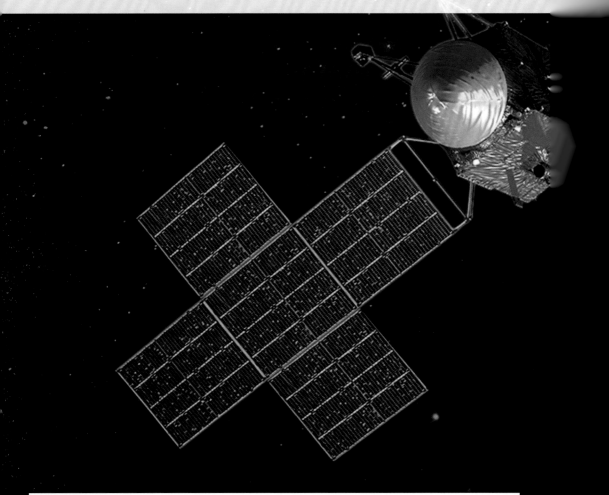

NASA's Psyche spacecraft with its five-panel solar arrays nears the metallic asteroid 16 Psyche, as seen in this illustration.

Noteworthy
ASTEROIDS

243 IDA
NASA's Galileo spacecraft passed by this asteroid more than a century after it was first discovered in 1884. Scientists observed a small natural satellite orbiting Ida, the first record of an asteroid hosting its own moon.

16 PSYCHE
Because its composition is similar to that of Earth's core, scientists have theorized that this asteroid could be the interior of an early planet, exposed after violent collisions wore away its rocky outer layers. NASA is currently planning a mission that would reach Psyche in 2026.

25143 ITOKAWA
In 2005, Japanese spacecraft Hayabusa collected a small amount of dust from this asteroid and five years later delivered the dust to Earth—the first samples of their kind. Evidence suggests that Itokawa is not solid, but instead a collection of rocks held together by shared gravity.

4 VESTA
The most massive object in the main asteroid belt, this asteroid formed one to two million years after the solar system itself. Its spherical shape and differentiated crust, mantle, and core are unusual qualities for an asteroid—Vesta nearly qualifies as a dwarf planet.

162173 RYUGU
In 2019, Japanese spacecraft Hayabusa2 landed on this asteroid, collecting photos, videos, and material samples. Using explosives to make a crater, Hayabusa2 has been able to collect subsurface materials to bring back to Earth to help scientists better understand this and other asteroids.

2000 QW7
The more our telescopes scan the heavens, the more we know about asteroids coming close. This one, estimated at twice the height of the Empire State Building, came about 3.3 million miles (5.3 million km) away from Earth in September 2019. Despite sensational headlines, it didn't hit.

A COMET IS MADE OF ICE, ROCK, AND DUST; AN ASTEROID IS MORE SOLID, MADE OF ROCK OR METAL. A METEOR IS A SPACE ROCK THAT HAS ENTERED A PLANET'S ATMOSPHERE.

MOONS BEYOND OURS

HUNDREDS OF PLANETARY SATELLITES

Scientists have identified nearly 200 moons within our solar system. These natural satellites come in many shapes, sizes, and types, but most are solid bodies and only a few are known to have their own atmospheres. They're widely distributed—Jupiter and Saturn have dozens of moons each, while here on Earth we have just one.

EARTH—MOON

Located some 230,000 miles (370,149 km) away, our only natural satellite likely formed about 4.5 billion years ago after a collision with Earth. The moon causes our tides and stabilizes the planet's climate.

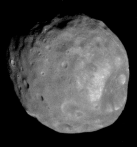

MARS—PHOBOS

The larger of Mars's two moons is on a collision course. Every century it gets about six feet (1.8 m) closer to the red planet, on track to collide within 50 million years or shatter as it nears the surface.

JUPITER—CALLISTO

The cratered surface of Jupiter's second-largest moon could hide a habitat capable of supporting life. Data collected by the Galileo spacecraft also suggest a deep underground ocean.

JUPITER—EUROPA

Europa is one of the most promising places to find life in our solar system. Beneath its solid-ice surface, there is an ocean that may hold up to twice the volume of Earth's oceans combined.

JUPITER—GANYMEDE

Largest moon in our solar system, Ganymede is the only one known to have a magnetic field. Caused by the moon's iron core, the field creates auroras in its polar regions.

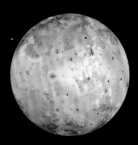

JUPITER—IO

The competing gravitational fields of nearby Jupiter, Europa, and Ganymede make this moon the most volcanically active place in the solar system.

SATURN—ENCELADUS

Fresh, clean ice covers Enceladus, giving it the most reflective surface in the solar system. Ice particles spray from the moon during its orbit, spreading out to form one of Saturn's rings.

SATURN—MIMAS

This smallest of Saturn's major moons is made almost entirely of ice, and a massive impact crater covers roughly a third of its surface. The crater is named for William Herschel, who discovered Mimas in 1789.

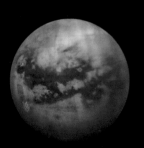

SATURN—TITAN

Saturn's largest moon, Titan is the only place in the solar system other than Earth known to have rivers, lakes, and seas— but containing liquid hydrocarbons like methane.

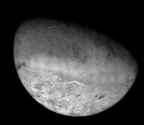

NEPTUNE—TRITON

A retrograde orbit (in opposition to its planet's rotation) is unique to the largest of Neptune's 13 moons. Surface temperatures reach minus 391° F (−235° C).

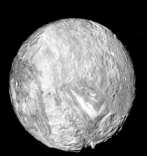

URANUS—MIRANDA

Miranda is one-seventh the size of Earth's moon, but its giant fault canyons are up to 12 times as deep as the Grand Canyon.

PLUTO—CHARON

First discovered in 1978, Charon is Pluto's largest moon, clocking in at nearly half the size of its parent. Some refer to Pluto and Charon as a double dwarf planet system.

SPACE SCIENCE
TIME LINE

14 BYA to 1 BC	AD 1 to 1600	1600 to 1700	1700 to 1800

■ 13.8 bya*
The universe forms in the big bang.

■ 13.2 bya
Our home galaxy, the Milky Way, forms.

■ 4.6 bya
Our solar system starts to emerge around the sun.

■ 4.6 bya
Planet Earth forms.

■ 4.5 bya
Earth's moon forms from debris.

■ 240 BC
Chinese astronomers make the first record of what becomes known as Halley's comet.

* billion years ago

■ 46
Roman emperor Julius Caesar introduces the Julian calendar.

■ ca 150
Ptolemy writes the *Almagest,* a standard guide to astronomy for over a thousand years.

■ 310
Chinese astronomers produce a comprehensive star map.

■ 1150
Astronomer Solomon Jarchus compiles the first celestial almanac.

■ 1610
Galileo observes four of Jupiter's moons.

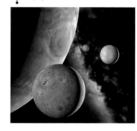

■ 1645
Flemish cartographer Michael Langrenus publishes the first map of the moon.

■ 1655
Dutch scientist Christiaan Huygens confirms that Saturn has rings.

■ 1664
English scientist Robert Hooke describes Jupiter's red spot.

■ 1676
Danish astronomer Ole Rømer makes the first quantitative measure of the speed of light.

■ 1725
Catalog of over 3,000 stars compiled by England's first Astronomer Royal, Rev. John Flamsteed, is published.

■ 1731
English astronomer John Bevis discovers the Crab Nebula.

■ 1771
Charles Messier publishes catalog of astronomical objects including galaxies, star clusters, and nebulae.

■ 1781
British astronomer William Herschel discovers the planet Uranus.

■ 1783
English physicist John Michell predicts the existence of black holes.

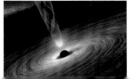

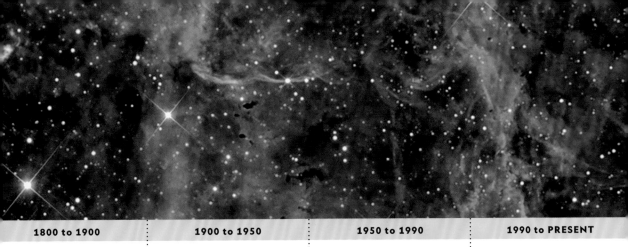

| **1800 to 1900** | **1900 to 1950** | **1950 to 1990** | **1990 to PRESENT** |

1838
Friedrich Bessel uses stellar parallax to estimate the distance to the star 61 Cygni.

1846
German astronomer Johann Galle is first to observe Neptune.

1872
American astronomer Henry Draper first photographs the spectrum of a star (Vega).

1877
Two moons of Mars, Phobos and Deimos, discovered by American astronomer Asaph Hall.

1889
American astronomer Edward Barnard takes first pictures of the Milky Way.

1915
Scottish astronomer Robert Innes locates Proxima Centauri, the nearest star to the sun.

1916
Albert Einstein publishes his paper on the general theory of relativity.

1927
Georges Lemaître proposes the big bang theory.

1930
Clyde Tombaugh discovers Pluto.

1957
U.S.S.R. launches Sputnik 1, first man-made satellite to orbit Earth.

1961
Russian astronaut Yuri Gagarin becomes first man in space.

1966
U.S.S.R. lands Luna 9, unmanned vehicle, on moon.

1969
U.S. Apollo 11 mission puts first men on moon.

1981
U.S. space shuttle *Columbia* completes maiden flight.

1990
Hubble Space Telescope launched into orbit.

2000
Two Russians and one American become the first crew to occupy the International Space Station.

2004
NASA lands two rovers, Spirit and Opportunity, on Mars.

2012
Mars Science Lab and Curiosity rover land on Mars.

2012
NASA's Voyager 1, launched in 1977, leaves the solar system and enters interstellar space.

2018
NASA's Voyager 2 also enters interstellar space, and is still sending data to Earth.

2019
China's Chang'e 4 lands on the far side of the moon and returns pictures to Earth.

BIRTH OF THE UNIVERSE

A HISTORY SHAPED BY DARK FORCES

Cosmologists have determined that the universe was born 13.8 billion years ago. But they've also concluded that what we see in the sky makes up only 5 percent of the observable universe. The invisible majority consists of 27 percent dark matter and 68 percent dark energy.

What's Dark Matter?

We can't see dark matter, but we can see the effects of its gravity. And dark matter can't just be inconspicuous

normal matter—in no plausible scenario would it add up to five times the mass of the bright stuff—hence scientists think it must be made of more exotic materials.

What's Dark Energy?

Dark energy, even more mysterious, refers to whatever is accelerating the rate at which the cosmos expands. It has been called a "general label for what we do not know about the large-scale properties of our universe."

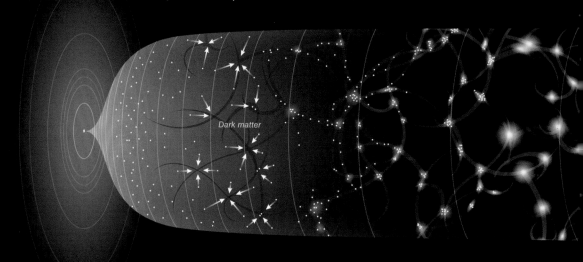

Dark matter

The big bang

13.8 billion years ago

Our universe blossoms from a hot, dense state smaller than an atom. Within milliseconds it inflates enormously.

Dark matter forms

First seconds of the universe

Dark matter also emerges in the first second. Interacting with particles of normal matter only through gravity, it begins to pull them together.

Stars light up

100 million years after the big bang

Clouds of hydrogen assembled by the gravity of dark matter collapse to form the first scattered stars. Nuclear fusion inside them creates heavier elements—and lights space.

Composition of the universe

Dark energy <1%

Dark matter <1%

Matter <1%   Radiation 99%*

86%

<1%   <1%

13%

A BELGIAN PRIEST NAMED GEORGES LEMAÎTRE FIRST SUGGESTED THE BIG BANG THEORY IN THE 1920S WHEN HE THEORIZED THAT THE UNIVERSE BEGAN FROM A SINGLE PRIMORDIAL ATOM.

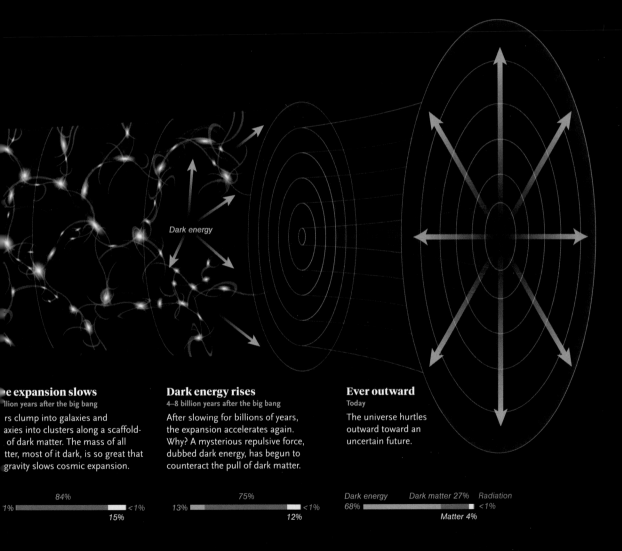

Dark energy

e expansion slows
llion years after the big bang

rs clump into galaxies and
axies into clusters along a scaffold-
of dark matter. The mass of all
tter, most of it dark, is so great that
gravity slows cosmic expansion.

84%

1% <1%

15%

Dark energy rises
4–8 billion years after the big bang

After slowing for billions of years,
the expansion accelerates again.
Why? A mysterious repulsive force,
dubbed dark energy, has begun to
counteract the pull of dark matter.

75%

13% <1%

12%

Ever outward
Today

The universe hurtles
outward toward an
uncertain future.

Dark energy   Dark matter 27%   Radiation
68%   <1%

                   Matter 4%

* Percentages do not add up to 100 due to rounding.

JENNIFER W. LOPEZ
SPACE TECHNOLOGIST

THE FUTURE OF SPACE

Seeing what lies beyond our planet isn't just for astronauts—there's plenty of exploring to be done from the surface. Jennifer Lopez is one of the people who make that exploration possible.

Lopez started early, attending a space-themed middle school and participating in a Young Astronauts Program.

F rom free-floating space laboratories to large-scale data analysis, Lopez works with emerging tech that will help us better understand the universe.

Exploration has long been a part of Lopez's life. She counts Indiana Jones among her childhood heroes and describes herself as "naturally curious about the world, our universe, and how things worked." Lopez's middle school was named for an astronaut, and she has come to take the school's motto— "Reach for the stars"—quite literally.

Lopez studied molecular biology in college, but her interest in business and space eventually took her outside the lab. In 2005, she founded Wisenn & Co., an agency focused on bringing groups together in science, technology, and exploration. Through it, she has worked with the International Space Station's U.S. National Laboratory and Johns Hopkins's astronomy program.

In 2019, she began working with Astrobotic Technology, a company developing robotic tools for space exploration. Astrobotic's Peregrine lander will soon deliver payloads to the moon as part of NASA's multifaceted effort to return to the lunar surface—a stepping stone to further space exploration.

CHALLENGING TRADITION

Lopez was also a founding member of NASA Datanauts. Their mission: to come up with new and creative ways to use NASA data. People of all nationalities and levels of experience are invited. Through this work, Lopez hopes to make space science accessible to anyone with a curious mind and the drive to answer the questions of the future.

“ I WANTED TO PROVE THEM WRONG AND SHOW THAT WOMEN DO BELONG IN TECH, WOMEN DO BELONG IN SCIENCE.”

Lopez and astronaut Buzz Aldrin share the concept of "overview"—the unique chance by those who orbit Earth to see it as a unified ecosystem.

KEY FACTS

NASA Datanaut
PROJECTS

■ **STARRY NIGHT**
This community project makes use of special conductive ink, a circuit board, and sensors to create instruments that play music based on NASA data. Datanauts have shared the project around the world.

■ **GLOBAL FOREST WATCH**
Using satellite imaging, open-source data, and crowd-sourcing, this interactive online system monitors forest landscapes and provides timely alerts about loss of tree cover.

■ **SPACE SHIELD**
Responding to a 2015 challenge, a team from Finland developed models that use NASA data to study the possible parameters of asteroids— orbits, sizes, colors, and spin, for example—to search for yet-undiscovered orbit types.

WHEN A STAR EXPLODES

THE LIFE CYCLE OF A STAR

Every star begins as a collapsing cloud of interstellar dust. Stars stabilize when the temperature in the core is hot enough to begin nuclear fusion: turning hydrogen into helium. From there, a star grows and changes, using the hydrogen at its core as fuel along the way. Eventually, there's nothing left to burn, and some of the star's mass flows into its core. Once the core reaches critical mass—becoming too heavy to withstand its own gravitational force—the star collapses in on itself, producing massive shock waves and the giant explosion of a supernova.

A WORD FROM

The Cosmic Dawn The Giant Magellan Telescope will have 10 times the resolution of the Hubble Space Telescope. It will be 20 million times more sensitive than the human eye. And it may, for the first time ever, be capable of finding life on planets outside of our solar system. It's going to allow us to look back at the first light in the universe—literally, the dawn of the cosmos.

—WENDY FREEDMAN, *astronomer*

The next supernova visible from Earth—as bright as Polaris—will be in Cygnus around 2022 and will last a year.

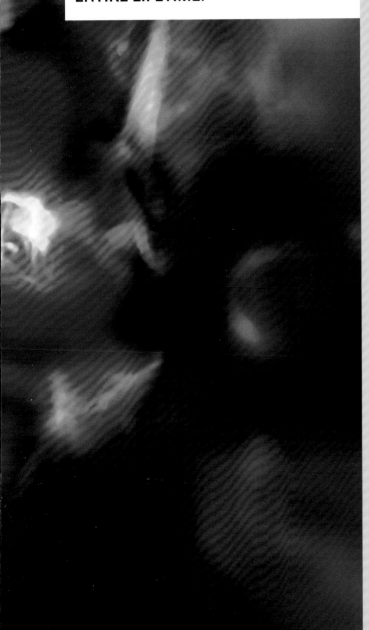

IN THE SPACE OF JUST A FEW YEARS A SUPERNOVA, A SPECIAL KIND OF EXPLODED STAR, RADIATES MORE ENERGY THAN OUR SUN DOES IN ITS ENTIRE LIFETIME.

Distances Out Into
THE UNIVERSE

■ **ASTEROID: 26,000 MILES**
A tiny asteroid, just 50–100 feet long and known as 2012 TC4, flew very close to Earth on Oct. 12, 2017, just above the orbit of communications satellites.

■ **COMET: 1.4 MILLION MILES**
Appearing about four times as large as a full moon to the naked eye in July 1770, comet Lexell (aka D/1770 L1) was six times as far away as the moon.

■ **NEXT STAR: 4.25 LIGHT-YEARS (LY)**
Proxima Centauri, our second nearest star (the sun is closer, obviously), is in the constellation of Centaurus. It is part of a three-star system with Alpha Centauri A and B.

■ **HABITABLE EXOPLANET: 4.25 LY**
Our nearest star has in its orbit an exoplanet (Proxima Centauri B) that could, based on its size and location, have liquid water.

■ **SUPERNOVA CANDIDATE: 150 LY**
The most likely star to become a supernova is the smaller partner in a binary system known as IK Pegasi at a not insignificant distance from Earth—but by the time it explodes, millions of years from now, the distance will be much greater.

■ **PLANETARY NEBULA: 650 LY**
Not actually home to planets, this celestial object is the glowing remnants of a sunlike star. The Helix Nebula, in the constellation of Aquarius, is likely the closest to us.

■ **BLACK HOLE: 3,000 LY**
Almost every galaxy has a supermassive black hole in its center. Ours is 27,000 ly from Earth. A stellar-mass black hole, V616 Monocerotis, is about 3,000 ly away.

■ **GALAXY: 25,000 LY**
The Canis Major dwarf galaxy, closest to us and to the center of the Milky Way (42,000 ly), is being unraveled by our galaxy's gravity.

SPACE RADIATION

FOLLOWING COSMIC RAYS THROUGH THE UNIVERSE

Pulsars emit particles along their two magnetic poles.

TRACING A PATH

WHERE DO THEY COME FROM?

By the time most cosmic rays reach Earth, many have been traveling for thousands or millions of years across the cosmos. But even when traveling near the speed of light, the universe is a big place. For scientists, the distance is less of a problem than the direction. Most cosmic radiation carries an electrical charge, which can be significantly affected by magnetic fields. A cosmic ray passing too close to a sun or large planet can find its path altered by its magnetic field. By the time the particle gets to Earth, it could be coming from a completely different direction than it started from, which means scientists can't necessarily match a cosmic ray to its cosmic source. Generating the ability to follow these pathways would give scientists new tools to explore and understand the universe.

UNDER SIEGE

HIGH-ENERGY INVASION

Earth is pelted with high-energy particles from outer space every second. These high-energy projectiles are atomic particles born in distant stars, many traveling near the speed of light. Cosmic radiation is a danger for astronauts, but for scientists, these aren't threats but atomic ambassadors from across the universe. Cosmic radiation helped science unlock the world beyond the atom, and understanding it better can help astronomers radically advance our understanding of the cosmos.

Particles of plasma lead to the aurora borealis.

Inside a Daya Bay neutrino detector

SOLAR WEATHER AFFECTS LEVELS OF RADIATION IN SPACE. EVERY 11 YEARS, THE SUN CYCLES THROUGH PERIODS OF HIGHER AND LOWER ACTIVITY, AND RADIATION LEVELS RISE WITH LEVELS OF SOLAR ACTIVITY.

An illustration of Earth's radiation belts

NEUTRINOS

A PECULIAR PARTICLE

One type of subatomic particle, the neutrino, rarely interacts with matter. Neutrinos can fly through magnetic fields, asteroids, and even planets without ever altering course. To catch a neutrino, scientists have buried storage tanks deep beneath lead mines or the Antarctic ice sheets and waited for the brief flash when a neutrino interacts with their contents. If scientists can find a way to successfully trace neutrinos, they will open up a new way of searching the universe for supernovae, black holes, and other wonders of the cosmos.

BLOCKING RADIATION

BEYOND THE SPHERE

Earth's magnetic field blocks 99.9 percent of space radiation , but humanity is safe only as long as we stay within our protective magnetic bubble. Beyond that layer, the radiation level rises, and so do health concerns for astronauts. High-energy cosmic rays can damage sensitive electronics, but even normal radiation could dramatically increase the risk of cancer. A single trip to Mars would be like undergoing an x-ray or MRI scan every week of the journey, and that covers only the voyage. Whether on the surface of Mars, the moon, or even the International Space Station, there is nowhere to hide from the cosmic storm. If humanity leaves the planet, understanding the cosmic storm will be vital.

A WORD FROM

The Human Body in Space On my previous flight to the space station, a mission of 159 days, I lost bone mass, my muscles atrophied, and my blood redistributed itself in my body, which strained and shrank the walls of my heart. More troubling, I experienced problems with my vision, as many other astronauts had. I had been exposed to more than 30 times the radiation of a person on Earth, equivalent to about 10 chest x-rays every day. This exposure would increase my risk of a fatal cancer for the rest of my life.

—**SCOTT KELLY,** *astronaut*

EXOPLANETS
IS THERE LIFE?

IN SEARCH OF GOLDILOCKS

When astronomers discuss planets that might support life, they refer to Goldilocks: Conditions have to be just right for life to happen. Once an exoplanet (a planet outside our solar system) is identified, astronomers assess its distance from the star it orbits and determine whether it is too close or too far to keep surface water in a liquid state. Size also matters: A planet that's too small cannot maintain an atmosphere; one that's too large will have a crushing atmosphere. "Goldilocks" planets have the right atmospheric pressure and the right temperature.

POP!

PLANETARY PLAYLIST

- "Aquarius (Let the Sunshine In)," The 5th Dimension
- "Fly Me to the Moon," Frank Sinatra
- "From Here to the Moon and Back," Dolly Parton
- "Gagarin," Public Service Broadcasting
- "Here Comes the Sun," The Beatles
- "Kuiper Belt," Sufjan Stevens, Bryce Dessner, Nico Muhly & James McAlister
- "Man on the Moon," R.E.M.
- "Pluto," Clare & the Reasons
- "Rocket Man," Elton John
- "Space Oddity," David Bowie
- "Stars Align," Lindsey Stirling
- "Supermassive Black Hole," Muse
- "We Are All Made of Stars," Moby

Imagine a planet with two nearby moons, visible day and night.

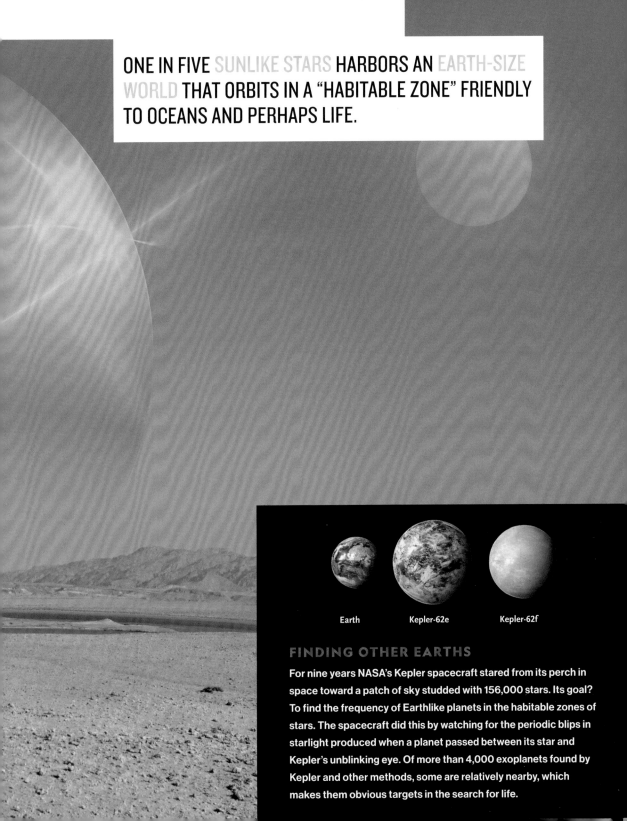

ONE IN FIVE SUNLIKE STARS HARBORS AN EARTH-SIZE WORLD THAT ORBITS IN A "HABITABLE ZONE" FRIENDLY TO OCEANS AND PERHAPS LIFE.

Earth   Kepler-62e   Kepler-62f

FINDING OTHER EARTHS

For nine years NASA's Kepler spacecraft stared from its perch in space toward a patch of sky studded with 156,000 stars. Its goal? To find the frequency of Earthlike planets in the habitable zones of stars. The spacecraft did this by watching for the periodic blips in starlight produced when a planet passed between its star and Kepler's unblinking eye. Of more than 4,000 exoplanets found by Kepler and other methods, some are relatively nearby, which makes them obvious targets in the search for life.

DARK MATTER

A MYSTERY AS BIG AS THE UNIVERSE

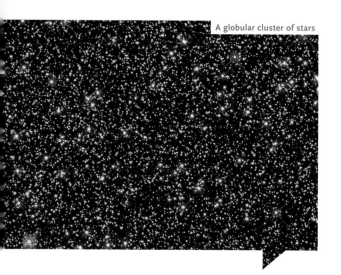

A globular cluster of stars

THE MISSING PIECE

A SEARCH FOR INVISIBLE MATTER

Astrophysics has a problem: The visible universe doesn't have enough stuff in it. Every star we see, every exoplanet and black hole we measure, every nebula we survey, is only 5 percent of what gravity tells us should be present in our universe. Hidden out in the vast reaches of space is a new type of matter—a new particle that neither emits nor reflects light but still makes up most of the universe. We can detect it only through its gravitational pushes and pulls on the visible universe we're familiar with. Scientists refer to it as the dark universe, a massive intergalactic web of dark matter and dark energy. A name is not an explanation, however, and scientists are still stumped for details.

DEFINING DARK MATTER

FILLING THE EMPTY SPACE

The idea of dark matter first appeared in the 1930s, when Swiss astronomer Fritz Zwicky focused on two galaxies orbiting each other in a distant stellar cluster. Without the galaxies containing much more mass than was seen, the galaxies should have spun away from each other. Zwicky theorized that galaxies must contain massive amounts of dark matter, many times greater than the visible matter we can detect. Other observations have only confirmed that hypothesis. In his planetary musings, Isaac Newton couldn't understand how gravity could pull Earth around the sun if the space between was totally empty. It turns out that empty space is far from empty. Our galaxy, and all the others, are filled with dark matter.

The Pinwheel galaxy

The Alpha Magnetic Spectrometer

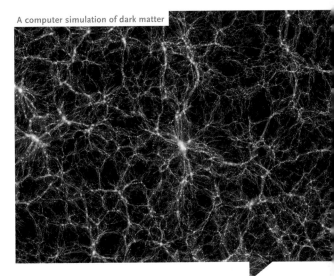

A computer simulation of dark matter

THEORETICAL PARTICLES

PICKING ON WIMPS

Scientists aren't certain what exactly dark matter is or where it comes from. Numerous theories have been formulated, but so far each one has been disputed. For decades scientists focused on a class of particles known as WIMPs—weakly interacting massive particles. Some researchers are using ever more powerful colliders to search for these elusive entities; some seek evidence of dark matter collisions in sunken tanks containing various chemicals; a third approach is to study cosmic rays for evidence of dark matter. Some of the biggest and most expensive science experiments, both on and off the planet, are dedicated to searching out this mysterious form of matter. From the two-billion-dollar Alpha Magnetic Spectrometer mounted on the International Space Station, to the Axion Dark Matter eXperiment (ADMX) in Seattle, Washington, the search is on.

SHINE A LIGHT

A NEW UNDERSTANDING

To reveal the secrets of dark matter would do more than unveil a new particle. It could rewrite our understanding of the universe. Dark matter is vital to create the universe around us; it is the soil where stars are born and the strings that connect galaxies. A simulated map of the dark universe we've identified reveals strands of the mystery material connecting stars, planets, and nebula in a vast intergalactic web. Some telescopes are able to study dark matter through its impact on light itself. Since dark matter affects gravity and gravity bends light, scientists have been able to literally "see" its effect. We can see it, but we do not know it. Not yet. So our universe is still literally held together by dark matter and mystery.

FURTHER

SALT-STREWN VISTA

Sunset casts a violet hue on the vast and mottled landscape of Utah's Bonneville Salt Flats, left behind after mineral-rich waters receded as the last Ice Age ended some 10,000 years ago. A salty crust blankets an area of about 46 square miles (119 sq km), fed in warmer weather by groundwater trickling up in fractal-like bumps and ridges. Flat and free of any vegetation, the terrain hosts some of the fastest auto races in the world. Once the cars and hubbub disappear, nature's deep silence returns.

The glow of Salt Lake City, more than a hundred miles (161 km) away, brushes the horizon over Utah's Bonneville Salt Flats.

> **" THERE ARE MOMENTS WHEN ALL ANXIETY AND STATED TOIL ARE BECALMED IN THE INFINITE LEISURE AND REPOSE OF NATURE. "**
>
> **—HENRY DAVID THOREAU,** AMERICAN TRANSCENDENTALIST

LIFE ON EARTH

ALL LIVING THINGS | OF THE EARTH

Africa's Ponta do Ouro Partial Marine Reserve is populated with some 250 bottlenose dolphins, known for their curiosity.

OF THE SEA | OF THE SKY | CARE FOR ALL LIFE

QUIZ MASTER

Life-forms Galore Millions of species of plants, animals, and other life-forms share the planet with us. Tease your brain with these questions, then turn to pages in this chapter to learn the answers and much more.

—**SUSAN TYLER HITCHCOCK,** *Nat Geo Quizmaster*

NAME THE ORGAN **THAT BUTTERFLIES** USE TO SIP **WATER AND NECTAR.**

p207

WHEN WAS THE FIRST EARTH DAY CELEBRATED: **IN 1970, 1980,** OR 1990?

p211

WHAT ANIMAL HAS THE BIGGEST BRAIN?

p189

WHAT YEAR DID SCOTTISH SCIENTISTS CLONE DOLLY THE SHEEP: **1986, 1996,** OR 2006?

p159

IS THE TAMARIN AN UNGULATE, A FELINE, OR A PRIMATE?

WHAT'S THE NAME OF THE SMALLEST BIRD IN THE WORLD?

p201

WHAT ANIMAL IS JANE GOODALL KNOWN FOR STUDYING?

p184

p182

WHAT DO ALL THESE ANIMALS HAVE IN COMMON: SOUTHERN CASSOWARY, KOALA, PLATYPUS, AND LAUGHING KOOKABURRA?

p181

LION'S MANE, WORLD'S LARGEST JELLYFISH, CAN GROW TO HOW LONG?

p191

p161

IN WHICH OF THE THREE DOMAINS OF LIFE DO PLANTS BELONG: ARCHAEA, BACTERIA, OR EUKARYA?

WHAT PIGMENT COLORS MANY PLANT CELLS, BY ABSORBING RED AND BLUE LIGHT AND REFLECTING GREEN?

p167

THE DOMESTICATION OF DOGS DATES BACK HOW MANY YEARS: 10,000, 5,000, OR 3,000?

p178

p183

WHAT IS THE ONLY APE FOUND OUTSIDE OF AFRICA?

TRUE OR FALSE: HUMMINGBIRDS CAN BEAT THEIR WINGS UP TO 500 TIMES A SECOND.

p201

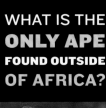

LIFE SCIENCE
TIME LINE

900 to 1 BC	AD 1 to 1100	1100 to 1600	1600 to 1800

ca 900 BC
Neolithic farmers use fertilizer and irrigation.

ca 800 BC
Egyptians use artificially heated incubators to hatch eggs.

ca 400 BC
Hippocrates of Kos describes human anatomy.

ca 350 BC
Aristotle draws up a classification scheme for plants and animals.

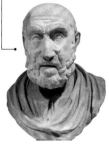

300 BC
Diocles of Carystus is credited with writing the first text on anatomy.

77
Roman scholar Pliny the Elder summarizes natural history as known to the Romans in his *Naturalis Historia*.

752
Chinese physician Wang Tao describes ailments including diabetes and malaria, along with remedies.

ca 900
Arab physician Rhazes distinguishes between measles and smallpox.

ca 1075
Female physician Trotula of Salerno writes about hygiene and women's disorders.

ca 1260
Arab physician Ibn al-Nafis describes the pulmonary circulation of the blood.

1276
Giles of Rome discusses the role of both parents in procreation in his work, *De Formatione Corporis.*

1410
Italian physician Benedetto Rinio catalogs more than 500 medicinal plants.

1517
Girolamo Fracastoro proposes that fossils are the petrified remains of once living organisms.

1583
Italian botanist Andrea Cesalpino devises a system of classifying plants by their structure.

1658
Dutch naturalist Jan Swammerdam describes red blood cells.

1665
Robert Hooke coins the word "cell" to describe individual units in plant tissues.

1677
Dutch scientist Antonie van Leeuwenhoek reports on his observations of bacteria.

1735
Swedish naturalist Carl Linnaeus introduces the binomial naming system.

1796
Georges Cuvier identifies "elephant" remains from Siberia as a separate and extinct species: "mammoth."

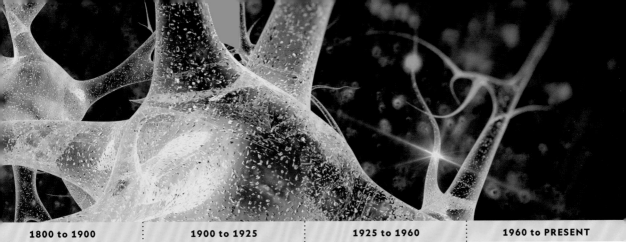

| 1800 to 1900 | 1900 to 1925 | 1925 to 1960 | 1960 to PRESENT |

1800 to 1900

■ 1822
Englishwoman Mary Ann Mantell discovers teeth from one of the first fossils to be recognized as a dinosaur.

■ 1831–1836
Darwin completes a five-year voyage on the H.M.S. *Beagle,* during which he conducted studies that lead to his theory of evolution.

■ 1860
The first fossil of *Archaeopteryx,* a birdlike prehistoric flying reptile, is found.

■ 1865
Gregor Mendel presents his ideas on inheritance.

■ 1876
Mitosis, the process of cell replication, is first described by Eduard Strasburger.

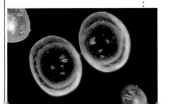

1900 to 1925

■ 1900
Cuban-American physiologist Aristides Agramonte y Simoni discovers that yellow fever is transmitted through mosquitoes.

■ 1901
Russian scientist Élie Metchnikoff determines the role of white blood cells in fighting infection.

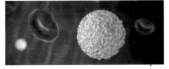

■ 1913
Alfred Sturtevant introduces the technique of chromosome mapping to record positions of genes.

■ 1919
Karl von Frisch describes the "bee's dance," the way in which honeybees communicate.

■ 1924
Fossils of human ancestor *Australopithecus* are discovered, helping establish Africa as the site of humankind's origins.

1925 to 1960

■ 1926
Walter Cannon introduces the concept of homeostasis, in which the body's systems work together to maintain balance.

■ 1944
Oswald Avery shows that nearly all organisms have DNA as their hereditary material.

■ 1953
Francis Crick, James Watson, and Rosalind Franklin determine the double-helix structure of DNA.

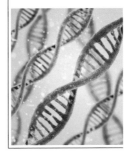

■ 1960
Jane Goodall begins her studies of chimpanzees in Gombe, Tanzania.

1960 to PRESENT

■ 1969
The first human eggs are fertilized using in vitro fertilization.

■ 1996
Scottish scientists clone a sheep named Dolly.

■ 2000
The Human Genome Project produces a rough draft of the human genome sequence.

■ 2006
Analysis of a 375-million-year-old fossil shows it to be a "missing link" between fish and four-legged vertebrates.

■ 2010
Genetic evidence shows that interbreeding between humans and Neanderthals took place and that some modern humans have Neanderthal genes.

DOMAINS OF LIFE

AN INVISIBLE WORLD

We share this planet with more than eight million other species, and each of them falls into one of only three types: Archaea, the ancient line; bacteria, the microbial line; and Eukarya, which includes plants, animals, fungus, and others.

ARCHAEA

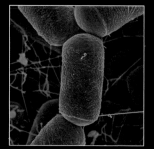

METHANOSARCINA SP.
A type of archaea
that produces methane

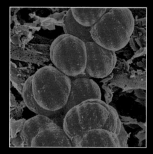

METHANOBREVIBACTER SP.
One of the archaea found
in the human gut

SULFOLOBUS SP.
Thrives in hot springs
>176°F (80°C)

ARCHAEA & BACTERIA

BACTERIA

MILLIONS OF MICROORGANISMS

Archaea are so difficult to detect that they were unknown until the 1970s. They resemble bacteria in their simple shape and lack of complex cellular organs, but they are as genetically distinct from bacteria as humans are. Their ancient genetic markers suggest that life may have started in the hydrothermal vents of the deep ocean.

Despite their microscopic size, bacteria make up most of the mass of life on Earth. There are as many bacteria on your skin and inside your body as there are human cells making it up. Although the battle against bacterial infection has been common for centuries, this microbial world represents an ecosystem scientists are only starting to approach cohesively.

MYCOBACTERIUM SP.
This bacterium
causes tuberculosis.

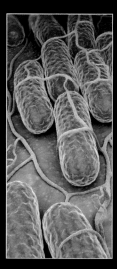

SALMONELLA SP.
Infected food causes
gastric disease.

POLYPORUS SP.
Shelf fungus, grows
on dead or dying trees

COOKEINA SP.
Tropical toadstool,
grows on trees

PLANTS

MAMMILLARIA SP.
Twin-spined cactus,
from Mexico

COSMOS
Annual seed-
bearing flower

POACEAE SP.
One of 8,000 species
of grasses

QUERCUS SP.
Southern live oak,
North America

EUKARYA

FROM FUNGI TO PRIMATES

Eukarya, which contain every complex multicellular organism on the planet, are divided into four taxonomic kingdoms: Plants, Animals, Fungi, and Protoctista. Despite their seeming diversity, Eukarya share a single set of characteristics: multicellular organisms with clearly defined cellular structures, such as a nucleus, mitochondria, and other organelles.

ANIMALS

TANGARA SP.
Golden-hooded tanager,
from Costa Rica

CHAETODON SP.
Masked butterfly fish,
from Asia

ELEPHANT
Two species,
Indian and African

CHIMPANZEE
In African rainforests,
woods, and grasslands

KEY DATES

Dates in the Evolution of
LIFE ON EARTH

■ **CA 4 BILLION YEARS AGO**
Life begins on planet Earth.

■ **CA 2.4 BILLION YEARS AGO**
Great oxidation event occurs, giving Earth its oxygen.

■ **1.5 BILLION YEARS AGO**
Plants, animals, and fungus separate into distinct types.

■ **500 MILLION YEARS AGO**
Life moves onto land.

■ **65 MILLION YEARS AGO**
The Cretaceous–Tertiary extinction wipes out the dinosaurs.

■ **7 TO 8 MILLION YEARS AGO**
Hominids share last common ancestor with bonobos and chimpanzees.

FOSSILS
PAST LIVES

Lasting Impressions Fossils are the preserved remains or imprints of ancient living things. They offer clues about past life-forms and environments and are keys to understanding the evolution of life on Earth.

> " I WANT YOU TO SEE THE WORLD THROUGH THE EYES OF TRILOBITES . . . MAKE A JOURNEY BACK THROUGH HUNDREDS OF MILLIONS OF YEARS."
>
> —RICHARD FORTEY,
> PALEONTOLOGIST

POP!

MOVIES STARRING DINOSAURS

- *The Lost World* (1925)
- *When Dinosaurs Ruled the Earth* (1970)
- *The Land Before Time* (1988)
- *Jurassic Park* (1993)
- *Walking With Dinosaurs* (1999)
- *Dinotopia* (2002)
- *King Kong* (2005)
- *Land of the Lost* (2009)
- *Jurassic World* (2015)

PLANT PARTS
Leaves, spores, pollen from as far back as 450 mya

PETRIFIED WOOD
Preserved when minerals fill pores in organic material

GRAPTOLITES
Wormlike marine animals from 500–315 mya

BRYOZOANS
Aquatic colonies in shallow limestone formations

CORALS
Main component of reefs; some date to 500 mya

TRILOBITES
Extinct animals that once dominated Earth's oceans

BRACHIOPODS
Tens of thousands of species of these once flourished.

BIVALVES
Ancestors of today's clams, mussels, oysters, and scallops

GASTROPODS
Remains of ancient snails and sea slugs

AMMONITES
Spiral-shelled creatures once prolific, extinct about 65 mya

ECHINODERMS
Five-point symmetry, like sand dollars of today

CRINOIDS
Marine animals: flexible stalk, head of waving filaments

FISH
First vertebrates in fossil record, starting 500 mya

SHARK TEETH
One ancient species left behind teeth 7 inches long.

INSECTS
Amber, fossilized tree resin, has preserved whole bodies.

A fossil from the Burgess Shale in Canada shows a trilobite's flattened, segmented shape.

TRILOBITES

ANCESTORS OF THE HORSESHOE CRAB

In Earth's early seas, trilobites roamed, only known to us now through their distinctive shapes in the fossil record. Though paleontologists have identified more than 20,000 species of trilobite, we know very little about their behavior, diet, or even how they moved. A particularly well-preserved specimen found in Morocco in 2017 gave scientists some insight into their diets, which likely consisted of a mix of sediment feeding and scavenging.

TRILOBITES FIRST APPEARED MORE THAN 500 MILLION YEARS AGO DURING THE CAMBRIAN PERIOD.

NODOSAUR

AN ARMORED WONDER

This astonishing creature is a nodosaur, an armored dinosaur we know now better than ever thanks to fossils found in Alberta, Canada, in 2017. Traces of red pigment found on its body and the armor plates that scattered during decomposition remain preserved, though the fossil is around 110 million years old. The process of fossilization often distorts the core shape of living things, but this nodosaur was well preserved. Paleobiologist Jakob Vinther noted the specimen was so complete that it "might have been walking around a couple of weeks ago." The new discovery could reveal how dinosaur armor functioned and provide new windows into dinosaur evolution and behavior.

Fossilized remains were so complete, illustrators and sculptors could envision the nodosaur in all its detail.

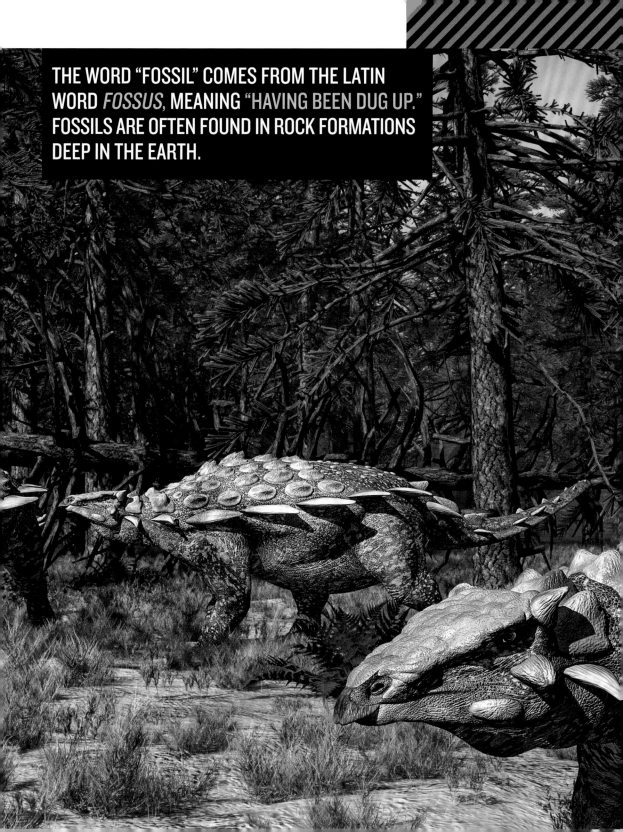

THE WORD "FOSSIL" COMES FROM THE LATIN WORD *FOSSUS*, MEANING "HAVING BEEN DUG UP." FOSSILS ARE OFTEN FOUND IN ROCK FORMATIONS DEEP IN THE EARTH.

PLANTS UP CLOSE

A WHOLE NEW LOOK AT ROSEMARY

When it comes to evolution, plants are anything but placid. At a microscopic scale, plants are dazzlingly varied and have astonishing structural complexity. Modern imaging reveals the incredible structures plants use to transform sunlight into energy and energy into everything else. Inside the cellular walls, chemical kitchens create oils, acids, and toxins that plants use to attract allies or keep away predators. If you've ever thought the kingdom of plants is boring, take a closer look. Here is a colorized microscopic look at a leaf of rosemary, a beloved kitchen herb.

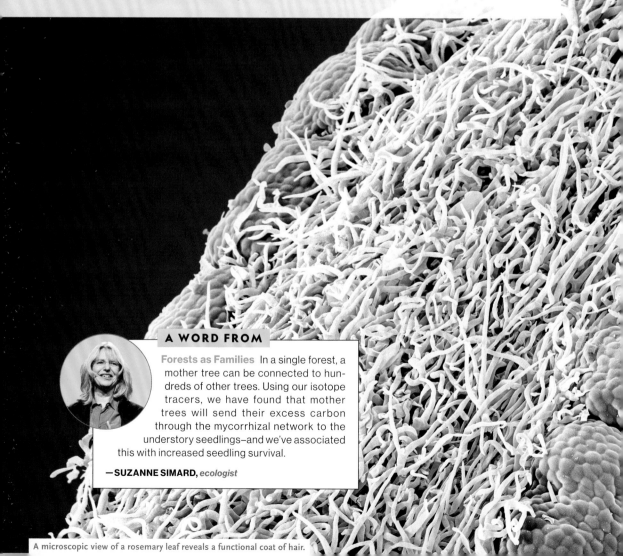

A WORD FROM

Forests as Families In a single forest, a mother tree can be connected to hundreds of other trees. Using our isotope tracers, we have found that mother trees will send their excess carbon through the mycorrhizal network to the understory seedlings—and we've associated this with increased seedling survival.

—**SUZANNE SIMARD,** *ecologist*

A microscopic view of a rosemary leaf reveals a functional coat of hair.

THROUGH PHOTOSYNTHESIS, PLANTS TURN SUNLIGHT, WATER, AND CARBON DIOXIDE INTO OXYGEN AND SUGARS. THIS NATURAL TURNAROUND RETURNS 100 BILLION NET TONS OF CARBON ANNUALLY TO THE PLANETWIDE SYSTEM AND GENERATES 40% OF THE PRECIPITATION THAT FALLS ON LAND.

Tiny repositories of oily essences help to fend off predators and give rosemary its distinctive flavor.

Under a microscope, the slight furriness of a rosemary leaf looks like a tangle of uncombed hairs.

Plant cells are mostly green because chlorophyll, the pigment central to photosynthesis, reflects green light and absorbs red and blue.

WILD FLOWERS

Weed or Wildflower? It depends on how you look at it. Some of the most common wildflowers, like chickweed and dandelion, appear throughout the North American continent. Others are more regional. Here are some of our most common wildflowers.

ASTER
Autumnal bloom pollinated by bees and butterflies

CARDINAL FLOWER
Late bloomer; hummingbird favorite

CHICKWEED
Edible winter greens, tiny starlike flowers

CHICORY
Blue morning blooms; roots roasted as coffee

COLUMBINE
Delicate spring flower; found in woodland shade

CONEFLOWER
Wild echinacea; favored treatment for colds and flu

DANDELION
Sunny blooms, bitter leaves, deep tap roots

DAY LILY
Orange flowers, many per stalk; bloom just a day

ELDERBERRY
Tall bushes hold white flowerheads then edible berries

GOLDENROD
Fall bloom mistakenly blamed for hay fever

HEAL-ALL
Non-fragrant mint; traditional remedy plant

HONEYSUCKLE
Climbing vine; tiny flowers perfume the springtime air

HORSE NETTLE
Prickly stem and leaves support white flower

INDIAN PIPE
All white, no green; depends on fungi in the soil

JIMSONWEED
Poisonous nightshade named for Jamestown

MORNING GLORY
Climbing vine with deep purple flowers

POKEWEED
Country folk cook sprouts; leaves and berries poisonous

QUEEN ANNE'S LACE
Wild carrot; scratch root to smell similarity

RED CLOVER
Common in fields and roadsides; nourishes the soil

ST. JOHN'S WORT
Summer blooms; herbal remedy for depression

SOAPWORT
Nicknamed Bouncing Bet; lathers up naturally

THISTLE
Prickly relative of the edible artichoke

TRILLIUM
Beloved forest flower; endangered in many areas

WOOD SORREL
Three-leaf mistaken for clover; sour and tangy

YARROW
Tough roadside weed; ancient healing plant

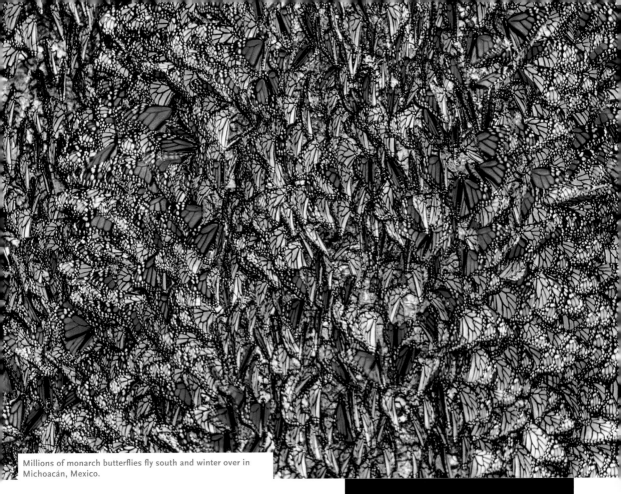
Millions of monarch butterflies fly south and winter over in Michoacán, Mexico.

MIGRATORY MIRACLE

BUTTERFLIES TRAVEL 3,000 MILES AS WINTER LOOMS
Every year millions of monarch butterflies make a cross-continental journey to warmer climes. Those that emerge in late summer leave northeastern United States and Canada and fly all the way to southwestern Mexico. They breed during their return north, and it may take four or five generations for their offspring to complete the journey. Then last year's migrators' great-grandchildren repeat the migratory trip.

Recently the monarch population has suffered a serious decline. One way to help is to plant more milkweed—either common milkweed or orange-flowered butterfly weed—in your garden. Milkweed is the only plant monarch caterpillars eat.

OBSERVERS ESTIMATE THAT THE MIGRATING MONARCH POPULATION ALONG THE U.S. PACIFIC COAST HAS DROPPED BY 99% SINCE THE 1980s.

BUTTERFLY WEED
Flat orange flower clusters; brilliant garden perennial

COMMON MILKWEED
Round pink flower clusters, pods full of winged seeds

Talking Trees

THE SECRETS WAYS OUR FORESTS ARE COMMUNICATING

Beneath a single patch of forest soil lies a vast interconnected web of life. Forest ecologist Suzanne Simard likens it to a kind of hidden intelligence. By tracking specific chemicals, she and other scientists observed how trees in the Douglas fir forests of Canada "talk," forming underground symbiotic relationships, called mycorrhizae, with fungi to relay stress signals and share resources.

Douglas fir
(hub tree)

Douglas fir
(younger tree)

Douglas fir
(seedling)

Understory nursery
Douglas fir trees use the network to identify and nurture related seedlings.

Excess sugar from photosynthesis

Symbiotic
fungal network

Resource pathways

→ Sugar from trees
→ Nutrients from soil
→ Mixed resources from network: nutrients and carbon (from sugar)
→ Chemical stress signals

Nitrogen, potassium, phosphorus, and other nutrients

Enlarged section of tree root tip

Resource-exchange pathway

Fungal thread

Tree root cell

1.
Excess production
Taller, older trees, called hub trees, often have more access to sunlight and produce more sugar through photosynthesis than they need.

2.
Exchange of goods
A mass of fungal threads, or mycelium, envelops the root tips of a hub tree, feeding it nutrients from the soil in exchange for sugar, which the fungus lacks.

“ FOREVER CHERISHED BE THE TREE . . .”

—EMILY DICKINSON, POET

Western spruce budworm
Paper birch
Douglas fir (hub tree)
Pine preparation
Fir trees infected with budworms send stress signals to nearby pines.
Chemical stress signals
Ponderosa pine
In spring and fall, firs share sugar with leafless birches.
In summer, birches return the favor to shaded firs.
Symbiotic fungal network
FOREST IN DISTRESS

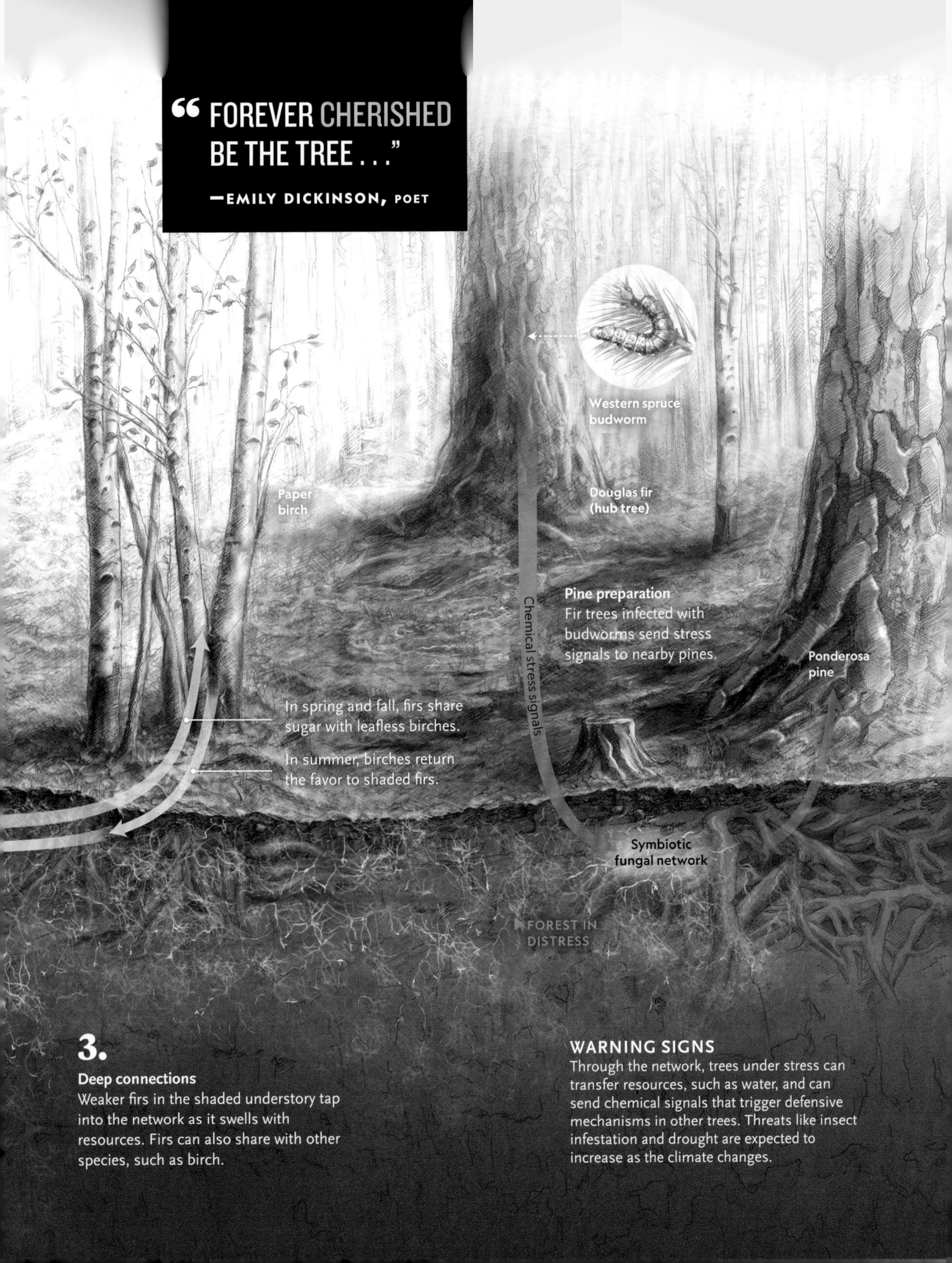

3.

Deep connections
Weaker firs in the shaded understory tap into the network as it swells with resources. Firs can also share with other species, such as birch.

WARNING SIGNS

Through the network, trees under stress can transfer resources, such as water, and can send chemical signals that trigger defensive mechanisms in other trees. Threats like insect infestation and drought are expected to increase as the climate changes.

BEST OF @NATGEO

TOP PHOTOS OF LIFE ON LAND

@thomaspeschak | THOMAS PESCHAK
About 100,000 endemic giant tortoises, a species eaten almost to extinction, survive on a remote Seychelles outpost.

@joelsartore | JOEL SARTORE
Caught in a bright spotlight, an endangered African lion perches tentatively, high in the treetops.

@stevewinterphoto | STEVE WINTER
A camera trap set amid known tiger territory results in a cameo portrait of this glorious individual.

@drewtrush | DREW RUSH
A mountain goat, native to the northern Rocky Mountains of North America, seems to pose for the camera.

@argonautphoto | AARON HUEY
A wolf from the Nenana River pack races its shadow across ice-crusted snow in Alaska's Denali National Park.

@amivitale | AMI VITALE
A curious panda peeks around a tree, appearing to say hello to a National Geographic photographer.

@beverlyjoubert | BEVERLY JOUBERT
This young elephant is learning to maneuver its tiny trunk, which has 100,000 distinct bundles of muscle fibers.

@stefanounterthiner | STEFANO UNTERTHINER
A Sulawesi crested black macaque, an endangered primate, lives in Indonesia's Tangkoko Nature Reserve.

RAE WYNN-GRANT
ECOLOGIST

A WILD LIFE

Rae Wynn-Grant wants to improve the relationship between people and the powerful wild animals that live around them. She has worked with lions in East Africa and bears in the American West, studying their environments and patterns of behavior. She's also dedicated to making science more welcoming to people of all backgrounds, working to dismantle institutional racism and break down barriers to achievement.

Wynn-Grant studies how grizzly bears reclaim their native habitats in grasslands by the Sierra Nevada and Rocky Mountains.

G rowing up in San Francisco, Wynn-Grant learned to love nature through television programs. It wasn't until college that she realized her love for ecology could be her career. She began studying conservation biology and spent a semester studying lions and their interactions with the Maasai people in Kenya.

Today, Wynn-Grant works to understand the movements of animals and how they interact with human communities. Lots of people depend on raising livestock for their livelihoods, and fear of the threat of large carnivores—wolves, for example— makes it hard for them to support conservation efforts. Wynn-Grant wants to change those perceptions.

LEVELING THE FIELD

In addition to her fieldwork, Wynn-Grant serves as the equity, inclusion, and diversity officer for the Society of Conservation Biology. She describes conservation as a mission critical field, and is committed to making it more diverse. "If we don't get it right, we're doomed," she says.

To solve the complex problems that they face, conservationists need to bring a range of backgrounds and perspectives to the table. Social justice is a significant part of that work, according to Wynn-Grant: "We won't see more scientists of color and from the developing world until we can alleviate poverty and make sure that families aren't struggling."

Wynn-Grant crouches by a tranquilized black bear in the Lake Tahoe Basin.

KEY FACTS

How You Can Support
CONSERVATION

EDUCATE YOURSELF
Visit zoos, explore parks, watch documentaries, and read books and stories about wildlife.

REDUCE DEMAND
Consider the impact of using plastics and eating animal products. Cut back where you can.

PUSH FOR CHANGE
Support the people and groups who are working to protect wildlife. Many conservation groups rely on their supporters not only for donations but also for spreading the word about the work that they do.

TELLTALE TRACKS

Who Goes There? There is a hidden world all around you: Animals you do not see may still leave traces of their lives behind. By studying animal tracks, scientists and guides can estimate population size, ages, and even what the animal was doing as it left the marks.

VIRGINIA OPOSSUM
North America's only marsupial

BLACK-TAILED PRAIRIE DOG
Complex tunnel town dwellers

NORTHERN FLYING SQUIRREL
Can glide up to 300 feet

EASTERN GRAY SQUIRREL
Tail serves as umbrella or wrap.

GROUNDHOG
Also called woodchuck

EASTERN CHIPMUNK
Caches food underground for winter

AMERICAN BEAVER
Incisors fell trees to build dams.

NORTH AMERICAN PORCUPINE
Sharp quills fend off predators.

MUSKRAT
Still trapped for fur

NORTH AMERICAN DEER MOUSE
Huddles together in cold weather

HOUSE MOUSE
Can have up to 14 litters a year

NORWAY RAT
Prefers to live near humans

ANTELOPE JACKRABBIT
Huge ears help it cool off.

EASTERN COTTONTAIL
Named for its powder-puff tail

NORTHERN SHORT-TAILED SHREW
Preys with poisonous bite

EASTERN MOLE
Flat, clawed forefeet dig tunnels.

BOBCAT
Most widespread cat in North America

MOUNTAIN LION
Solitary unless mating

COYOTE
So adaptable, now in cities

RED FOX
Imported from Europe for sport

AMERICAN BLACK BEAR
Males weigh up to 900 pounds.

NORTH AMERICAN RIVER OTTER
Playful swimmer

BLACK FOOTED FERRET
Nearly extinct; takes over prairie dog dens

STRIPED SKUNK
Spray can be smelled half mile away.

RACCOON
Handy thanks to dexterous fingers

Black bear cubs follow their mother along the water's edge in Alaska.

BLACK BEARS

MAMMAL MODEL OF ADAPTABILITY

You can find the American black bear in forests across North America. As the smallest of the three American bears, the black bear may lack the massive size of polar bears or brown bears (better known as grizzlies), but it makes up for it in adaptability. There are estimated to be as many as 950,000 black bears living in North America—in Mexico, Canada, and 40 of the 50 states. They also aren't all black. Black bears' coats can come in red, brown, blond, and, rarely, blue and white. The secret to their success is adaptability. Black bears happily eat berries, insects, fish, mammals—almost anything they can get their paws on, even human trash.

A WORD FROM

Among the Bears There's only so much you can learn by measuring a tranquilized bear and putting dots on a map . . . Because if you want to learn about their habitat use, social organization, language—everything that makes a bear a bear—you have to at least see the animal that you're studying, and it can't be tranquilized. I knew I had to get close, and do more of a Jane Goodall kind of research.

—**LYNN ROGERS**, *biologist*

DOMESTICATION
TRANSFORMATION

ONCE WILD, NOW OUR FAITHFUL COMPANIONS

Playtime in a park

SHAPING EVOLUTION

MAKING OUR BEST FRIENDS

Today they're our best friends, but we are still unraveling the process that transformed wild cats into house cats and wolves into springer spaniels. Domestication isn't just about behavior or tameness; the friendliest wild animal is still wild in ways our pets can never be again. As humans worked with animals, our domesticated friends underwent a remarkable transformation, human-led evolution that changed behavior, size, and coloration. Cats and dogs, cows and mice—dozens of species have undergone domestication, each one with a suite of physical changes. A puppy's floppy ears and curly tail, a cow's white spots and massive size, and the orange coat of a tabby cat are all physical manifestations of this transformation.

SHAPING DOGS

FROM WOLF TO WOOF

The process of domesticating dogs began at least 10,000 years ago, and it may have happened simultaneously in different parts of the world. It likely began by accident, as wolves followed human hunters, scavenging their kills or eating scraps. While no one is certain exactly what the early relationship looked like, the transformation from fearful antagonist to companion and guardian happened remarkably quickly. Social transformation led to genetic change as humans began selecting for preferential traits. Some dogs were bred for strength, others for speed, but virtually all of them were chosen based on their behavior toward humans—survival of the friendliest. It was a genetic experiment that we're now seeing in the DNA and behavior of modern dogs around the world.

A wolf and a Maltese

Loving foxes

A few genes govern breed variability.

HOW TO MAKE A PET

EFFORTS TO REENACT EVOLUTION

In 1959, Russian geneticist Dmitry Belyaev began to study 130 silver foxes, breeding together the tamest individuals and those most responsive to humans. The goal was to re-create in miniature the long journey from wolves to dogs.

After six generations, the foxes were eager for human contact and attention. Physical changes also occurred. The foxes' tails shrank, the pups' ears stayed floppy, their tails began to wag, they began to lick their humans' faces, and they acted more like trusting young kits than wary adult foxes: a suite of genetic changes that have become known as the domestication phenotype.

EARTH DAY EVERY DAY

House Cats Versus
WILD BIRDS

According to the American Bird Conservancy, domesticated cats allowed to roam outdoors kill some 2.4 billion birds each year. The World Conservation Union (IUCN) includes house cats on their list of the world's 100 worst invasive species. By keeping pet cats indoors, you can help save biodiversity and beloved songbird species.

PET GENETICS

UNRAVELING THE DNA

When Belyaev's experiment began, genetic sequencing was a distant dream. But he believed that genetic changes could contain the answers he sought. Because dog breeds have almost always been governed by human selection, the deliberate creation and cultivation of traits has left clues in the genome that can be traced. Just a single gene can change a dog's size from Dachshund scale to Rottweiler scale. Hair length, ear shape, coat color, even fur type are all controlled by about 50 genetic switches. The diversity of dogs and their domestication is not a natural wonder. We have shaped our animal companions to be as amazing as they are. They are our perfect companions because we made them that way.

MEET THE QUOLL

A MARSUPIAL ON THE MEND

This cat-size marsupial is a quoll, once native to Australia. Depleted habitat and introduced predators including cats drove them to the edge of extinction. Three subspecies survive in Australia, but one, the eastern quoll, persisted only in Tasmania. In 2017, 20 eastern quolls were released into southeastern Australia in the hope that these creatures will reestablish themselves in their original homeland.

TOXIC CANE TOADS, UNWITTINGLY INTRODUCED TO AUSTRALIA IN 1935, ACCOUNT FOR RECENT QUOLL DEATHS, BUT CARETAKERS HAVE BEEN TRAINING TASTE AVERSION IN SOME OF THE QUOLLS BEFORE REINTRODUCING THEM INTO THE WILD.

Quolls usually spend daytime in their dens, but sometimes they venture out to forage.

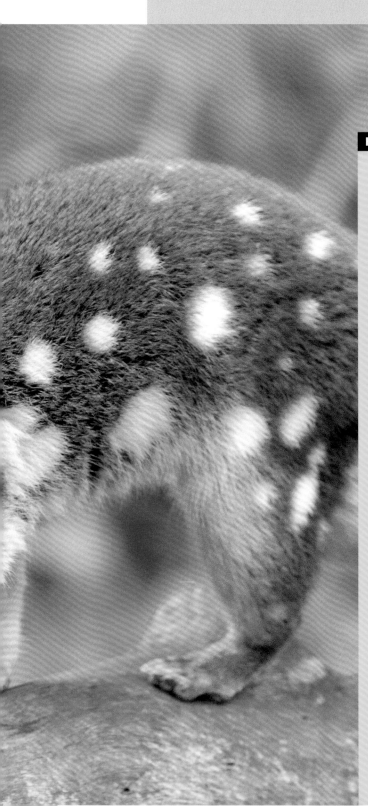

Wildlife Found Only in
AUSTRALIA

■ SOUTHERN CASSOWARY
Cassowaries are large, flightless birds—relatives to emus, ostriches, and kiwis. The southern cassowary is the largest of three species, standing up to six feet tall and weighing up to 160 pounds.

■ TASMANIAN DEVIL
These feisty mammals have one of the most powerful bites relative to their size in the animal kingdom. They were once common across the continent of Australia, but now their range is limited to the island of Tasmania.

■ KOALA
Though they're often called koala bears, these small gray animals are actually marsupials. Their diet is almost exclusively made of leaves from eucalyptus trees—a single koala can eat up to three pounds of leaves in a single day.

■ RED KANGAROO
One of the most recognizable Australian species, the red kangaroo is the largest marsupial in the world. With their powerful hind legs, they can jump up to six feet high and cover 25 feet in a single leap.

■ PLATYPUS
One of the few egg-laying mammals in the world, platypuses look like a mixture of a duck and a beaver. They're amphibious creatures that feed on frogs and fish and burrow into muddy riverbanks.

■ LAUGHING KOOKABURRA
Found in the eastern forests, the laughing kookaburra has a distinctive call that sounds a bit like manic laughter. Their long, distinctive beaks help them catch the small lizards, snakes, and insects that their diet comprises.

PRIMATE FAMILY TREE

OUR DISTANT COUSINS

Humans have many characteristics that make each of us unique, but biologically, we're not a class unto ourselves. Among the more than 500 different species of primate, we humans are just one. And these days, our family could use some help: Most of our cousins live in the shrinking tropical rainforest, and two-thirds of us are at risk of extinction.

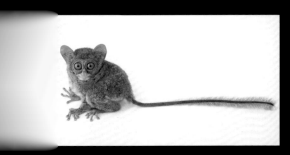

SPECTRAL TARSIER

One of the smallest primates in the world is a scant three and a half inches in length. Although they may look adorable, tarsiers are the only truly carnivorous primates, grabbing beetles, bats, and even snakes—often in midair—before devouring them.

GOLDEN LION TAMARIN

These iconic creatures live in the forests of Brazil. Tamarin juveniles, which are raised by the entire community, are sometimes twins—rare among primates. Once on the edge of extinction, tamarins have been saved by intensive conservation efforts.

HAMADRYAS BABOON

These amazingly social creatures can often be seen in troops numbering in the hundreds. Though found across northeast Africa and the Arabian Peninsula, they are locally extinct in Egypt, where they were once revered as favorites of Thoth, the ancient Egyptian god of learning.

ORANGUTAN

Orangutans are the only great apes found outside of Africa: They live in the forests of Borneo and Sumatra, where they spend almost all of their time aloft. Like many primates, they have been seen creating and using simple tools when hunting and are chimpanzees' closest genetic relatives.

GORILLA

The largest of the primates, gorillas may look intimidating, but these herbivorous apes are more Curious George than King Kong. They spend most of their day wandering about, eating plants, and building new nests every night. A group of gorillas, called a "troop," can be as large as 30 individuals.

CHIMPANZEE

One of our closest genetic relatives, chimps live in tightly bonded families, use tools, and even eat medicinal plants when injured. Generally fruit and plant eaters, they also consume insects, eggs, and meat, including carrion. With such a varied diet, they can habituate themselves to African rainforests, woodlands, and grasslands. They are known to make weapons, commit murder, and even coordinate attacks on other tribes.

WE ARE, INDEED, UNIQUE PRIMATES, WE HUMANS, BUT WE'RE SIMPLY NOT AS DIFFERENT FROM THE REST OF THE ANIMAL KINGDOM AS WE USED TO THINK."

—JANE GOODALL, **PRIMATOLOGIST**

A WORD FROM

Compassionate Conservation
Working with the gorillas taught me how readily our emotions, our sense of compassion, and our humanity influence conservation decisions. I finally understood that conservation is more than a science. I realized it was time to shift gears in my career and start teaching. I no longer wanted to work to save the last of a species or focus just on the science of veterinary medicine. I wanted to help inspire the next generation of conservationists.

—LUCY SPELMAN, *wildlife biologist*

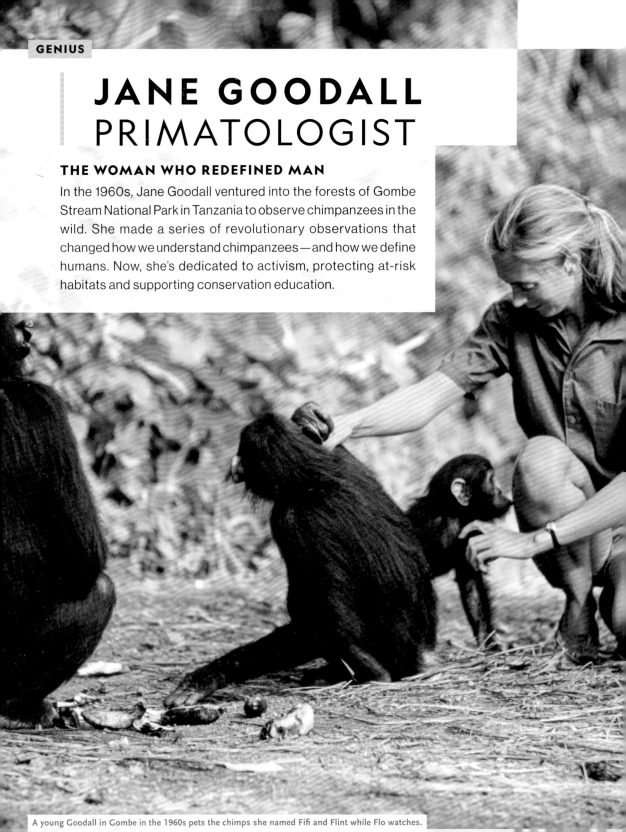

JANE GOODALL
PRIMATOLOGIST

THE WOMAN WHO REDEFINED MAN

In the 1960s, Jane Goodall ventured into the forests of Gombe Stream National Park in Tanzania to observe chimpanzees in the wild. She made a series of revolutionary observations that changed how we understand chimpanzees—and how we define humans. Now, she's dedicated to activism, protecting at-risk habitats and supporting conservation education.

A young Goodall in Gombe in the 1960s pets the chimps she named Fifi and Flint while Flo watches.

As a girl, Goodall read Doctor Doolittle and Tarzan stories and dreamed of living among the animals in Africa. In her early 20s, she visited Kenya and sought out renowned archaeologist Louis Leakey, who gave her a job at his dig site in Olduvai Gorge, where he and his wife had been finding remarkable artifacts of early human ancestors. Impressed with her work, Leakey asked Goodall if she would be interested in studying primates. Soon she set off for Gombe to observe chimpanzees.

"I knew that to find out about the chimps, I would have to get their trust," Goodall says. She observed them making and using tools—a trait previously believed to be uniquely human.

In 1962, wildlife photographer Hugo van Lawick came to Gombe to document the work at Gombe. His film and photographs made Jane Goodall a household name. It also led to marriage—Goodall married van Lawick and had a son, Hugo, who grew up in the camp. In total, Goodall spent 26 years living and working in Gombe.

SPEAKING OUT

Though she says activism didn't come to her naturally, Goodall couldn't stay quiet once she learned how poaching, medical testing, and habitat loss were affecting chimpanzees.

These days, campaigning to protect the wild is her main job. She travels more than 300 days a year, spreading the word about disappearing habitats and training the next generation of conservationists to take up her mantle.

> " ONLY IF WE UNDERSTAND CAN WE CARE. ONLY IF WE CARE WILL WE HELP. ONLY IF WE HELP SHALL THEY BE SAVED."

Recognizing the threats to biodiversity worldwide, Goodall now speaks out on behalf of the planet.

KEY DATES

Goodall's Major
MILESTONES

■ **1960**
Goodall arrives in Gombe. Within three months she observes chimps making and using tools.

■ **1965**
The documentary *Miss Goodall and the Wild Chimpanzees* airs to an estimated audience of 25 million viewers.

■ **1977**
She founds the Jane Goodall Institute, an NGO devoted to protecting the rapidly disappearing chimp habitat.

■ **2005**
The Jane Goodall Institute establishes its first formal conservation plan around Gombe Stream National Park.

■ **2017**
Jane, a documentary film about her life, is released.

BEST OF @NATGEO

TOP PHOTOS OF SEA LIFE

@andy_mann | ANDY MANN
A sleepy and charismatic Weddell seal lifts its head as an Antarctic sunset blazes in the background.

@daviddoubilet | DAVID DOUBILET
Stingrays belong to a group of ocean ambassadors that gently greet tourists in Bora Bora, French Polynesia.

@brianskerry | BRIAN SKERRY
A group of Atlantic spotted dolphins swim together in the waters around Bimini in the Bahamas.

@enricsala | ENRIC SALA
Blacktip reef sharks gather in the Pacific Ocean's Southern Line Islands, a pristine marine wilderness.

> ## "WE KNOW THAT WHEN WE PROTECT OUR OCEANS, WE'RE PROTECTING OUR FUTURE."
>
> —**BILL CLINTON,** U.S. PRESIDENT, 1993-2001

@thomaspeschak | **THOMAS PESCHAK**
A whale shark and its entourage of yellow jacks traverse the western reaches of the Indian Ocean.

@bertiegregory | **BERTIE GREGORY**
A female harp seal nuzzles her pup, whom she knows by scent, on an ice floe in the Gulf of St. Lawrence.

@mitty | **CRISTINA MITTERMEIER**
A sea anemone sways to the rhythm of the British Columbia coastal waters, extending its tentacles to feed.

@paulnicklen | **PAUL NICKLEN**
In Svalbard, Norway, a walrus swings its three-foot-long (1 m) tusks toward the sky as he adjusts his position.

WHALES

LEARNING FROM THESE GIANTS OF THE SEA

A sperm whale tail

OCEAN ELDERS

A SPECTACLE OF SIZE & LONGEVITY

Whales are some of the largest animals in the history of Earth, and some of the most graceful. Blue whales, which can weigh up to 150 tons and measure as long as the boats sent to watch them, glide with seemingly no effort. They leap from the water, spin, and dive with casual elegance.

Some whales can dive more than 10,000 feet into the darkest depths, going hours between breaths. The rewards for these astonishing dives are squid, krill, and crustaceans. The whale's massive size comes with a long life span. Baby whales can take a decade to reach adulthood, and even the shortest lived whales can live for 40 years, the longest for more than 200.

WHALE SONG

SOUNDS OF THE SEA

In the deep sound channel of the open ocean, the clicks and songs of whales filter in from thousands of miles away. For many, it is the song of the sea, and all whales are part of its chorus. These animals, including the blue whale, the largest mammal on Earth, fill the ocean with their haunting melody.

Like bats or dolphins, some whales can echolocate, using their calls to "see" objects through reflected soundwaves. Other whale songs are used to show off for mates or rivals, while mothers and calves whisper to each other to avoid aquatic eavesdroppers. Sometimes whale pods sing in something near conversation across hundreds of miles. Still, evolutionarily, this is a recent soundtrack, and the song of the whales wasn't always aquatic.

A humpback whale calf

A mother blue whale and her calf

SPERM WHALES HAVE THE LARGEST BRAINS EVER KNOWN TO EXIST ON EARTH, MEASURING NEARLY 500 CUBIC INCHES. A HUMAN BRAIN IS ABOUT 80 CUBIC INCHES.

A pod of sperm whales

EVOLUTIONARY HISTORY

THE EARLIEST WHALES

Pakicetus was an ancient ancestor of the massive blue whales and all other cetaceans, a group of marine mammals that includes dolphins and porpoises. With a hairy coat, four legs, a long tail, and a long, narrow mouth, this distant relative looked more like a German shepherd than a cetacean. It lived alongside the ocean, not in it, but over millions of years it evolved into more and more of an ocean dweller. Archaeologists have reconstructed the story piece by piece, watching the slow transformation of ankles to fins, and long snouts to massive mouths.

A WORD FROM

Creating Crittercam I conceived of Crittercam as a scientific tool, a way of studying animal behavior in places people access. What I didn't expect was the tremendous attraction the resulting images hold for people. Every time we deploy, Crittercam brings home the animal's point of view . . . a perspective that allows people to connect with the animal and its struggles to survive. It's this empathic experience that I didn't necessarily expect when I invented Crittercam.

—**GREG MARSHALL,** *biologist and cinematographer*

PROTECTING WHALES

KEEPING MARINE MAMMALS SAFE

They may be titans in the sea, but whales are under threat. Commercial whaling continues in countries like Iceland, Norway, and Japan, and traditional indigenous spear hunting is still a practice in some regions. Whales often meet with accidental threats as well—entanglement in fishing lines or nets, strikes by oceangoing vessels. Changes in the temperature and water quality of the ocean can also affect their survival.

Climate change, the threat for most animals, hits some species harder than others. Some whales like the vaquita live in specialized climates, with no escape, while global wanderers like the gray whales are thriving in warmer waters and venturing into new regions.

SPINELESS
SWIMMERS

THE FASCINATING INNER WORKINGS OF A JELLYFISH

Jellyfish have been drifting through Earth's oceans for hundreds of millions of years, sweeping in or happening upon their food, which includes microscopic zooplankton, tiny crustaceans, and even other jellies. Many, like the Atlantic bay nettle pictured below, hunt not by sight but by direct contact. They spread tentacles and appendages called oral arms to contact prey and then pulse, thereby creating vortices to pull in their prey.

1. Swimming
Many jellies hunt by direct contact, spreading tentacles and oral arms wide.

2. Stinging
Tentacles have millions of stinging cells (A) with barbed tubules (B) that uncoil and eject venom (C).

3. Ingesting
Hairlike cilia on the oral arms convey prey to the mouth. Larger prey can take hours to digest.

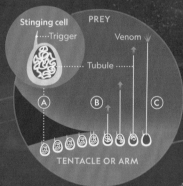

Stinging cell
Trigger
PREY
Venom
Tubule
(A) (B) (C)
TENTACLE OR ARM

Cilia

24 TENTACLES
4 ORAL ARMS

Small prey
Zooplankton

Big prey
Mnemiopsis comb jelly

Rhopalia
These structures sense light and gravity and convey information to the nerves on the bell, driving behavior.

3 ft

120 ft long

GIANTS OF THEIR KIND

Tentacles of the lion's mane, world's largest jellyfish species, can reach 120 feet (37 m) long. It lives in the cold waters of the Arctic and northern Atlantic and Pacific Oceans.

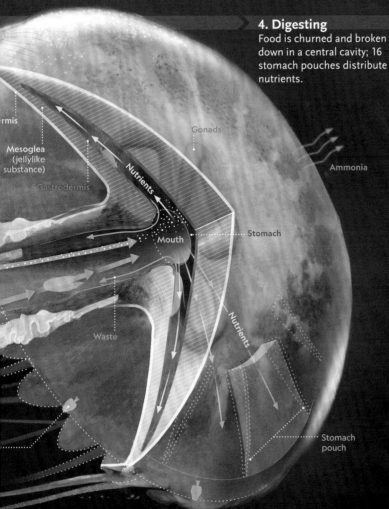

4. Digesting

Food is churned and broken down in a central cavity; 16 stomach pouches distribute nutrients.

rmis

Mesoglea (jellylike substance)

Gastrodermis

Gonads

Nutrients

Ammonia

Mouth

Stomach

Waste

Nutrients

Stomach pouch

ONE JAPANESE JELLYFISH SPECIES GROWS TO SIX FEET ACROSS AND CAN WEIGH 440 POUNDS.

KEY FACTS

Stages in Jellyfish GROWTH

SPERM & EGGS
Both are released into the water, up to 40,000 eggs a day.

LARVAE
Fertilized eggs become larvae that attach to a hard surface.

POLYPS
Also attached, polyps can take days or years to reproduce. They look like sea anemones.

CLONES
Clones bud off the polyps through asexual reproduction and begin to float free.

ADULTS
Clones develop rapidly into adult jellyfish.

SEA SHELLS

A Home in the Sea Creatures started building shells around 500 million years ago. Since then, they have evolved spirals, spines, and ridges, but the purpose is still the same: to protect the delicate animal living inside it.

FLORIDA FIGHTING CONCH
Spurred foot for defense, burrowing

FRILLED DOGWINKLE
Preys with tongue and poison

KNOBBED WHELK
Like conch, can be made into a horn

LETTERED OLIVE
Used by Native Americans for jewelry

ATLANTIC PLATE LIMPET
Attaches to rocks by suction

ATLANTIC SLIPPER SHELL
Shells stack for reproduction

BAY SCALLOP
Senses predators with 18 pairs of eyes

PACIFIC LITTLENECK CLAM
Abundant in U.S. West Coast shallows

EASTERN OYSTER
Must attach to hard surface to mature

PACIFIC RAZOR CLAM
Meaty edible bivalve

ATLANTIC JACKKNIFE CLAM
Digs itself down into sand or mud

ATLANTIC AUGER
Stuns prey with poisonous barb

PACIFIC GEODUCK
Can age to more than 150 years

NORTHERN QUAHOG
Harvested for clam chowder

MARINE MUSSEL
One of many edible mussel species

BLACK TURBAN SNAIL
Feeds on algae, has many predators

COMMON MARSH SNAIL
Breathes air, feeds on marsh grasses

COMMON PERIWINKLE
Two antennae, one foot

RED ABALONE
Long valued for pearlescent colors

VIOLET SEA SNAIL
Churns bubbles and floats to survive

> **" NATURE IS THE MOST BEAUTIFUL ENGINEER AND IT ALWAYS HAS A REASON FOR CHOOSING ANY SHAPE."**
>
> **—DR. CHANDRA TIWARY,** INDIAN INSTITUTE OF SCIENCE

A man wades through a bed of giant clams in Kiribati, Polynesia.

CLAMMING UP

MARINE MARVELS

Clams, snails, and giant squids all are mollusks, one of the most diverse groups of life on Earth. There are more than 100,000 known species, but the number may be twice that, found in every aquatic environment from freshwater lakes to deep-sea trenches. Mollusks are invertebrates, with a mantle covering the soft body. Some possess a biological glue stronger than any other substance in nature, and some can survive briefly outside their aquatic environment. Their abundance and versatility has made them desirable food. In fact, early American waters had so many oysters, they were considered peasant food. Today they are an expensive gourmet treat.

THE AMAZING
OCTOPUS

UNDERWATER GENIUSES

The octopus is a strange animal. Its three hearts pump blue blood through a bone-less frame. Some can compress their bodies from three feet across to the size of a quarter. Other species mimic textures and shapes like ridges, bumps, or spines. It takes a common octopus approximately two seconds to fully camouflage itself with its surroundings. Octopuses may have been the first intelligent creature on Earth, yet of their 500 million neurons, two-thirds are located in their arms, not their heads.

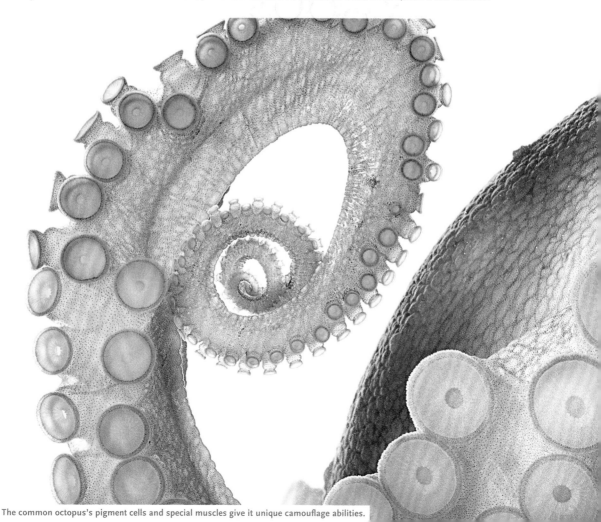

The common octopus's pigment cells and special muscles give it unique camouflage abilities.

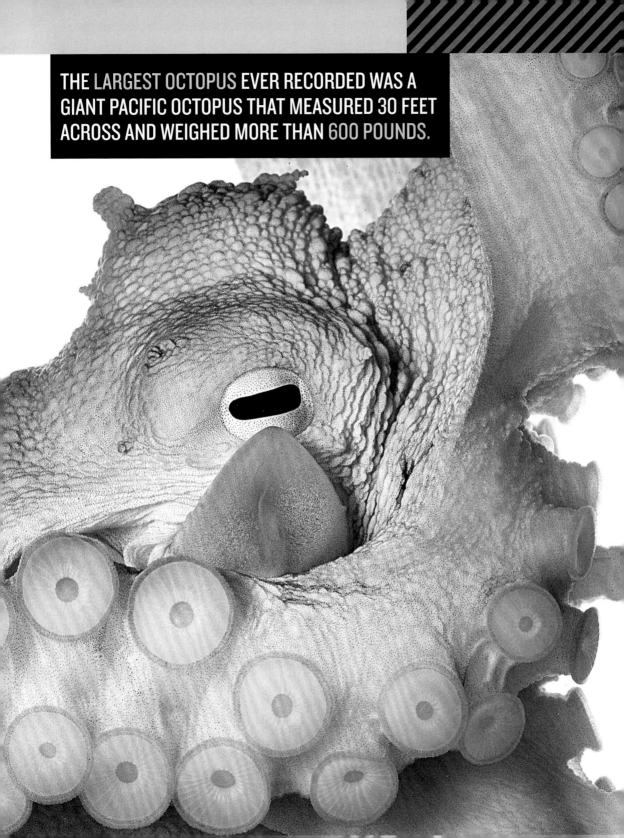

THE LARGEST OCTOPUS EVER RECORDED WAS A GIANT PACIFIC OCTOPUS THAT MEASURED 30 FEET ACROSS AND WEIGHED MORE THAN 600 POUNDS.

BEST OF @NATGEO

TOP PHOTOS OF LIFE ON THE WING

@kengeiger | KEN GEIGER
The grey crowned crane, its numbers falling, is more than three feet tall (1 m), its wingspan more than six feet (1.8 m).

@anandavarma | ANAND VARMA
Water droplets fly from the body of an Anna's hummingbird, perched on a branch as it shakes itself dry.

@timlaman | TIM LAMAN
This Vogelkop superb is a bird-of-paradise and global ambassador for Papua forest conservation in Indonesia.

@franslanting | FRANS LANTING
Two emperor penguins stand over their young, which must fledge before the ice melts, in Antarctica.

> **"THE MOMENT YOU DOUBT WHETHER YOU CAN FLY, YOU CEASE FOREVER TO BE ABLE TO DO IT."**
>
> —J. M. BARRIE, PLAYWRIGHT & AUTHOR OF *PETER PAN*

@ronan_donovan | RONAN DONOVAN
Migrating sandhill cranes and snow geese fill the sky in New Mexico's Bosque del Apache National Wildlife Refuge.

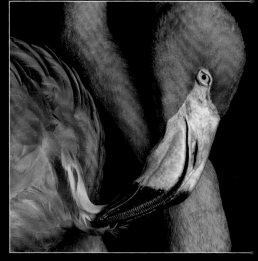

@jasperdoest | JASPER DOEST
Curaçao's Flamingo Bob, who got a concussion after flying into a window, brings awareness to Caribbean flamingos.

@lucasfogliaphoto | LUCAS FOGLIA
A female honeybee pollinates a flower. A hive has one queen and 100 female workers for every male drone.

@carltonward | CARLTON WARD
A burrowing owl snacks on a mole cricket on a ranch in the Everglades area of the Florida Wildlife Corridor.

BACKYARD
BIRDS

Flights of Fascination Birds wing their way through everyone's landscape, on every continent, whether hot or cold, rural or urban. Birding is about more than checking lists: Birders turn their love of these avians into real science.

AMERICAN GOLDFINCH
One of the few vegan birds

HOUSE FINCH
Males have rose-colored breast.

BALTIMORE ORIOLE
Weaves hanging nest of fibers

AMERICAN ROBIN
Traditional sign of spring

BLACK-CAPPED CHICKADEE
Chirps its own name

WESTERN BLUEBIRD
Nests in knotholes or birdhouses

EASTERN BLUEBIRD
Eats primarily insects and grubs

SONG SPARROW
May raise two or more broods a year

TUFTED TITMOUSE
Hoards food for winter

WARBLING VIREO
Melodious, recognizable song

NORTHERN CARDINAL
Males bright red, females olive

HOUSE SPARROW
Prefers to live near to humans

NORTHERN FLICKER
Digs in soil for ants and beetles

HOUSE WREN
Wide range, Canada through S. America

RED-WINGED BLACKBIRD
Winter flocks in the millions

RUBY-THROATED HUMMINGBIRD
Sips from red and orange flowers

GREAT HORNED OWL
Head swivels to look in all directions.

EASTERN PHOEBE
Perching, tail wags up and down

EUROPEAN STARLING
Mimics calls of other birds

CLIFF SWALLOW
Creates gourd-shaped nest of mud

AMERICAN CROW
Crafts tools to get at food

PURPLE MARTIN
Will move into erected nesting boxes

NORTHERN MOCKINGBIRD
May learn 200 different songs

WHITE-BREASTED NUTHATCH
Creeps along tree trunks, often head down

BLUE JAY
Throat pouch can hold 2–3 acorns.

Common ravens are the largest perching birds in North America.

CORVIDS

A family that includes ravens, crows, and magpies, corvids are often recognized as some of the most intelligent birds in the world. Their abilities run the gamut from mimicking other animal sounds to using tools and other problem-solving skills. Researchers studying animal cognition have found that ravens are able to preplan tasks, a skill once thought to be unique to humans and great apes. The Eurasian magpie, with its distinct black and white plumage, recognizes its own reflection in a mirror. Some species of crow recognize human faces, and sometimes they are more comfortable with humans they have interacted with before than with strangers.

MYTHICAL BIRDS

Corvids feature prominently in folklore across cultures and religions. In the Old Testament, it is said that Noah sent out both a raven and a dove to see if floodwaters had receded. In some Native American traditions, a raven swallowed the sun out of jealousy. The Norse God Odin had two ravens, named Huginn and Muninn— thought and memory.

> **❝ IF YOU TAKE CARE OF BIRDS, YOU TAKE CARE OF MOST OF THE ENVIRONMENTAL PROBLEMS IN THE WORLD.❞**
>
> **—THOMAS E. LOVEJOY,**
> **CONSERVATION BIOLOGIST**

A WORD FROM

Better Together [Crows] have this family unit, but they also have a neighborhood that they have some allegiance to as well. You keep your territory and you don't let the neighbors in, but if a predator is attacking them, you go help. They all know everybody in the neighborhood; they know what's happening by what everybody else is saying.

—KEVIN MCGOWAN, *ornithologist*

HUMMINGBIRDS
WINGED WONDERS

FIREWORKS IN FLIGHT

Hummingbirds fly like magical fairies and shimmer like jewels in the sky, but scientists have never fully understood these glorious birds. The hummingbird can fly backward, hover, and even fly sideways—all at incredible speed. But how? The answer comes in unique biological adaptations only recently discovered: larger brains to process information, symmetrical wing strokes, and longer "hands" for greater flexibility and movement. Despite their diminutive size—the smallest of 340 species weighs less than two grams—their brain represents 4.2 percent of their body weight, making it proportionally one of the largest in the animal kingdom.

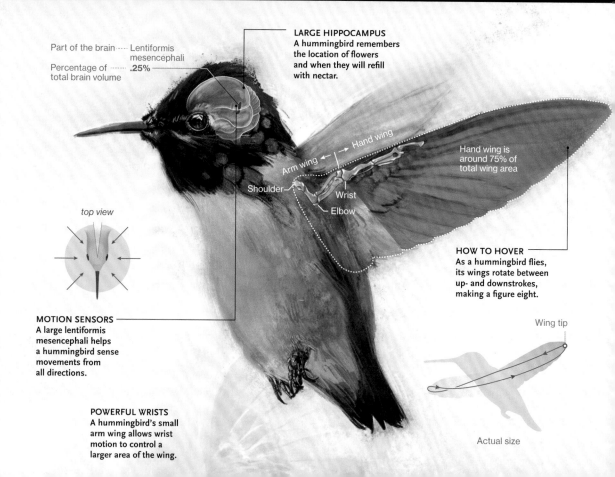

Part of the brain ···· Lentiformis mesencephali

Percentage of ······ .25%
total brain volume

LARGE HIPPOCAMPUS
A hummingbird remembers the location of flowers and when they will refill with nectar.

Arm wing ← → Hand wing

Hand wing is around 75% of total wing area

Shoulder

Wrist

Elbow

top view

MOTION SENSORS
A large lentiformis mesencephali helps a hummingbird sense movements from all directions.

HOW TO HOVER
As a hummingbird flies, its wings rotate between up- and downstrokes, making a figure eight.

Wing tip

Actual size

POWERFUL WRISTS
A hummingbird's small arm wing allows wrist motion to control a larger area of the wing.

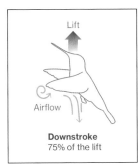

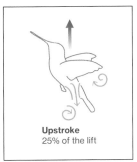

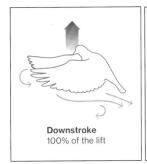

Downstroke 75% of the lift	**Upstroke** 25% of the lift	**Downstroke** 100% of the lift	**Upstroke** 0% of the lift

DOWNSTROKE
Hummingbirds produce lift with both upward and downward wing strokes.

UPSTROKE
They can beat their wings up to 100 times a second.

PROPULSION
In larger birds, all the propulsion comes from downward wing strokes.

FORWARD
Larger birds tend to fly forward rather than hovering.

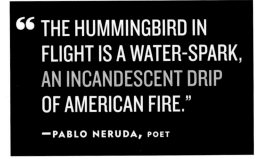

> ## " THE HUMMINGBIRD IN FLIGHT IS A WATER-SPARK, AN INCANDESCENT DRIP OF AMERICAN FIRE."
>
> **—PABLO NERUDA,** POET

SEEING EVERY MOVE

FLIGHT OF HANDS

By using super-high-speed cameras to slow down time, scientists are finally unlocking the secrets of the world's smallest bird. Hummingbirds have, proportionally, the longest hands and shortest arms of any bird. Arm wings are often used for gliding, while hand wings provide the lift. With a larger hand wing, hummingbirds can rotate the shape of their wing on every stroke, generating precise and constant lift, at the cost of constant flapping. Moving at this speed and control takes massive brainpower. Here too, the hummingbird is unique, having proportionally the second largest brain in the animal kingdom. Speed, smarts, and control are vital for the birds to access the nectar they so desperately need.

TOP FIVE

Best Flowers for HUMMINGBIRDS

1 **SCARLET BEE BALM**
Hummingbirds love this hardy perennial. Its red, pink, or lavender petals catch a wandering bird's eye.

2 **CARDINAL FLOWER** This 48-inch-tall flower is loaded with long-lasting deep-red blossoms providing nectar and height to any garden.

3 **TRUMPET VINE** The bright orange flowers on this creeping vine delight hummingbirds and other avians but can take over small areas.

4 **LUPINE** This early blooming flower attracts the first hummingbirds of the season.

5 **BUTTERFLY BUSH** True to its name, the thick clusters of flowers on this bountiful bush attract insects as well as hummingbirds.

PARROTS

MORE THAN JUST POLLY & HER CRACKER

A row of macaws

SUCH DIVERSITY

A PLETHORA OF PARROTS

From the streets of San Francisco to the tip of South Africa, the Peruvian Amazon to the jungles of New Guinea, you can find parrots on five of the seven continents. The extensive range of these birds has led to incredible biodiversity. There are over 350 kinds of parrot scattered across the globe, appearing in all sizes: A tiny pygmy parrot measures just three inches across, while the hyacinth macaw's wingspan stretches more than three feet when fully spread.

Most are a riot of colors—pale greens and teal blues, deep blacks and violent reds—though others, like the African grays, are more muted. These birds aren't just beautiful flashes in the wilderness. Some of the larger species of parrots can live for over 80 years.

SOCIAL CREATURES

FLOCKING TOGETHER

At night in the tropics, the oldest, tallest trees in the forest resound with the singsong conversation of flocks of parrots. Tree canopies form the heart of a parrot's social life, and parrot parents often nest in the hollowed-out core of the tree below. Lorikeets, lovebirds, and cockatoos gather in flocks of hundreds or even thousands.

Unfortunately, this socialization has made them a prime target of trappers, who often gather numerous birds at once. In Mexico alone, up to 75,000 birds were harvested in a single year, and more than 75 percent of the birds harvested die before they even make it into trade. In the pet market, they often face a life of stress and isolation and develop symptoms of anxiety and depression.

Scarlet macaws

A crimson-fronted parakeet

PARROTS HAVE TASTE BUDS ON THE INSIDE OF THEIR BEAKS AS WELL AS ON THEIR TONGUES.

Australian king parrots

LANGUAGE LEARNERS

AN INSTINCT FOR IMITATION

While many birdcalls are biologically hardwired, parrots learn language from their flock. Some flocks develop unique accents and dialects. Certain calls can act as passwords, with parrot calls identifying outsiders to the flock. While parrots are famous for their mimicry—several species can accurately mimic other birdcalls, fire alarms, and even human speech—it's not limited to copying. Parrots have shown complex reasoning skills on the same scale as chimpanzees or small children.

WILDLIFE TRADE

A WILDLIFE DISASTER

No order of birds has been more exploited in the wild than the parrot, and no individual bird more than the African gray parrot. More than 1.3 million African grays were removed from the continent legally, and it's unknown how many others were smuggled out or died in transit. In Ghana, the population of African grays has been reduced by 99 percent, and a bird once as common as a pigeon is now exceedingly rare. Australian palm cockatoos can fetch up to $30,000 per bird and have attracted the types of organized crime usually associated with elephant and rhino poaching. The international pet trade means we may be loving these animals to death.

A WORD FROM

Bird Brain He [the African gray parrot Alex] was not supposed to be able to name objects and categories, understand "bigger" and "smaller," "same" and "different," because his was a bird brain. But, of course, Alex did do such things. I knew that Alex was proving a profound truth: Brains may look different, and there may be a spectrum of ability that is determined by anatomical details, but brains and intelligence are a universally shared trait in nature—the capacity varies, but the building blocks are the same.

—**IRENE PEPPERBERG,** *animal behaviorist and psychologist*

J. DREW LANHAM
ORNITHOLOGIST

LEARNING TO FLY

Drew Lanham has always been fascinated by flight. As a kid, he tried making wings out of cardboard boxes, but as an adult, he leaves flying to the birds—and shares his fascination with his students. For more than 20 years, he's been studying songbird ecology and the ways that humans interact with the environment, with a close eye to how race informs our relationship with nature.

Lanham seeks to bring birders and hunters together for conservation efforts.

L anham works with his head and his heart—combining emotion and data to get people to really see and appreciate the world around them. He's a poet and artist as well as a professor of ornithology at Clemson University, and he looks to the way different methods of storytelling can inspire and inform each other. "The science is the art and the art is the science," he says. He has his students write in haiku and other nontraditional forms of science communication to test how best to convey what they are learning.

HIS HOME PLACE

Lanham's study of birds leads him back to the land, so closely tied up with the life of humans. "Our plights are intertwined," Lanham says, and points out that the South Carolina rice fields, important nesting sites for waterfowl, wouldn't even be there if not for slaves. Lanham feels a connection to the rich ecological diversity of his home state and doesn't shy away from discussing the legacy of slavery or the implications of race today. Though he loves to travel, he's always drawn back home—and he's written a book about it: *The Home Place: Memoirs of a Colored Man's Love Affair with Nature*.

Lanham is the first to point out that within the huge community of birders, few are people of color—witness his 2013 article "9 Rules for the Black Bird Watcher," which includes Rule #1: "Be prepared to be confused with the other black birder." Through his teaching and writing, he hopes to change that landscape and inspire others—of all colors—to become what he calls himself: an "eco-addict."

" I MAY ANTHROPOMORPHIZE A BIT, BUT I HEAR JOY IN BIRDSONG."

Lanham surrounded by his art and work at home in Clemson, South Carolina

KEY DATES

Milestones in
SAVING BIRDS

1896
The Massachusetts Audubon Society is formed to advocate for the protection of wild birds. The National Audubon Society follows in 1905.

1903
Theodore Roosevelt declares Florida's Pelican Island the first federal bird reservation.

1918
The Migratory Bird Treaty Act identifies species federally protected from harm.

1973
The Endangered Species Act secures federal protection for at-risk animals and plants.

1995
The African-Eurasian Migratory Waterbird Agreement ensures protections for birds migrating across Africa, Europe, and Asia.

WHOSE CATERPILLAR?

MIRACULOUS TRANSFORMATION

The famous transformation from caterpillar to butterfly looks a little different to scientists studying the creatures than to poets writing about them. To change their structure so completely, caterpillars almost completely dissolve themselves into a stem cell soup inside the cocoon. They rebuild themselves from scratch using pockets of specialized imaginal cells before emerging in their new form.

GREAT PURPLE HAIRSTREAK
Seeks mistletoe, eats leaves and male flowers

PIPEVINE SWALLOWTAIL
Eats leaves of pipevine

WESTERN TIGER SWALLOWTAIL
Spins silk for shelter

BLACK SWALLOWTAIL
When threatened, forked gland spews odor

CABBAGE WHITE
Hatches from eggs laid on garden greens

GRAY HAIRSTREAK
Tended and defended by ants

GULF FRITILLARY
Eats only passionflower plants

MOURNING CLOAK
Eats leaves of hardwood trees and shrubs

RED ADMIRAL
Eats tender inside stem of nettles

AMERICAN LADY
Seeks sunflowers to eat

COMMON BUCKEYE
Metallic-blue branching spines

MONARCH
Turns distasteful to predators by eating milkweed

VICEROY
Mottled body resembles bird dropping

REGAL MOTH
Called hickory-horned devils, but harmless

IO MOTH
Prickly green spines that can sting

LUNA MOTH
Spins papery brown cocoon

BUTTERFLIES SIP WATER, NECTAR, AND EVEN ANIMAL BLOOD USING A LONG, THIN PROBOSCIS. ALTHOUGH IT LOOKS LIKE A STRAW, BUTTERFLIES DO NOT SUCK THROUGH IT. INSTEAD, THE ORGAN SOAKS UP FLUID BY CAPILLARY ACTION, AS IF IT WERE A TUBE MADE OUT OF PAPER TOWEL.

GREAT PURPLE HAIRSTREAK
Brilliant blue on upper wing

PIPEVINE SWALLOWTAIL
Poisons from pipevine deter predators.

WESTERN TIGER SWALLOWTAIL
Clusters in mud puddles

BLACK SWALLOWTAIL
Courting pairs flutter before landing.

CABBAGE WHITE
One of spring's first butterflies

GRAY HAIRSTREAK
3–4 generations a year in the southern U.S.

GULF FRITILLARY
Migrates south to escape cold

MOURNING CLOAK
Long life span of 11–12 months

RED ADMIRAL
Prefers dung and carrion to nectar

AMERICAN LADY
Males are territorial.

COMMON BUCKEYE
Wing eyespots may scare predators.

MONARCH
State insect or butterfly in seven U.S. states

VICEROY
Mirrors bitter-tasting monarch as defense

REGAL MOTH
Adults do not eat at all.

IO MOTH
When disturbed, spreads wings to show eyespots

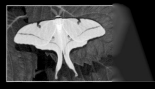

LUNA MOTH
Wing tails distract bats from preying on body.

PLIGHT OF
THE HONEYBEE

POLLINATOR IN PERIL

One of tens of thousands of pollinating species, honeybees do more than their share: It's estimated that one out of eight nonagricultural plants around the world was pollinated by honeybees. But honeybees face many threats: habitat loss, monoculture farming, pesticides, and parasitic mites, to name several. Since wild bees often don't produce honey, commercial honeybees are imported, but these nonnative bees can spread disease to wild populations or turn invasive. Wild bees are suffering as a result, some seeing population drops of 70 percent and others going completely extinct. The humble workers of the bee world can't seem to catch a break.

Worker bees forage for pollen and nectar; they are the only bees that most people see.

IN SUMMER, A HONEYBEE QUEEN LAYS UP TO 2,500 EGGS A DAY.

How to Help
HONEYBEES

■ PLANT A POLLINATOR GARDEN
Green lawns are deserts for bees. Add flowering plants and gardens to your yard.

■ BUY LOCAL RAW HONEY
Local honey supports local bees and promotes local beekeeping.

■ DON'T REMOVE NATURAL WEEDS AND LOCAL PLANTS
A field of dandelions is a feast for the bees. Let the weeds live!

■ AVOID PESTICIDES ON LAWNS AND PLANTS
These chemicals kill off insects and bugs, already at risk.

■ PROVIDE A SMALL, SHALLOW WATER BASIN
Bees can get thirsty too. Offering water helps them stay productive.

CONSERVATION
TIME LINE

8000 to 1 BC	AD 1 to 1850	1850 to 1900	1900 to 1950

8000 BC
Organized agriculture begins: cultivated plants and herded animals.

6000 BC
Animal manure is used as fertilizer.

6000 BC
Maize is domesticated in the Americas.

ca 1500 BC
Aztec build chinampas, floating gardens, on edges of Mexican lakes.

1661
London's Vauxhall Gardens open to the public.

1701–1731
Jethro Tull invents seed drill, improves plow, and makes other farming innovations.

1730
British statesman-farmer Charles Townshend develops four-year crop rotation.

1789
Englischer Garten opens in Munich, Germany.

1849
The U.S. Department of Interior is established.

1854
Henry David Thoreau's *Walden* is published.

1858
Construction of New York City's Central Park, the first major urban park in the U.S., is under way.

1863
Britain's Alkali Act curbs acid gas emissions.

1872
Yellowstone National Park, the first legislated national park, is established.

1892
The Sierra Club is founded, with John Muir as its first president.

1913
German People's Park Association (Deutscher Volksparkbund) is founded in Germany.

1916
U.S. and Canada sign Migratory Birds Treaty, first international conservation effort.

1916
The U.S. National Park Service is established.

1918
Fritz Haber receives Nobel Prize for synthesizing ammonia, used for fertilizer.

1940s
High-yield wheat is introduced in Mexico, starting "green revolution."

| 1950 to 1970 | 1970 to 1980 | 1980 to 2000 | 2000 to PRESENT |

1962
Rachel Carson's *Silent Spring* is published.

1970
About 20 million participate in first Earth Day, April 22.

1980
Green Party is established in West Germany.

2000
In U.S., Green Party presidential candidate Ralph Nader receives 2.7% of vote.

1970
The U.S. Environmental Protection Agency is established.

1987
Montreal Protocol, which reduces emissions that deplete the ozone layer, is signed by 140 nations.

1964
U.S. legislates Wilderness Act, protecting lands from development.

1970
Monsanto develops glyphosate herbicide, soon known as Roundup.

1968
Apollo 8 astronauts create "Earthrise" photo.

1971
Greenpeace begins as protest against nuclear testing in Alaska.

1988
First GMO crops, Roundup-resistant soybeans, developed.

2008
Svalbard Global Seed Vault is established in Norwegian Arctic.

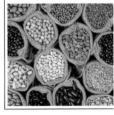

1968
First edition of the *Whole Earth Catalog* is published.

1972
Apollo 17 astronauts create "Blue Marble" photo.

1973
U.S. Congress approves Endangered Species Act.

2011
The population of humans on Earth reaches 7 billion, according to estimates from the United Nations.

1992
United Nations convenes Earth Summit in Rio de Janeiro, Brazil.

2016
Paris Agreement is ratified, joining nations in combating climate change.

1968
Paul R. Ehrlich's *The Population Bomb* is published.

1979
An accident occurs at Three Mile Island nuclear power plant.

PHOTO ARK

SAVING THEM BEFORE THEY DISAPPEAR

The number of animals going extinct is growing exponentially, warn the experts. Witnessing the problem firsthand, Joel Sartore decided he would use his photography to make a difference. He is now creating the National Geographic Photo Ark, collecting portraits of every animal species under human care, in zoos, wildlife centers, and private collections around the world. He figures they number some 15,000—and he has created stunning photographs of more than three-quarters of those already.

These playful Sumatran tiger cubs live at Tierpark Berlin, a landscape animal park that houses more than 8,000 animals.

Sartore pokes through his portable studio, set up to photograph a frill-necked lizard in Australia.

KEY NUMBERS

Species & Subspecies
PHOTOGRAPHED

■ **AMPHIBIANS**
842 species

■ **BIRDS**
2,559 species

■ **FISH**
2,533 species

■ **INVERTEBRATES
(TERRESTRIAL & AQUATIC)**
1,381 species

■ **MAMMALS**
1,209 species

■ **REPTILES**
1,611 species

■ **TOTAL**
10,135 species and subspecies
photographed as of March 2020

PLASTIC
IN OUR WORLD

AN ENDURING THREAT

Since it was first mass-produced in the 1940s, plastic has made its way into every corner of life, from soda bottles and IV bags, to car parts and insulation, and even soaps and shampoos. It has revolutionized our society—but at a cost. Plastic takes more than 400 years to degrade, so most of it still exists in some form. Only 12 percent has been incinerated, and only 9 percent has been recycled. Of the 8.3 billion metric tons produced to date, 6.3 billion has become plastic waste.

The vast majority of plastic waste—79 percent—is accumulating in landfills or sloughing off in the natural environment as litter.

NEARLY HALF OF ALL PLASTIC EVER MANUFACTURED HAS BEEN MADE SINCE 2000.

Ways You Can Help
REDUCE PLASTIC

TAKE A MUG Carry a mug into your favorite coffee shop to cut down on single-serving cups and tops.

SHOP LOCAL Frequent farmers markets and local food purveyors and bring your own containers.

LOOSE PRODUCE Steer clear of pre-wrapped fruits and vegetables; fill your own fabric bags instead.

JUICE YOUR OWN Juice whole fruit rather than drinking from single-serve containers.

CAN OVER BOTTLE If you're buying soda or other drinks, reach for the cans, not the plastic bottles.

REUSABLE STRAWS You can say "no straw, please" when you carry your own reusable one.

GO FOR THE BAR Forget liquid hand and body cleanser and return to old-fashioned bars of soap.

IT'S A MATCH Abandon plastic lighters and go back to matches to light your candles.

LONG-LASTING SHAVE Instead of throwaway razors, use stainless steel razors that last for years.

RECYCLE PLASTIC KNOWINGLY Learn which plastics your community collects and rinse before recycling.

FURTHER

POISON FOR SOME, LIFE-GIVING FOR OTHERS

Three-quarters of the world's lesser flamingos breed at Tanzania's Lake Natron, whose chemistry mummifies other animals that hazard into it. But flamingos' leathery leg skin resists the salt. Other species avoid the site, making Lake Natron a safe nesting place for flamingos. The lake water turns red with the bloom of cyanobacteria. Flamingos dip their curved beaks into the muck to eat these microscopic creatures, whose high carotenoid content keeps feathers bright pink.

Lesser flamingos fly over the Ewaso Ng'iro River Delta in Kenya. The river feeds into Tanzania's Lake Natron, whose high-alkaline waters deter many other species.

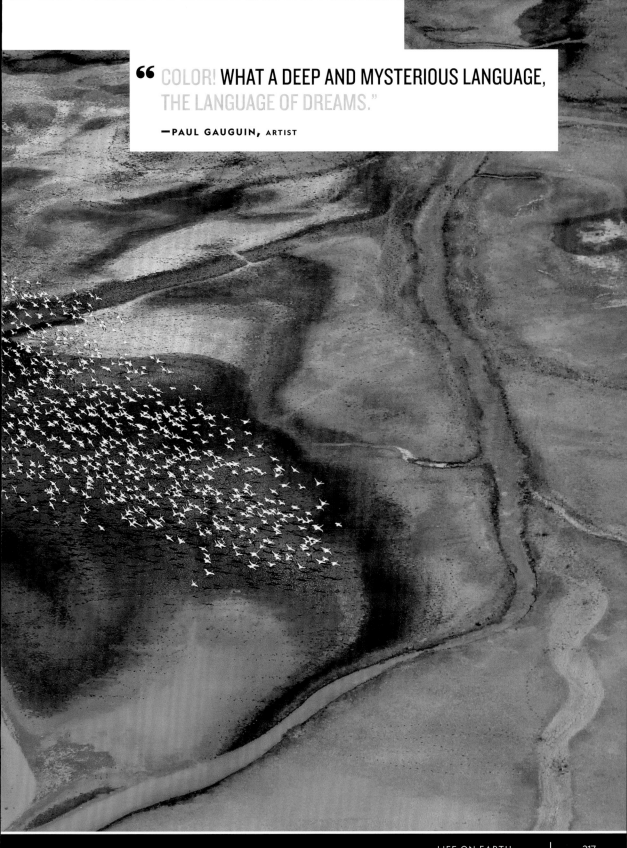

> **"COLOR! WHAT A DEEP AND MYSTERIOUS LANGUAGE, THE LANGUAGE OF DREAMS."**
>
> —PAUL GAUGUIN, ARTIST

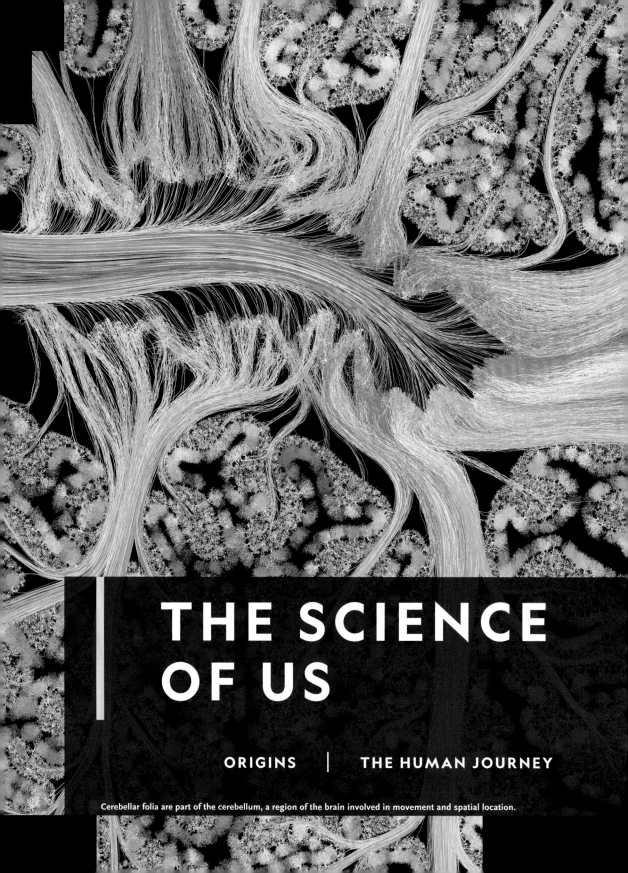

THE SCIENCE OF US

ORIGINS | THE HUMAN JOURNEY

Cerebellar folia are part of the cerebellum, a region of the brain involved in movement and spatial location.

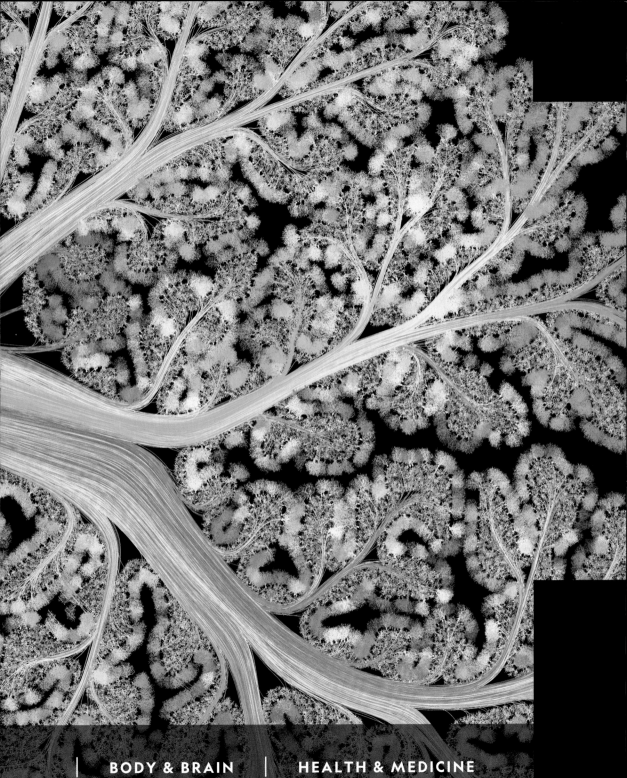

Getting to Know You Whether it's genome, family, or culture, the varieties of human health and behavior are endlessly fascinating. Use these questions to lead the way into learning more about yourself and others.

—SUSAN TYLER HITCHCOCK, *Nat Geo Quizmaster*

p263

WHAT ARE THE THREE TYPES OF MEMORY?

WHICH WORLD RELIGION OBSERVES THE MOST HOLIDAYS?

p248

NAME THE CLOSEST PREHISTORIC RELATIVE TO MODERN-DAY HUMANS.

p231

p243

WHAT PROPORTION OF PEOPLE IN THE WORLD LIVE IN CITIES: 1 IN 8, 1 IN 20, OR 1 IN 100?

p275

HOW MANY DIFFERENT LANGUAGES ARE SPOKEN BY HUMANS TODAY?

MACE IS THE OUTER HUSK OF WHAT OTHER COMMON SPICE?

WHAT DO LIMBURGER CHEESE AND BODY ODOR HAVE IN COMMON?

WHAT IS THE ORIGIN OF THE WORD "CARNIVAL"?

p223

p235

IN 1863, WHO INVENTED **PASTEURIZATION AS A** STERILIZATION **PROCESS FOR MILK AND** OTHER FOODS?

p264

WHAT IS THE **TITLE OF THE** BOOK IN WHICH CHARLES DARWIN PUT FORTH HIS THEORY OF EVOLUTION?

p247

IN 1856, IN WHAT COUNTRY WERE THE **FIRST** REMAINS OF NEANDERTHALS DISCOVERED: **SOUTH AFRICA,** ESTONIA, **OR** GERMANY?

p223

WHERE WILL YOU FIND THE MOST MICROBE SPECIES: **ON YOUR FOOT,** FOREARM, **OR FACE?**

p272

WHAT RIVER IS HELD SACRED IN THE HINDU RELIGION?

WHAT PROPORTION OF **THE WORLD'S POPULATION** EATS INSECTS **IN** THEIR EVERYDAY DIET: 1 IN 4, 1 IN 7, **OR** 1 IN 10?

p254

HUMAN EVOLUTION
TIME LINE

4 MYA to 80,000 YA	80,000 YA to 8000 BC	8000 to 1500 BC	1500 to 1 BC

3.5 mya*
Upright bipedalism—walking on two legs—evolves.

ca 1.75 mya
Homo erectus, an early ancestor of modern humans, uses stone tools.

ca 400,000 ya**
Neanderthals use fire as a tool in some areas.

ca 160,000 ya
Homo sapiens, the modern human race, first appears.

ca 120,000 ya
Neanderthals live in modern-day Europe.

ca 80,000 ya
Early humans begin moving out of Africa onto other continents.

* *million years ago*
** *years ago*

---

ca 80,000 ya
Modern humans move into Europe and live alongside Neanderthals.

ca 65,000 ya
Modern humans reach the Australian continent.

ca 40,000 ya
Neanderthals die out.

ca 25,000 ya
A small figurine called the Venus of Willendorf is crafted. It is the oldest known art in Europe.

ca 15,000 ya
The first human settlements appear in North America.

ca 11,000 ya
Agricultural systems begin to emerge in the Middle East, as humans cultivate plants and domesticate animals.

---

ca 6500 BC
Farming begins in the Indus Valley in modern-day Pakistan and western India.

ca 5000 BC
Rice is cultivated as a crop in central and eastern China.

ca 3500 BC
First wheels appear in Mesopotamia, used for pottery and later for vehicular use.

2630 BC
The Egyptians begin building pyramids.

ca 2300 BC
The earliest known maps are produced in Mesopotamia.

ca 2000 BC
Austronesians settle on islands in the South Pacific.

---

ca 1550 BC
The Mesopotamian empire begins to grow from the city of Mittani.

ca 1050 BC
Ironworking is introduced to Greece.

1000 BC
The Phoenicians develop an alphabet.

ca 600 BC
The Maya use cacao to make a chocolate drink.

ca 400 BC
Hippocrates of Kos describes human anatomy and various diseases.

ca 300 BC
The Maya build pyramids in modern-day Mexico.

| AD 1 to 1850 | 1850 to 1900 | 1900 to 1975 | 1975 to PRESENT |

■ 1677

Dutch scientist Antonie van Leeuwenhoek observes and describes both bacteria and human sperm cells.

■ 1691

John Ray suggests that fossils are the remains of creatures from the distant past.

■ 1735

Swedish naturalist Carolus Linnaeus introduces the binomial naming system.

■ 1836

English naturalist Charles Darwin completes his five-year voyage on the H.M.S. *Beagle*.

■ 1856

Workmen digging in the valley of the Neander River near Düsseldorf, Germany, discover remains of Neanderthal man.

■ 1859

Charles Darwin publishes *On the Origin of Species*, the book in which he puts forward his theory of evolution.

■ 1865

Austrian monk Gregor Mendel presents his research on inheritance.

■ 1868

French paleontologist Louis Lartet excavates fossils of Cro-Magnon man in southwestern France.

■ 1891

Dutch anthropologist Eugene Dubois discovers fossils of the human ancestor "Java man," now known as *Homo erectus*.

■ 1924

Raymond Dart discovers the first fossils of human ancestor *Australopithecus* in Africa.

■ 1933

Anthropologists discover a 92,000-year-old fossil of *Homo sapiens* in Israel.

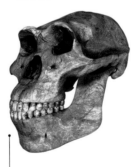

■ 1948

English anthropologist Mary Leakey discovers fossils of possible ape ancestor *Proconsul africanus* in Africa.

■ 1960

Anthropologist Jonathan Leakey discovers the remains of *Homo habilis* in Tanzania.

■ 1972

Anthropologist Richard Leakey finds an intact skull of *Homo habilis*.

■ 1974

Donald Johanson unearths "Lucy," a fossil of *Australopithecus afarensis*, in Ethiopia.

■ 1993

Anthropologists from Berkeley discover remains of oldest known hominoid, *Ardipithecus ramidus*.

■ 2004

An 80,000-year-old skeleton of a small humanoid called *Homo floresiensis* is found in Indonesia.

■ 2008

Fossil of a new hominid, *Australopithecus sediba*, is discovered by Lee Berger in South Africa.

■ 2013

Multiple remains of a newly discovered species, *Homo naledi*, are found in a cave in South Africa.

MEET OUR HUMAN ANCESTORS

HOW WE GOT TO WHERE WE ARE NOW

Scientists no longer use a family tree to depict relationships among early humans. It is now understood that several lines of early humans evolved at the same time. We also know that chimpanzees (or other apes) didn't evolve into humans. Instead, both lineages descended from a common ancestor and went their separate ways.

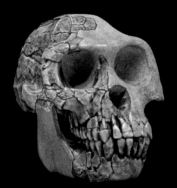

ARDIPITHECUS RAMIDUS (4.4 MYA)

Found in northeastern Ethiopia in 1992–1994, the partial skeleton of a female *Ar. ramidus* (nicknamed "Ardi") is more like a human—and less like a chimpanzee—than was expected in the human-ape record. For example, some believe foot and pelvis characteristics indicate that *Ar. ramidus* walked upright when on the ground. It is not clear yet whether it is an ancestor of *H. sapiens*.

AUSTRALOPITHECUS AFARENSIS (3.85–2.95 MYA)

"Lucy" *(Au. afarensis),* the most famous of our fossilized ancestors, was discovered in 1974 in eastern Africa. Scientists have concluded that *Au. afarensis* climbed trees, though it was mostly bipedal. Despite having a brain about one-third of modern humans', this tenacious species lived for over 900,000 years.

PARANTHROPUS BOISEI (2.3–1.2 MYA)

P. boisei, discovered in 1955, was immediately distinctive, because of its large jaw. This indicates a diet that required heavy chewing, though other evidence that it consumed hard substances (like nuts) is lacking. A recent report identified another exceptional characteristic: It may have carried HSV2, the virus causing genital herpes.

HOMO HABILIS (2.4-1.4 MYA)

H. habilis (aka "handy man") was discovered in 1960 at Tanzania's Olduvai Gorge at the same site and by the same team that found *P. boisei*. Its appearance reoriented the search for human origins from Asia, where *H. erectus* had been found, to Africa. A prominent researcher recently argued that it is different enough from other *Australopithecus* and *Homo* specimens to merit its own genus.

HOMO ERECTUS (1.89 MYA-143,000 YA)

H. erectus has proportions similar to modern humans', including shorter arms and longer legs in relation to the torso. Tools such as hand axes have been found near to and in the same sediment layers as *H. erectus*, marking an important moment in evolution. *H. erectus* was also migratory. In fact, it was first discovered in Indonesia in 1891.

HOMO SAPIENS IS NOW THE ONLY SPECIES OF HUMAN ON EARTH. BUT THAT'S BEEN TRUE FOR LESS THAN 30,000 YEARS.

POP!

PREHISTORY ON-SCREEN

- *One Million Years B.C.* (1966)
- *The Land That Time Forgot* (1974)
- *At the Earth's Core* (1976)
- *Quest for Fire* (1981)
- *Iceman* (1984)
- *The Clan of the Cave Bear* (1986)
- *Encino Man* (1992)
- *10,000 B.C.* (2008)
- *The Croods* (2013)
- *Early Man* (2018)

SHARED TIME ON EARTH?

These hand bones are among thousands recently found by paleoanthropologist Lee Berger and his team in South Africa. They belong to an all-new hominid species, *Homo naledi*, which likely lived alongside *Homo sapiens* less than 500,000 years ago.

OUR NEW ANCESTOR

HOMO NALEDI CHANGES THE STORY

In 2013, two spelunkers dropped into a narrow, uncharted chamber in South Africa's Rising Star cave system and stumbled upon a massive collection of fossils. Paleoanthropologist Lee Berger led an excavation of the site—the richest of its kind ever found—and uncovered a new species with a tiny brain, shoulders and a torso like an ape's, but humanlike teeth and hands. His team named the species *Homo naledi*, after the local word for "star." Analysis of the fossils put them between 236,000 and 335,000 years old, suggesting that *H. naledi* coexisted with early *Homo sapiens*. Discovery of more specimens in a nearby chamber, equally hard to access, has helped fill in some gaps but raises more questions about this newest member of our human family tree.

DID THEY BURY THEIR DEAD?

So how did more than 1,500 *Homo naledi* bones wind up in these deep, remote, nearly inaccessible caves? The chambers lie far from the cave entrance, past two nauseatingly tight passages, one of which includes a 40-foot (12.2 m) vertical drop. There are no tooth marks on the bones to suggest that a scavenging animal brought them into the cave, and no rocks, rubble, or other remains to suggest that they were swept into the cave by wind or water. Berger and his team theorize that the site was a burial chamber, with bodies deposited over a long period of time. The idea is controversial—if true, the Rising Star fossils would represent the earliest known evidence of deliberate burial.

A paleoartist's reconstruction of *H. naledi*

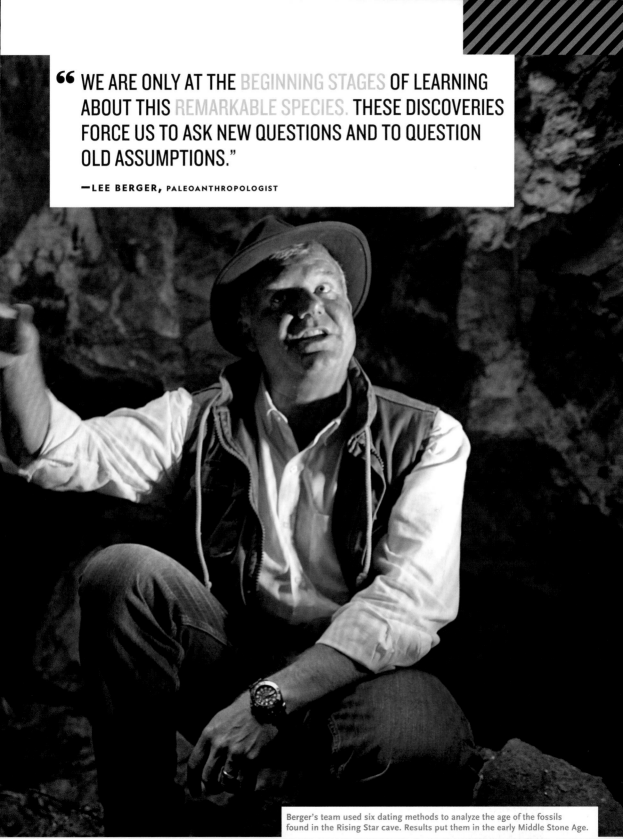

"WE ARE ONLY AT THE BEGINNING STAGES OF LEARNING ABOUT THIS REMARKABLE SPECIES. THESE DISCOVERIES FORCE US TO ASK NEW QUESTIONS AND TO QUESTION OLD ASSUMPTIONS."

—LEE BERGER, PALEOANTHROPOLOGIST

Berger's team used six dating methods to analyze the age of the fossils found in the Rising Star cave. Results put them in the early Middle Stone Age.

OUR DEEP ANCESTRY

STAGES OF HUMAN MIGRATION

The character of a person's mitochondrial DNA (passed down intact from mother to child) and, in each male, of the Y chromosome (passed intact from father to son) are only two threads in the vast tapestry of genetic information in any individual's genome. Studies like the years-long National Geographic Genographic Project now allow us to map human migration over tens of thousands of years by comparing the mtDNA and Y chromosomes of people from various populations.

What Stories Do Our Genes Tell?

Between 70,000 and 50,000 years ago, a small group of *Homo sapiens*—perhaps as few as 1,000, to whom all modern non-Africans are related—emigrated from Africa. One group continued along the coast to southern Asia, reaching a super-continent made up of Tasmania, Australia, and New Guinea. Recent DNA research confirms that Aboriginal civilization is one of the longest continuous human occupations outside Africa.

EARLY HUMAN MIGRATIONS

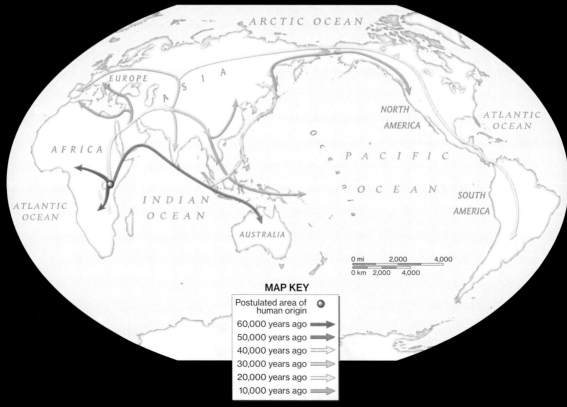

MAP KEY

Postulated area of human origin ●

60,000 years ago ➡
50,000 years ago ➡
40,000 years ago ⇨
30,000 years ago ⇨
20,000 years ago ⇨
10,000 years ago ➡

FINDING YOUR ROOTS

TRACKING THE HUMAN JOURNEY

These days it's possible to learn more about your own deep ancestry through projects like National Geographic Genographic Project or commercial offerings from companies like Ancestry.com or 23andMe. A swab of cells from inside your cheek provides enough to learn what your genetic makeup tells about the path your long-ago ancestors took in the massive human migrations over tens of thousands of years. You may find your ancestors coming from one of several directions.

AFRICA

The diversity of genetic markers is greatest in the African continent, the earliest home of modern humans. "The genetic makeup of the rest of the world is a subset of what's in Africa," says Yale geneticist Kenneth Kidd.

ASIA

As some modern humans pushed into Central Asia, others traveled through Southeast Asia and China, eventually reaching Japan and Siberia. Humans in northern Asia eventually migrated to the Americas.

EUROPE

Genetic data show that the DNA of today's western Eurasians resembles that of people in India. It's possible that an inland migration from Asia seeded Europe between 40,000 and 30,000 years ago.

THE AMERICAS

When sea levels were low and the first humans crossed the land bridge between Siberia and Alaska, ice sheets covered the interior of North America, forcing the new arrivals to travel down the west coast.

> **" I THINK [EARLY HUMANS] WERE MAINLY MOTIVATED BY CURIOSITY AND THE DESIRE FOR EXPLORATION."**
>
> **—ELENI PANAGOPOULOU,** ARCHAEOLOGIST

Immigrants gather at a Sikh festival in Barcelona.

KEY FACTS

Natural Reasons for
MIGRATION

CLIMATE CHANGE Modern humans' departure from Africa around 60,000 years ago was likely in response to a deteriorating climate, growing cooler and drier and less hospitable to human life.

LAND BRIDGES Climate changes can determine access between regions, such as the sea-level drop about 40,000 years ago that exposed a lowland area connecting Australia to Tasmania.

COMPETITION Despite arriving in Europe hundreds of thousands of years before their modern relatives, Neanderthals went extinct not long after modern humans' arrival.

SEAFARING Axes found on Crete in 2010 may be evidence that early humans had the knowledge and technology to sail across the Mediterranean to the island.

AGRICULTURE Farming and herding developed around 12,000 years ago in the Near East and then, as farmers migrated to Europe and elsewhere, quickly replaced the hunter-gatherer lifestyle.

NEANDERTHALS
JOIN THE FAMILY

NOT-SO-DISTANT RELATIVES

When our ancestors emerged from Africa into Eurasia around 45,000 years ago, they found the landscape already inhabited. Neanderthals were 99.5 percent genetically identical to modern humans *(Homo sapiens)* but had evolved distinctive anatomy—such as wide bodies to conserve heat—during hundreds of thousands of years in the cold Eurasian climate.

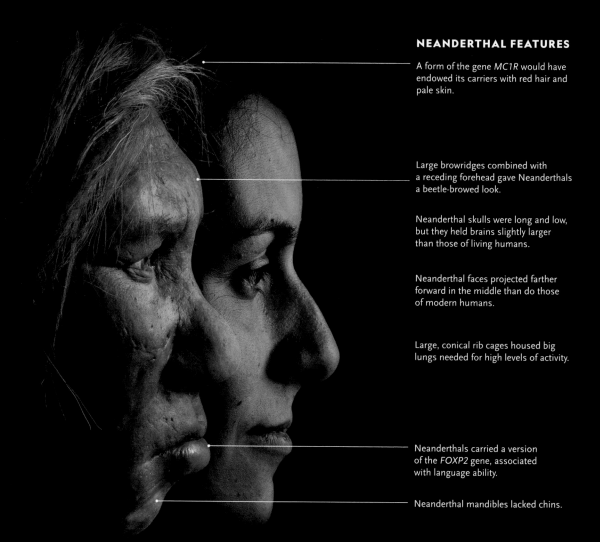

NEANDERTHAL FEATURES

A form of the gene *MC1R* would have endowed its carriers with red hair and pale skin.

Large browridges combined with a receding forehead gave Neanderthals a beetle-browed look.

Neanderthal skulls were long and low, but they held brains slightly larger than those of living humans.

Neanderthal faces projected farther forward in the middle than do those of modern humans.

Large, conical rib cages housed big lungs needed for high levels of activity.

Neanderthals carried a version of the *FOXP2* gene, associated with language ability.

Neanderthal mandibles lacked chins.

DIVERGENT LINES REUNITE

Neanderthals, our closest prehistoric relatives, dominated Eurasia for the better part of 200,000 years. During that time, they poked their famously large and protruding noses into every corner of Europe and beyond. But climate swings and competition with newcomers may have combined to push Neanderthals into a few outposts before they went extinct, mysteriously dying out about 30,000 years ago.

Friend or Foe?

Scientists posit that the lineages of Neanderthals and their European successors diverged long before modern humans migrated out of Africa, as far back as 370,000 years ago. But until recently, questions lingered: Did modern humans replace Neanderthals, or did they interbreed with them?

Then, in 2010, scientists uncovered the first solid genetic evidence that "modern" humans interbred with their Neanderthal neighbors. Today, we know that genomes of people currently living outside Africa are composed of 1.8 to 2.6 percent Neanderthal DNA. Some parts of non-African genomes are totally devoid of Neanderthal DNA, but other regions abound with it, including those containing genes that affect our skin and hair. This hints that those Neanderthal gene versions conferred some benefit and were retained during evolution. Other genes, however, match segments now closely associated with various health concerns, including blood cholesterol levels and rheumatoid arthritis.

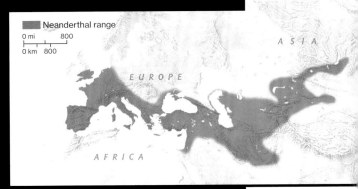

250,000–45,000 YEARS AGO
Neanderthals before the arrival of modern humans in Eurasia

45,000–28,000 YEARS AGO
Period of Neanderthal and modern human overlap in Eurasia

DIGGING DEEPER

At-Home
DNA TESTING

Today it is possible to collect a DNA sample, send it in, and have it analyzed for ancestry markers. Some organizations will link you up with other contemporary individuals who are a match and have a good probability of being related to you. National Geographic's Genographic Project, which has more than 800,000 participants, probes further, providing regional and deep ancestry going back hundreds of generations—even identifying two hominin species, Neanderthals and Denisovans. The project has found that most non-Africans are about 2 percent Neanderthal and slightly less than 2 percent Denisovan.

INTANGIBLE CULTURE

MORE THAN MONUMENTS & ARTIFACTS

Communities worldwide are working to identify and preserve practices, events, skills, and knowledge—intangibles—passed down by ancestors.

Dancers perform the *Ramayana*.

PERFORMING ARTS

THE RAMLILA, INDIA

An epic poem recounting the eventful life of Rama, an important Hindu god, the *Ramayana* is reenacted each fall in northern India. During Ramlila ("Rama's play"), which can last up to a month, seasoned storytellers are joined on stage by audience members—who also help create masks, costumes, and sets.

SHADOW PUPPETS, SYRIA

In these performances, a puppeteer voices characters in traditional stories and situations depicting current social issues with humor, satire, and music. Shadows of two-dimensional handmade puppets enact scenarios starring two characters—one clever, the other naive. As of 2018, only one puppeteer remained active in the country.

CULTURAL PRACTICES

SACRED KAYA FORESTS, KENYA

The Mijikenda of coastal Kenya believe that their ancestors reside in sacred forest *kayas*—village sites that date back to the 16th century, uninhabited but still tended and protected. Stories and ritual ceremonies honor and maintain the forest even as urban development encroaches.

Q'ESWACHAKA ROPE BRIDGE, PERU

Beyond facilitating transportation, the Q'eswachaka bridge serves as a sacred connection for Quechua-speaking people in the southern Andes. They congregate to restore the rope suspension bridge over a three-day gathering that includes ritual ceremonies and a festival. Families make ropes that bridge builders attach to ancient stone pillars.

A Quechua woman crosses the Q'eswachaka bridge.

Celebrants dress up for Día de los Muertos.

TO SAFEGUARD THE WORLD'S INTANGIBLE HERITAGE, UNESCO CURRENTLY RECOGNIZES 508 PRACTICES, ARTS, AND CULTURAL EXPRESSIONS FROM 122 COUNTRIES.

A woman extracts scents from processed flowers.

CELEBRATIONS

DÍA DE LOS MUERTOS, MEXICO

Flower petals strewn from homes to cemeteries, ancestors' favorite foods placed at tombs — these are part of Day of the Dead celebrations, combining precolonial religious rites and Catholic practices.

CATALAN HUMAN TOWERS, SPAIN

Costumed men and young children — surrounded by a base of tightly packed adults (the *pinya*) — rise up into human towers. Music featuring the *gralla,* a traditional Catalonian reed instrument, tells *castellers* how far a tower has progressed.

ARTS & CRAFTS

PERFUME, FRANCE

For over 400 years, the community of Pays de Grasse in southern France has cultivated plants and created fragrances. This artisanal, community-based approach stands in contrast to more commercial enterprises, which import oils and create synthetic perfumes.

WASHI PAPER, JAPAN

Just three communities produce authentic washi — paper used as stationery and in iconic Japanese room dividers, doors, and screens. Washi is made by hand using fibers from mulberry plants, clear river water, and bamboo screens. Members of the community participate at every stage, strengthening community bonds.

EARTH DAY EVERY DAY

The Ancient Arts of
PLANTS

Ethnobotanists are trying to preserve the indigenous knowledge about medicinal plants that is disappearing along with plant species and habitats. They interview practitioners to learn their treatments for everything from infections and heart disease to mental illness and cancer.

PLAY
CARNIVAL

CELEBRATION OF MISCHIEF & FREEDOM

In festivities around Christmas and just before Lent, African slaves combined tribal traditions with those of their plantation overlords. Carnivals continue today as ways to celebrate emancipation, embrace native traditions, and disrupt cultural norms.

Brazilian actress Grazielli Massafera, Queen of the Drummers of Acadêmicos do Grande Rio samba school, parades during carnival celebrations in Rio de Janeiro.

THE WORD "CARNIVAL" COMES FROM THE LATIN *CARNE*—FLESH—AND *VALE*—FAREWELL—IN HONOR OF THE TRADITION OF GIVING UP MEAT DURING LENT.

Traditions Across the CARIBBEAN

TRINIDAD & TOBAGO Historians believe the modern Carnival originated here in the late 18th century. Festivities start after Christmas and culminate on Fat Tuesday with parades and extravagant costumes.

CAYMAN ISLANDS Batabano is the national carnival here, celebrating African history. The name comes from the Cayman Islanders' term for tracks left in the sand by baby sea turtles.

MARTINIQUE Ash Wednesday marks the climax of the Carnival season, when a "Vaval," a mannequin made out of reeds and wood representing the king of the Carnival, is burned in a massive bonfire at nightfall.

DOMINICAN REPUBLIC El Diablo Cojuelo is the main character in Dominican Carnival. He wears a horned mask and a colorful cloaked suit adorned with small mirrors, rattles, ribbons, and cowbells, and carries a whip.

HAITI During Carnival season, participants masquerade to highlight the historical and current struggles of Haitian society. The Haitian Defile Kanaval is one of the larger carnivals in the Caribbean, extending across multiple cities.

BRAZIL The heart of Brazilian Carnival is the samba—music and dance that blend African and Caribbean influences. Top samba schools compete in an event called the Sambodromo, where they are evaluated on dance, music, costume, and cultural significance.

CARRIACOU Close to Grenada, the island of Carriacou hosts a unique tournament preceding Lent, with masked and caped contenders reciting speeches from Shakespeare.

THE BAHAMAS Parades, costumes, drums, horns, and whistles: Junkanoo starts at midnight Christmas night and ends at dawn—traditionally explained as the hours when slaves could celebrate freely.

BEST OF @NATGEO

TOP PHOTOS OF WORLD TRADITIONS

@anastasiatl | ANASTASIA TAYLOR-LIND
Girls wear ceremonial drumming uniforms at the Ataman
Platov Cossack cadet school in Southern Russia.

@limauricio | MAURICIO LIMA
Near the Eiffel Tower, French football fans celebrate a win
over Croatia during the World Cup's final match.

@lynseyaddario | LYNSEY ADDARIO
Jmmey Ahmed, a Bengali-American bride, poses for a
portrait before her wedding celebration in Michigan.

@nicholesobecki | NICHOLE SOBECKI
Kenyans celebrate the opening of a solar-powered pump tha
brings water to the country's remote northwest.

> **"CULTURE IS ALL THE** THINGS AND IDEAS **EVER DEVISED BY** HUMANS **WORKING AND LIVING TOGETHER."**
>
> **—PETER FARB,** WRITER

@pete_k_muller | PETE MULLER
Indigenous Quechuan men gather around a fire during an annual pilgrimage into the Peruvian Andes.

@mitty | CRISTINA MITTERMEIER
A Porgera man from Papua New Guinea proudly wears a headdress adorned with wild boar tusks and cassowary feathers.

@davidalanharvey | DAVID ALAN HARVEY
Hot summer nights and cool waters beckon beachgoers to Rio de Janeiro's Ipanema waterfront at all hours.

@edkashi | ED KASHI
A group of Nigerian men relax in the Emir of Kano's palace, a striking example of traditional Hausa architecture.

DISAPPEARING
LANGUAGES

WE MAY LOSE OVER HALF OF OUR 7,000 LANGUAGES BY 2100

Language defines a culture, through the people who speak it and what it allows speakers to say. Words that describe a particular cultural practice or idea may not translate precisely into another language. To lose those words is to lose those treasures.

HAIDA
100 speakers
Northern and southern versions spoken on the Haida Gwaii (Queen Charlotte Islands) off the coast of British Columbia

RESIGARO
Nearly extinct
Language of the Peruvian Amazon that has blended in with those of other tribes in this rainforest region

CHOROTE
Few speak only this language
More than 2,000 speakers of two related languages in Argentina, Paraguay, and Chile, 750 of whom speak only this language

NORTH AMERICA

SOUTH AMERICA

EU

A

> ## "EVERY TIME A LANGUAGE DIES, WE LOSE PART OF THE PICTURE OF WHAT OUR BRAINS CAN DO."
> —K. DAVID HARRISON, LINGUIST AND ANTHROPOLOGIST

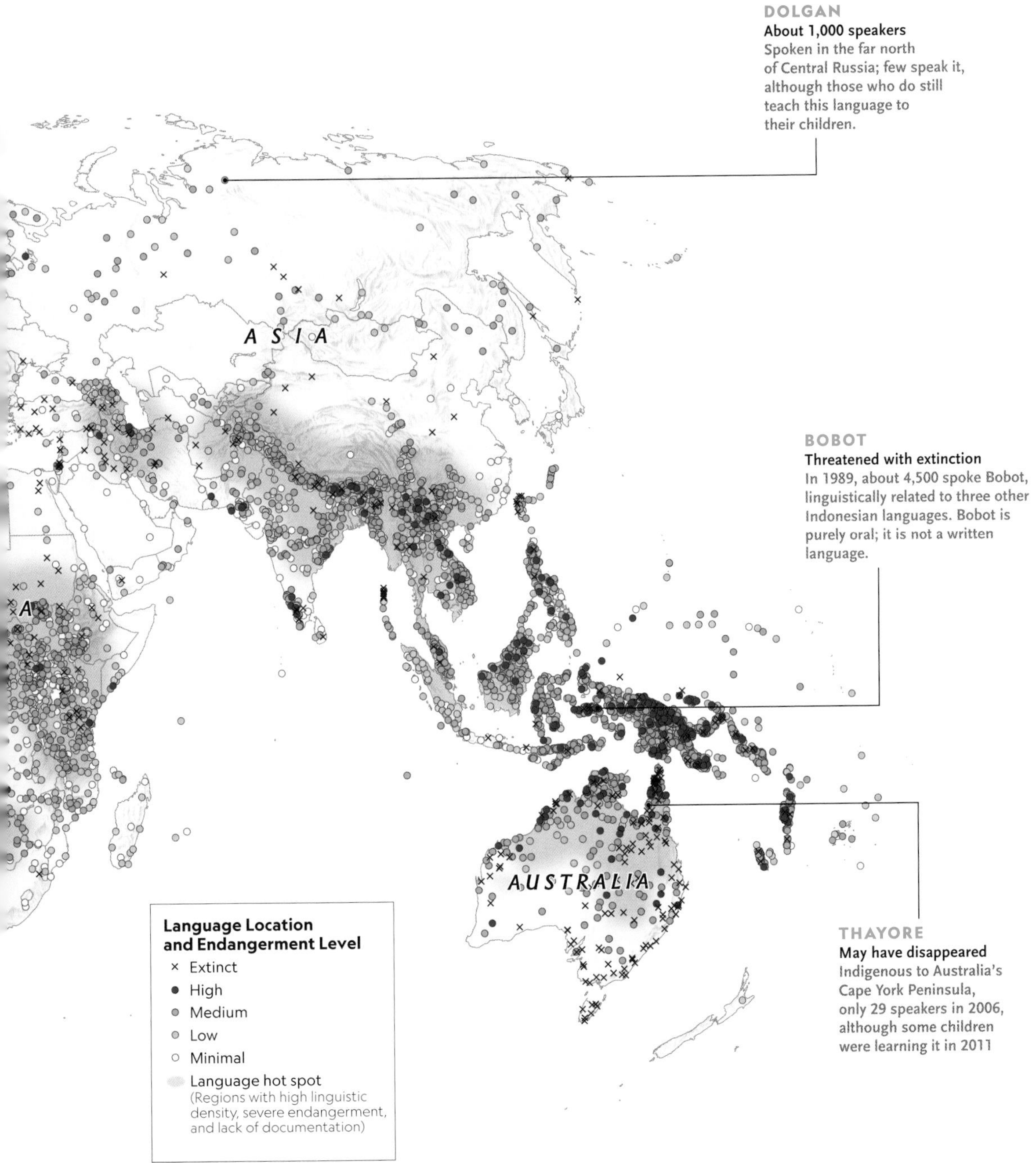

DOLGAN
About 1,000 speakers
Spoken in the far north of Central Russia; few speak it, although those who do still teach this language to their children.

A S I A

BOBOT
Threatened with extinction
In 1989, about 4,500 spoke Bobot, linguistically related to three other Indonesian languages. Bobot is purely oral; it is not a written language.

A

AUSTRALIA

Language Location and Endangerment Level
× Extinct
● High
● Medium
○ Low
○ Minimal
▨ Language hot spot
(Regions with high linguistic density, severe endangerment, and lack of documentation)

THAYORE
May have disappeared
Indigenous to Australia's Cape York Peninsula, only 29 speakers in 2006, although some children were learning it in 2011

WADE DAVIS
ANTHROPOLOGIST

CULTURES FROM INSIDE

Wade Davis has spent the last 40 years traveling and living among indigenous peoples in the Amazon, the Arctic, and in between. From Polynesian navigation to Haitian voudon, Davis has experienced the diversity of human culture. Trained in botany and anthropology, seeking to link the study of science and the spirit, he is uniquely tuned in to the forces that weave nature and culture together.

Davis visits with Buddhist monk Matthieu Ricard during his 2016 journey from Namche Bazaar to Tenpoche in Nepal.

D avis studied under the great ethnobotanist Richard Evans Schultes, following his lead by plunging into the South American rainforest and living among native people there in order to learn their ways. His first book, *The Serpent and the Rainbow,* told of his search for the substance used in Haitian rituals to create zombies—the living dead. (Spoiler: They didn't use only plants; they used poison from fish and toads as well.)

Ever after, Davis has continued to dive deeply into indigenous cultures, gaining the trust of those he visits and participating in their daily lives and ceremonial rituals. His work has taken him from his home in Canada to every inhabited continent of the world. He has written and created documentary films in Mongolia, Greenland, the Australian outback, the Andes and the Himalaya, and, most recently, Colombia and its major river, the Magdalena.

CONNECTING WITH ALL CULTURES

As much an activist as an anthropologist, Wade Davis urges us to reconsider the wisdom of every culture—to discover, as he once wrote, "a new appreciation for the diversity of the human spirit as expressed by culture."

The way we think about the world is neither the only nor the best, Davis reminds us. "Other cultures aren't failed attempts at being modern," he writes. There is no "civilized versus primitive"; all cultural traditions are "unique expressions of the human imagination and heart."

> " WHAT DOES IT MEAN TO BE HUMAN AND ALIVE? EACH CULTURE HAS SOMETHING TO SAY TO US AND EACH ONE DESERVES TO BE HEARD."

Davis (center) holds his godson Armando, now a tailor in Cusco, in Chinchero, Peru, in 1982.

KEY TITLES

Books From a Life of
EXPLORATION

■ *THE SERPENT AND THE RAINBOW* (1987) **An investigation of Haitian voudon, this book inspired a 1988 film**

■ *ONE RIVER* (1996) **Following Richard Evans Schultes's path in the Amazon**

■ *LIGHT AT THE EDGE OF THE WORLD* (2001) **An exploration of traditional cultures, many disappearing**

■ *INTO THE SILENCE* (2011) **The story of George Mallory and his 1920s Everest team**

■ *WADE DAVIS PHOTOGRAPHS* (2018) **Images made during Davis's many travels**

■ *MAGDALENA, RIVER OF DREAMS* (2020) **The story of Colombia, symbolized through its great river**

URBANIZATION

MOVING TO THE CITY

By 2050, almost 70 percent of the global population will live in cities. As recently as 1950, these figures were reversed, and 70 percent lived in rural areas. The number of people living in rural areas has changed little, however, indicating that cities have been absorbing the world's exponential population growth since the mid-20th century—from 2.5 billion in 1950 to almost eight billion today.

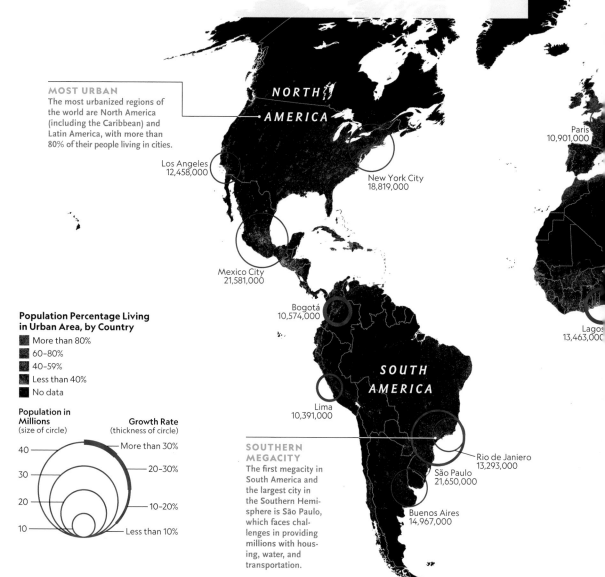

MOST URBAN
The most urbanized regions of the world are North America (including the Caribbean) and Latin America, with more than 80% of their people living in cities.

NORTH AMERICA

Paris
10,901,000

Los Angeles
12,458,000

New York City
18,819,000

Mexico City
21,581,000

Bogotá
10,574,000

Lagos
13,463,000

Population Percentage Living in Urban Area, by Country
- More than 80%
- 60–80%
- 40–59%
- Less than 40%
- No data

SOUTH AMERICA

Lima
10,391,000

Population in Millions
(size of circle)

Growth Rate
(thickness of circle)

- 40 — More than 30%
- 30 — 20–30%
- 20 — 10–20%
- 10 — Less than 10%

SOUTHERN MEGACITY
The first megacity in South America and the largest city in the Southern Hemisphere is São Paulo, which faces challenges in providing millions with housing, water, and transportation.

Rio de Janiero
13,293,000

São Paulo
21,650,000

Buenos Aires
14,967,000

IN 2000, THE WORLD COUNTED 19 CITIES OVER 10 MILLION, 10 OF WHICH WERE IN ASIA. BY 2018, THERE WERE 33 MEGACITIES—HOME TO ONE IN EIGHT PEOPLE ON THE PLANET.

WHERE WE LIVE

The world's urban population passed 55% in 2018, but the size and location of population centers varies. North Americans and Europeans tend to spread out among small and medium-size cities, with relatively few migrating to megacities of more than 10 million people. Nations as diverse as Iceland, Kuwait, and Uruguay are more than 90% urban, while Liechtenstein, Burundi, and Papua New Guinea are among the most rural.

Moscow 12,410,000

ASIA

Tianjin 13,215,000

Beijing 19,618,000

ROPE

Lahore 11,738,000

Delhi 28,514,000

Chongqing 14,838,000

Osaka 19,281,000

Tokyo 37,468,000

Istanbul 14,751,000

Kolkata 14,681,000

Karachi 15,400,000

Dhaka 19,578,000

Shanghai 25,582,000

Cairo 20,076,000

Shenzhen 11,908,000

C A

Manila 13,482,000

Mumbai 19,980,000

SHRINKING CITIES
Japan's low population growth affects its cities: Osaka is the only megacity with a declining population, and Delhi will displace Tokyo as the world's largest by 2030.

Bangalore 11,440,000

Bangkok 10,156,000

Guangzhou 12,638,000

Chennai 10,456,000

Kinshasa 13,171,000

RURAL-URBAN BALANCE
India has the world's largest rural population—at almost 900 million—and the most rapidly growing urban population, adding over 400 million city dwellers by 2050.

Jakarta 10,517,000

AUSTRALIA

URBAN ISLANDS
Indonesia is urbanizing at lightning speed, and it expects to see over 60% of its people living in cities by 2025—including the new megacity of Jakarta.

MOST RURAL
In 2018, 57% of Africa's population was still rural, but some cities are growing rapidly, including Kinshasa, which may be the most populous African city by 2030.

URBAN NATURE

MAKING METRO MEAN HEALTHY

Cities around the world are striving to improve air quality and provide better transit options to their citizens by embracing environmentally friendly practices such as creating bike lanes, using alternative fuels, and offering incentives for electric vehicles. A recent survey of a hundred international cities ranks how well municipal governments are doing at helping people get where they need to go while also making cities more livable and attractive—and sustainable.

A jogger and a bike rider enjoy Manhattan's Central Park in the fall.

TOWARD GREENER CITIES

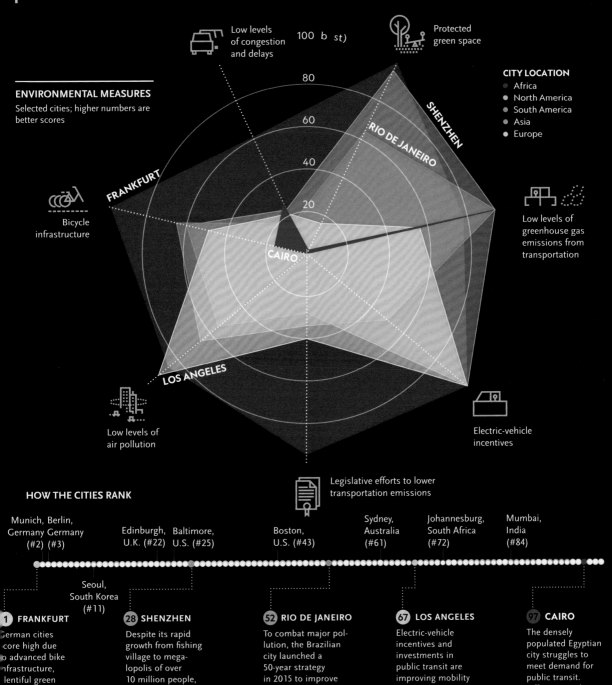

ENVIRONMENTAL MEASURES
Selected cities; higher numbers are better scores

Low levels of congestion and delays

Protected green space

100 b st)

80

60

40

20

SHENZHEN

RIO DE JANEIRO

FRANKFURT

CAIRO

LOS ANGELES

Bicycle infrastructure

Low levels of greenhouse gas emissions from transportation

Electric-vehicle incentives

Low levels of air pollution

Legislative efforts to lower transportation emissions

CITY LOCATION
- Africa
- North America
- South America
- Asia
- Europe

HOW THE CITIES RANK

Munich, Berlin, Germany Germany (#2) (#3)

Edinburgh, U.K. (#22)

Baltimore, U.S. (#25)

Boston, U.S. (#43)

Sydney, Australia (#61)

Johannesburg, South Africa (#72)

Mumbai, India (#84)

Seoul, South Korea (#11)

1 FRANKFURT
German cities score high due to advanced bike infrastructure, plentiful green spaces, and low greenhouse gas emissions.

28 SHENZHEN
Despite its rapid growth from fishing village to megalopolis of over 10 million people, the Chinese city has developed sustainable transit.

52 RIO DE JANEIRO
To combat major pollution, the Brazilian city launched a 50-year strategy in 2015 to improve air quality and local ecosystems by using cleaner fuels.

67 LOS ANGELES
Electric-vehicle incentives and investments in public transit are improving mobility in the U.S. city, which is known for its epic traffic jams.

97 CAIRO
The densely populated Egyptian city struggles to meet demand for public transit. Offering a wider variety of transit options could help.

RELIGION
AROUND THE WORLD

CULTURE & MEANING

Religion's great power comes from its ability to speak to the heart and longings of individuals and societies. In time, an untold number of local religious practices yielded to just a few widespread traditions.

CHACO CANYON
A ceremonial site for the Pueblo peoples between AD 850 and 1250, the complex remains here are protected as a U.S. National Historical Park and a UNESCO World Heritage site.

NORTH AMERICA

MEXICO CITY
The Basilica of Our Lady of Guadalupe in Mexico City is the most visited Catholic pilgrimage site in the world. Accounts state that a vision of the Virgin Mary appeared there in 1531.

SOUTH AMERICA

GUYANA
Although most of South America is predominantly Christian, Guyana is predominantly Hindu; nearby Suriname includes both Christian and Hindu adherents, yet neither represents the majority religion.

EARTH DAY EVERY DAY

When Beliefs Drive
ACTION

Many find their religious faith fueling conservation efforts. For example, A Rocha is an international network of environmental projects—from freshwater filtration in Africa to bird-watching tours in Australia, meadow assessment in Switzerland to tree planting in Lebanon—consciously linked to principles of Christianity.

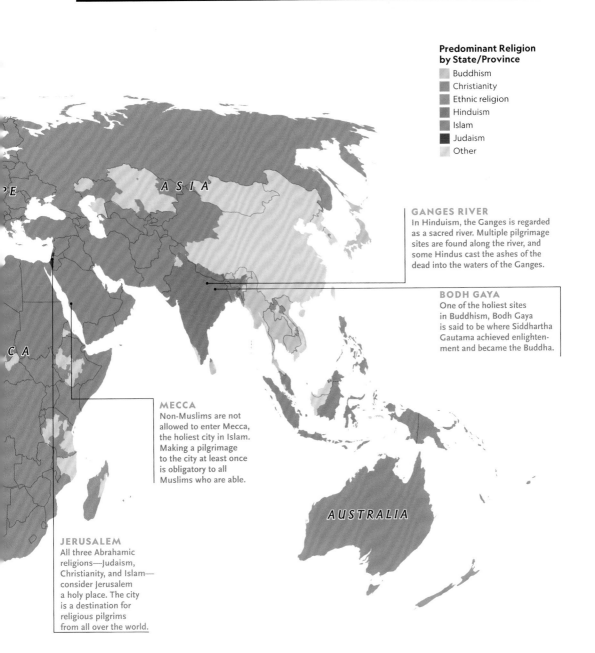

> **"THERE ARE WAYS IN WHICH WE CAN CONSCIOUSLY WORK TO DEVELOP FEELINGS OF LOVE AND KINDNESS. FOR SOME OF US, THE MOST EFFECTIVE WAY TO DO SO IS THROUGH RELIGIOUS PRACTICE."** —THE 14TH DALAI LAMA

Predominant Religion by State/Province

- Buddhism
- Christianity
- Ethnic religion
- Hinduism
- Islam
- Judaism
- Other

GANGES RIVER
In Hinduism, the Ganges is regarded as a sacred river. Multiple pilgrimage sites are found along the river, and some Hindus cast the ashes of the dead into the waters of the Ganges.

BODH GAYA
One of the holiest sites in Buddhism, Bodh Gaya is said to be where Siddhartha Gautama achieved enlightenment and became the Buddha.

MECCA
Non-Muslims are not allowed to enter Mecca, the holiest city in Islam. Making a pilgrimage to the city at least once is obligatory to all Muslims who are able.

JERUSALEM
All three Abrahamic religions—Judaism, Christianity, and Islam—consider Jerusalem a holy place. The city is a destination for religious pilgrims from all over the world.

ASIA

AUSTRALIA

Religious Holidays

SOMEWHERE IN THE WORLD, a meal, ritual, or offering is being prepared in religious observance — most likely by the busy adherents of Roman Catholicism or Hinduism. If Catholics celebrated every saint's day or Hindus commemorated each deity's birthday, nearly the entire year would be accounted for.

WHO CELEBRATES THE MOST?
With feasts, fasts, and prayers, the world's nine largest religions can collectively observe more than a hundred holidays in a year.

HINDUS LEAD THE FESTIVITIES
Hinduism recognizes the birthdays and milestones of hundreds of deities. It also commemorates the changing of the seasons, the harvest, and lunar phases.

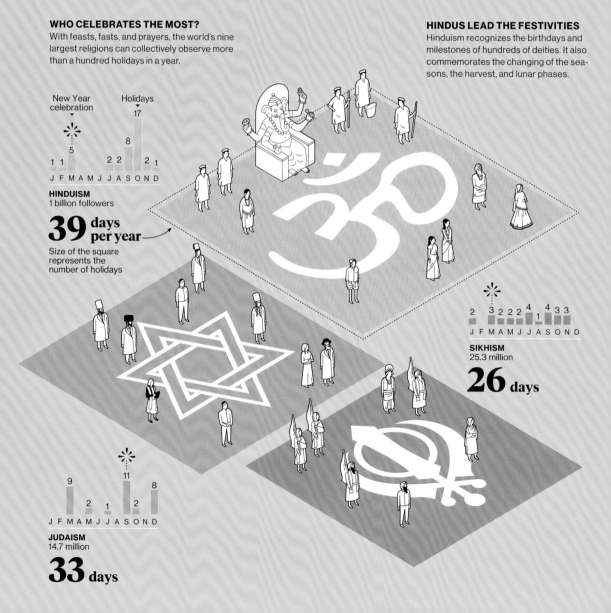

New Year celebration

Holidays
17

5

8

2 2

2 1

1 1

J F M A M J J A S O N D

HINDUISM
1 billion followers

39 days per year

Size of the square represents the number of holidays

2   3 2 2 2   4   4 3 3
                1
J F M A M J J A S O N D

SIKHISM
25.3 million

26 days

9

11

8

2   1   2

J F M A M J J A S O N D

JUDAISM
14.7 million

33 days

The Jewish calendar has dozens of holidays — but the Torah only mandates strict observance of the five holiest. Muslims, too, are holiday minimalists. In Islam the biggest celebrations are saved for the last days of its two major holidays: Id al-Fitr for Ramadan and Id al-Adha to end the hajj pilgrimage.

Compiling a schedule of the holidays most widely observed by the world's nine largest religions is no simple task. Different countries and regions, as well as denominations, celebrate their own versions of the holidays, and some religions follow a unique calendar.

China's lunar calendar runs on a 60-year cycle; India uses several types of calendars.

The establishment of the international date line in 1884 pushed holidays that used to begin at sunset to the next day in many countries. Today holiday scheduling can be influenced by things like economic productivity, which is the reason some celebrations move around each year to bookend a weekend.

NEW YEARS ALL YEAR ROUND
While Christians follow the Gregorian calendar, many traditions follow other calendar systems and celebrate the New Year during different months.

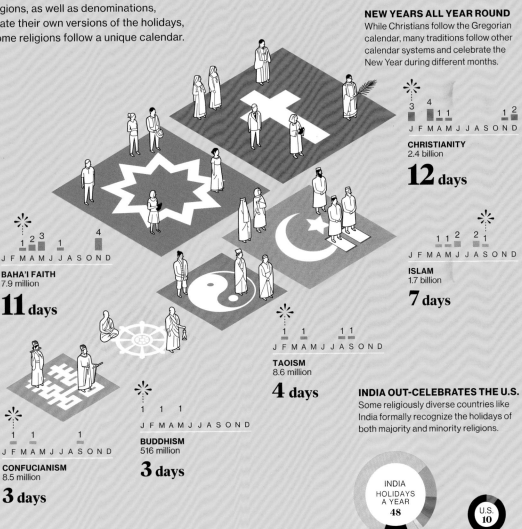

CHRISTIANITY
2.4 billion

12 days

BAHA'I FAITH
7.9 million

11 days

ISLAM
1.7 billion

7 days

TAOISM
8.6 million

4 days

BUDDHISM
516 million

3 days

CONFUCIANISM
8.5 million

3 days

INDIA OUT-CELEBRATES THE U.S.
Some religiously diverse countries like India formally recognize the holidays of both majority and minority religions.

INDIA
HOLIDAYS
A YEAR
48

SECULAR
5

U.S.
10

SECULAR
9

BEST OF @NATGEO

TOP PHOTOS OF PEOPLE

@coryrichards | CORY RICHARDS
Dorje, a Tibetan yak herder, stands for a high-altitude portrait on the north side of Mount Everest.

@amytoensing | AMY TOENSING
Dhakti Dashi, a Bangladeshi widow, stands at the back of an ashram—her home for more than a quarter century.

@sarahyltonphoto | SARA HYLTON
Tracey George Heese sits on buffalo skin that recalls her mother, whose murder decades ago is unsolved.

@mitty | CRISTINA MITTERMEIER
A child wears face paint and a headdress of colored chicken feathers at a festival in the New Guinea highlands.

" CULTURE DOES NOT MAKE PEOPLE. PEOPLE MAKE CULTURE."

—CHIMAMANDA NGOZI ADICHIE, WRITER

@hammond_robin | ROBIN HAMMOND
Eleven-year-old twins Millie (left) and Marcia—called "rainbow twins" by their mother—in Birmingham, England

@markosian | DIANA MARKOSIAN
Two Muslim girls pick flowers pensively in an open field in Chechnya in the North Caucasus.

@mike_hettwer | MIKE HETTWER
A man sits in the hands of a temporary giant sculpture at Burning Man in Nevada's Black Rock Desert.

@noralorek | NORA LOREK
Kila Jani sits by a *milaya,* a traditional hand-decorated bedsheet, in Uganda's Bidibidi Refugee Settlement.

THE SCIENCE
OF SLEEP

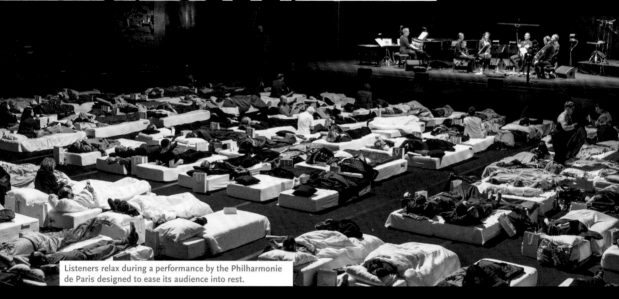

Listeners relax during a performance by the Philharmonie de Paris designed to ease its audience into rest.

THE NECESSITY OF SLEEP

Everything we've learned about sleep has emphasized its importance to our mental and physical health. Our sleep-wake pattern is a central feature of human biology—an adaptation to life on a spinning planet, with its endless wheel of day and night. The 2017 Nobel Prize in medicine was awarded to three scientists who, in the 1980s and 1990s, identified the molecular clock inside our cells that aims to keep us in sync with the sun. When this circadian rhythm breaks down, recent research has shown, we are at increased risk for illnesses such as diabetes, heart disease, and dementia.

There is evidence that sleep is essential for maintaining a healthy immune system, body temperature, and blood pressure. Without enough of it, we can't regulate our moods well or recover swiftly from injuries. Sleep may be more essential to us than food. Animals will die of sleep deprivation before starvation.

Good sleep likely also reduces one's risk of developing dementia. It appears that while we're awake, our neurons are packed tightly together, but when we're asleep, some brain cells deflate by up to 60 percent, widening the spaces between them. These intercellular spaces are dumping grounds for the cells' metabolic waste—notably a substance called beta-amyloid, which disrupts communication between neurons and is closely linked to Alzheimer's. Only during sleep can spinal fluid slosh like detergent through these broader hallways of our brain, washing beta-amyloid away.

WHILE YOU'RE SLEEPING

Our brains aren't less active when we sleep, just differently active. Sleep literally makes connections you might never have formed consciously, as we all intuitively realize. No one says, "I'm going to eat on a problem." We sleep on it. The waking brain is optimized for collecting external stimuli, the sleeping brain for consolidating information. At night we switch from recording to editing, a change that can be measured on the molecular scale. We're not just rotely filing our thoughts—the sleeping brain actively curates which memories to keep and which to toss.

A seven-year-old falls asleep watching cartoons on his iPad.

KEY FACTS

Understanding the
IMPORTANCE OF SLEEP

MEMORY FORMATION As we fall into sleep, our brain stays active and fires into its editing process—deciding which memories to keep and which ones to toss.

FITNESS Lack of sleep is directly tied to obesity: Without enough sleep, the stomach and other organs overproduce ghrelin, the hunger hormone, causing us to overeat.

BY THE NUMBERS Sleep-deprived consumers paid $66 billion in 2016 for devices, medications, and sleep studies. The figure could rise to $85 billion by 2021.

OTHER SPECIES Dolphins sleep one brain hemisphere at a time, allowing them to swim continuously. Great frigatebirds can nap while gliding.

DAYLIGHT SAVINGS The Monday after a daylight saving time change in the U.S., there's a 24 percent increase in heart attacks, compared with other Mondays, and a jump in fatal car crashes, too.

BAD COP Sleep-deprived suspects held by the police, it's been shown, will confess to anything in exchange for rest.

THE WAKING BRAIN IS OPTIMIZED FOR COLLECTING INFORMATION, THE SLEEPING BRAIN FOR CONSOLIDATING. AT NIGHT WE SWITCH FROM RECORDING TO EDITING.

Eating Insects

As incomes rise in developing countries, so too does the demand for meat. But raising livestock uses a lot of resources. Eating insects—already common in many tropical countries—could be an alternative. Beetles and crickets, for example, are packed with nutrients and provide protein at a low environmental cost.

Palatability poses a problem. "People have an emotional response to bugs—it's the yuck factor," says Arnold van Huis of Wageningen University in the Netherlands. To disguise their form, insects can be processed into powders or pastes. What's next? Protein-rich "bug flours" that are part flour and part ground insect are starting to appear on the market.

EFFICIENT PROTEIN

Edible insects provide a sustainable alternative to meat. They are a healthy food source with a high protein and fat content, but their nutritional value varies by species.

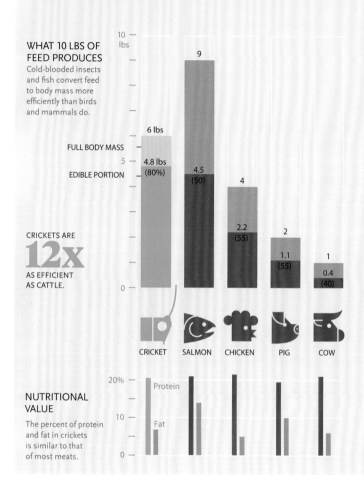

WHAT 10 LBS OF FEED PRODUCES
Cold-blooded insects and fish convert feed to body mass more efficiently than birds and mammals do.

FULL BODY MASS

EDIBLE PORTION

CRICKETS ARE
12x
AS EFFICIENT AS CATTLE.

CRICKET   SALMON   CHICKEN   PIG   COW

6 lbs — 4.8 lbs (80%)
9 — 4.5 (50)
4 — 2.2 (55)
2 — 1.1 (55)
1 — 0.4 (40)

NUTRITIONAL VALUE
The percent of protein and fat in crickets is similar to that of most meats.

Protein

Fat

MOST COMMONLY CONSUMED
Beetles are the most consumed species; mealworms are beetle larvae.

BEETLES — 31%
CATERPILLARS — 18%
15% — ANTS, BEES, WASPS
13% — CRICKETS, GRASSHOPPERS, LOCUSTS
OTHER — 23% — DRAGONFLIES, FLIES, TERMITES

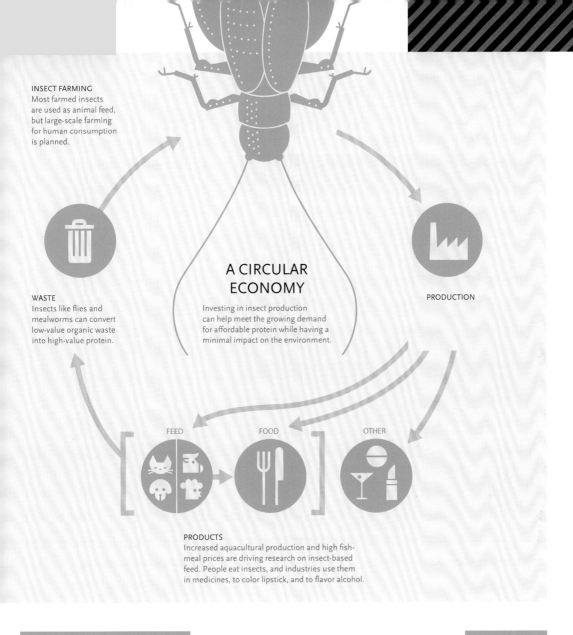

INSECT FARMING
Most farmed insects are used as animal feed, but large-scale farming for human consumption is planned.

WASTE
Insects like flies and mealworms can convert low-value organic waste into high-value protein.

A CIRCULAR ECONOMY

Investing in insect production can help meet the growing demand for affordable protein while having a minimal impact on the environment.

PRODUCTION

FEED   FOOD   OTHER

PRODUCTS
Increased aquacultural production and high fish-meal prices are driving research on insect-based feed. People eat insects, and industries use them in medicines, to color lipstick, and to flavor alcohol.

ENVIRONMENTAL IMPACT

Insects emit fewer greenhouse gases and require less land to produce than livestock such as pigs and cattle.

GREENHOUSE GAS PRODUCTION
Pounds of CO_2-eq* generated from producing a pound of protein

14 — MEALWORM
38 — PIG

LAND USE
Square feet needed to produce a pound of protein

88 — MEALWORM
269 — PIG

A DELICACY

IN UGANDA A POUND OF GRASSHOPPERS COSTS

40%

MORE THAN A POUND OF BEEF

* CO_2-equivalents: the sum of carbon dioxide, methane, and nitrous oxide emissions

INTERNAL CLOCK

INTERNAL TIMEKEEPER
The suprachiasmatic nucleus (SCN) spontaneously generates a near-24-hour rhythm. Sunlight synchronizes it each day.

HOW LIGHT AFFECTS SLEEP PATTERNS

Our sleep-wake pattern is a central feature of human biology—an adaptation to life on a spinning planet, with its endless wheel of day and night—and it's important for physical and mental health. The pattern depends on the interaction of two processes: Sleep pressure, thought to be created by sleep-promoting substances that accumulate in the brain during waking hours, and our circadian rhythm, the internal clock that keeps brain and body in sync with the sun. The clock can be set backward or forward by light. We're particularly sensitive to blue (short-wavelength) light, the kind that brightens midday sunlight and our computer screens but can disrupt our cycle—especially at night, when we need the dark to cue us to sleep.

SUNRISE

PHASE SHIFT
(Sleep delay at night)

Tablet	Smartphone	E-reader*	Incandescent	Candle
96 min	67 min	58 min	55 min	0 minutes

Brightness — ●●●●●● ●●●● ●●●● ●●● ○

MORE BLUE ← LIGHT SOURCE RANGE → LESS BLUE

*with backlit display

SLEEP DRIVERS

— CIRCADIAN CYCLE

··· SLEEP PRESSURE

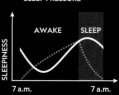

AWAKE   SLEEP

SLEEPINESS

7 a.m.   7 a.m.

SLEEP DRIVERS

The pressure to sleep builds throughout the day. Light sets our internal clock and artificial light disrupts it. Some ganglion cells have blue-light-sensitive receptors that set our circadian clock to night or day. The bluer and brighter the light, the more likely it is to suppress melatonin release and shift our sleep cycle—especially when we're exposed to it at night and up close on electronic screens.

CLOCK WITHOUT LIGHT

Some blind people who have no light information reaching their brains use melatonin products every 24 hours as cues to try to stay in sync.

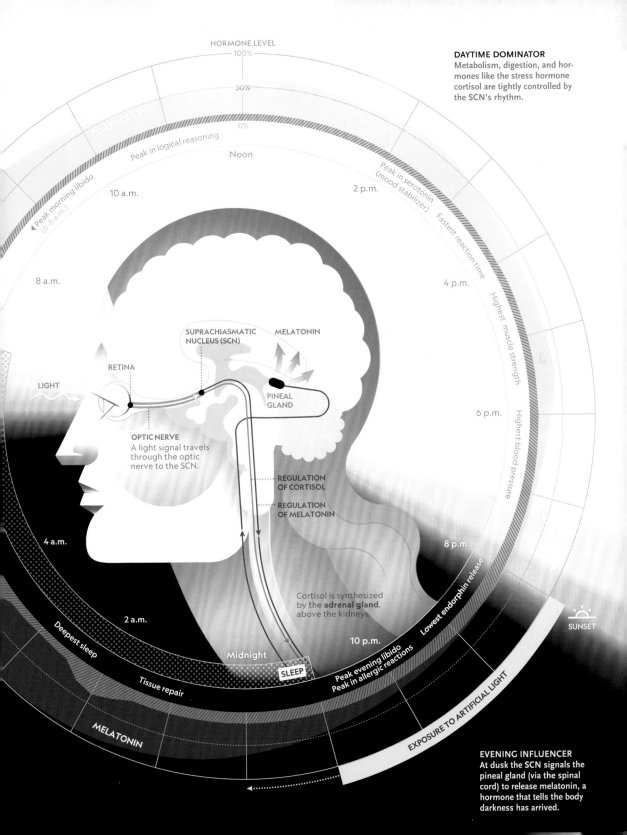

HORMONE LEVEL
100%
50%
0%

DAYTIME DOMINATOR
Metabolism, digestion, and hormones like the stress hormone cortisol are tightly controlled by the SCN's rhythm.

Peak in logical reasoning

Noon

CONNECTIVE TISSUE

Peak morning libido
(6–8 a.m.)

10 a.m.

Peak in serotonin
(mood stabilizer)

2 p.m.

Fastest reaction time

8 a.m.

4 p.m.

Highest muscle strength

SUPRACHIASMATIC NUCLEUS (SCN)

MELATONIN

RETINA

PINEAL GLAND

6 p.m.

LIGHT

Highest blood pressure

OPTIC NERVE
A light signal travels through the optic nerve to the SCN.

REGULATION OF CORTISOL

REGULATION OF MELATONIN

4 a.m.

8 p.m.

Cortisol is synthesized by the **adrenal gland**, above the kidneys.

2 a.m.

Lowest endorphin release

10 p.m.

SUNSET

Midnight

SLEEP

Deepest sleep

Peak evening libido
Peak in allergic reactions

Tissue repair

MELATONIN

EXPOSURE TO ARTIFICIAL LIGHT

EVENING INFLUENCER
At dusk the SCN signals the pineal gland (via the spinal cord) to release melatonin, a hormone that tells the body darkness has arrived.

UNDERSTANDING
GENDER

NO LONGER SIMPLY MALE OR FEMALE

Our society is in the midst of a conversation about gender issues, with evolving notions about what it means to be a woman or a man. At the same time, scientists are uncovering new complexities in the biological understanding of sex. Whereas genital differentiation takes place in the first two months of fetal development, sexual differentiation of the brain comes months later.

IN A SURVEY OF A THOUSAND MILLENNIALS AGES 18 TO 34, HALF AGREED THAT "GENDER IS A SPECTRUM, AND SOME PEOPLE FALL OUTSIDE CONVENTIONAL CATEGORIES."

More children are opting for new gender identities, like this young transgender artist.

Glossary of Terms for
GENDER

CISGENDER A term describing one whose gender identity matches the biological sex assigned at birth.

GENDER BINARY The idea that gender is strictly either male/man/masculine or female/woman/feminine based on sex assigned at birth, rather than a continuum or spectrum of gender identities and expressions.

GENDER CONFORMING One whose gender expression is consistent with cultural norms expected for that gender.

GENDER DYSPHORIA The medical diagnosis for being transgender. It is controversial because it implies that being transgender is a mental illness, rather than a valid identity.

GENDER EXPRESSION One's outward gender presentation: clothing, hairstyle, makeup, vocal inflection, body language.

GENDERFLUID One whose gender identity or expression shifts between man/masculine and woman/feminine or falls somewhere along this spectrum.

GENDER IDENTITY One's deep-seated, internal sense of who one is as a gendered being; the gender with which one identifies.

INTERSEX Any mix of male and female chromosomes, testicular and ovarian tissue, genitals, or other sexual characteristics.

NONBINARY A spectrum of gender identities and expressions. Terms include genderqueer, genderfluid, and pangender.

QUEER An umbrella term for a range of people who are not heterosexual and/or cisgender. Some consider the term derogatory.

TRANSGENDER An adjective describing one whose gender identity does not match the biological sex assigned at birth. Sometimes abbreviated as trans.

INSIDE YOUR BRAIN

ANATOMY OF A NERVE CELL

Cell body
The neuron's powerhouse, responsible for generating energy and synthesizing proteins

Dendrites
Branching projections that pick up signals from other neurons

An image a millimeter high—less than four-hundredths of an inch—shows nerve cells arranged in orderly layers and columns.

1 mm = 1,000 microns*

*The 1-mm image is from a different data set than the other images.

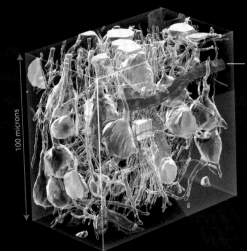

Blood vessels

100 microns

10 microns

Deep Brain Dive

For the first time scientists can visualize how neurons actually connect with one another. The three blocks at right have been colorized but are not an artist's conception: They show, at increasing levels of magnification, real neurons in part of a mouse's brain receiving signals from the face. Technology may soon make possible a similar reconstruction of an entire mouse brain—and eventually of the vastly more complicated architecture of the human brain, opening the way for advances in understanding schizophrenia, depression, and other mental diseases.

A section a hundredth the size reveals blood vessels among pink cell bodies and a tangle of their axons and dendrites.

HALF THE WORLD'S HARD DRIVES
Visualizing neurons at the level of detail shown in these images requires unprecedented computing power. Producing an image of an entire human brain at the same resolution would consume nearly half the world's digital storage capacity.

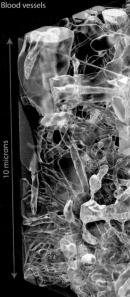

Magnified again by 100, this section more clearly shows axons (blue) and dendrites (yellow). Budlike dendritic spines receive information from other cells' axons across gaps called synapses.

Storage capacity needed to produce mouse brain image
450,000 terabytes

Storage capacity needed to produce human brain image
1.3 billion terabytes

Global digital storage, 2012:
2.7 billion terabytes

A SEGMENT OF A MOUSE'S BRAIN THE SIZE OF A GRAIN OF SALT HOLDS 100 TERABYTES OF DATA—THE AMOUNT IN ABOUT 25,000 HIGH-DEFINITION MOVIES.

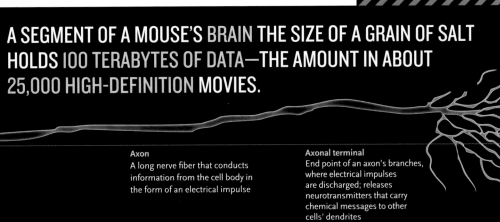

Axon
A long nerve fiber that conducts information from the cell body in the form of an electrical impulse

Axonal terminal
End point of an axon's branches, where electrical impulses are discharged; releases neurotransmitters that carry chemical messages to other cells' dendrites

Glial cells
The glue of the nervous system, supporting, feeding, and protecting neurons

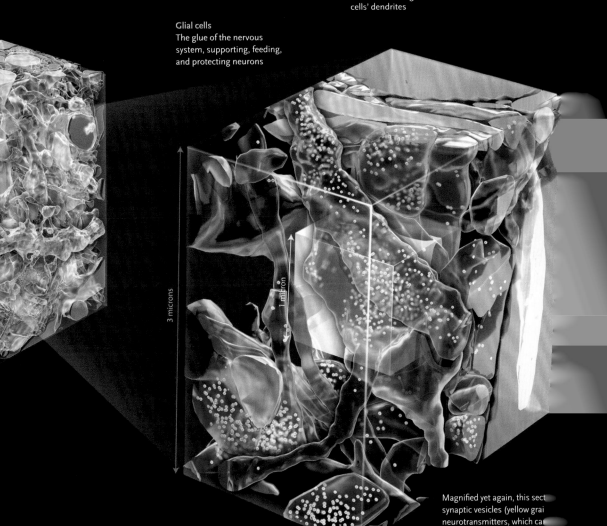

3 microns

1 micron

Magnified yet again, this sect
synaptic vesicles (yellow grai
neurotransmitters, which ca
messages across synapses, s
receiving nerve cell to fire or

STEVE RAMIREZ
NEUROSCIENTIST

UNDERSTANDING THE BRAIN

From Shakespeare to astronomy to piano to Boston sports, Steve Ramirez is a man of many interests. In college, he realized that the common denominator between all those different subjects was the brain. Today, he's trying to figure out exactly how it works. In his lab at Boston University, Ramirez is studying the physical basis of memories, and how we might be able to modify them.

Son of immigrants from El Salvador and his family's first Ph.D., Ramirez attributes much of his work ethic and curiosity to his parents.

Memory, says Ramirez, is like having a time machine stuck between your ears. Think about what you had for dinner last night and you're transported to that moment—different parts of your brain working to recall the taste and smell of the food, the feeling of being full, and the room you were in.

HOW TO CHANGE A MIND

The work in Ramirez's lab is twofold: to learn how memory works in the brain and to discover whether it can be manipulated. To answer the first question, they're building a 3-D map, finding where different senses and emotions link up within our brains as we remember. Memories aren't static, and they're not stored in a single place, which makes them challenging to map.

When it comes to modifying memories, Ramirez and his team are exploring ways to dull the experience of a negative memory and activate a positive one. He and his team genetically engineer mice for brain cells that respond to light. Then they give the mice a mild electric shock—creating a bad memory—and observe which cells respond. Deactivating those cells could make the bad memory inaccessible or allow it to be overwritten by a good memory.

So far they only use mice with genetically modified brain cells, but the results of this work may have human applications in treating conditions like PTSD, depression, or anxiety. Imagine being able to turn off trauma and replace it with joy: a scene out of science fiction, happening in Steve Ramirez's lab.

Microimagery from Ramirez's lab shows the proteins (lit in green) in a mouse's brain that bind to a specific memory.

KEY DATES

Milestones in
MEMORY SCIENCE

1904
Evolutionary biologist Richard Semon proposes that experience leaves a trace on neurons.

1950
Karl Lashley summarizes his research on the storage of memories throughout the brain.

1968
Richard Atkinson and Richard Shiffrin propose three types of memory: sensory, short-term, and long-term.

1980S & 1990S
Computer models simulate memory.

2013
The Human Brain Project, a 10-year undertaking to advance neuroscience, begins.

MEDICINE TIME LINE

6500 to 1 BC	AD 1 to 1500	1500 to 1850	1850 to 1900

ca 6500 BC
The first known surgery is completed.

ca 3000 BC
The Ayurveda, a Hindu medical treatise, establishes a holistic medical system still in use today.

ca 2500 BC
Chinese doctors use acupuncture to heal ailments.

ca 2000 BC
In Syria and Babylon, medicine becomes an important practice; recipes for ointments and poultices are recorded on clay tablets.

ca 1550 BC
Egyptians have about 700 drugs and medications in use.

440 BC
The Hippocratic Corpus, a collection of medical treatises from ancient Greece, is compiled.

ca 30
Roman doctors use splints and bandages stiffened with starch to set broken bones.

77
Pedanius Dioscorides writes a guide to medicinal herbs and drugs that remains authoritative until the 15th century.

1012
Persian physician Ibn Sina publishes an influential medical text, *The Canon of Medicine*.

ca 1286
Eyeglasses are invented in Italy.

1347–1351
The Black Death spreads across Europe and Asia in one of the most devastating pandemics in history.

1628
English physician William Harvey explains the circulation of blood in the body.

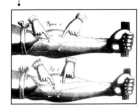

1796
English physician Edward Jenner introduces the smallpox vaccination in Europe.

1805
Japanese physician Hanaoka Seishu performs the first surgery on a patient using general anesthesia.

1824
Louis Braille invents the Braille alphabet to aid blind people in reading and writing.

1840
Jakob Henle proposes the germ theory of disease.

1854
English physician John Snow connects cholera and contaminated water.

1863
Louis Pasteur invents a sterilization process now known as pasteurization.

1867
Joseph Lister publishes a paper on the use of antiseptic surgical methods.

1885
Sigmund Freud begins developing his theories of psychoanalysis.

1893
Surgeon Daniel Hale Williams performs the first heart surgery.

1895
German physicist Wilhelm Röntgen takes the first x-ray.

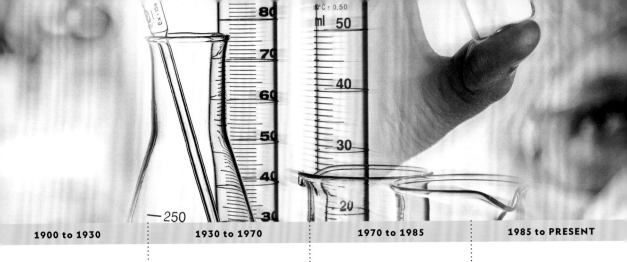

| 1900 to 1930 | 1930 to 1970 | 1970 to 1985 | 1985 to PRESENT |

1917

Margaret Sanger opens a birth control clinic in the United States.

1921

Psychiatrist Hermann Rorschach introduces his inkblot test for studying personality.

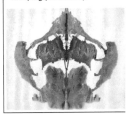

1922

Vitamins D and E are first discovered.

1925

Biologist Ernest Just demonstrates that UV radiation can cause cancer.

1928

Scottish bacteriologist Alexander Fleming discovers penicillin.

1937

Italian scientist Daniel Bovet identifies the first antihistamine effective in treating allergies.

1948

The World Health Organization is founded.

1950

Link between smoking and lung cancer is shown.

1952

Jonas Salk develops the first polio vaccine.

1953

Francis Crick, James Watson, and Rosalind Franklin determine the double-helix structure of DNA.

1967

South African surgeon Christiaan Barnard performs the first successful heart transplant.

1973

American and English physicians begin to develop magnetic resonance imaging (MRI) scanning.

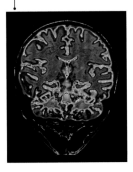

1976

The Ebola virus is first identified after outbreaks in Africa.

1978

The first "test tube" baby is born in England.

1982

The first genetically engineered insulin is produced.

1983

Luc Montagnier and Robert Gallo discover the human immunodeficiency virus (HIV).

1998

Researchers at Johns Hopkins University successfully grow human stem cells in a lab.

2001

American researchers successfully clone a human embryo.

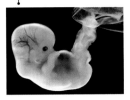

2007

Geneticist J. Craig Venter publishes his entire genetic sequence—the first genome published of a single person.

2010

World's first all-robotic surgery takes place in Canada.

2013

Researchers develop a 3-D printed prosthetic hand that can be produced at a low cost.

INSIDE
CHEESE

THE ART & SCIENCE OF FERMENTED DAIRY

Like sourdough, kombucha, and other fermented foods, cheese is the product of bacteria and yeast, plus mold. These microbial cultures turn regular milk into the many varieties of cheese we know and love. Microbiologist Benjamin Wolfe's lab at Tufts University studies the mini ecosystems inside cheese. Understanding these microbes could help engineer more effective medicines and new agricultural methods—not to mention tastier cheese.

Specific bacteria and fungi determine the unique textures and flavors of different cheeses.

THE STRONG SMELL OF LIMBURGER CHEESE COMES FROM *BREVIBACTERIUM LINENS*—ONE OF THE BACTERIA ALSO RESPONSIBLE FOR BODY AND FOOT ODOR.

COUPOLE

The rind of this creamy Vermont cheese is dominated by *Geotrichum candidum,* a fungus that gives it a wrinkled appearance. The inside is mild and lemony; the rind is potent and intense.

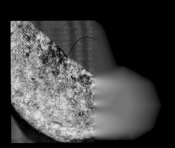

TOMME DE SA

On this French a cheese, bacteri *proteamaculans (Mucor lanceola* friction highway across the chee

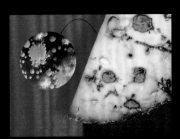

BAYLEY HAZEN BLUE

In this cheese, fungi *(Penicillium commune)* produce antibacterial compounds to fight off bacteria *(Staphylococcus succinus, S. xylosus),* resulting in blue veins.

WINNIMERE

This cheese co *(Vibrio casei)* an *(Psychrobacter* spp.). Some are and the moist, s their ideal enviro

Antibiotic Resistance

THE POULTRY CASE STUDY

Americans today eat three times as much poultry as they did in 1960. Since most U.S. chickens are raised in large, crowded facilities, farmers feed them antibiotics to prevent disease as well as speed their growth.

Decades of Antibiotics

Since the 1950s, farmers have fed antibiotic growth promoters (AGPs) to livestock. Overusing these substances can create superbugs, pathogens that are resistant to multiple drugs and could be passed along to humans. Mindful of that, companies such as Perdue Farms have stopped using the drugs to make chickens gain weight faster. Since Denmark banned AGPs in the 1990s, the major pork exporter says it's producing more pigs— and the animals get fewer diseases. Says Centers for Disease Control and Prevention epidemiologist Tom Chiller, "Antibiotics are miracle drugs that should only be used to treat diseases."

MEAT CONSUMPTION IN THE U.S.

100 pounds per person per year

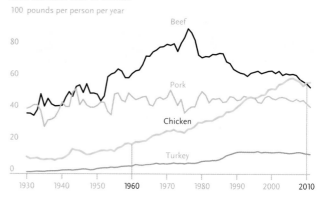

Antibiotics as Growth Promoters

They help chickens grow bigger faster, making the meat . . .

. . . cheaper for the consumer.

In 1960 it took 63 days to grow a 3.4-pound broiler.

$3.24* a pound

In 2011 it took 47 days to grow a 5.4-pound one.

$1.29 a pound

* 2011 dollars, adjusted for inflation

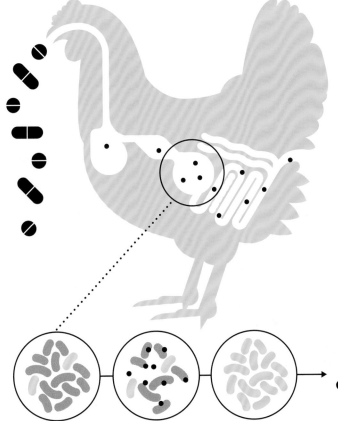

How Resistance Develops and Spreads

1.

Antibiotics can be given to livestock in their feed or sprayed on them, to be ingested when the animals groom themselves.

2.

The bacteria causing an infection are usually not resistant to drugs.

But some of them can be naturally drug resistant.

When antibiotics kill the nonresistant bacteria . . .

. . . the resistant ones, the superbugs, can flourish.

53%

of grocery store chicken sampled in a 2013 study had resistant *E. coli.*

3.

Superbugs can be passed to humans in many ways.

Farmworkers often have direct contact with animals.

Drug-resistant bacteria can linger on improperly cooked meat.

Fertilizer or water containing animal feces can spread superbugs to food crops.

THE STORY
OF A FACE

A REVOLUTIONARY TRANSPLANT

In 2014, Katie Stubblefield tried to end her life in a moment of desperation. She survived, but lost her face—and thus became one of the subjects in the study of the experimental surgery of face transplantation. Over the next three years, Katie was hospitalized more than a dozen times and underwent 22 surgeries. In 2017, she became the youngest person in the U.S. to receive a full-face transplant.

> " **WHEN I TOUCH MY FACE NOW WITH MY HAND, I FEEL WHOLE AGAIN. I WANTED MY FACE BACK, AND I WAS WILLING TO DO WHATEVER IT TOOK.**"
>
> —**KATIE STUBBLEFIELD,** FACE TRANSPLANT RECIPIENT

Eight months and 22 days after Katie received her face transplant, she meets Sandra, the woman who donated her granddaughter Adrea's face for the procedure.

Katie's Transplant
TIME LINE

MARCH 2014 After a self-inflicted gunshot wound, Katie is hospitalized, and surgeons stabilize her through a series of operations.

MAY 2014 Katie is transferred to Cleveland Clinic, where doctors construct a new nasal cavity and rebuild her jaw.

AUGUST 2014 After several more procedures, Katie is discharged and begins physical, occupational, speech, and vision therapy and undergoes evaluation for face transplant candidacy.

AUGUST 2015 To protect her brain from infection, Katie undergoes several more operations. Her evaluation for a possible face transplant continues.

MARCH 2016 Katie is officially listed as a candidate for a face transplant.

APRIL 2016 To prepare her skull to fit a donor face, surgeons reshape the bones of Katie's face, controlling for shape and length as it regrows.

MAY 2017 A donor with matching tissue type, sex, and a similar face size becomes available. Surgeons planned on a partial transplant, but after evaluating the donor switch to a full-face transplant.

AUGUST 2017 Katie is discharged from the Cleveland Clinic and begins therapy to learn how to use her new facial muscles.

JULY 2018 A post-transplant revision surgery corrects Katie's jaw and tongue placement to make it easier for her to talk.

FEBRUARY 2019 Katie undergoes her fourth revision surgery, aimed at continuing to improve her speech and function.

PSYCHOBIOME

THE BRAIN-GUT CONNECTION

The human body contains as many microbes as it does cells—nearly 30 trillion of them. Several ecosystems are found on our skin: Your forearm has the richest community, with an average of 44 species. The human gut teems with bacteria, which help us digest food, absorb nutrients, and protect our intestinal walls. The more we learn about our microbes, the more we realize their profound effect on mental health, attitudes, and emotions—which is why many now call that population inside us our "psychobiome."

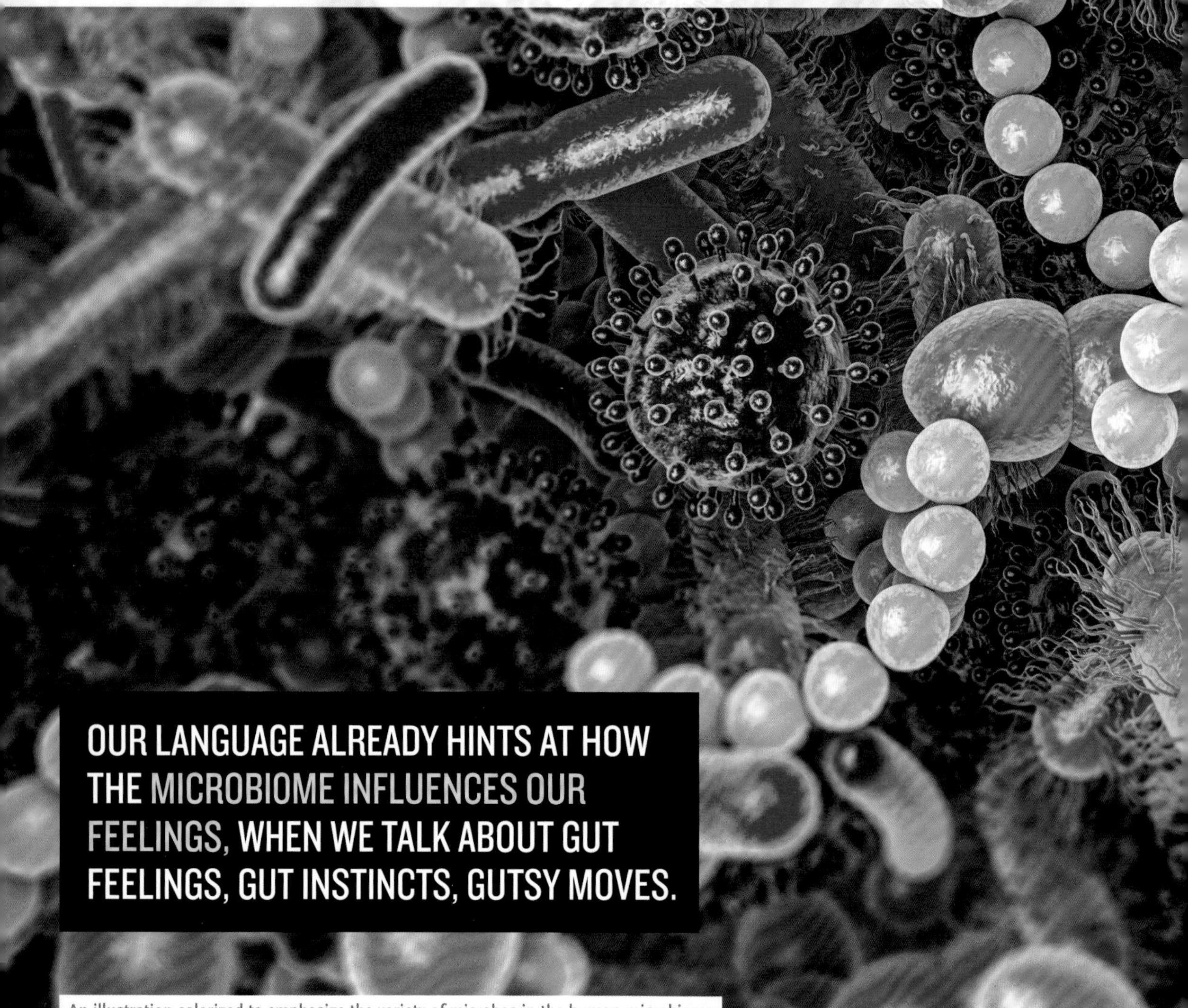

OUR LANGUAGE ALREADY HINTS AT HOW THE MICROBIOME INFLUENCES OUR FEELINGS, WHEN WE TALK ABOUT GUT FEELINGS, GUT INSTINCTS, GUTSY MOVES.

An illustration colorized to emphasize the variety of microbes in the human microbiome

Five Ways the Gut Affects
WELL-BEING

INFECTIONS & DEPRESSION In 2000, following a contamination of the water supply, an infection spread among 5,000 residents of a single town, Walkerton, Ohio. In addition to causing gastrointestinal illness, the related inflammation resulted in widespread depression and anxiety.

STRESS & INFLAMMATION Stress hormones are part of our fight-or-flight response. But they also quiet the immune system, allowing gut pathogens such as *Salmonella* and *E. coli* to flourish, which means people who are stressed become more susceptible to infection and inflammation.

TEENAGE HABITS & DECISION-MAKING The sheathing of the brain's nerve fibers (myelination), a process governed by the microbiome, spreads to the frontal lobes in our teen years. This means executive function and thought processes are shaped in part by youthful eating habits and stressors.

FERMENTED FOODS & MEMORY The psychobiotic *Lactobacillus plantarum*, found in foods such as kimchi and sauerkraut, has anti-inflammatory properties. Evidence from animal studies indicates that it improves memory even in cases of memory loss related to aging.

JUNK FOOD & ANXIETY Foods with added sugars boost harmful bacteria in the gut and have been shown to bring on depression. In a study involving 23,000 mothers and children, junk food in a mother's diet while pregnant or in a child's own diet was a predictor of psychological problems in the children.

HERBS & SPICES
FOR HEALTH

BASIL
Fragrant annual
native to India

BAY
Aromatic shrub leaf
flavors soups.

CHERVIL
Delicate relative
of parsley

CHIVES
Tender stalks
in onion family

CILANTRO
Leaves of plant whose
seeds are coriander

DILL
Ancient cure
for indigestion

FENNEL
Seeds, leaves, stalks,
bulbs all tasty

LEMONGRASS
Southeast Asian native,
citrus flavor

MARJORAM
Sweet herb, makes
a calming tea

OREGANO
Classic herb in
Mediterranean cuisines

PARSLEY
Edible garnish high
in antioxidants

PEPPERMINT
Tea is a favorite
stomach soother.

ROSEMARY
Research affirms
tradition as pain reliever.

SAGE
Honeybees love
sage flowers.

TARRAGON
Fragile flavor best captured
in vinegar

THYME
Good in cooking;
tea also calms a cough.

> **"A GREEN BOOM IS SWEEPING OUR LAND. SCIENTISTS AND COMMERCIAL DRUG PRODUCERS ARE DISCOVERING THAT THERE IS GOLD AMONG THE GREENS."**
>
> —**EUELL GIBBONS,** *STALKING THE HEALTHFUL HERBS*

ALLSPICE
Ground from dried berries, Caribbean native

BLACK PEPPER
Native to India, spurred spice trade in 1600s

CARDAMOM
Ancient Egyptians chewed it for clean breath.

CAYENNE
Powdered hot peppers, rich in vitamins and minerals

CINNAMON
Inner bark of tropical tree, lowers blood sugar

CLOVES
Ground tree buds, antioxidant and mildly anesthetic

CORIANDER
Seed of cilantro plant, often used in curries

CUMIN
Aromatic seed essential to Mexican and Indian cuisines

GINGER
Ground root, traditional remedy for seasickness

MACE
Outer covering of nutmeg; both appetite stimulants

PAPRIKA
Bright red, made of dried peppers, typical in Hungary

TURMERIC
Related to ginger, provides many health benefits

ANCIENT WISDOM

Herbs and spices add flavor, aroma, color, texture, and nutrients to food—and many improve health as well. Herbs are leaves or stems of plants from temperate zones, used fresh or dried. Spices come from many parts of tropical plants—dried seeds, flowers, fruit, bark, or roots—and are used either whole or ground fine. Most of these provide vitamins and minerals, and many have healing properties.

A WORD FROM

Passing on Knowledge Interviewing people is a standard method in ethnobotanical research. Through individual interviews with several people in the community who self-medicate with "bush medicines," I am hoping to develop a database of locally useful plants and to understand the myriad of ways in which these plants are used ... The ultimate goal is to give back that information to the community, so that these precious oral traditions do not disappear.

—**INA VANDEBROEK,** *ethnobotanist*

MINDFULNESS

THE SCIENCE OF PAYING ATTENTION

Even just one generation ago, traits like compassion and focus were thought to be inherent and predetermined. But scientists have come to understand that mental patterns are malleable: Through practice and repetition, the brain's circuitry can be rerouted, and one's reactions and habits can be intentionally redirected. This is known as neuroplasticity.

Meditation is a deliberate approach to mindfulness in which one remains present and reflects on internal thoughts, physical responses, and external stimuli. Practitioners have been found to have better control of their attention and emotions. Meditation also appears to slow loss of the brain's gray matter and age-related cognitive decline.

A woman sits mindfully at the edge of the Trolltunga rock formation in Norway.

> **"THE BEST WAY TO CAPTURE MOMENTS IS TO PAY ATTENTION. THIS IS HOW WE CULTIVATE MINDFULNESS."**
>
> —JON KABAT-ZINN, AUTHOR AND MINDFULNESS TEACHER

10 Principles of Living
MINDFULLY

These interconnected principles both facilitate and are the fruit of mindful meditation.

ACCEPTANCE By choosing to not force change, you are in a better position to release what needs to be let go of.

CALM Calm is a steadiness and freedom that prevails in distressing or disruptive situations, regardless of the emotions involved.

CLARITY Consistent habits of observation and openness yield deep wisdom and the ability to see yourself rightly.

COMPASSION When you're able to identify suffering and to have empathy with those in pain—whether yourself or others—you can act compassionately to bring relief.

CONNECTEDNESS We are connected to everything around us. Consider and celebrate the ways we need one another and the natural world.

CONSCIOUSNESS Practice being aware of what is immediately present and of what you're experiencing in the moment. Do not need to judge it as right or wrong. Just name it.

GRATEFULNESS Acknowledge the world's goodness and beauty and be receptive to these gifts. By cultivating gratitude, you reap great connection and joy.

IMPERMANENCE Being present in each moment is key in a changing, temporary world, where grasping at what is passing brings only grief and regret.

JOY Deep-seated bliss transcends the situations in which we find ourselves and guides us toward truth and health.

NEWCOMER'S EYES Observe yourself and what's around you with curiosity, wonder, and openness, as if seeing it for the first time—setting aside presumptions and previous experiences.

FURTHER

DANCING DAY

On the fourth Sunday of January, the city of Iloilo, Philippines, on the island of Panay, erupts in costume, dance, and drumming during the annual Dinagyang Festival. Inspired by a centuries-old celebration among Panay's indigenous Ati people, Dinagyang "tribes"—neighborhood teams—prepare for months, creating magnificent costumes and choreography. Dinagyang honors not only its Ati origins but also the deeply felt Catholicism of the region and includes parades honoring the Santo Niño, an icon of the Christ child.

Filipinos celebrate the Dinagyang Festival, an annual religious and sociocultural gathering.

"LOVE EXALTS OUR EARTHLY BODIES TO HEAVEN, AND MAKES THE VERY HILLS TO DANCE WITH JOY!"

—RUMI, 13TH-CENTURY SUFI POET

YESTERDAY TO TOMORROW

WORLD HISTORY | U.S. HISTORY

Colonial-era sculpture contrasts with the modern skyline of Lujiazui, Shanghai's financial district, at sunrise.

QUIZ MASTER

The Past Shapes the Future History tells us about who we are, where we have been, and where we might be going. Delve back into the past for endless details that are surprising and enlightening—and start here, to see what you already know.

—SUSAN TYLER HITCHCOCK, *Nat Geo Quizmaster*

WHICH HAPPENED FIRST: THE AMERICAN OR THE FRENCH REVOLUTION?

p295

p284

NAME THE LEGENDARY **PAIR OF BROTHERS** SAID TO HAVE **FOUNDED THE CITY OF ROME.**

WHICH WAS **BUILT** FIRST: **THE SPHINX OR STONEHENGE?**

p304

IN WHAT LANGUAGE WAS THE **MAGNA CARTA, ISSUED BY ENGLAND'S KING JOHN IN 1215, WRITTEN?**

p294

WHO MADE THE **WORLD'S FIRST** LONG-DISTANCE **TELEPHONE** CALL?

p290

WHAT WAS THE NORTH-SOUTH BOUNDARY **CALLED** THE TORDESILLAS **LINE?**

WHEN WERE CHINA'S **TERRA-COTTA WARRIORS** DISCOVERED: 1924, 1954, OR 1974?

p300

p305

IN WHAT YEAR DID AMELIA EARHART DISAPPEAR AS SHE ATTEMPTED TO FLY AROUND THE WORLD?

p309

HOW OLD WAS TUTANKHAMUN WHEN HE ASCENDED TO THE THRONE?

p302

IN WHAT MODERN COUNTRY ARE **EXCAVATIONS** UNDER WAY AT **NURI, THE ANCIENT** CAPITAL OF THE **KINGDOM OF KUSH:** EGYPT, ALGERIA, OR SUDAN?

p296

IN WHAT YEAR **DID THE** *CLOTILDA,* LAST KNOWN SHIP **KNOWN TO CARRY SLAVES TO THE** UNITED STATES, ARRIVE IN MOBILE BAY?

p306

SIMÓN BOLÍVAR IS **FAMOUS** FOR HIS **LETTER** FROM WHICH **CARIBBEAN ISLAND:** JAMAICA, CUBA, OR ARUBA?

p292

p293

FOR HOW MANY YEARS WAS **NELSON MANDELA** IN PRISON?

WHAT WERE THE **WORDS** ON THE WARNER BROS. **SHOP SIGN** DAMAGED IN THE 9/11 ATTACK **ON THE WORLD** TRADE CENTER?

p315

PREHISTORY TO 1600
TIME LINE

PREHISTORY	3000 to 1000 BC	1000 to 500 BC	500 to 1 BC

ca 100,000 ya*
Early humans migrate from Africa to other continents.

ca 80,000 ya
Neanderthals and modern humans live alongside each other in Europe.

ca 14,500 ya
Human populations are present in North and South America.

ca 10,000 ya
Agriculture develops in the Yellow River Valley and other places in China.

ca 3200 BC
Sumer, the first known civilization, emerges in modern-day Iraq.

* years ago

---

ca 2575 BC
Ancient Egypt's Old Kingdom begins.

ca 2500–1900 BC
The Indus civilization thrives in modern-day Pakistan and northwest India.

ca 1766–1122 BC
The Shang dynasty rules in ancient China.

ca 1500 BC
Olmec culture develops in modern-day Mexico.

ca 1200 BC
Proto-Celtic people of Indo-European origin settle in central Europe.

---

753 BC
Rome is founded by Romulus and Remus, according to legend.

ca 700 BC
Athens and other Greek city-states become centers of learning and maritime trade.

ca 560 BC
Siddhartha Gautama is born in the Himalayan foothills; he is later known as the Buddha.

509 BC
The Roman Republic is established.

---

ca 500 BC
Iron tool technology spreads across Africa.

334 BC
Alexander the Great invades Persia and carves out an empire stretching from Greece to northwestern India.

ca 100 BC
Buddhism spreads into Central Asia along the Silk Road.

27 BC
Augustus becomes the first emperor of Rome.

AD 1 to 500	500 to 1090	1090 to 1400	1400 to 1600

■ 79
Mount Vesuvius erupts, destroying Pompeii and Herculaneum.

■ ca 300
Maya in South America develop a script and a calendar.

■ 312
Constantine I becomes the emperor of Rome and expands legal rights for religions.

■ 441
Attila the Hun launches a massive attack on the Eastern Roman Empire.

■ ca 500
The empire of Ghana gains prominence in West Africa.

■ 570
Muhammad, the Prophet and future messenger of Islam, is born in Mecca.

■ 800
Charlemagne is crowned the Holy Roman Emperor.

■ 960
The Song dynasty reunifies China and ushers in economic, social, and cultural change.

■ ca 1000
Leif Eriksson sails to North America.

■ 1054
The schism between the Roman and Eastern Christian churches becomes permanent.

■ 1095
The First Crusade begins, inaugurating a series of religious wars that would last for hundreds of years.

■ 1206
Genghis Khan becomes leader of the Mongol confederation.

■ 1337
The Hundred Years' War begins between England and France.

■ 1368
Zhu Yuanzhang founds the Ming dynasty in China.

■ 1440
Moctezuma I becomes ruler of the Aztec.

■ 1478
The Spanish Inquisition begins.

■ 1517
Martin Luther instigates the Protestant Reformation.

■ 1519–1521
Spain conquers the Aztec Empire, beginning a century-long colonial period.

■ 1560s
The transatlantic slave trade grows in West Africa.

■ 1577–1580
English explorer Sir Francis Drake circumnavigates the globe.

TALES OLDER
THAN THE HILLS

A BOY STEALS THE OGRE'S TREASURE
4,500 years old
A boy trespasses into a giant's house to steal his treasure. When the giant comes home, the boy hides and then manages to evade the giant's pursuit. Finally the boy kills the giant and takes his treasure.

THE SMITH AND THE DEVIL
6,000 years old
A blacksmith trades his soul to the devil for the power to weld any materials together. With his wish granted, the man traps the devil, sticking him to the ground until the evil spirit releases him from the bargain.

THE ANIMAL BRIDEGROOM
3,000 years old
Picking a rose lands a father in debt to a beast. In exchange for his freedom, his daughter is taken prisoner. After falling in love with the beast, she must overcome a curse to transform him into a prince.

FAIRY TALES—OLDER THAN YOU MIGHT THINK

As Wilhelm and Jacob Grimm collected Germanic folktales in the 19th century, they realized that many were similar to stories told in distant parts of the world. The brothers wondered whether similarities indicated a shared ancestry thousands of years old.

To test the Grimms' theory, anthropologist Jamie Tehrani and literary scholar Sara Graça da Silva traced 76 basic plots back to their oldest linguistic ancestor. If a similar tale was told in German and Hindi, the researchers concluded its roots lay in the languages' last common ancestor. "The Smith and the Devil," a story about a man who trades his soul for blacksmith skills, was first told some 6,000 years ago in Proto-Indo-European. In the United States, we tell a similar tale about blues guitarist Robert Johnson.

FRIENDS IN LIFE AND DEATH
2,000 years old
A man invites his dead friend to his wedding. When the groom accompanies his friend to the underworld, 400 years pass and he misses his own nuptials.

THE SUPERNATURAL HELPER
2,500 years old
A peasant falsely tells the king his daughter can spin gold out of straw. An elfin creature appears, offering the real skill in exchange for her firstborn child. The only way out is to guess his name—which she does.

MODERN TAKES

FRIENDS IN LIFE AND DEATH
A dead man accepts Don Juan's invitation to a banquet in exchange for Don Juan's attendance at another event—in the underworld.

THE ANIMAL BRIDEGROOM
In Disney's *Beauty and the Beast*, a witch's curse traps the prince in a beast's body until Belle's love breaks the spell.

THE SMITH AND THE DEVIL
Fictional scholar Faust and blues guitarist Robert Johnson are among the modern figures said to have sold their souls to the devil for knowledge.

A BOY STEALS THE OGRE'S TREASURE
Magic beans grow to great heights in "Jack and the Beanstalk," allowing Jack to climb up into a giant's lair and steal his treasures.

THE SUPERNATURAL HELPER
Trapped in an agreement to give Rumpelstiltskin her first child, a young queen overhears him chanting his name and gets out of the deal.

FOLKTALES
ARE PASSED DOWN ORALLY, OBSCURING THEIR AGE AND ORIGIN.

SEMIRAMIS
QUEEN OF BABYLON

THE ASSYRIAN EMPIRE'S ONLY WOMAN RULER

In the Neo-Assyrian regime of the ninth century BC, one woman commanded an entire empire—stretching from Asia Minor to today's western Iran. She was Sammu-ramat, thought to mean "high heaven," and she inspired universal respect. Centuries after her brief five-year reign, Greeks wrote about Semiramis, as they called her, and her achievements. From there, the Assyrian queen passed into the realm of legend. What stands out is how both the woman and the myth were celebrated for things traditionally associated with male rulers: scoring military triumphs, building architectural wonders, and ruling with wisdom.

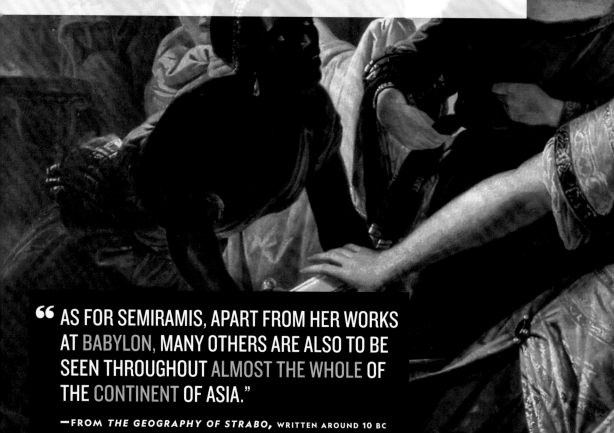

❝ AS FOR SEMIRAMIS, APART FROM HER WORKS AT BABYLON, MANY OTHERS ARE ALSO TO BE SEEN THROUGHOUT ALMOST THE WHOLE OF THE CONTINENT OF ASIA."

—FROM *THE GEOGRAPHY OF STRABO*, WRITTEN AROUND 10 BC

Queen Sammu-ramat of history begat Queen Semiramis of legend, whose civic accomplishments are lauded on the same level as her beauty.

Semiramis's
LIFE & LEGEND

■ **MARRIAGE**
According to artifacts, Queen Sammu-ramat was married to King Shamshi-Adad V, who reigned 823–811 BC, and was the mother of King Adad-nirari III.

■ **INHERITING THE THRONE**
When the king died, his son, Adad-nirari III, was too young to rule, leaving Queen Sammu-ramat to govern Assyria through her regency.

■ **BATTLE**
One monument mentions that the queen accompanied her son into battle, which indicates her actions were honored and respected.

■ **EARNING RESPECT**
Another monument bears this exceptional dedication: "Sammu-ramat, Queen of Shamshi-Adad, King of the Universe, King of Assyria; Mother of Adad-nirari, King of the Universe, King of Assyria."

■ **A PLACE IN HISTORY**
In the fifth century BC, the historian Herodotus perpetuated memory of Sammu-ramat using the Greek form of her name, Semiramis, by which she is best known today.

■ **MYTHIC ORIGINS**
In the account perpetuated by Diodorus Siculus in the first century BC, Semiramis was the child of a Syrian goddess and a young Syrian man.

■ **ANCIENT WONDERS**
Greek historians said the queen ordered a new city, with fabulous hanging gardens, to be built on the banks of the Euphrates—Babylon. No historical evidence supports their claims.

■ **CIRCLES OF HELL**
She inspired the Italian medieval poet Dante, who placed her in his *Inferno,* where she is punished for her "sensual vices."

■ **A LASTING LEGACY**
The French Enlightenment writer Voltaire wrote a tragedy about her, which was later made into Rossini's 1823 opera, *Semiramide.*

MAPPING HISTORY

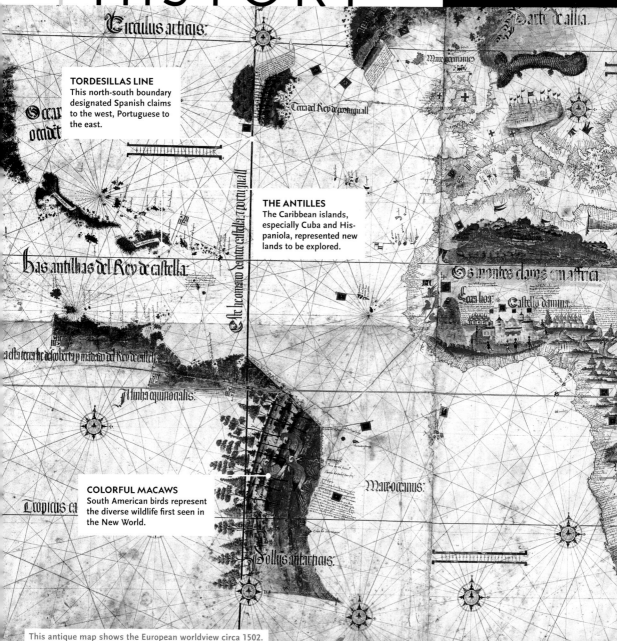

TORDESILLAS LINE
This north-south boundary designated Spanish claims to the west, Portuguese to the east.

THE ANTILLES
The Caribbean islands, especially Cuba and Hispaniola, represented new lands to be explored.

COLORFUL MACAWS
South American birds represent the diverse wildlife first seen in the New World.

This antique map shows the European worldview circa 1502.

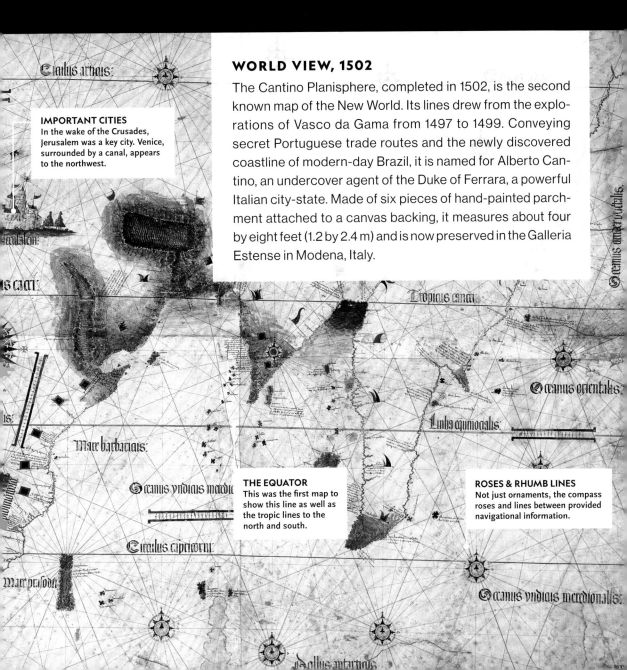

THIS MAP DISAPPEARED IN THE MID-19TH CENTURY, ONLY TO BE FOUND BY A LIBRARY DIRECTOR SOME YEARS LATER IN A BUTCHER SHOP.

WORLD VIEW, 1502

The Cantino Planisphere, completed in 1502, is the second known map of the New World. Its lines drew from the explorations of Vasco da Gama from 1497 to 1499. Conveying secret Portuguese trade routes and the newly discovered coastline of modern-day Brazil, it is named for Alberto Cantino, an undercover agent of the Duke of Ferrara, a powerful Italian city-state. Made of six pieces of hand-painted parchment attached to a canvas backing, it measures about four by eight feet (1.2 by 2.4 m) and is now preserved in the Galleria Estense in Modena, Italy.

IMPORTANT CITIES
In the wake of the Crusades, Jerusalem was a key city. Venice, surrounded by a canal, appears to the northwest.

THE EQUATOR
This was the first map to show this line as well as the tropic lines to the north and south.

ROSES & RHUMB LINES
Not just ornaments, the compass roses and lines between provided navigational information.

1600 TO RECENT PAST
TIME LINE

| 1600 to 1700 | 1700 to 1800 | 1800 to 1860 | 1860 to 1900 |

1600 to 1700

■ 1600s
European powers expand their colonization around the world.

■ ca 1600
Algonquin tribes unite to form the Powhatan Confederacy in North America.

■ 1633
For his theory that Earth circles the sun, Galileo goes on trial for heresy.

■ 1649
Civil war in England results in the execution of King Charles I.

■ 1661
Swedish banknotes become the first paper currency in use in Europe.

1700 to 1800

■ 1701
The Asante kingdom expands in West Africa under the reign of Osei Tutu.

■ 1762
Catherine II proclaims herself empress of Russia.

■ 1770
Aboard the *Endeavour*, James Cook claims Australia for Britain.

■ 1776
Americans post their Declaration of Independence.

■ 1789
A mob storms the Bastille, marking the beginning of the French Revolution.

1800 to 1860

■ 1801
A slave rebellion succeeds, leading to Haiti's independence from France three years later.

■ 1815
Simón Bolívar writes his "Letter From Jamaica," outlining his vision of South America freed of colonial rule.

■ 1833
Slavery is abolished throughout the British Empire.

■ 1837
Queen Victoria begins her 63-year reign.

■ 1845–1851
Irish potato famine causes poverty and mass starvation; millions emigrate to North America.

1860 to 1900

■ 1861
Tsar Alexander II frees serfs in Russia.

■ 1863
Abraham Lincoln issues the Emancipation Proclamation, freeing slaves in 10 states.

FREEDOM TO SLAVES!

■ 1867
Provinces in Canada unite into a single country.

■ 1884–1885
The Berlin Conference divides Africa among various European powers.

■ 1897
First Zionist Congress convenes in Basel, Switzerland.

| 1900 to 1925 | 1925 to 1950 | 1950 to 1975 | 1975 to 2000 |

■ 1914
The Panama Canal opens, enabling faster transoceanic shipping.

■ 1914
Assassination of Archduke Ferdinand sparks years-long World War I.

■ 1917
Lenin and the Bolsheviks overthrow the tsar in Russian Revolution.

■ 1920
Mohandas Gandhi becomes India's leader in its struggle for independence.

■ 1929
Wall Street stock market crashes, beginning the Great Depression.

■ 1933
Adolf Hitler is appointed chancellor of Germany.

■ 1939–1945
In World War II, Allied powers (including U.K., U.S., Soviet Union, France, and China) battle Axis powers (Germany, Italy, and Japan).

■ 1945
United Nations is founded.

■ 1949
Marxist leader Mao Zedong transforms China into Communist People's Republic of China.

■ 1955
Rosa Parks's arrest in Alabama sets the American civil rights movement in motion.

■ 1957
European Economic Community, precursor to the European Union, is established.

■ 1959
Fidel Castro takes over Cuba after leading a Marxist revolution.

■ 1973
Organization of Petroleum-Exporting Countries (OPEC) embargoes oil supplies, causing a worldwide energy crisis.

■ 1979
Muslim cleric Ayatollah Ruhollah Khomeini seizes power in Iran.

■ 1986
Disastrous accident at Chernobyl nuclear power plant in Ukraine forces massive resettlement.

■ 1989
Thousands of students occupy Beijing's Tiananmen Square, advocating democracy in China.

■ 1989
Built in 1961 to encircle Germany's West Berlin, the Berlin Wall falls, a sign of the end of the Cold War.

■ 1990
Nelson Mandela is released after 27 years in prison, signifying end of apartheid in South Africa.

A HISTORY OF DEMOCRACY

THE QUEST FOR EQUAL RIGHTS

Raphael's "School of Athens"

ANCIENT HISTORY

FIRST GRANTING OF RIGHTS, CA 594 BC
Solon of Athens institutes economic and political reforms, including granting all citizens the right to participate in the ecclesia (general assembly), which has legislative and judicial powers.

REFORMING POWER STRUCTURE, 508 BC
Athenian statesman Cleisthenes encourages participation in government by extending the right to participate to all free adult men born in townships—and becomes the father of democracy.

COMMON GOOD, 4TH CENTURY BC
Aristotle describes a "polity" as government by consent and for the common good—which resembles what comes to be known as a constitutional democracy.

EARLY TIMES

OLDEST PARLIAMENT, 930
During the Viking era and predating Iceland's written language, the first parliament, Althing, is established at Thingvellir, a place-name literally meaning "parliament plains." It has become the world's longest-running representative democracy.

LEVELS OF REPRESENTATION, CA 11TH TO 15TH CENTURIES
The Igbo society in what is now Nigeria has representative bodies at the village level that seek consensus under the leadership of elders. This decentralized, chiefless system endures until colonialism.

INDIVIDUAL FREEDOM, 1215
The Magna Carta—"Great Charter"—is issued in Latin by England's King John in the context of power struggles between the pope and the king of England. Reaffirmed by John's successors, it ensures basic individual rights and guarantees justice and the right to a fair trial, thus granting protection to individuals from higher authorities.

SELF-GOVERNANCE, 1620
Most of the men arriving on the *Mayflower* sign a compact that will influence governance in the Plymouth colony. The Mayflower Compact has inclinations toward democratic values of self-government and common consent.

The U.S. Constitution

Tunisian demonstrators during election, 2011

REVOLUTIONARY ERA

ALL CREATED EQUAL, 1776
Colonists in the Americas draft the Declaration of Independence—asserting "that all men are created equal, that they are endowed by their Creator with certain unalienable Rights, that among these are Life, Liberty and the pursuit of Happiness." This becomes a globally recognized document of self-governance and the fundamental rights of human beings.

BALANCE OF POWER, 1787
The U.S. Constitution is presented to the states for ratification. It outlines the workings of a federal democratic government, including the balance of power in a tripartite government, individual rights versus the state, and the limits of centralized government versus the state sovereignty. Amendments known as the Bill of Rights are added in 1789.

RIGHTS OF THE CITIZEN, 1789
As the French Revolution begins, France's National Assembly adopts the Declaration of the Rights of Man and of the Citizen, which is later revised and incorporated into subsequent constitutions.

MODERN TIMES

END TO COLONIALISM, 1950
India becomes a democratic republic when its new constitution takes effect—the world's largest democracy.

CIVIL PROTEST, 1989
Hundreds of thousands occupy China's Tiananmen Square to demand democratic reform. After a tense few months, the government responds with violence, martial law, and criminal prosecutions.

BRINGING DOWN APARTHEID, 1996
Following centuries of occupation by the Dutch and British, including decades of apartheid, the government of South Africa transitions to majority rule.

ARAB SPRING, 2010
The first of several pro-democracy protests takes place in Tunisia, inspiring uprisings across North Africa and the Middle East. Some countries suppress the movement; others, like Morocco, implement reforms.

PEARCE PAUL CREASMAN
ARCHAEOLOGIST

DIVING INTO PYRAMIDS

A wetsuit isn't normally needed for archaeological surveys in the desert, but rising groundwater has flooded a number of ancient burial sites—and archaeologist Pearce Paul Creasman is diving in. The royal cemetery and necropolis at Nuri, in northern Sudan, sprawls across more than seven million square feet (650,321 sq m) near the east bank of the Nile. Its watery tombs may tell a new story about the ancient Kushite culture ruled by the so-called black pharaohs.

Nubian pyramids some 2,500 years old spread across Nuri, a region of Sudan just south of the Egyptian border.

Nuri is home to some 20 pyramids built between 650 BC and 300 BC. They are the burial sites of Kushite royals who operated on the southern edges of the Egyptian empire. Archaeologists first visited the site more than a century ago, but as water levels rose and filled the site, excavations became too difficult, and they turned their attention to the many other sites along the Nile.

JOURNEY TO THE PAST

Creasman and his team won't let the water stop them. They don masks and air hoses and swim through muddy water into the inner sanctum of these sites. They've started with the smallest pyramid in the necropolis. It's the tomb of Nastasen, the last king to be buried at Nuri.

It took Creasman's team the entire 2018 field season (and part of 2019) to dig out a staircase leading into the pyramid. The entrance to the tomb is now completely underwater, likely due to the combination of rising groundwater caused by climate change, agriculture near the site, and modern dams along the Nile.

The team is working to excavate Nastasen's royal burial chambers. Although they are filled with water, Creasman believes he has seen the royal sarcophagus there. "There are three chambers, with these beautiful arched ceilings," he says. They've found bits of gold foil floating in the water, suggesting the opulence of their quarry. "I think we finally have the technology to be able to tell the story of Nuri," says Creasman. "It's a story that deserves to be told."

> **AT THE SITE THERE ARE THESE BEAUTIFUL SAND DUNES, AND PYRAMIDS THAT LOOK AS IF THEY ARE BEING ENGULFED BY THE DUNES. IT'S OUT OF SOME SORT OF ROMANCE NOVEL. IT'S GORGEOUS."**

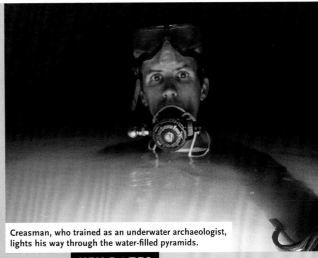

Creasman, who trained as an underwater archaeologist, lights his way through the water-filled pyramids.

KEY DATES

A Brief History of
NUBIA

CA 5000 BC
People move from the Sahara toward the Nile in Nubia.

CA 760 BC
The Nubian king Piye invades Egypt, establishing a dynasty.

760 BC TO 650 BC
Five Kushite pharaohs rule all of Egypt, from Nubia to the Mediterranean.

CA 200 BC
Nubians develop alphabetic writing systems called Meroitic language.

CA 350 AD
The Nubian capital of Meroë is invaded and eventually abandoned.

BEST OF @NATGEO

TOP PHOTOS OF HISTORIC PLACES

@simonnorfolkstudio | SIMON NORFOLK
Work began on Apadana, an audience hall now in ruins, in Persepolis by Persian King Darius I in 518 BC.

@pedromcbride | PETE MCBRIDE
Flower-bearing boughs frame the Jefferson Memorial in Washington, D.C., during cherry blossom season.

@geosteinmetz | GEORGE STEINMETZ
A rare snowfall graces the Jinshanling section of China's Great Wall, built during the Ming dynasty.

@yamashitaphoto | MICHAEL YAMASHITA
A double rainbow shines on a forest of chortens, or stupas—Tibetan Buddhist monuments.

> ❝ **MAN IS A** HISTORY-MAKING **CREATURE WHO CAN NEITHER REPEAT HIS PAST NOR LEAVE IT BEHIND.**❞
>
> **—W. H. AUDEN,** POET

@babaktafreshi | BABAK TAFRESHI
A 13th-century stained-glass window shines in Notre Dame Cathedral. The window survived the 2019 fire.

@renaeffendiphoto | RENA EFFENDI
Satellite imaging technology sheds new light on Egyptian archaeological sites like the Great Pyramid of Giza.

@JimRichardsonNG | JIM RICHARDSON
The Stones of Stenness, 700 years older than Stonehenge, anchor the Heart of Neolithic Orkney in Scotland.

@irablockphoto | IRA BLOCK
A balloon flies over a centuries-old Buddhist temple in Bagan, Myanmar, now a UNESCO World Heritage site.

TERRA-COTTA
WARRIORS

A LEGION FOR ETERNITY

Workers digging a well outside the city of Xi'an, China, in 1974 struck upon one of the greatest archaeological discoveries in the world: a life-size clay soldier poised for battle. Government archaeologists arrived to find not one but thousands of clay soldiers, each with unique facial expressions and positioned according to rank, in trenchlike underground corridors. In some of the corridors, clay horses are aligned four abreast; behind them are wooden chariots. The terra-cotta army, we now know, was part of an elaborate mausoleum created to accompany the first emperor of China, Qin Shi Huang Di, into the afterlife.

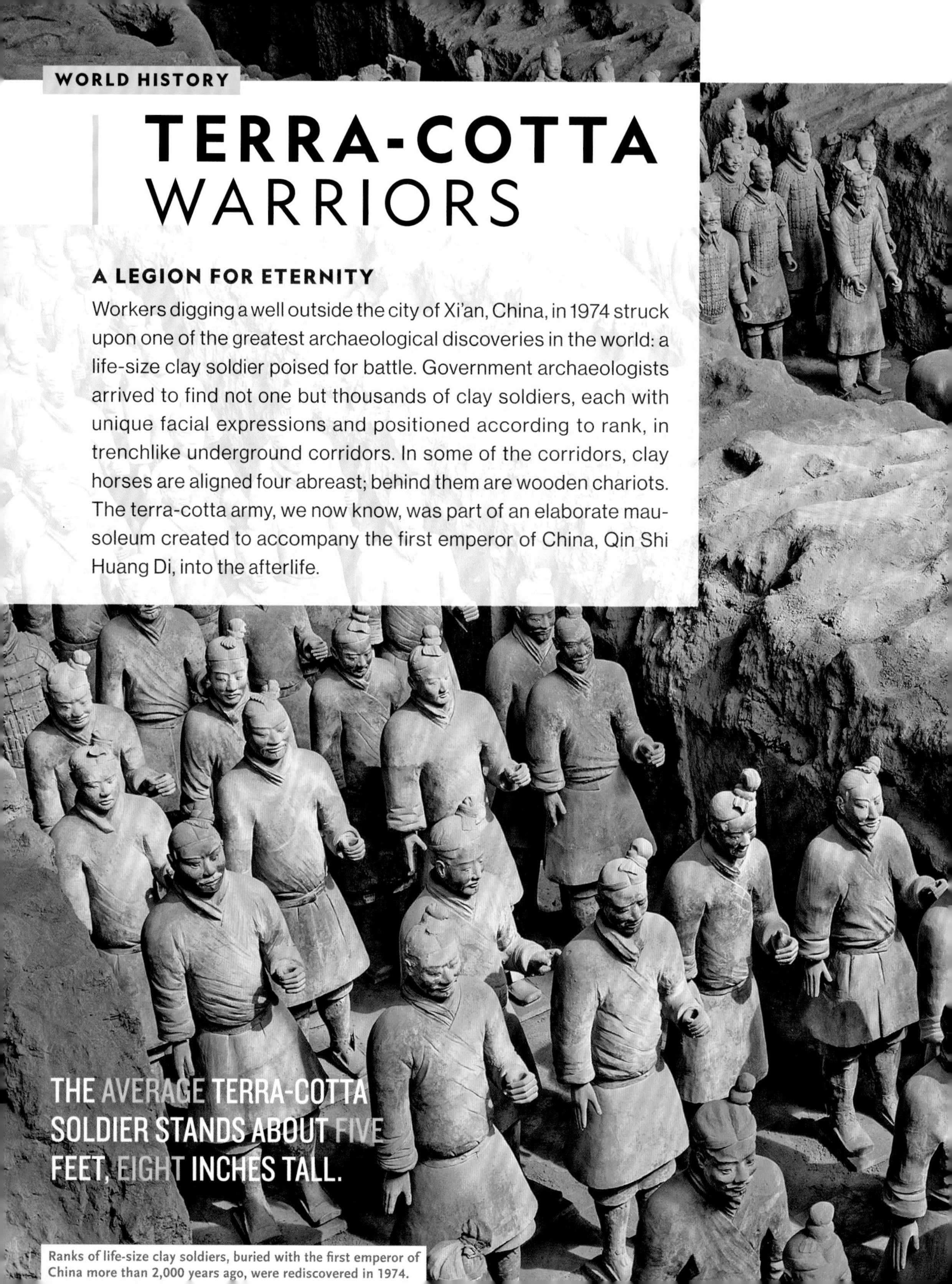

THE AVERAGE TERRA-COTTA SOLDIER STANDS ABOUT FIVE FEET, EIGHT INCHES TALL.

Ranks of life-size clay soldiers, buried with the first emperor of China more than 2,000 years ago, were rediscovered in 1974.

The Emperor's
ARMY FOR
THE AFTERLIFE

■ **FIRST EMPEROR**
Ying Zheng took the throne in 246 BC at the age of 13. By 221 BC, he had unified a collection of warring kingdoms and took the name of Qin Shi Huang Di—the First Emperor of Qin.

■ **LABOR**
Court historian Sima Qian of the following Han dynasty claims that more than 700,000 laborers worked on the project, though modern scholars doubt that figure.

■ **BURIAL GUARDS**
An estimated 8,000 statues of warriors were buried in three pits less than a mile from the emperor's tomb.

■ **TOMB**
The burial complex covers almost 38 square miles.

■ **BURIED ALONGSIDE**
Artisans, craftsmen, and laborers—likely including shackled convicts—who died during the 36 years it took to build this complex were buried here.

■ **BURSTS OF COLOR**
Qin's army of soldiers and horses was a supernatural display swathed in a riot of bold colors: red and green, purple and yellow.

■ **PRESERVING EARTH**
The original paint degrades on exposure but adheres to dirt, so preservationists are now trying to preserve the earth itself.

■ **OTHER CULTURES**
Terra-cotta acrobats and bronze figures of ducks, swans, and cranes uncovered at the grand funerary complex may show evidence of Greek influence.

■ **EXCAVATION**
Archaeologists have no plans to unearth the first emperor's tomb, waiting instead for new conservation technologies.

GENOME CLUES IN EGYPT

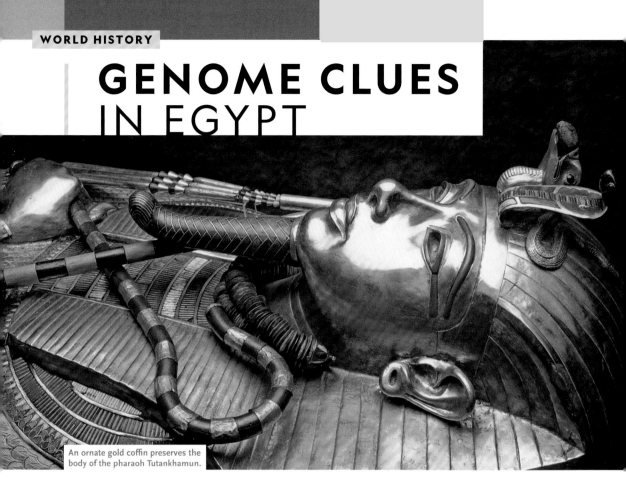

An ornate gold coffin preserves the body of the pharaoh Tutankhamun.

ANCIENT RIDDLES, MODERN SCIENCE

Tutankhamun was a pharaoh during ancient Egypt's New Kingdom era, about 3,300 years ago. He ascended to the throne at the age of nine but ruled for only 10 years before dying at 19, around 1324 BC. Despite his brief reign, King Tut is perhaps Egypt's best known pharaoh because of the treasures—including a solid gold death mask—found in his tomb in 1922.

Yet while King Tut may be seen as the golden boy of ancient Egypt today, he wasn't exactly a strapping sun god during his reign. Instead, a DNA study says, King Tut was a frail pharaoh, beset by malaria and a bone disorder—his health possibly compromised by his incestuous origins.

The study could be conducted on ancient Egyptian royal mummies because the embalming method the ancient Egyptians used seems to have protected DNA as well as flesh. Using DNA samples taken from the mummies' bones, scientists were able to create a five-generation family tree for the boy pharaoh.

One genealogical mystery lingers: Some Egyptologists have speculated that King Tut's mother was Akhenaten's chief wife, Queen Nefertiti, who was also Akhenaten's cousin. Others claim that DNA shows his mother was the daughter of Amenhotep III and Tiye and thus the sister of her husband, Akhenaten.

LASTING LEGACIES

In addition to using DNA to identify royalty, scientists are evaluating the genetic makeup of mummies spanning 1,300 years. One surprising finding is that modern Egyptians have sub-Saharan ancestry not found in the ancient population, which was similar genetically to people from the Levant.

It had been thought that Egyptians acquired European and Middle Eastern ancestry over time, following conquests and contact with those populations. But scientists have determined that about 700 years ago, the amount of sub-Saharan DNA in Egyptians' makeup population increased. What facilitated this change is not clear. What is clear, however, is that Europeans are more closely related to ancient Egyptians than are modern Egyptians.

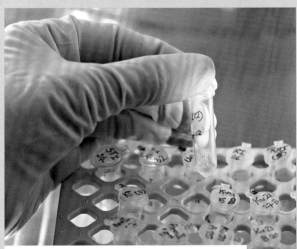

DNA samples from King Tut shed light on the royal lineage.

KEY FACTS

Ancient Egypt
THEN & NOW

■ DUSTING FOR PRINTS
To dust for prints at a crime scene, modern investigators use Egyptian blue, a pigment formulated some 5,250 years ago—in the time of the pharaohs.

■ EMBALMING
A decade-long investigation of prehistoric mummy wrappings roughly 6,600 years old established that Egyptians embalmed their dead thousands of years earlier than previously thought.

■ FEMALE FIGURE
Historians had speculated that Akhenaten's feminine features—such as wide hips, a pot-belly, and female-like breasts—were caused by a genetic disorder, but none has been found. It is now believed that these features, evident in statues, were created for religious and political reasons.

■ ANCIENT BEERS
Archaeologists have excavated a tomb belonging to Khonso Im-Heb, who was head of granaries and beer brewing for the worship of the Egyptian mother goddess, Mut.

■ METEORIC METAL
Researchers have confirmed that the iron of a dagger placed on King Tutankhamun's mummified body has meteoric origins. This follows an earlier identification of 5,000-year-old Egyptian beads made of meteoric iron—the earliest known sign of metalwork.

■ SATELLITE
Using high-resolution satellite images near Lisht, at the edge of the Sahara, archaeologists identified looted pits that turned out to be an interlocking mortuary system housing at least 4,000 individuals in the afterlife.

INNOVATIONS
TIME LINE

6000 to 1500 BC	1500 to 1 BC	AD 1 to 1000	1000 to 1600

6000 to 1500 BC

ca 6000 BC
The world's first known city, Çatalhöyük, is built in Anatolia.

ca 3500 BC
Wheeled vehicles are in use in the Middle East.

ca 3000 BC
Egyptians have developed a process for making paper from the papyrus plant.

ca 2500 BC
The Great Pyramids and the Sphinx are completed in Egypt.

ca 2500 BC
Peruvians use a canal system to irrigate crops.

ca 1525 BC
Stonehenge is completed in England.

1500 to 1 BC

ca 1400 BC
Iron weapons are in use by the Hittites of modern-day Turkey.

ca 500 BC
The abacus, earliest calculating tool, is in use in China.

ca 300 BC
The Maya begin constructing their monumental pyramids in Mexico and Central America.

214 BC
The main section of the Great Wall of China is completed.

ca 120 BC
Romans use concrete to create paved streets, aqueducts, and bridges.

AD 1 to 1000

ca 200
Porcelain is being produced in Han dynasty China.

350
Antioch, in today's Turkey, becomes the first city to have a system of street lighting.

ca 600
Chatrang, an early version of chess, is popular in parts of Central Asia.

607
Japan's Horyuji Temple, the world's oldest wooden building, is completed.

ca 800
Islamic scientists use the astrolabe for celestial observation.

1000 to 1600

ca 1000
Fireworks, made of a bamboo tube filled with gunpowder, are invented in China.

ca 1040
Chinese explorers use magnetic compasses to navigate.

ca 1286
In Italy, the first known eyeglasses are manufactured to correct vision.

ca 1450
The Inca construct a 20,000-mile-long roadway to unite their empire.

1455
Johannes Gutenberg prints the Bible on a movable type press.

| 1600 to 1800 | 1800 to 1900 | 1900 to 1950 | 1950 to PRESENT |

■ 1609–1610
Galileo first observes Earth's moon and four moons of Jupiter with a telescope.

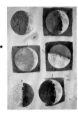

■ 1626
St. Peter's Basilica is completed in Rome after 120 years of construction.

■ 1716
The first lighthouse in North America is built, in Boston Harbor.

■ 1752
After demonstrating the electrical nature of lightning, Benjamin Franklin invents the lightning rod.

■ 1775
Inventor Alexander Cummings patents the first flushing toilet.

■ 1843
Ada Lovelace and Charles Babbage collaborate on the world's first computer.

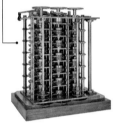

■ 1844
Samuel Morse sends the first telegraph message in the United States.

■ 1867
Alfred Nobel patents dynamite in Britain.

■ 1876
Alexander Graham Bell invents the telephone and makes the first long-distance call.

■ 1898
German chemist Hans von Pechmann synthesizes polyethylene, the world's first plastic.

■ 1901
Italian scientist Guglielmo Marconi makes the first transatlantic radio broadcast.

■ 1904
German engineer Christian Hülsmeyer patents the first radar system, used to prevent collisions among shipping vessels.

■ 1931
The Empire State Building in New York City becomes the world's tallest building.

■ 1943
Jacques Cousteau begins using the Aqua-Lung, which he designed with engineer Émile Gagnan, for underwater diving.

■ 1945
Americans manufacture, test, and deploy the atom bomb.

■ 1954
The first solar cells, converting sunlight to electricity, are developed.

■ 1959
Unimate #001, the first industrial robot, is deployed in a General Motors engine plant.

■ 1959
The microchip, key component of computers, is invented.

■ 1989
The World Wide Web is initiated by British computer scientist Tim Berners-Lee.

■ 2000
The International Space Station begins operating with a crew.

CLOTILDA'S
PAINFUL PAST

AMERICA'S LAST SLAVE SHIP FOUND

From the early 1600s to 1860, an estimated 389,000 Africans came to America as slaves. Very few of the thousands of vessels involved in the transatlantic slave trade have been found, but in 2019 archaeologists uncovered the remains of the last ship known to bring enslaved Africans to America. Importing slaves was made illegal in 1808, but in March of 1860, Alabama landowner Timothy Meaher made a plan to smuggle in more slaves. Four months later, the schooner *Clotilda* brought 103 slaves to Mobile Bay. The crew burned the ship to hide the evidence, but a century and a half later, archaeologists located what remains. Now, the descendents of those slaves hope to memorialize the site as a place to reflect on slavery's role in American history.

African captives survived a brutal passage in *Clotilda*'s cramped hold. Some 150 years later, *Clotilda*'s design and dimensions helped archaeologists identify the wreck, as shown in this artist's re-creation.

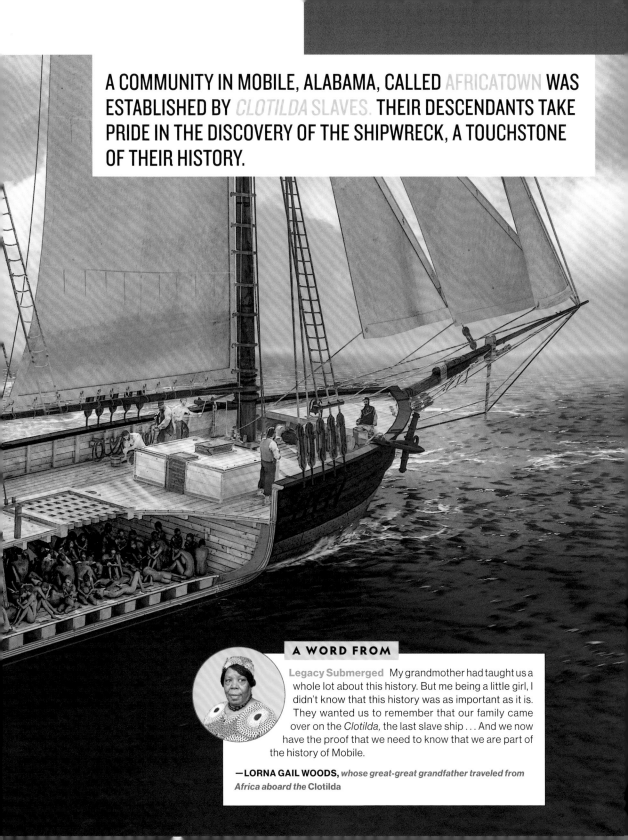

A COMMUNITY IN MOBILE, ALABAMA, CALLED AFRICATOWN WAS ESTABLISHED BY *CLOTILDA* SLAVES. THEIR DESCENDANTS TAKE PRIDE IN THE DISCOVERY OF THE SHIPWRECK, A TOUCHSTONE OF THEIR HISTORY.

A WORD FROM

Legacy Submerged My grandmother had taught us a whole lot about this history. But me being a little girl, I didn't know that this history was as important as it is. They wanted us to remember that our family came over on the *Clotilda,* the last slave ship . . . And we now have the proof that we need to know that we are part of the history of Mobile.

—LORNA GAIL WOODS, *whose great-great grandfather traveled from Africa aboard the* **Clotilda**

AMELIA EARHART
AVIATOR

DISAPPEARED BUT NOT FORGOTTEN

At the age of 25 Amelia Earhart had flown the highest any woman had: 14,000 feet (4,267 m). She was the first woman to fly across the Atlantic (as a passenger) and followed that record soon after by piloting a plane solo across the Atlantic, then across the United States, and then from California to Hawaii. By 1937, she had set seven solo women's aviation records. She was a celebrity, known and loved by all.

Earhart stands in front of her new Lockheed Electra, the plane she and navigator Fred Noonan flew in their attempt to circle the world.

"Women, like men, should try to do the impossible," Earhart said—and in 1937 flying all the way around the world was nigh unto impossible. Wiley Post had done it in 1933, and there were women making other aviation achievements, but as she set out on her journey, Amelia Earhart intended to be the first woman to fly the globe.

Earhart and navigator Fred Noonan took off in her twin-engine Lockheed Electra from Oakland, California. Even with extra fuel tanks, her plane could only fly 20 hours at a time, with a cruising speed of about 200 miles an hour (322 km/h). They crossed North America, skirted South America, transected Africa and Asia, through Indonesia to Australia, and then headed across the Pacific back toward California.

Her last stop was in Papua New Guinea, from which she departed on July 2, 43 days into the journey. Her last radio transmission cited a position that put her near two tiny Pacific islands, Howland and Nikumaroro. Then she disappeared.

THE SEARCH CONTINUES

Theories abound, search missions multiply, all in the quest for what happened. In 2019, ocean explorer Robert Ballard took his research vessel E/V *Nautilus* to Nikumaroro, now part of the Micronesian nation of Kiribati, and spent weeks combing the nearby ocean floor with high-tech remotely operated submarines. But no luck. "Now I know where she isn't," said Ballard, who hopes to continue the search in years to come. Amelia Earhart's fate remains a mystery.

Earhart, circa 1925—already a record-holding aviator

KEY DATES

Amelia Earhart's
ACHIEVEMENTS

1921
Bought first plane, *The Canary*

1922
Set women's altitude record, flying to 14,000 feet (4,267 m)

1928
First woman to fly across the Atlantic

1930
Set several women's flight speed records

1932
First woman to fly solo across the Atlantic and across North America

1935
First person to fly solo nonstop Mexico City to Newark, NJ

UNITED STATES
TIME LINE

1500 to 1650	1650 to 1770	1770 to 1800	1800 to 1850

1587
English colonists settle briefly at Roanoke Island.

1607
Capt. John Smith founds the Jamestown settlement on behalf of England.

1619
The Virginia Assembly, the oldest governing body in the modern United States, first meets.

1620
The *Mayflower* lands in modern-day Massachusetts.

1625–1643
The colonies of New Hampshire, Massachusetts, Rhode Island, Connecticut, Maryland, and Delaware are established.

1636
Harvard College is founded.

1692
The Salem witch trials occur in Massachusetts.

1720s–1740s
A religious revival, the Great Awakening, sweeps through the British colonies.

1754
The French and Indian War breaks out between Britain and France.

1763
Chief Pontiac leads a Native American rebellion against British settlers near Detroit.

1763–1767
Surveyors Charles Mason and Jeremiah Dixon lay out the boundary between Pennsylvania, Maryland, and Delaware.

1775
Fighting at Lexington and Concord begins the American Revolution; the next year, the Continental Congress adopts the Declaration of Independence.

1781
At the Battle of Yorktown, American and French forces defeat the British Army.

1783
By the Treaty of Paris, Britain accepts American independence.

1789
George Washington becomes the first president of the United States of America.

1800
Washington, D.C., becomes the seat of the U.S. government.

1803
Napoleon sells the lands between the Mississippi River and the Rocky Mountains to the U.S. for $15 million in the Louisiana Purchase.

1812–1814
The War of 1812 is fought between the U.S. and the British; British forces burn down the White House.

1825
The Erie Canal opens, allowing boats to travel from the Great Lakes to the Atlantic.

1830s
The Cherokee, Chickasaw, Choctaw, Creek, and Seminole tribes are forced west on the Trail of Tears.

1841
The first wagon trains to cross the Rocky Mountains arrive in California.

| 1850 to 1900 | 1900 to 1940 | 1940 to 1970 | 1970 to PRESENT |

1850 to 1900

1850
Harriet Tubman returns to Maryland after escaping from slavery.

1857
The Dred Scott decision makes the Missouri Compromise unconstitutional, increasing tension over slavery between the North and the South.

1861
The American Civil War begins when Confederates fire on Fort Sumter.

1863
President Abraham Lincoln signs the Emancipation Proclamation, freeing slaves in the Confederate states.

1865
Robert E. Lee surrenders at Appomattox Court House, ending the Civil War.

1900 to 1940

1903
Orville and Wilbur Wright fly a powered airplane at Kitty Hawk, North Carolina.

1908
Teddy Roosevelt undertakes the first inventories of public lands and their resources in the United States.

1917
The U.S. enters World War I.

1920
The 19th Amendment gives women the right to vote.

1929
The Wall Street stock market crash signals the beginning of the Great Depression.

1940 to 1970

1941
Japanese planes bomb the American base at Pearl Harbor; the following day the U.S. joins the Allies in World War II.

1945
The U.S. drops atomic bombs on Hiroshima and Nagasaki; World War II ends soon after.

1963
President John F. Kennedy is assassinated in Dallas, Texas.

1968
Martin Luther King, Jr., is assassinated in Memphis, Tennessee.

1969
Apollo 11 lands the first men on the moon.

1970 to PRESENT

1973
The U.S. and South Vietnam sign a cease-fire agreement with North Vietnam and the last U.S. troops are withdrawn.

1974
The Watergate scandal forces Richard Nixon to resign.

2001
Planes hijacked by al Qaeda terrorists crash into the World Trade Center and Pentagon, sparking the current U.S. conflict in the Middle East.

2008
Barack Obama is the first African American to be elected president of the United States.

WOMAN SUFFRAGE

FIGHTING FOR GENDER EQUALITY IN POLITICS

The Sewall-Belmont House, now a National Park Service property

THE HOUSE THAT SUFFRAGE BUILT

In 1929, suffragist Alice Paul moved the National Woman's Party (NWP) to a brick house on Constitution Avenue in Washington, D.C. Its members were political participants and needed—in the words of suffragist Elsie Hill—"a vantage point from which they may keep Congress under perpetual observation." The house, located near Capitol Hill, was just that place.

The women of the NWP campaigned for female candidates and legislation that addressed issues like property rights, divorce, and the ability for women to keep their birth name after marriage. Alice Paul herself drafted the Equal Rights Amendment, which activists have been trying to pass since 1923.

THE EQUALITY STATE

Leading the way, Wyoming gave women the right to vote on December 10, 1869. A few months before, Congress had proposed the 15th Amendment (ratified in 1870), giving all men the right to vote. The Wyoming Territory's woman suffrage bill—granting women the rights to vote, sit on juries, and run for political office—was introduced in the legislature's first session and quickly signed by the governor, hoping to increase the territory's population. "We now expect at once quite an immigration of ladies to Wyoming," wrote the *Cheyenne Leader,* a local newspaper. This is how Wyoming earned its nickname—the Equality State—and why the state seal includes a banner bearing the words "Equal Rights."

Women voting in 1869

Suffragettes campaign in New Jersey, 1915.

THINK GLOBALLY, VOTE LOCALLY

Around the world, women have won suffrage only because they demanded it. The first country to grant the full right to vote was New Zealand, in 1893. In 2015, Saudi Arabia, the last holdout, finally enfranchised women—though they still cannot move about freely.

Challenges to participating in the political process remain. In many countries, women lack access to the institutions, experiences, and resources needed to hold office. Even more frequently, they face discrimination and intimidation. To address this problem, the United Nations set goals for women's inclusion. It also offers training to candidates and runs campaigns urging voters to elect qualified women.

As of 2017, the head of government or head of state was a woman in 15 countries, and Bolivia and Rwanda were the only countries in which at least 50 percent of the members of parliament were women. The worldwide average was just 23 percent.

PHOENIX
AT GROUND ZERO

REBUILDING & REDEDICATION TWO DECADES AFTER 9/11

Twenty years after the worst attack on American soil, New York's World Trade Center has risen from the ashes. At its center is the National September 11 Memorial & Museum, with eternal waterfalls where the twin towers stood and thought-provoking exhibits underground, deep as bedrock. Sleek skyscrapers have shot up all around, and the dramatic oculus, designed by architect Santiago Calatrava, tops a transportation hub serving trains and subways. In 2019, the Memorial Glade opened, dedicated to all who have suffered illness or death as a result of hazards or toxins during recovery operations.

Every September 11, the glorious Tribute in Light, visible for miles around, shines up from New York's World Trade Center.

In the Collection of the
MUSEUM

■ LADY LIBERTY
Fiberglass replica of the Statue of Liberty, 10 feet (3 m) tall, left anonymously at Manhattan firehouse, soon affixed with cards, notes, rosary beads, and other memorial items

■ WEDDING RING
A gold band with inset diamonds belonging to Robert Joseph Gschaar, working as an insurance underwriter on the 92nd floor of the South Tower on 9/11

■ THE LAST COLUMN
Steel column, 36 feet (12 m) tall and weighing 58 tons (53 t), the last structural piece to be removed; by then it was covered with messages, memorials, stickers, and photographs.

■ FIRE TRUCK
Parked nearby on 9/11, a demolished fire truck: cab sheared off, ladder crushed, body melted and deformed

■ WARNER BROS. SIGN
Damaged but legible, a sign from a store inside the World Trade Center concourse with the Warner Bros. cartoon phrase: "That's all, Folks"

■ BLACK PURSE
Warped and discolored but still containing lipstick and glasses, a purse belonging to Patricia Mary Fagan, executive at Aon Corporation, who worked on the 98th floor of the South Tower

■ SURVIVOR'S SHOES
Scuffed and dust-coated high heels worn by Joanne Capestro as she evacuated from the 87th floor of the North Tower; she donated them and the clothing she was wearing to the museum.

■ WALKIE-TALKIE
Handheld radio used by Fire Chief Peter James Ganci, Jr., as he directed FDNY response; Ganci was last seen near the North Tower after ordering others to evacuate.

■ AFGHAN TAPESTRY
Wall hanging showing the Manhattan skyline, figures in black, and doves surrounding the Afghan flag, hand embroidered and given as a gift of peace from the people of Afghanistan

THE 9/11 MEMORIAL MUSEUM DISPLAYS MORE THAN 900 PERSONAL AND MONUMENTAL OBJECTS AND HAS A COLLECTION OF MORE THAN 60,000 ARTIFACTS, FROM DAMAGED RESCUE VEHICLES TO HATS, KEYS, AND ID CARDS FOUND IN THE RUBBLE.

STARS & STRIPES
THROUGH THE CENTURIES

NO COUNTRY HAS CHANGED ITS FLAG AS MUCH AS THE UNITED STATES

The Continental Colors (below, top left) represented the colonies during the early years of the American Revolution. Its British Union Jack, which signified loyalty to the crown, was replaced on June 14, 1777, by a flag designed by New Jersey Congressman Francis Hopkinson to include 13 stars for the 13 colonies, "representing a new constellation," as was said at the time. In 1817, Congressman Peter Wendover of New York wrote the current flag law, which retains 13 stripes permanently but adds stars as new states join the union. The original "Star-Spangled Banner," which inspired Francis Scott Key during the War of 1812 to write what became our national anthem, is elegantly preserved at the Smithsonian's National Museum of American History in Washington, D.C.

1/1/1776–6/14/1777

6/15/1777–4/30/1795

5/1/1795–7/3/1818

7/4/1818–7/3/1819

7/4/1822–7/3/1836

7/4/1836–7/3/1837

7/4/1837–7/3/1845

7/4/1847–7/3/1848

7/4/1848–7/3/1851

7/4/1851–7/3/1858

7/4/1858–7/3/1859

7/4/1859–7/3/1861

7/4/1865–7/3/1867

7/4/1867–7/3/1877

7/4/1877–7/3/1890

7/4/1890–7/3/1891

7/4/1891–7/3/1896

7/4/1896–7/3/1908

7/4/1908–7/3/1912

7/4/1912–7/3/1959

7/4/1959–7/3/1960

FUTURE (51-STAR)?

> **" THIS FLAG, WHICH WE HONOR AND UNDER WHICH WE SERVE, IS THE EMBLEM OF OUR UNITY, OUR POWER, OUR THOUGHT AND PURPOSE AS A NATION. IT HAS NO OTHER CHARACTER THAN THAT WHICH WE GIVE IT FROM GENERATION TO GENERATION."**
>
> **—PRESIDENT WOODROW WILSON, 1917**

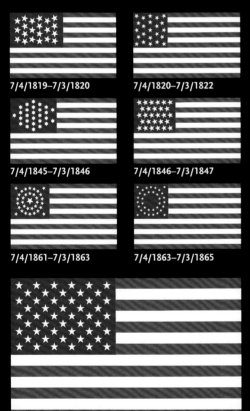

7/4/1819–7/3/1820

7/4/1820–7/3/1822

7/4/1845–7/3/1846

7/4/1846–7/3/1847

7/4/1861–7/3/1863

7/4/1863–7/3/1865

7/4/1960–PRESENT

KEY DATES

The Evolution of the U.S. FLAG

1776
The Grand Union Flag is replaced by the first true American flag, said to have been sewn by Betsy Ross.

1779
According to tradition, with stars now in rows, the Serapis flag or John Paul Jones flag flew through the War of 1812.

1821
Missouri joined the Union as the 24th state, and the 24-star flag lasted for 14 years and through three presidencies.

1837
Many versions of a Great Star Flag, with a star made of stars, flew in the 19th century.

1847
When Iowa joined the United States, it was time to design a 29-star flag. It lasted only one year.

1863
During the Civil War, the 34 stars were arranged in several designs: rows, circles, stars, even a flower.

1876
A centennial flag arranged 80 stars to spell out the numerals 1776 and 1876.

1892
The Pledge of Allegiance, written by Francis Bellamy, first appears in a magazine called *The Youth's Companion*.

1912
President Howard Taft signs an executive order specifying proportions and design of the U.S. flag.

1960
The addition of Alaska and Hawaii gives the U.S. flag the design we know today, with 50 stars for 50 states and 13 stripes for the 13 original colonies.

FLAGS OF THE
UNITED STATES

ALABAMA
Became a state in 1819
A simple design, crimson cross
on a field of white; until 1987 it could
be either square or rectangular.

ALASKA
Became a state in 1959
Against the blue of sea and sky,
the Big Dipper and Polaris,
signifying Alaska's northernmost position;
designed by a 13-year-old Alaskan.

ARIZONA
Became a state in 1912
A copper star, signifying Arizona's copper
industry, on a blue field in the face of
a setting sun with 13 rays
for the original colonies.

ARKANSAS
Became a state in 1836
Diamond signifies its status
as the sole diamond-producing state;
ring of 25 stars since it was
the 25th state to join the union.

CALIFORNIA
Became a state in 1850
Grizzly bear, also the state animal,
on red and white for bravery and purity;
first flown by settlers resisting
Mexican rule in 1846.

COLORADO
Became a state in 1876
White for snow-covered mountains, gold
for sunshine, red for red soil,
blue for clear blue skies,
and a C for the state's name.

CONNECTICUT
Became a state in 1788
Three fruiting grapevines and
the state motto, "*Qui transtulit sustinet*
—He who transplanted still sustains."

DELAWARE
Became a state in 1787
Coat of arms with a ship, farmer,
militiaman, and ox; below, the date
when Delaware ratified the Constitution
and became the first state.

FLORIDA
Became a state in 1845
Red cross on white, in the center
the state seal: Seminole woman,
palmetto pine, and steamboat
in nearby water.

GEORGIA
Became a state in 1788
Thick red and white stripes,
a blue square on which 13 stars
encircle the state seal; three pillars
represent three branches of government.

HAWAII
Became a state in 1959
Eight horizontal stripes representing
the eight major islands; a Union Jack
in the upper left, reflecting past
British rule.

IDAHO
Became a state in 1890
A robed woman represents liberty
and justice; a miner holds a pick
and shovel; wheat sheaves and cornucopia
represent plentiful harvests.

ILLINOIS
Became a state in 1818
State seal centered on white
udes bald eagle holding banner
ith motto, "State Sovereignty,
National Union."

INDIANA
Became a state in 1816
Torch of enlightenment circled
by stars: 13 for the first states,
five for the next, and a large one
for Indiana, 19th state.

IOWA
Became a state in 1846
An eagle flies amid red, white
and blue, carrying a banner:
"Our liberties we prize and
our rights we will maintain."

KANSAS
Became a state in 1861
sunflower atop the state seal,
scenes of farming, a wagon train,
e Americans, buffalo, steamboat,
and the rising sun.

KENTUCKY
Became a state in 1792
A pioneer and a statesman
shake hands, surrounded
by the motto "United we stand,
divided we fall."

LOUISIANA
Became a state in 1812
White pelican nurtures her
nestling young with her own blo
beneath them, the motto
"Union Justice Confidence."

MAINE
Became a state in 1820
rmer and sailor flank a crest
th an evergreen and a moose;
e, the North Star atop the motto
"*Dirigo*—I lead."

MARYLAND
Became a state in 1788
Checkerboard of two family arms:
Calvert, state founders, and Crossland,
mother of George Calvert,
the first Lord Baltimore.

MASSACHUSETTS
Became a state in 1788
Native American holds bow and
arrow pointing down, symbolizing p
star at his shoulder means this w
one of the first 13 states.

MICHIGAN
Became a state in 1837
se, elk, and bald eagle surround
st with explorer at water's edge,
un rising, topped with word
"*Tuebor*—I will defend."

MINNESOTA
Became a state in 1858
Native American and farmer,
tree stump for timber industry,
waterfall for wilderness.
"*L'Etoile du Nord*—the North Star State."

MISSISSIPPI
Became a state in 1817
In upper left, square canton
containing 13 stars for 13 colonies
three broad stripes in red,
white, and blue.

MISSOURI
Became a state in 1821
...ars circle grizzlies clasping seal
...American eagle, crescent moon,
...and grizzly within; above,
...other 24 stars, since 24th state.

MONTANA
Became a state in 1889
Mountains, cliffs, trees, and river
represent the landscape; tools represent
farming and mining, as does motto:
"*Oro y plata*—gold and silver."

NEBRASKA
Became a state in 1867
On blue, state seal with
blacksmith in foreground, steam...
and train in background,
farm and homestead in betwee...

NEVADA
Became a state in 1864
...ht blue and in corner, silver star,
...of sagebrush, with banner reading
...attle Born," since state entered
union during Civil War.

NEW HAMPSHIRE
Became a state in 1788
On blue field, seal portraying frigate
Raleigh, one of the first American
Revolutionary warships,
built in Portsmouth.

NEW JERSEY
Became a state in 1787
On a buff background, seal inclu...
plows for agriculture, helme...
for courage, and figures of Lib...
and Ceres, harvest goddess...

NEW MEXICO
Became a state in 1912
Red symbol for the sun,
sacred to the Zia Indians,
...n a bright yellow background.

NEW YORK
Became a state in 1788
On blue, the seal portrays ships
of commerce flanked by the figures
of Liberty and Justice. Below,
the motto "*Excelsior*—ever upward."

NORTH CAROLINA
Became a state in 1789
Broad stripes—top red, bottom w...
alongside a blue bar with "N...
a star, and two key dates a...
the colony declared independe...

NORTH DAKOTA
Became a state in 1889
...ald eagle, wings spread, holds
...ve branch and arrows in its talons;
...stars for 13 colonies spread
out into sun rays.

OHIO
Became a state in 1803
Swallowtail burgee with
red and white stripes, blue triangle
with 17 stars, since the 17th state
to join the Union.

OKLAHOMA
Became a state in 1907
An Osage warrior's rawhi...
shield hung with eagle feath...
across which sit an olive bra...
and a peace pipe.

OREGON
Became a state in 1859
...Blue flag with yellow insignia.
...On front, state seal including
...on train, ships, and setting sun.
...back, the state animal: a beaver.

PENNSYLVANIA
Became a state in 1787
An eagle and two horses surround
a crest with a ship, a plow, and wheat
sheaves; below, the motto "Virtue Liberty
and Independence."

RHODE ISLAND
Became a state in 1790
White flag bearing a gold...
anchor, circled by 13 gold s...
and beneath it a blue ban...
with the simple motto "Ho...

SOUTH CAROLINA
Became a state in 1788
...escent, from local Revolutionary
War uniforms, and a palmetto
...ree—white designs against
deep blue.

SOUTH DAKOTA
Became a state in 1889
Farmer, livestock, factory,
and steamboat on the state seal,
circled by yellow sun rays
on a field of bright blue.

TENNESSEE
Became a state in 1796
A circle containing three white s...
representing East, Middle,
and West, all against red,
with blue and white edge.

TEXAS
Became a state in 1845
The famous "Lone Star"
...hite against a blue background
...ith broad horizontal panels
of white and red.

UTAH
Became a state in 1896
Beehive, symbol of industry,
surrounded by U.S. flags and a spread eagle.
Two dates: 1847, Mormons arrived,
and 1896, statehood.

VERMONT
Became a state in 1791
A field with sheaves, pine,
and cow stretches back to mount...
pine boughs on either side,
antlered buck atop.

VIRGINIA
Became a state in 1788
...nale Virtus (Virtue) stands over
...fallen man, his crown toppled;
...n, the motto "Sic semper tyrannis—
Thus always to tyrants."

WASHINGTON
Became a state in 1889
Portrait of George Washington
circled by yellow on a field of green—
the only U.S. flag with a
historical figure on it.

WEST VIRGINIA
Became a state in 1863
A farmer and a miner lean aga...
a rock inscribed with the dat...
of gaining statehood;
rhododendrons drape the sea...

WISCONSIN
Became a state in 1848
Against a bright blue background,
sailor and miner dominate the state seal,
topped by a badger
and the motto "Forward."

WYOMING
Became a state in 1890
State seal in blue against
the silhouette of a bison in white,
background blue with red,
and white borders top and bottom.

> " I SALUTE THE FLAG OF THE STATE OF
> NEW MEXICO, THE ZIA SYMBOL OF PERFECT
> FRIENDSHIP AMONG UNITED CULTURES."

—OFFICIAL PLEDGE TO NEW MEXICO'S FLAG

TERRITORIES OF THE UNITED STATE

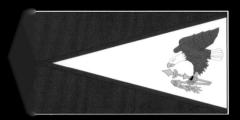

AMERICAN SAMOA
Became a U.S. territory in 1900
Blue with red-edged white triangle;
bald eagle gripping native symbols of authority:
war club and coconut fiber whisk.

GUAM
Became a U.S. territory in 1898
Dark blue flag with red border; central emblem
shaped like native sling stone, encloses palm tr
outrigger canoe, and beach.

PUERTO RICO
Became a U.S. territory in 1898
Five bands of red and white; triangle of blue,
for sky and waters, with central white star,
which symbolizes Puerto Rico.

NORTHERN MARIANA ISLANDS
Became a U.S. territory in 1976
Blue flag containing gray foundation stones,
white star, and floral head wreath
representing native Chamorro culture.

TEREST IN PACIFIC ISLANDS
BACK TO THE 1856 GUANO
OS ACT, BY WHICH CONGRESS
ED RIGHTS TO UNINHABITED
OS IN ORDER TO MINE GUANO—
ROPPINGS—FOR GUNPOWDER
RTILIZER.

U.S. VIRGIN ISLANDS
Became a U.S. territory in 1917
On field of white, yellow eagle holds olive
branch and arrows; modified U.S. coat of arms
in center, initials "V" and "I" on either side.

NOT QUITE STATES

BUT STILL PART OF THE U.S.

The U.S. Constitution gives Congress the power to incorporate new federal territories, organize them, and admit them as new states. The most recent territories to become states were Alaska and Hawaii, in 1959. Present-day U.S. territories range from uninhabited specks in the Pacific Ocean to the organized Caribbean island of Puerto Rico. Some of the small islands in the Pacific were once military bases, but many now function as wildlife refuges. American Samoa, Puerto Rico, and the Northern Mariana Islands all possess their own constitutions. The people living in these territories are U.S. citizens, but they are not allowed to vote in presidential elections.

DISTRICT OF COLUMBIA

NATION'S CAPITAL

"End Taxation Without Representation" reads the license plates of those who live in the District of Columbia, created in 1790 as a federal district for the new nation's capital city. Residents of the District have voted in presidential elections since 1964, but they do not have any representatives in Congress. Since the 1970s, many have been pushing for D.C. statehood.

FURTHER

SILENT SPACE

Called a "work of human creative genius" by UNESCO in designating it a World Heritage site, Germany's Cologne Cathedral has literally stood the test of time. Begun in 1248 to house relics representing the Three Kings, patron saints of the city, not until 1880 was the final stone laid, following plans from the 13th century. Its two towers withstood World War II bombings. To this day, ancient arches and light filtering through brilliant stained-glass windows invite contemplation for believers and non-believers alike.

In a clever illusion, artist Berndnaut Smilde created a cloud that hovers momentarily inside Cologne Cathedral.

> **" SPIRITUAL SILENCE IS AVAILABLE TO EVERYBODY."**
>
> **—J. BRENT BILL,** AUTHOR & QUAKER MINISTER

OUR
WORLD

WORLD VIEWS | CONTINENTS & OCEANS

The view from space only intensifies the turquoise of the Bahamas' waters.

QUIZ MASTER

Mapping Facts Geography is a key to understanding the world, past, present, and future. Each map holds rich details, each answer leads to more questions. Start here on your journey to knowing more about our world.

—**SUSAN TYLER HITCHCOCK,** *Nat Geo Quizmaster*

NAME THE MOST DENSELY POPULATED COUNTRY IN THE WESTERN HEMISPHERE.

p332

P357

SALAS Y GÓMEZ LIES CLOSE TO WHAT OTHER PACIFIC ISLAND AND POPULAR TOURIST DESTINATION?

WHICH TWO COUNTRIES HAVE THE MOST DEPENDENCIES OR TERRITORIES?

p373

DO THE ISLANDS MAKING UP INDONESIA NUMBER IN THE DOZENS, HUNDREDS, OR THOUSANDS?

p331

THE NARWHAL LIVES IN ONLY ONE OF EARTH'S OCEANS—WHICH ONE?

p361

WHAT IS THE LARGEST CITY IN AFRICA?

p346

AS OF 2018, HOW MANY PEOPLE IN THE WORLD WERE URBAN DWELLERS: 40%, 55%, OR 66%?

p379

WHAT COUNTRY IS HOME TO THE **GLOBAL SEED BANK:** DENMARK, AUSTRIA, OR NORWAY?

p342

WHAT COUNTRY WAS THE **FIRST** IN THE **WORLD** TO GIVE **WOMEN** THE VOTE?

p333

MYANMAR'S GOLDEN ROCK **IS A PILGRIMAGE SITE** REVERED BY PRACTITIONERS OF WHICH WORLD RELIGION?

p344

WHAT OTHER **PACIFIC ISLAND** WAS BOMBED BY **THE JAPANESE** JUST HOURS AFTER **PEARL HARBOR?**

p348

CENTRAL AMERICA HAS ONLY ONE SUBWAY SYSTEM. IN WHAT COUNTRY **IS IT FOUND?**

p338

WHICH OCEAN CONTAINS THE WORLD'S **LONGEST** UNDERWATER **CABLE?**

p358

NAME THE MEDITERRANEAN ISLAND, NOW AN INDEPENDENT **REPUBLIC,** THAT HAS BEEN RULED BY SEVEN DIFFERENT ENTITIES **OVER THE CENTURIES.**

p342

OUR PHYSICAL
WORLD

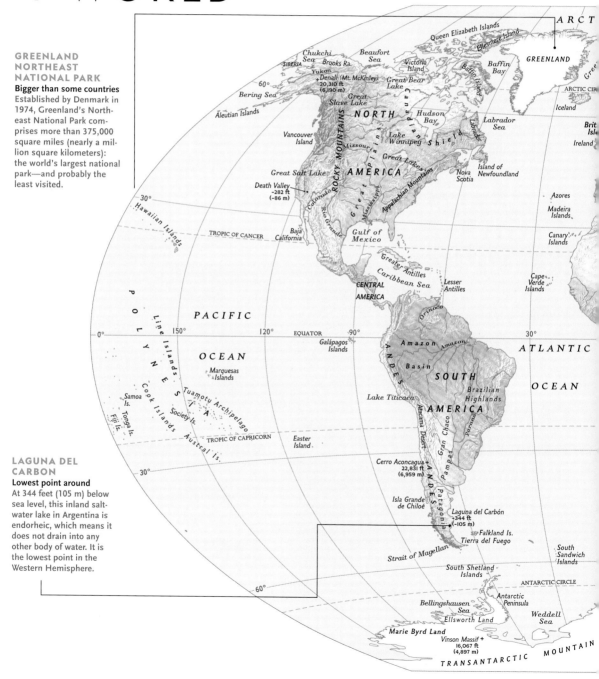

GREENLAND NORTHEAST NATIONAL PARK

Bigger than some countries
Established by Denmark in 1974, Greenland's Northeast National Park comprises more than 375,000 square miles (nearly a million square kilometers): the world's largest national park—and probably the least visited.

LAGUNA DEL CARBON

Lowest point around
At 344 feet (105 m) below sea level, this inland saltwater lake in Argentina is endorheic, which means it does not drain into any other body of water. It is the lowest point in the Western Hemisphere.

ARCT

Queen Elizabeth Islands
Ellesmere Island
Chukchi Sea
Beaufort Sea
GREENLAND
SIBERIA Brooks Ra.
Yukon
Victoria Island
Baffin Bay
Gree
Denali (Mt. McKinley)
20,310 ft
(6,190 m)
Great Bear Lake
ARCTIC CIR
60°
Bering Sea
Great Slave Lake
Baffin Island
Iceland
Aleutian Islands
NORTH
Hudson Bay
Labrador Sea
Brit
Isl
Vancouver Island
Lake Winnipeg
Labrador
Ireland
ROCKY MOUNTAINS
Canadian Shield
AMERICA
Great Lakes
Island of Newfoundland
Great Salt Lake
Missouri
Nova Scotia
Death Valley
-282 ft
(-86 m)
Great Plains
Appalachian Mountains
Azores
30°
Colorado
Mississippi
Madeira Islands
Hawaiian Islands
Rio Grande
TROPIC OF CANCER
Baja California
Gulf of Mexico
Canary Islands
Greater Antilles
Caribbean Sea
Lesser Antilles
Cape Verde Islands
CENTRAL AMERICA
Orinoco
P
O
L
Y
N
E
S
I
A
PACIFIC
Amazon
Amazon
ATLANTIC
150°
120°
EQUATOR
90°
Galápagos Islands
Basin
Line Islands
OCEAN
SOUTH
OCEAN
Marquesas Islands
Brazilian Highlands
Samoa Is.
Tuamotu Archipelago
ANDES
Lake Titicaca
AMERICA
Cook Islands
Society Is.
Fiji Is.
Tonga Is.
Austral Is.
TROPIC OF CAPRICORN
Easter Island
Atacama Desert
Gran Chaco
Paraná
Cerro Aconcagua
22,831 ft
(6,959 m)
Pampas
30°
Isla Grande de Chiloé
Patagonia
Laguna del Carbón
-344 ft
(-105 m)
Falkland Is.
Tierra del Fuego
South Sandwich Islands
Strait of Magellan
60°
South Shetland Islands
ANTARCTIC CIRCLE
Bellingshausen Sea
Antarctic Peninsula
Weddell Sea
Ellsworth Land
Marie Byrd Land
Vinson Massif
16,067 ft
(4,897 m)
MOUNTAIN
TRANSANTARCTIC

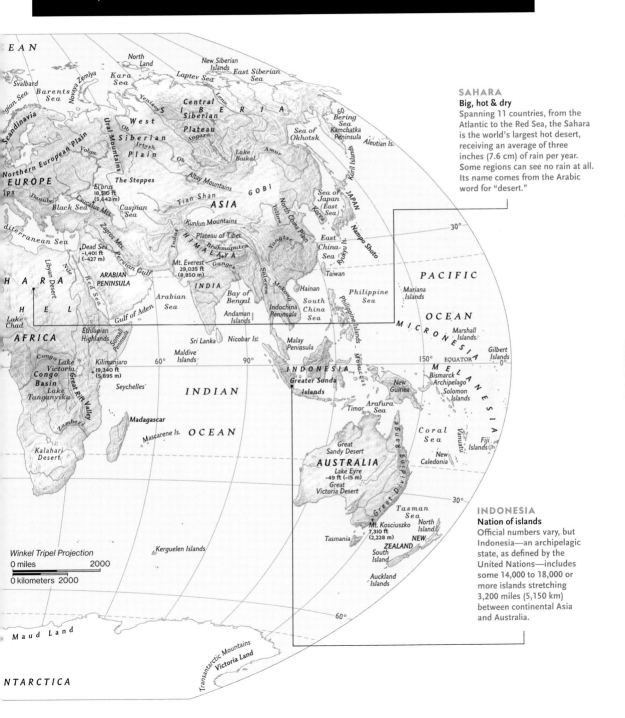

SAHARA
Big, hot & dry

Spanning 11 countries, from the Atlantic to the Red Sea, the Sahara is the world's largest hot desert, receiving an average of three inches (7.6 cm) of rain per year. Some regions can see no rain at all. Its name comes from the Arabic word for "desert."

INDONESIA
Nation of islands

Official numbers vary, but Indonesia—an archipelagic state, as defined by the United Nations—includes some 14,000 to 18,000 or more islands stretching 3,200 miles (5,150 km) between continental Asia and Australia.

Winkel Tripel Projection

0 miles 2000

0 kilometers 2000

OUR POLITICAL
WORLD

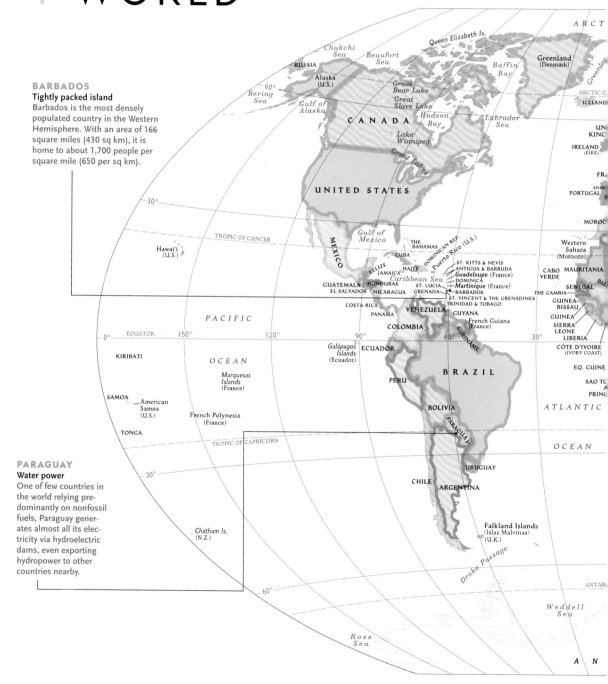

BARBADOS

Tightly packed island

Barbados is the most densely populated country in the Western Hemisphere. With an area of 166 square miles (430 sq km), it is home to about 1,700 people per square mile (650 per sq km).

PARAGUAY

Water power

One of few countries in the world relying predominantly on nonfossil fuels, Paraguay generates almost all its electricity via hydroelectric dams, even exporting hydropower to other countries nearby.

Map labels:

ARCT

Queen Elizabeth Is.

Chukchi Sea

Beaufort Sea

RUSSIA

Baffin Bay

Greenland (Denmark)

Alaska (U.S.)

Bering Sea

Great Bear Lake

ARCTIC C

ICELAND

Gulf of Alaska

Great Slave Lake

CANADA

Hudson Bay

Labrador Sea

UN
KINC

Lake Winnipeg

IRELAND (ÉIRE)

Great Lakes

FR

UNITED STATES

ANDC
PORTUGAL

30°

MOROC

TROPIC OF CANCER

Gulf of Mexico

THE BAHAMAS

DOMINICAN REP.

Puerto Rico (U.S.)

Western Sahara (Morocco)

Hawai'i (U.S.)

MEXICO

CUBA

ST. KITTS & NEVIS
ANTIGUA & BARBUDA
Guadeloupe (France)
DOMINICA
Martinique (France)
BARBADOS

CABO VERDE

MAURITANIA

BU

BELIZE
JAMAICA
HAITI
Caribbean Sea
ST. LUCIA

SENEGAL

GUATEMALA
EL SALVADOR
HONDURAS
NICARAGUA

GRENADA
ST. VINCENT & THE GRENADINES
TRINIDAD & TOBAGO

THE GAMBIA

GUINEA-
BISSAU

COSTA RICA
PANAMA

VENEZUELA

GUYANA

GUINEA

PACIFIC

COLOMBIA

French Guiana (France)

SIERRA
LEONE
LIBERIA

EQUATOR

150°

120°

90°

SURINAME

60°

30°

CÔTE D'IVOIRE
(IVORY COAST)

Galápagos Islands (Ecuador)

ECUADOR

EQ. GUINE

OCEAN

Marquesas Islands (France)

PERU

BRAZIL

SAO TO

PRIN

SAMOA

American Samoa (U.S.)

French Polynesia (France)

BOLIVIA

PARAGUAY

ATLANTIC

TONGA

TROPIC OF CAPRICORN

OCEAN

30°

URUGUAY

Chatham Is. (N.Z.)

CHILE

ARGENTINA

Falkland Islands (Islas Malvinas) (U.K.)

Drake Passage

ANTAR

60°

A N

Weddell Sea

Ross Sea

KIRIBATI

0°

RUSSIA & CHINA
Neighboring nations
Asia, the world's largest continent in both area and population, includes both Russia, the world's largest country, and China, the world's most populous country.

TAIWAN
The People's Republic of China claims Taiwan as its 23rd province. Taiwan's government (Republic of China) maintains that there are two political entities.

NEW ZEALAND
Early suffrage success
In 1893, New Zealand, self-governing and yet still a British colony, became the first country in the world to give women the vote.

Winkel Tripel Projection
0 miles   2000
0 kilometers 2000

BEST OF @NATGEO

TOP PHOTOS OF LANDSCAPES

@enricsala | ENRIC SALA
n Abu Dhabi, the Rub' al Khali (the Empty Quarter) is considered one of the driest places in the world.

@dguttenfelder | DAVID GUTTENFELDER
The sun sets over bustling Tokyo and its sparkling lights,
which reach the foothills of a looming Mount Fiji.

@richardbarnes | RICHARD BARNES
The Vermilion Cliffs National Monument and its geological
features straddle the Arizona and Utah borders.

@michaelchristopherbrown | MICHAEL CHRISTOPHER BR
The Arrigetch Peaks are clusters of rugged granite spires in
the Brooks Range region of northern Alaska.

> # "WILDNESS REMINDS US WHAT IT MEANS TO BE HUMAN, WHAT WE ARE CONNECTED TO RATHER THAN WHAT WE ARE SEPARATE FROM."
>
> **—TERRY TEMPEST WILLIAMS,** AUTHOR & CONSERVATIONIST

@pedromcbride | PETE MCBRIDE
Blue hour falls over Monument Valley, which is overseen by the Navajo Nation, on the Utah-Arizona border.

@franslanting | FRANS LANTING
Hot lava oozes down an erupted volcano, demonstrating one of the complex processes of natural tectonics.

@stephenwilkes | STEPHEN WILKES
A lone tree punctuates an epic Serengeti landscape that spans 12,000 square miles (31,080 sq km) in northern Tanzania.

@dzalcman | DANIELLA ZALCMAN
Water flows out of Havasu Falls on the Havasupai Reservation, which lies at the bottom of the Grand Canyon.

THE CONTINENTS

LANDFORMS CHANGE SHAPE OVER MILLENNIA

With the unceasing movement of Earth's tectonic plates, continents "drift" over geologic time—breaking apart, reassembling, and again fragmenting to repeat the process. Three times during the past billion years, Earth's drifting landmasses have merged to form so-called supercontinents. Rodinia, the earliest known supercontinent, began breaking apart in the late Precambrian, about 750 million years ago (mya).

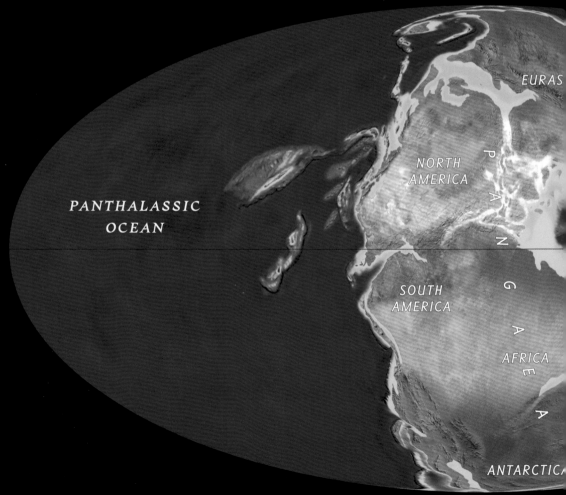

EURAS

NORTH
AMERICA

PANTHALASSIC
OCEAN

P
A
N
G
A
E
A

SOUTH
AMERICA

AFRICA

ANTARCTICA

PANGAEA, 240 MILLION YEARS AGO
Even when most of Earth's landmass was a single continent, named Pangaea, surrounded by a single ocean, the Panthalassic (predecessor to the Pacific), configurations began taking shape that presaged the continents of today. The Tethys Ocean ultimately became the Mediterranean.

DINOSAURS ROAMED POLE TO POLE ON PANGAEA, BUT OVER TIME THE CONTINENTS SPLIT AND DISTINCT DINOSAUR SPECIES EVOLVED SEPARATELY IN DIFFERENT LOCATIONS.

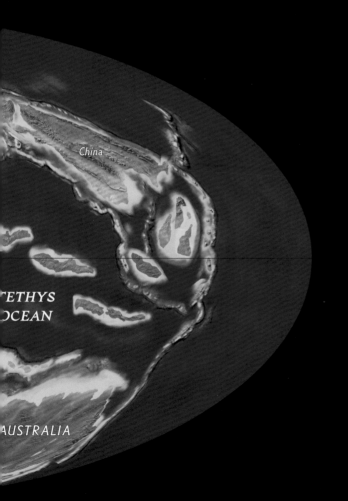

China

TETHYS OCEAN

AUSTRALIA

KEY DATES

Stages in Earth's
EVOLUTION

■ **PRECAMBRIAN TIME (4,500–542 MYA)**
Archaean eon (ca 3,800–2,500 mya)
First life-forms appear on Earth.

Proterozoic eon (2,500–542 mya)
In latter part of this eon, continental fragments join into one: Pannotia.

■ **PHANEROZOIC EON (542 MYA–PRESENT)**
Paleozoic era (542–251 mya)
Includes Cambrian, 500 mya: Multicellular animals leave abundant fossil evidence.

Includes Devonian, 400 mya: Freshwater fish migrate freely; plants colonize land.

Mesozoic era (251–65.5 mya)
Includes Triassic, 240 mya: Geologic catastrophes cause massive extinctions; surviving lizards evolve into dinosaurs.

Cenozoic era (65.5 mya–present)
Includes K-T extinction event, 65 mya: Half the plant and animal species become extinct.

Includes last great ice age, 18,000 ya: North and south are locked in ice; continents as we know them begin to form, further defined by retreating glaciers.

NORTH AMERICA

CITY DWELLERS
One third of all citizens of Greenland live in the city of Nuuk, located on the south corner of the mostly ice-co island. With a population of about 16,000, Nuuk is one the world's smallest capita

FAILED PASSAGE
In 2014 and 2016, marine archaeologists found the sunken wrecks of the H.M.S. *Erebus* and *Terror,* British ships that tried in 1845 to navigate the Northwest Passage, an Arctic route from the Atlantic to the Pacific.

PARADISE LOST
In September 2019, Hurricane Dorian demolished the northernmost islands of the Bahamas: the Abacos, a chain of islands 120 miles (193 km) long, and Grand Bahama, which includes the popular tourist destination of Freeport.

UNDERGROUND CONNECTIONS
The Metro de Panamá, Central America's only subway system, runs north and south through Panama City and costs less than half a U.S. dollar per ride. Opened in 2014, it currently links 14 stations, including its southernmost stop near the Panama Canal.

Greenland (Denmark)

ALASKA
U.S.

C A N A D A

UNITED STATES

MEXICO

THE BAHAMAS

CUBA

HAITI

DOM.REP.

JAMAICA

Puerto Rico (U.S.)

ANTIGUA & BARBUDA

ST. KITTS & NEVIS

DOMINICA

ST. LUCIA

BARBADOS

ST. VINCENT & THE GRENADINES

GRENADA

TRINIDAD & TOBAGO

BELIZE

GUATEMALA

HONDURAS

EL SALVADOR

NICARAGUA

COSTA RICA

PANAMA

New York's Midtown Manhattan illuminated in the twilight

Continental FACTS

TOTAL NUMBER OF COUNTRIES
23

TOTAL AREA
9,449,000 square miles (24,474,000 sq km)

MOST POPULOUS COUNTRY
United States: 329,256,000

LEAST POPULOUS COUNTRY
Saint Kitts and Nevis: 53,000

LARGEST COUNTRY BY AREA
Canada: 3,855,101 square miles (9,984,670 sq km)

SMALLEST COUNTRY BY AREA
Saint Kitts and Nevis: 101 square miles (261 sq km)

HIGHEST ELEVATION
Denali (Mount McKinley),
United States: 20,310 feet (6,190 m)

LOWEST ELEVATION
Death Valley, United States: −282 feet (−86 m)

SOUTH AMERICA

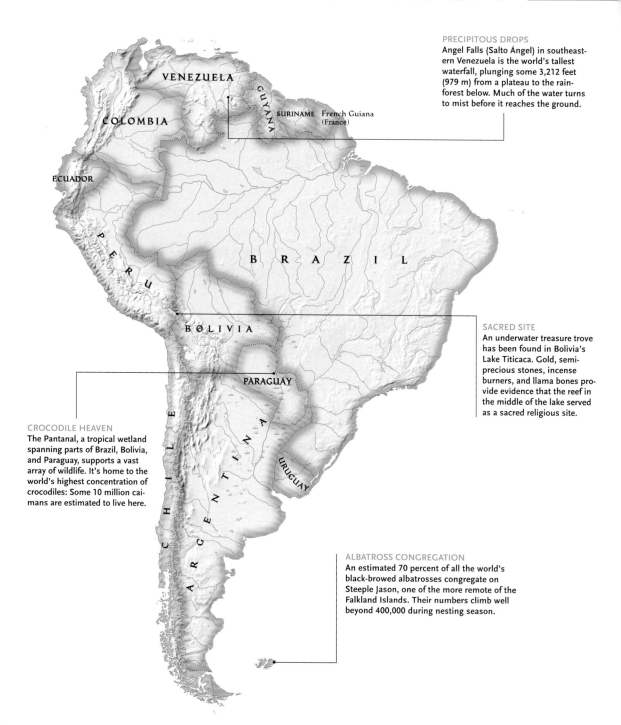

PRECIPITOUS DROPS
Angel Falls (Salto Ángel) in southeastern Venezuela is the world's tallest waterfall, plunging some 3,212 feet (979 m) from a plateau to the rainforest below. Much of the water turns to mist before it reaches the ground.

SACRED SITE
An underwater treasure trove has been found in Bolivia's Lake Titicaca. Gold, semiprecious stones, incense burners, and llama bones provide evidence that the reef in the middle of the lake served as a sacred religious site.

CROCODILE HEAVEN
The Pantanal, a tropical wetland spanning parts of Brazil, Bolivia, and Paraguay, supports a vast array of wildlife. It's home to the world's highest concentration of crocodiles: Some 10 million caimans are estimated to live here.

ALBATROSS CONGREGATION
An estimated 70 percent of all the world's black-browed albatrosses congregate on Steeple Jason, one of the more remote of the Falkland Islands. Their numbers climb well beyond 400,000 during nesting season.

Continental
FACTS

TOTAL NUMBER OF COUNTRIES
12

TOTAL AREA
6,880,000 square miles (17,819,000 sq km)

MOST POPULOUS COUNTRY
Brazil: 208,847,000

LEAST POPULOUS COUNTRY
Suriname: 598,000

LARGEST COUNTRY BY AREA
Brazil: 3,287,596 square miles (8,515,770 sq km)

SMALLEST COUNTRY BY AREA
Suriname: 63,251 square miles (163,820 sq km)

HIGHEST ELEVATION
Cerro Aconcagua, Argentina: 22,834 feet (6,960 m)

LOWEST ELEVATION
Laguna del Carbón, Argentina: −344 feet (−105 m)

Autumn at Fitz Roy Mountain in Patagonia, Argentina

EUROPE

SAVING SEEDS
More than 800,000 seed samples are stored underground in Norway's Svalbard Global Seed Vault, established to protect the genetic diversity of seeds, especially for food crops such as wheat, rice, and barley.

NEOLITHIC TECHNOLOGY
Recent searches of crannogs—human-made islands found in the waterways of Scotland's Outer Hebrides—have brought up Neolithic artifacts, suggesting the deliberate marine constructions date back to the Stone Age.

A FITTING CENTENNIAL
La Sagrada Família, Antoni Gaudí's intricate and monumental Roman Catholic basilica in Barcelona, Spain, has been under construction for more than 130 years. Completion is planned for 2026, a century after the Spanish architect's death.

INTENSE HISTORY
Now an independent republic, Malta has been ruled by Phoenicians, Greeks, Carthaginians, Romans, Byzantines, Arabs, and the Roman Catholic Order of the Knights of St. John. UNESCO describes its capital, Valletta, as "one of the most concentrated historic areas in the world."

ICELAND

Svalbard
(Norway)

NORWAY
SWEDEN
FINLAND
ESTONIA
LATVIA
LITHUANIA
RUSSIA
BELARUS
RUSSIA

(ÉIRE) IRELAND
UNITED KINGDOM
DENMARK

NETH.
BELG.
LUX.
GERMANY
POLAND
UKRAINE
KAZAKHSTAN

CZECHIA
(CZECH REP.)
SLOVAKIA
LIECH
SWITZ.
AUSTRIA
HUNGARY
MOLD.
FRANCE
SLOV.
CROATIA
ROMANIA
CRIMEA
MONACO
SAN MARINO
BOSN. &
HERZG.
SERBIA
PORTUGAL
ANDORRA
ITALY
MONTEN.
KOS.
BULGARIA
SPAIN
VATICAN
CITY
NORTH MACED.
TURKEY
ALBANIA
GREECE
MALTA

Sunset at the village of Oia in Santorini, a Greek Island in the Aegean Sea

Continental FACTS

TOTAL NUMBER OF COUNTRIES
46

TOTAL AREA
3,841,000 square miles (9,947,000 sq km)

MOST POPULOUS COUNTRY
*Russia: 142,123,000

LEAST POPULOUS COUNTRY
Vatican City: 1,000

LARGEST COUNTRY BY AREA
*Russia: 6,601,665 square miles (17,098,242 sq km)

SMALLEST COUNTRY BY AREA
Vatican City: 0.17 square mile (0.44 sq km)

HIGHEST ELEVATION
El'brus, Russia: 18,510 feet (5,642 m)

LOWEST ELEVATION
Caspian Sea: −92 feet (−28 m)

* Area and population figures reflect the total of Asian and European regions.

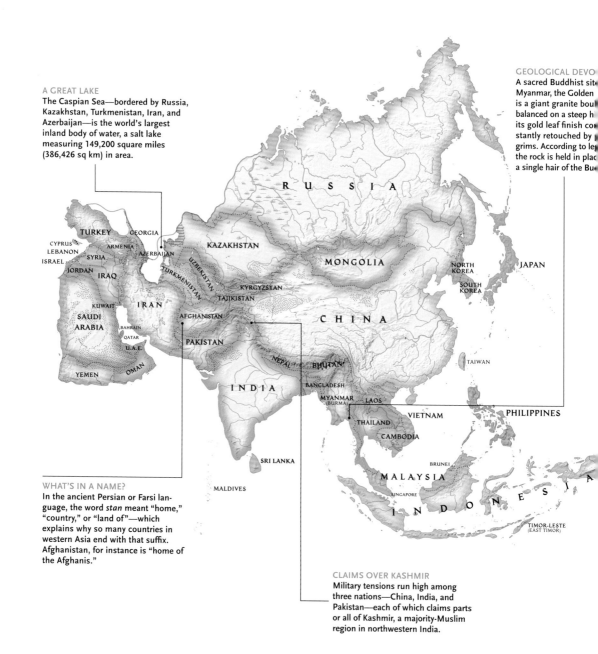

A GREAT LAKE
The Caspian Sea—bordered by Russia, Kazakhstan, Turkmenistan, Iran, and Azerbaijan—is the world's largest inland body of water, a salt lake measuring 149,200 square miles (386,426 sq km) in area.

GEOLOGICAL DEVO
A sacred Buddhist site Myanmar, the Golden is a giant granite bou balanced on a steep h its gold leaf finish co stantly retouched by grims. According to le the rock is held in plac a single hair of the Bu

WHAT'S IN A NAME?
In the ancient Persian or Farsi language, the word *stan* meant "home," "country," or "land of"—which explains why so many countries in western Asia end with that suffix. Afghanistan, for instance is "home of the Afghanis."

CLAIMS OVER KASHMIR
Military tensions run high among three nations—China, India, and Pakistan—each of which claims parts or all of Kashmir, a majority-Muslim region in northwestern India.

RUSSIA

TURKEY
CYPRUS
LEBANON
ISRAEL
GEORGIA
ARMENIA
AZERBAIJAN
SYRIA
JORDAN
IRAQ
KUWAIT
SAUDI
ARABIA
BAHRAIN
QATAR
U.A.E.
YEMEN
OMAN
IRAN
KAZAKHSTAN
UZBEKISTAN
TURKMENISTAN
KYRGYZSTAN
TAJIKISTAN
AFGHANISTAN
PAKISTAN
MONGOLIA
CHINA
NORTH KOREA
SOUTH KOREA
JAPAN
NEPAL
BHUTAN
INDIA
BANGLADESH
MYANMAR (BURMA)
LAOS
VIETNAM
THAILAND
CAMBODIA
TAIWAN
PHILIPPINES
SRI LANKA
MALDIVES
BRUNEI
MALAYSIA
SINGAPORE
INDONESIA
TIMOR-LESTE (EAST TIMOR)

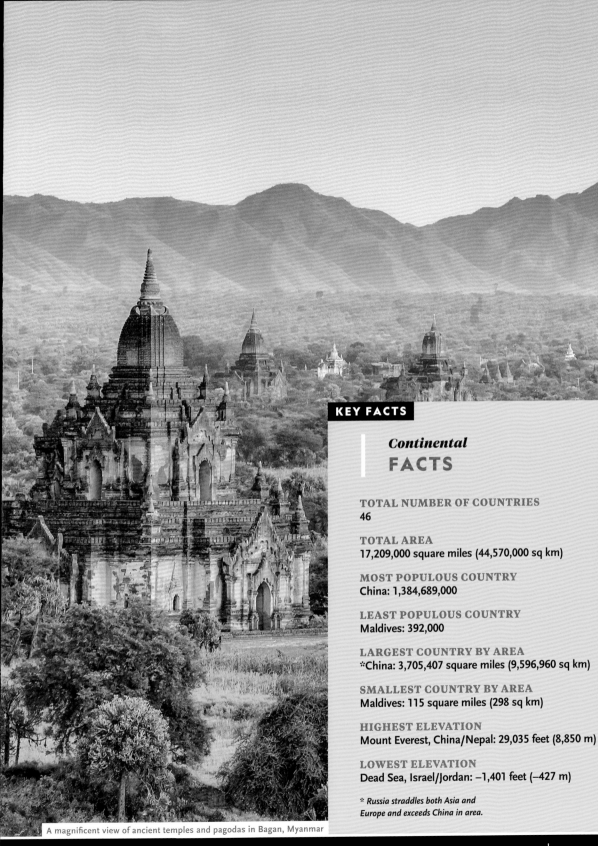

A magnificent view of ancient temples and pagodas in Bagan, Myanmar

Continental
FACTS

TOTAL NUMBER OF COUNTRIES
46

TOTAL AREA
17,209,000 square miles (44,570,000 sq km)

MOST POPULOUS COUNTRY
China: 1,384,689,000

LEAST POPULOUS COUNTRY
Maldives: 392,000

LARGEST COUNTRY BY AREA
*China: 3,705,407 square miles (9,596,960 sq km)

SMALLEST COUNTRY BY AREA
Maldives: 115 square miles (298 sq km)

HIGHEST ELEVATION
Mount Everest, China/Nepal: 29,035 feet (8,850 m)

LOWEST ELEVATION
Dead Sea, Israel/Jordan: –1,401 feet (–427 m)

* Russia straddles both Asia and
Europe and exceeds China in area.

AFRICA

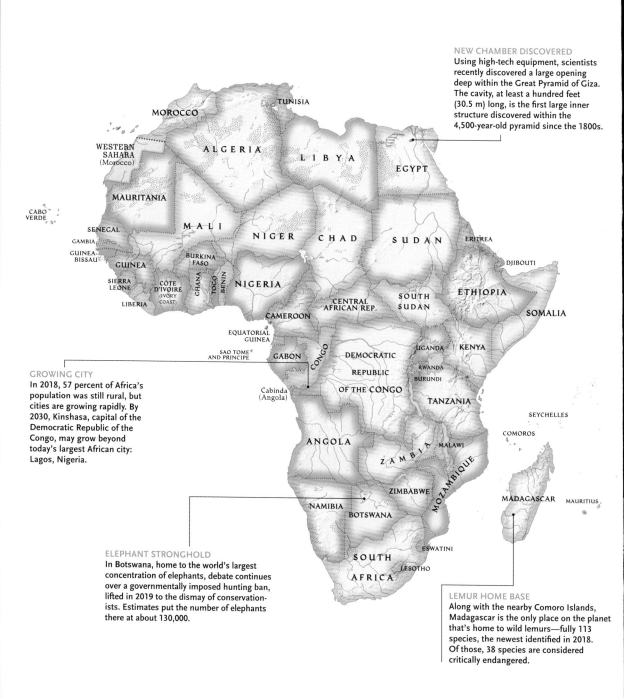

NEW CHAMBER DISCOVERED
Using high-tech equipment, scientists recently discovered a large opening deep within the Great Pyramid of Giza. The cavity, at least a hundred feet (30.5 m) long, is the first large inner structure discovered within the 4,500-year-old pyramid since the 1800s.

GROWING CITY
In 2018, 57 percent of Africa's population was still rural, but cities are growing rapidly. By 2030, Kinshasa, capital of the Democratic Republic of the Congo, may grow beyond today's largest African city: Lagos, Nigeria.

ELEPHANT STRONGHOLD
In Botswana, home to the world's largest concentration of elephants, debate continues over a governmentally imposed hunting ban, lifted in 2019 to the dismay of conservationists. Estimates put the number of elephants there at about 130,000.

LEMUR HOME BASE
Along with the nearby Comoro Islands, Madagascar is the only place on the planet that's home to wild lemurs—fully 113 species, the newest identified in 2018. Of those, 38 species are considered critically endangered.

AUSTRALIA & OCEANIA

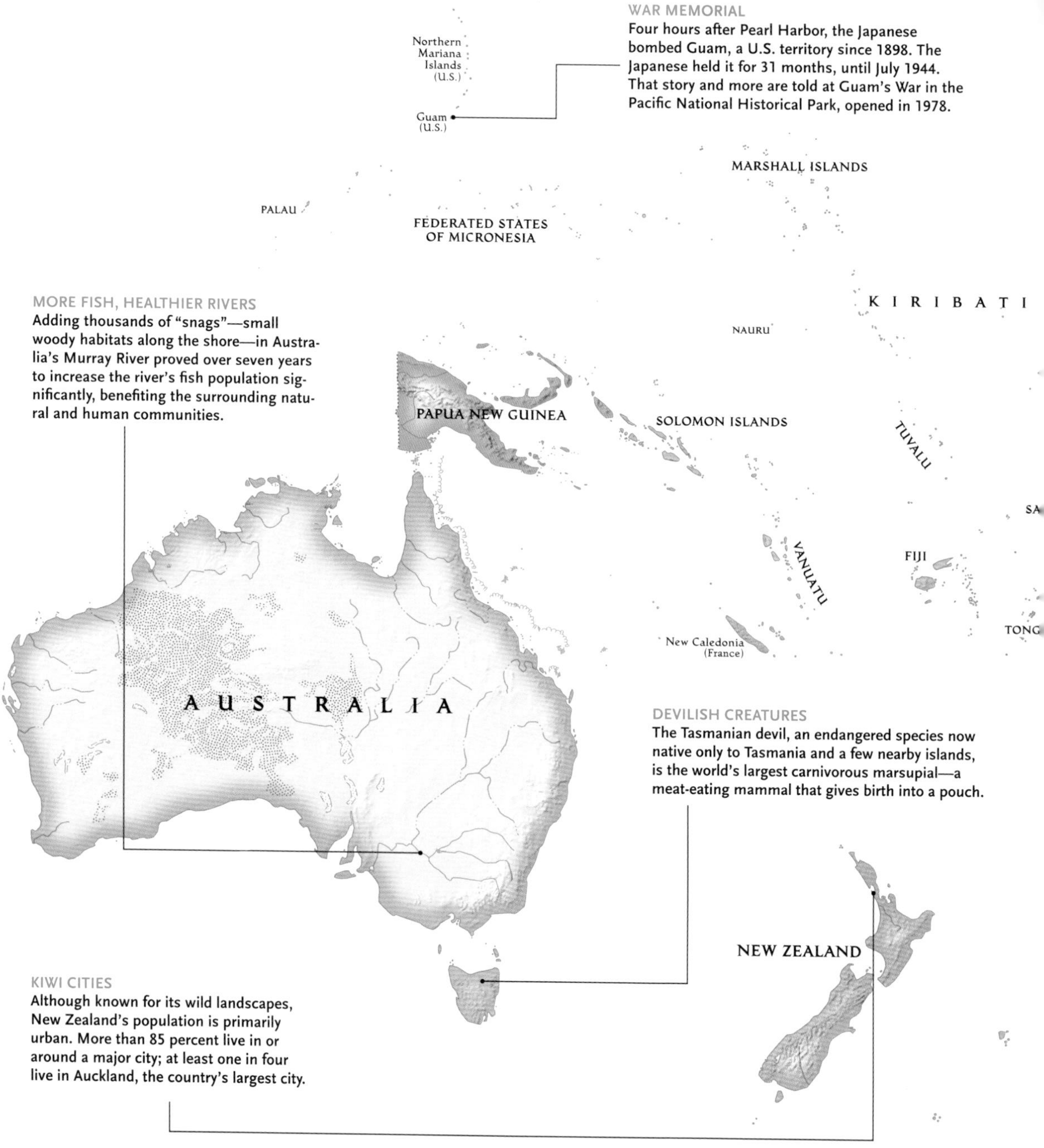

Northern
Mariana
Islands
(U.S.)

Guam
(U.S.)

WAR MEMORIAL
Four hours after Pearl Harbor, the Japanese bombed Guam, a U.S. territory since 1898. The Japanese held it for 31 months, until July 1944. That story and more are told at Guam's War in the Pacific National Historical Park, opened in 1978.

MARSHALL ISLANDS

PALAU

FEDERATED STATES
OF MICRONESIA

K I R I B A T I

NAURU

MORE FISH, HEALTHIER RIVERS
Adding thousands of "snags"—small woody habitats along the shore—in Australia's Murray River proved over seven years to increase the river's fish population significantly, benefiting the surrounding natural and human communities.

PAPUA NEW GUINEA

SOLOMON ISLANDS

TUVALU

SA

VANUATU

FIJI

New Caledonia
(France)

TONG

A U S T R A L I A

DEVILISH CREATURES
The Tasmanian devil, an endangered species now native only to Tasmania and a few nearby islands, is the world's largest carnivorous marsupial—a meat-eating mammal that gives birth into a pouch.

NEW ZEALAND

KIWI CITIES
Although known for its wild landscapes, New Zealand's population is primarily urban. More than 85 percent live in or around a major city; at least one in four live in Auckland, the country's largest city.

Mount Otemanu, surrounded by coral reefs, on Tahititi's Bora Bora

ANTARCTICA

VISITORS ONLY
Antarctica remains Earth's one uninhabited continent, with neither indigenous people nor endemic land animals. Tens of thousands of tourists visit each year, but rarely more than 1,000 scientists work here through the winter.

DRY ICE
Antarctica's precipitation averages less than two inches (5 cm) a year, a measurement that closely parallels the amount of rain received in the driest part of the Sahara.

ANTARCTIC
PENINSULA

RITSCHER
UPLAND

QUEEN MAUD LAND

Riiser–Larsen
Peninsula

ENDERBY LAND

COATS LAND

VALKYRIE
DOME

MAWSON COAST

MAC. ROBERTSON
LAND

TRANSANTARCTIC MOUNTAINS

AMERICAN
HIGHLAND

DOME ARGUS

ELLSWORTH
LAND

POLAR
PLATEAU

EAST
ANTARCTICA

WEST
ANTARCTICA

HOLLICK–KENYON
PLATEAU

TITAN DOME

MARIE BYRD LAND

WILKES LAND

LAW
DOME

VICTORIA LAND

TALOS
DOME

USARP
MTS.

TALLEST PEAK
Vinson Massif, at 16,066 feet (4,897 m) above sea level Antarctica's highest mountain, is named for Carl G. Vinson, a Georgia Democrat who served in the U.S. Congress for 26 terms and advocated for Antarctic exploration.

LONGSTANDING TREATY
Thanks to the Antarctic Treaty, originally drafted in 1959, 54 countries now agree to dedicate the continent to peaceful use, freely exchange scientific data gathered there, and ban all territorial claims.

A boat of tourists moving under an iceberg arch in Antarctica

OCEANS
OF THE WORLD

A BLUE PLANET

Earth's predominant physical feature is the vast, continuous body of water that accounts for more than two-thirds of its surface, totaling some 139 million square miles. The global ocean is a dominant climate factor, with currents carrying heat from the Equator toward the poles, and a vital resource providing food to much of the world's population and serving as a key transportation route between continents.

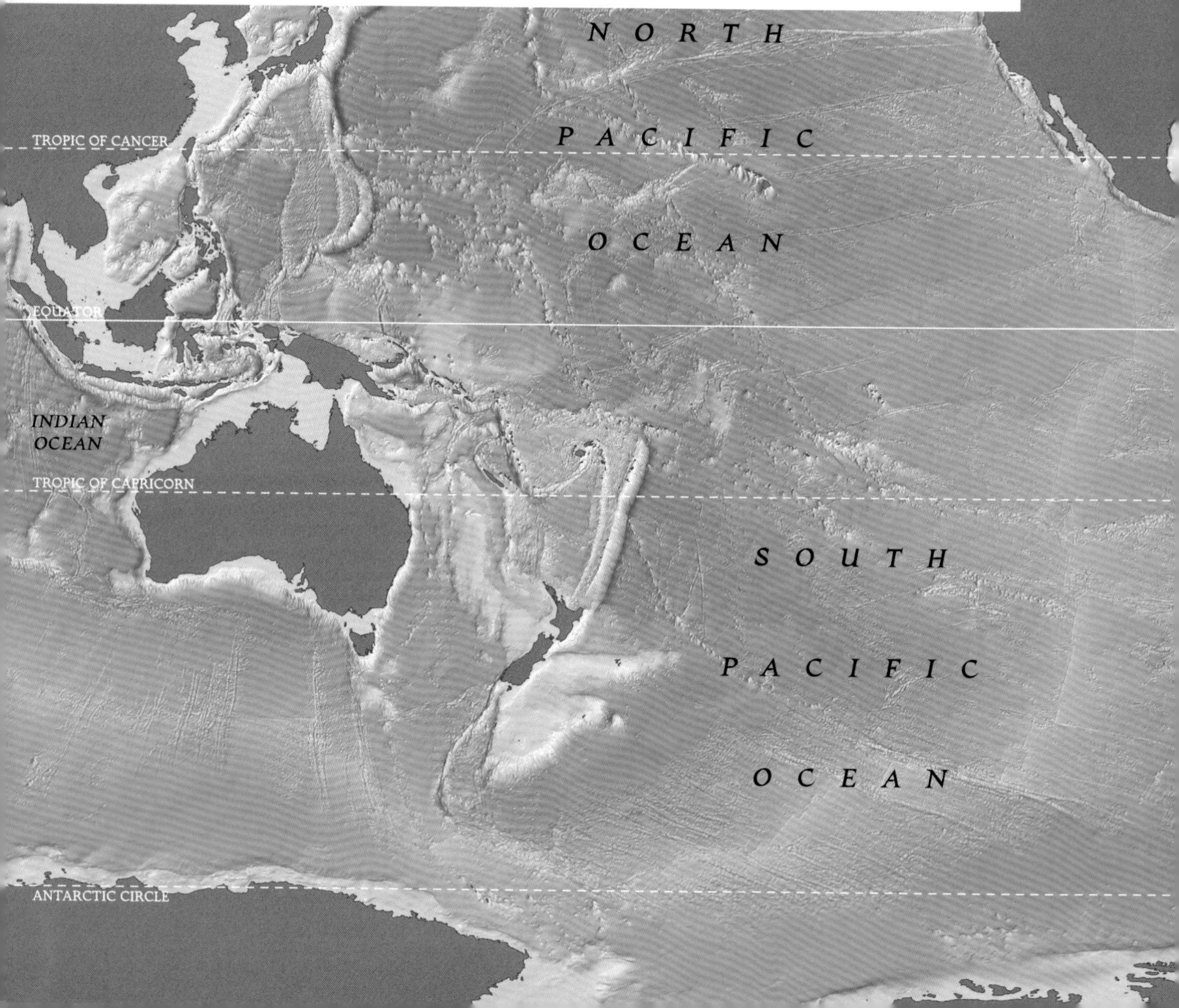

NORTH

TROPIC OF CANCER

PACIFIC

OCEAN

EQUATOR

INDIAN
OCEAN

TROPIC OF CAPRICORN

SOUTH

PACIFIC

OCEAN

ANTARCTIC CIRCLE

ARCTIC CIRCLE

WHEREVER TWO CURRENTS MEET . . . THERE ARE ZONES OF GREAT TURBULENCE AND UNREST . . . AT SUCH PLACES THE RICHNESS AND ABUNDANCE OF MARINE LIFE REVEALS ITSELF MOST STRIKINGLY.

—RACHEL CARSON, IN *THE SEA AROUND US*

NORTH ATLANTIC OCEAN

TROPIC OF CANCER

EQUATOR

SOUTH ATLANTIC OCEAN

INDIAN OCEAN

TROPIC OF CAPRICORN

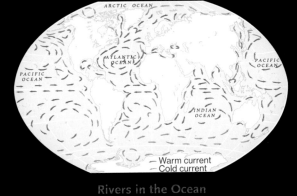

Warm current
Cold current

Rivers in the Ocean

Great surface currents circle the major ocean basins, ferrying the heat of the tropical sun north to warm and expand the temperate zones.

ANTARCTIC CIRCLE

ATLANTIC OCEAN

OCEAN TRENDS

Oceans are living things, with environments and processes that affect us all. They play huge roles in our lives as highways for travel and sources of food. Their vitality shapes the future of life on this planet. Here are a few indicators of ocean well-being today.

Coral Reefs

Reefs protect coasts from erosion and surges, and one-eighth of the world relies on fish from them. Yet coral reefs around the world are among the most at-risk ecosystems, with many species threatened by rising water temperatures and acidification.

Coral Reef Distribution

- ~17% Australia
- ~16% Indonesia
- ~9% Philippines
- 58% rest of the world

Fishing Activity

Roughly one billion people depend on fish as their main protein source. As demand has risen, the global fishing industry has grown, and overfishing threatens ocean ecosystems. Crude fishing techniques can result in unintentional bycatch, which accounts for more than 40 percent of all marine catch globally.

Fishing Hours, 2 (hours per km2)
- 100 or more
- 0.1
- 0

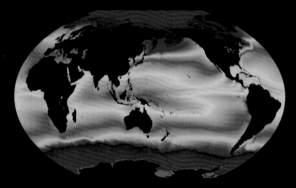

Sea Surface Temperatures

Destructive tropical storms are generated and sustained in areas where the ocean has high surface temperatures. Higher ocean temperatures mean more frequent and destructive storms.

Sea surface temperature, July 2002–Aug. 2013 average
- High
- Low

KEY FACTS

About the ATLANTIC

TOTAL AREA
35,400,000 square miles (91,700,000 sq km)

AVERAGE DEPTH
10,925 feet (3,300 m)

DEEPEST POINT
Puerto Rico Trench: −28,232 feet (−8,605 m)

LARGEST ISLAND
Greenland

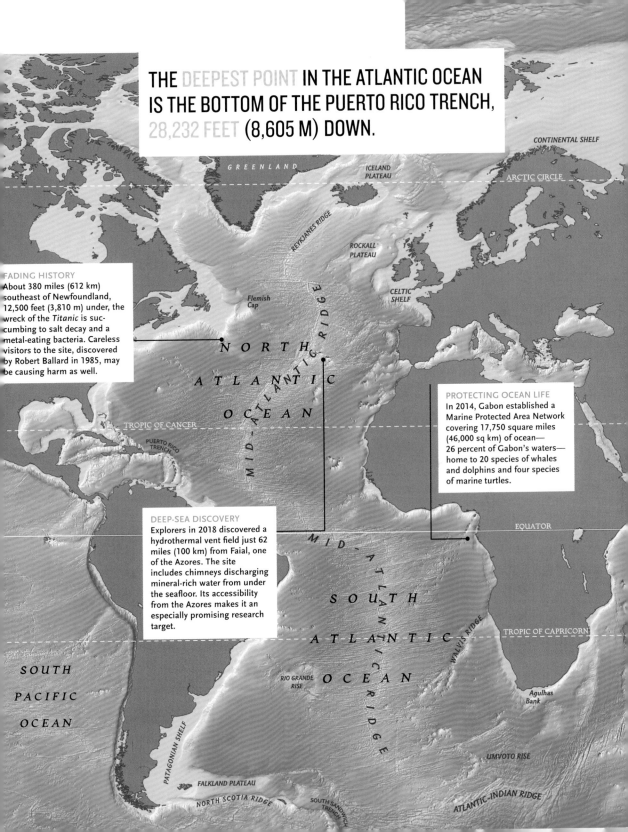

THE DEEPEST POINT IN THE ATLANTIC OCEAN IS THE BOTTOM OF THE PUERTO RICO TRENCH, 28,232 FEET (8,605 M) DOWN.

FADING HISTORY
About 380 miles (612 km) southeast of Newfoundland, 12,500 feet (3,810 m) under, the wreck of the *Titanic* is succumbing to salt decay and a metal-eating bacteria. Careless visitors to the site, discovered by Robert Ballard in 1985, may be causing harm as well.

PROTECTING OCEAN LIFE
In 2014, Gabon established a Marine Protected Area Network covering 17,750 square miles (46,000 sq km) of ocean—26 percent of Gabon's waters—home to 20 species of whales and dolphins and four species of marine turtles.

DEEP-SEA DISCOVERY
Explorers in 2018 discovered a hydrothermal vent field just 62 miles (100 km) from Faial, one of the Azores. The site includes chimneys discharging mineral-rich water from under the seafloor. Its accessibility from the Azores makes it an especially promising research target.

GREENLAND

ICELAND PLATEAU

ARCTIC CIRCLE

CONTINENTAL SHELF

REYKJANES RIDGE

ROCKALL PLATEAU

CELTIC SHELF

Flemish Cap

NORTH

ATLANTIC

OCEAN

MID-ATLANTIC RIDGE

TROPIC OF CANCER

PUERTO RICO TRENCH

EQUATOR

MID-ATLANTIC RIDGE

SOUTH

ATLANTIC

OCEAN

WALVIS RIDGE

TROPIC OF CAPRICORN

SOUTH PACIFIC OCEAN

RIO GRANDE RISE

Agulhas Bank

PATAGONIAN SHELF

UMVOTO RISE

FALKLAND PLATEAU

NORTH SCOTIA RIDGE

SOUTH SANDWICH TRENCH

ATLANTIC-INDIAN RIDGE

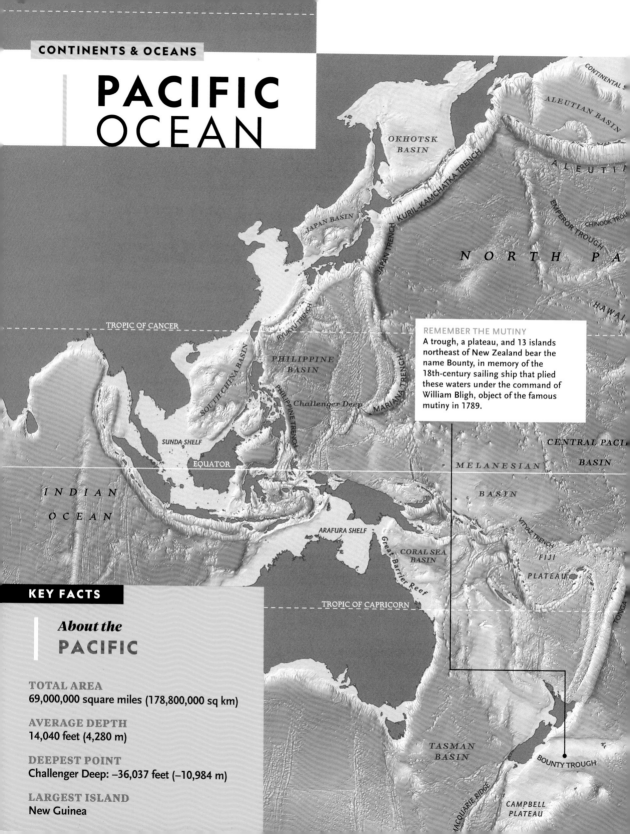

PACIFIC OCEAN

OKHOTSK BASIN

ALEUTIAN BASIN

CONTINENTAL S

ALEUTIAN

ALEUTIA

KURIL-KAMCHATKA TRENCH

JAPAN BASIN

JAPAN TRENCH

EMPEROR TROUGH

CHINOOK TRO

N O R T H   P A

HAWAI

TROPIC OF CANCER

RYUKYU TRENCH

PHILIPPINE BASIN

SOUTH CHINA BASIN

PHILIPPINE TRENCH

Challenger Deep

MARIANA TRENCH

REMEMBER THE MUTINY
A trough, a plateau, and 13 islands northeast of New Zealand bear the name Bounty, in memory of the 18th-century sailing ship that plied these waters under the command of William Bligh, object of the famous mutiny in 1789.

CENTRAL PACI
BASIN

SUNDA SHELF

EQUATOR

MELANESIAN
BASIN

I N D I A N
O C E A N

VITIAZ TRENCH

FIJI
PLATEAU

TONGA

ARAFURA SHELF

CORAL SEA BASIN

Great Barrier Reef

TROPIC OF CAPRICORN

KEY FACTS

About the
PACIFIC

TOTAL AREA
69,000,000 square miles (178,800,000 sq km)

AVERAGE DEPTH
14,040 feet (4,280 m)

DEEPEST POINT
Challenger Deep: −36,037 feet (−10,984 m)

LARGEST ISLAND
New Guinea

TASMAN BASIN

BOUNTY TROUGH

MACQUARIE RIDGE

CAMPBELL PLATEAU

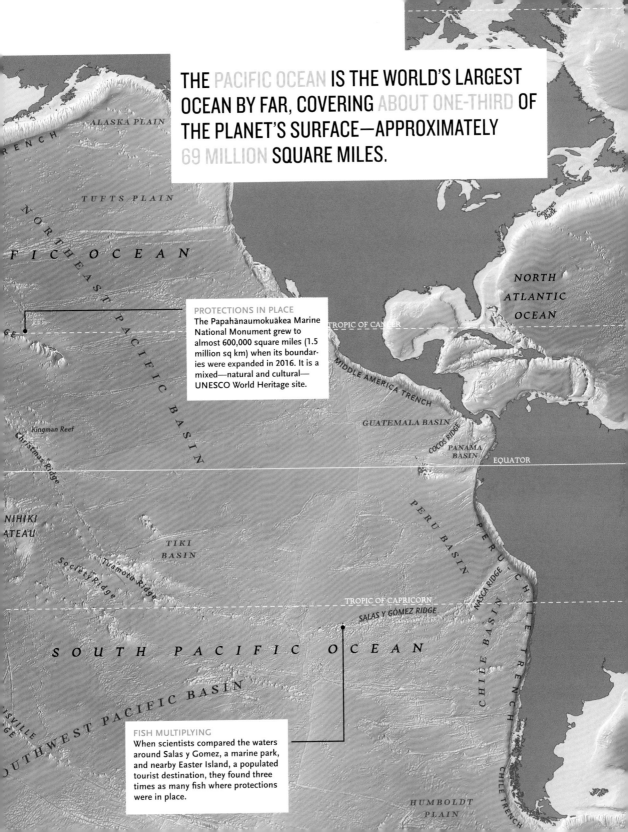

THE PACIFIC OCEAN IS THE WORLD'S LARGEST OCEAN BY FAR, COVERING ABOUT ONE-THIRD OF THE PLANET'S SURFACE—APPROXIMATELY 69 MILLION SQUARE MILES.

ALASKA PLAIN

TUFTS PLAIN

FIC OCEAN

NORTHEAST PACIFIC BASIN

RENCH

NORTH ATLANTIC OCEAN

Georges Bank

TROPIC OF CANCER

MIDDLE AMERICA TRENCH

Kingman Reef

Christmas Ridge

GUATEMALA BASIN

COCOS RIDGE

PANAMA BASIN

EQUATOR

NIHIKI ATEAU

TIKI BASIN

Society Ridge

Tuamotu Ridge

PERÚ BASIN

PERU-CHILE TRENCH

NASCA RIDGE

CHILE BASIN

TROPIC OF CAPRICORN

SALAS Y GÓMEZ RIDGE

SOUTH PACIFIC OCEAN

SVILLE GE

SOUTHWEST PACIFIC BASIN

CHILE TRENCH

HUMBOLDT PLAIN

PROTECTIONS IN PLACE
The Papahānaumokuākea Marine National Monument grew to almost 600,000 square miles (1.5 million sq km) when its boundaries were expanded in 2016. It is a mixed—natural and cultural—UNESCO World Heritage site.

FISH MULTIPLYING
When scientists compared the waters around Salas y Gomez, a marine park, and nearby Easter Island, a populated tourist destination, they found three times as many fish where protections were in place.

INDIAN OCEAN

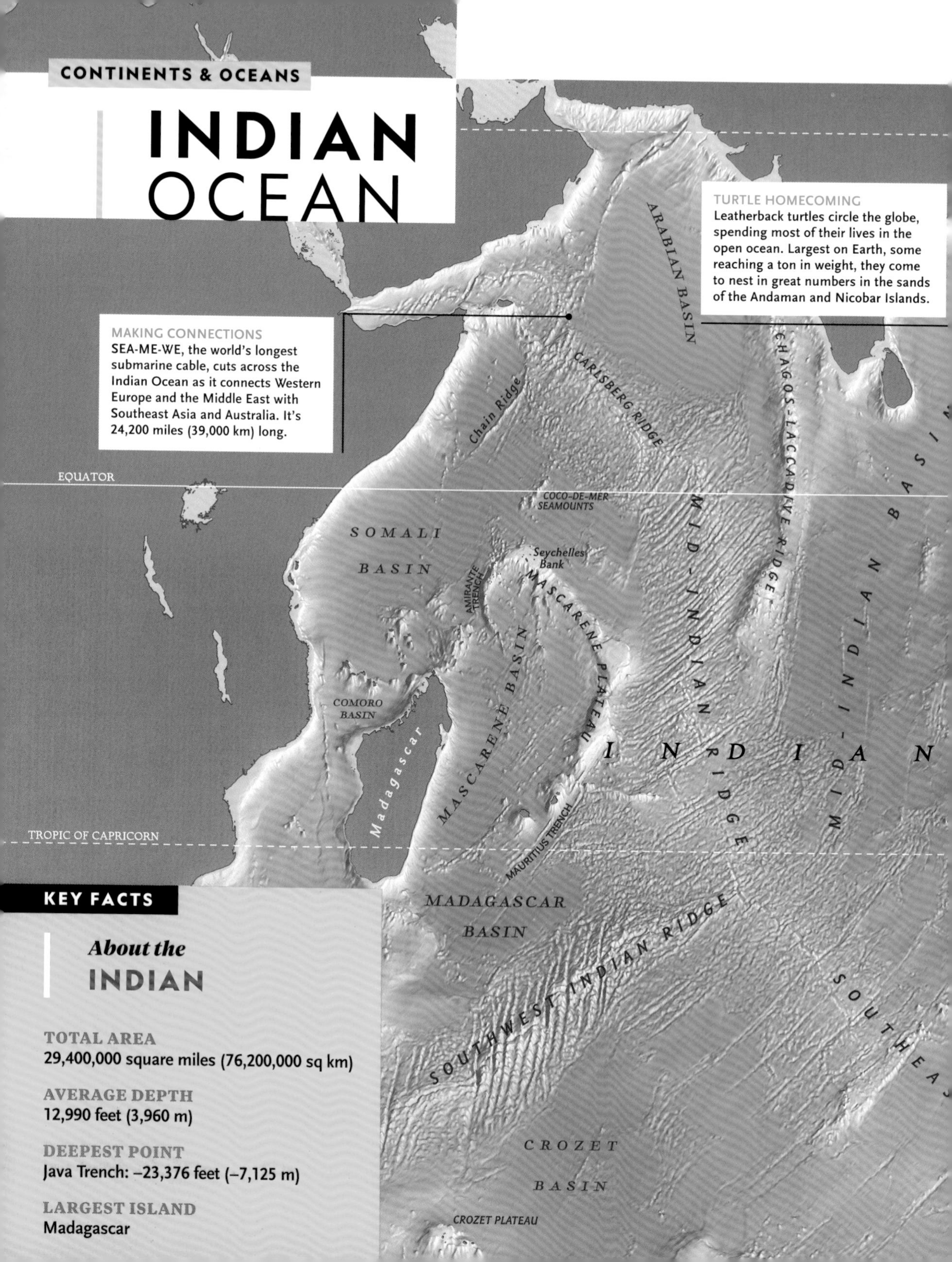

TURTLE HOMECOMING
Leatherback turtles circle the globe, spending most of their lives in the open ocean. Largest on Earth, some reaching a ton in weight, they come to nest in great numbers in the sands of the Andaman and Nicobar Islands.

MAKING CONNECTIONS
SEA-ME-WE, the world's longest submarine cable, cuts across the Indian Ocean as it connects Western Europe and the Middle East with Southeast Asia and Australia. It's 24,200 miles (39,000 km) long.

EQUATOR

TROPIC OF CAPRICORN

ARABIAN BASIN

CHAGOS-LACCADIVE RIDGE

MID-INDIAN BASIN

Chain Ridge

CARLSBERG RIDGE

COCO-DE-MER SEAMOUNTS

SOMALI BASIN

Seychelles Bank

AMIRANTE TRENCH

MASCARENE PLATEAU

MID-INDIAN RIDGE

COMORO BASIN

MASCARENE BASIN

Madagascar

I N D I A N

MAURITIUS TRENCH

MADAGASCAR BASIN

SOUTHWEST INDIAN RIDGE

SOUTHEAS

CROZET BASIN

CROZET PLATEAU

KEY FACTS

About the
INDIAN

TOTAL AREA
29,400,000 square miles (76,200,000 sq km)

AVERAGE DEPTH
12,990 feet (3,960 m)

DEEPEST POINT
Java Trench: −23,376 feet (−7,125 m)

LARGEST ISLAND
Madagascar

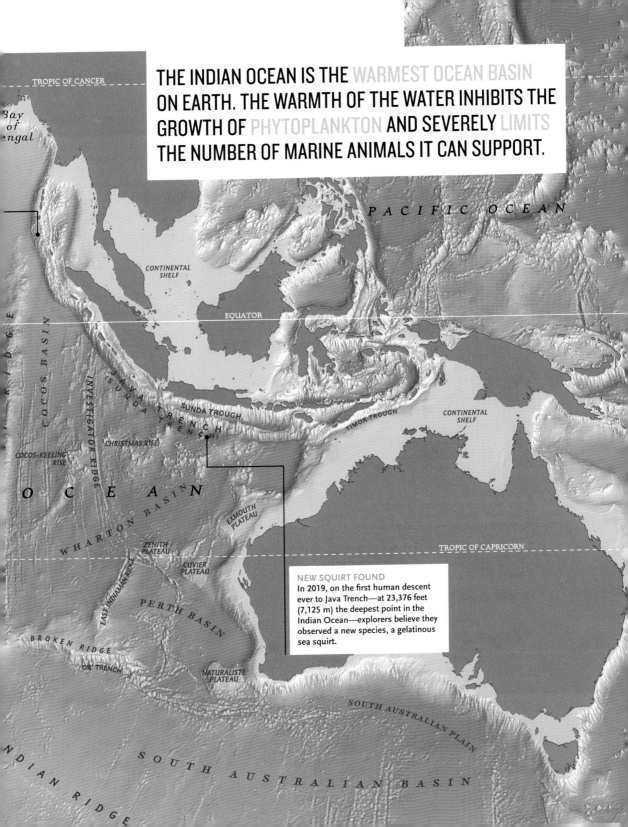

THE INDIAN OCEAN IS THE WARMEST OCEAN BASIN ON EARTH. THE WARMTH OF THE WATER INHIBITS THE GROWTH OF PHYTOPLANKTON AND SEVERELY LIMITS THE NUMBER OF MARINE ANIMALS IT CAN SUPPORT.

TROPIC OF CANCER

Bay of Bengal

PACIFIC OCEAN

CONTINENTAL SHELF

EQUATOR

RIDGE

COCOS BASIN

INVESTIGATOR RIDGE

JAVA TRENCH (SUNDA TRENCH)

SUNDA TROUGH

CHRISTMAS RISE

TIMOR TROUGH

CONTINENTAL SHELF

COCOS-KEELING RISE

O C E A N

WHARTON BASIN

EXMOUTH PLATEAU

ZENITH PLATEAU

TROPIC OF CAPRICORN

CUVIER PLATEAU

EAST INDIAMAN RIDGE

PERTH BASIN

NEW SQUIRT FOUND
In 2019, on the first human descent ever to Java Trench—at 23,376 feet (7,125 m) the deepest point in the Indian Ocean—explorers believe they observed a new species, a gelatinous sea squirt.

BROKEN RIDGE

'OB' TRENCH

NATURALISTE PLATEAU

SOUTH AUSTRALIAN PLAIN

INDIAN RIDGE

SOUTH AUSTRALIAN BASIN

ARCTIC OCEAN

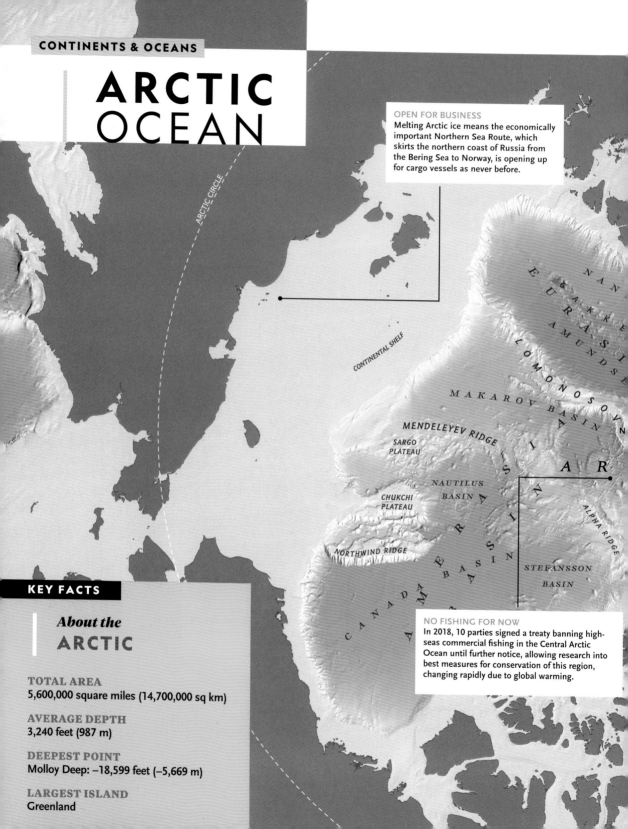

OPEN FOR BUSINESS
Melting Arctic ice means the economically important Northern Sea Route, which skirts the northern coast of Russia from the Bering Sea to Norway, is opening up for cargo vessels as never before.

ARCTIC CIRCLE

CONTINENTAL SHELF

N A N

GAKKE

E U R A S I

A M U N D S E

L O M O N O S

M A K A R O V   B A S I N

MENDELEYEV RIDGE

SARGO
PLATEAU

NAUTILUS
BASIN

A R

CHUKCHI
PLATEAU

R A S I N

ALPHA RIDGE

NORTHWIND RIDGE

B A S I N

STEFANSSON
BASIN

C A N A D A

A M E R

NO FISHING FOR NOW
In 2018, 10 parties signed a treaty banning high-seas commercial fishing in the Central Arctic Ocean until further notice, allowing research into best measures for conservation of this region, changing rapidly due to global warming.

KEY FACTS

About the ARCTIC

TOTAL AREA
5,600,000 square miles (14,700,000 sq km)

AVERAGE DEPTH
3,240 feet (987 m)

DEEPEST POINT
Molloy Deep: –18,599 feet (–5,669 m)

LARGEST ISLAND
Greenland

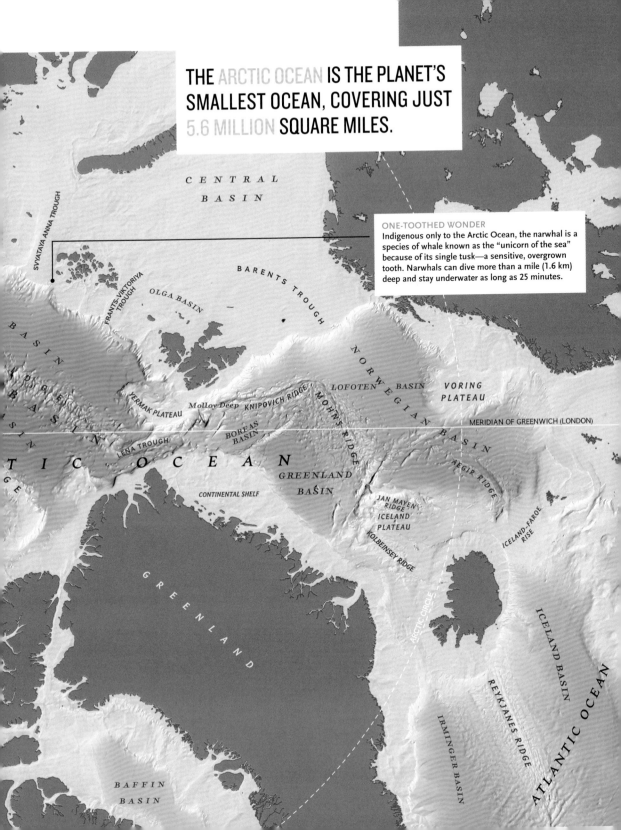

THE ARCTIC OCEAN IS THE PLANET'S SMALLEST OCEAN, COVERING JUST 5.6 MILLION SQUARE MILES.

CENTRAL BASIN

SVATAYA ANNA TROUGH

FRANTS-VIKTORIYA TROUGH

OLGA BASIN

BARENTS TROUGH

ONE-TOOTHED WONDER
Indigenous only to the Arctic Ocean, the narwhal is a species of whale known as the "unicorn of the sea" because of its single tusk—a sensitive, overgrown tooth. Narwhals can dive more than a mile (1.6 km) deep and stay underwater as long as 25 minutes.

BASIN

NORWEGIAN BASIN

VORING PLATEAU

LOFOTEN BASIN

YERMAK PLATEAU

Molloy Deep KNIPOVICH RIDGE

MOHNS RIDGE

MERIDIAN OF GREENWICH (LONDON)

BOREAS BASIN

LENA TROUGH

AEGIR RIDGE

TIC OCEAN

GREENLAND BASIN

CONTINENTAL SHELF

JAN MAYEN RIDGE

ICELAND PLATEAU

KOLBEINSEY RIDGE

ICELAND-FAROE RISE

GREENLAND

ARCTIC CIRCLE

ICELAND BASIN

REYKJANES RIDGE

IRMINGER BASIN

ATLANTIC OCEAN

BAFFIN BASIN

OCEAN AROUND
ANTARCTICA

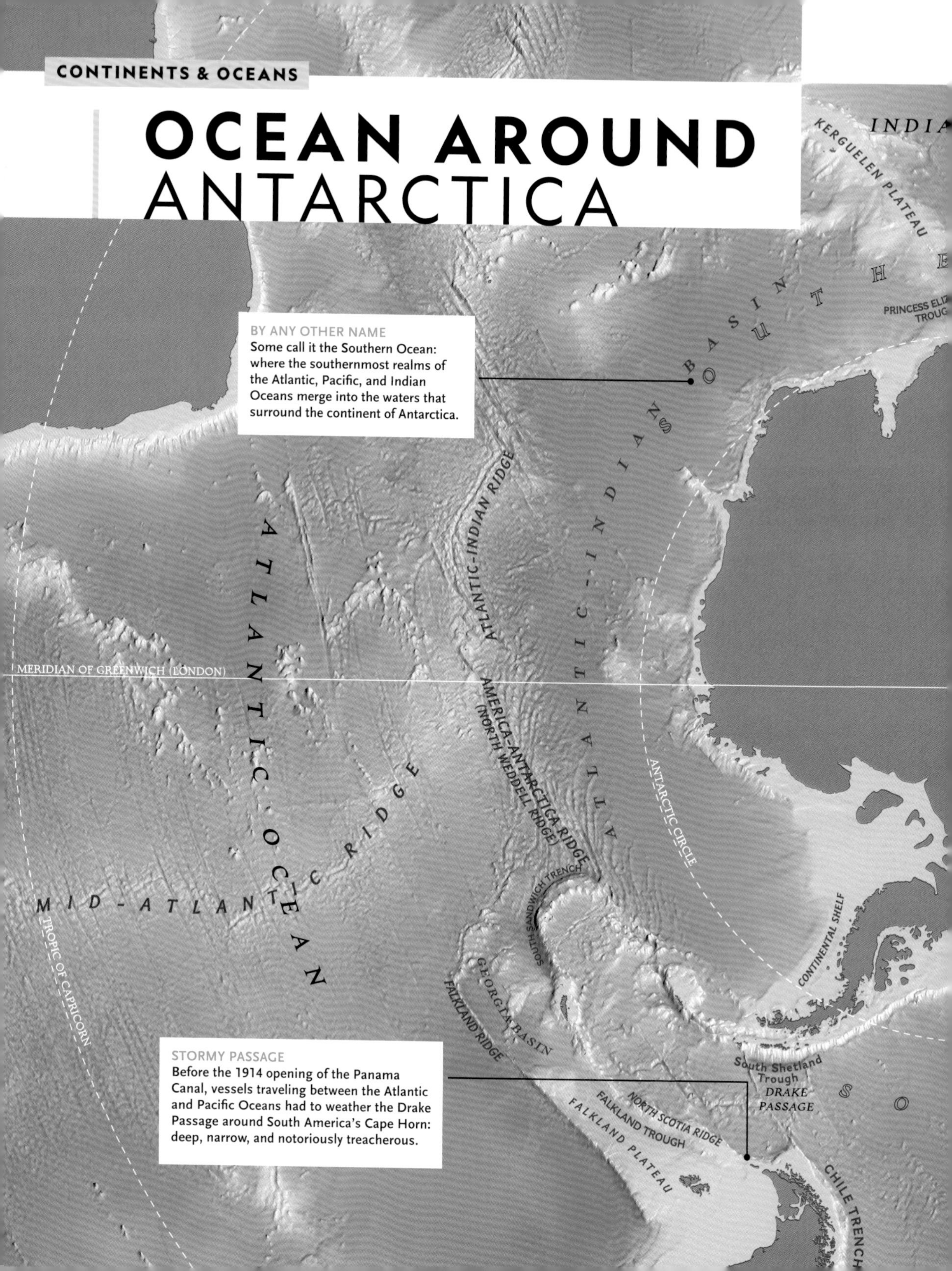

BY ANY OTHER NAME
Some call it the Southern Ocean: where the southernmost realms of the Atlantic, Pacific, and Indian Oceans merge into the waters that surround the continent of Antarctica.

STORMY PASSAGE
Before the 1914 opening of the Panama Canal, vessels traveling between the Atlantic and Pacific Oceans had to weather the Drake Passage around South America's Cape Horn: deep, narrow, and notoriously treacherous.

INDIA

KERGUELEN PLATEAU

PRINCESS ELIZ... TROUG...

SOUTHE...

BASIN

ATLANTIC-INDIAN RIDGE

ATLANTIC-INDIAN

ATLANTIC OCEAN

MERIDIAN OF GREENWICH (LONDON)

AMERICA-ANTARCTICA RIDGE (NORTH WEDDELL RIDGE)

ANTARCTIC CIRCLE

ATLANTIC RIDGE

MID-ATLANTIC

SOUTH SANDWICH TRENCH

TROPIC OF CAPRICORN

GEORGIA BASIN

FALKLAND RIDGE

NORTH SCOTIA RIDGE

FALKLAND TROUGH

FALKLAND PLATEAU

CONTINENTAL SHELF

South Shetland Trough

DRAKE PASSAGE

CHILE TRENCH

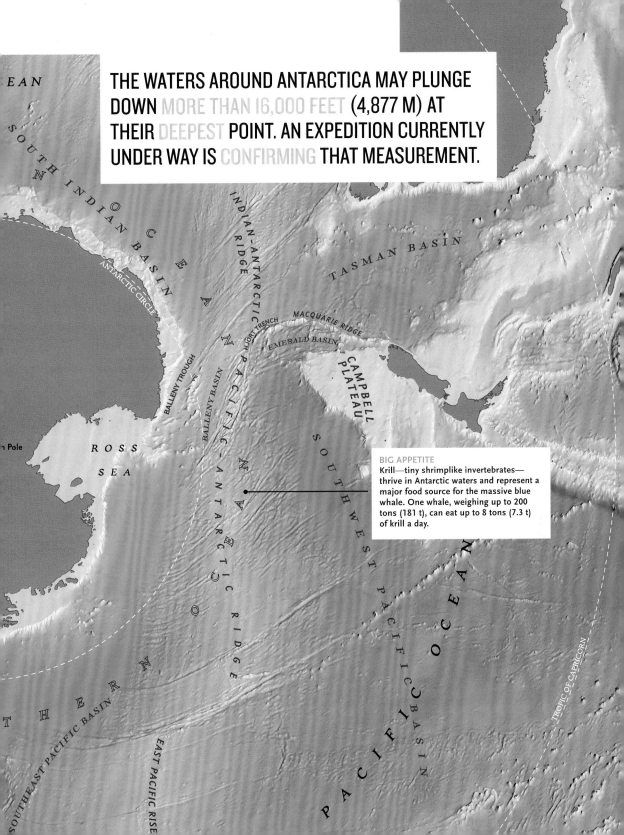

THE WATERS AROUND ANTARCTICA MAY PLUNGE DOWN MORE THAN 16,000 FEET (4,877 M) AT THEIR DEEPEST POINT. AN EXPEDITION CURRENTLY UNDER WAY IS CONFIRMING THAT MEASUREMENT.

EAN

SOUTH INDIAN OCEAN

SOUTH INDIAN BASIN

ANTARCTIC CIRCLE

INDIAN-ANTARCTIC RIDGE

TASMAN BASIN

MACQUARIE RIDGE

HJORT TRENCH

EMERALD BASIN

CAMPBELL PLATEAU

BALLENY TROUGH

BALLENY BASIN

PACIFIC-ANTARCTIC RIDGE

n Pole

ROSS SEA

SOUTHWEST PACIFIC BASIN

BIG APPETITE
Krill—tiny shrimplike invertebrates—thrive in Antarctic waters and represent a major food source for the massive blue whale. One whale, weighing up to 200 tons (181 t), can eat up to 8 tons (7.3 t) of krill a day.

SOUTHERN OCEAN

PACIFIC OCEAN

SOUTHEAST PACIFIC BASIN

EAST PACIFIC RISE

TROPIC OF CAPRICORN

BEST OF @NATGEO

TOP PHOTOS OF OCEANSCAPES

@simonnorfolkstudio | SIMON NORFOLK
This beach at Detwah Lagoon is part of Yemen's Socotra, an archipelago of four islands in the Arabian Sea.

@paulnicklen | PAUL NICKLEN
Dark clouds and distant hail pellets predict a storm quickly engulfing the Gardens of the Queen in Cuba.

@ronan_donovan | RONAN DONOVAN
Spots along Maine's coast are great for watching sunsets over the Atlantic—like this one on Deer Isle.

@stephenwilkes | STEPHEN WILKES
A sunrise and double rainbow illuminate the water as hundreds of albatrosses gather on the Falkland Islands.

> **"EVERYONE, EVERYWHERE IS INEXTRICABLY CONNECTED TO AND UTTERLY DEPENDENT UPON THE EXISTENCE OF THE SEA."** —SYLVIA EARLE, OCEANOGRAPHER

@andy_mann | ANDY MANN
Under a wave off Selvagem Pequena Island, 200 miles (322 km) from the Morocco coast, lies a seamount full of life.

@jimmy_chin | JIMMY CHIN
A pristine moment of peace and tranquility between wild squalls on the west coast of Greenland.

@james_balog | JAMES BALOG
Photography can be used to document the severe impact of global warming on glacial ice in the Arctic.

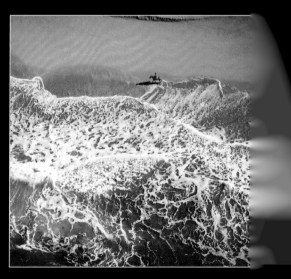

@irablockphoto | IRA BLOCK
A horse and rider enjoy the beauty of Puerto Rico's northeast coastline, which in 2017 felt the brunt of Hurricane Maria.

FLAGS OF THE WORLD

EACH OF TODAY'S 195 COUNTRIES FLIES AN HONORED AND SYMBOLIC FLAG

AFGHANISTAN

AREA 251,827 sq mi
(652,230 sq km)
POPULATION 34,941,000
CAPITAL Kabul

ALBANIA

AREA 11,100 sq mi
(28,748 sq km)
POPULATION 3,057,000
CAPITAL Tirana

ALGERIA

AREA 919,590 sq mi
(2,381,741 sq km)
POPULATION 41,657,000
CAPITAL Algiers

ANDORRA

AREA 181 sq mi
(468 sq km)
POPULATION 86,000
CAPITAL Andorra la Vella

ANGOLA

AREA 481,351 sq mi
(1,246,700 sq km)
POPULATION 30,356,000
CAPITAL Luanda

ANTIGUA AND BARBUDA

AREA 171 sq mi
(443 sq km)
POPULATION 96,000
CAPITAL St. John's

ARGENTINA

AREA 1,073,518 sq mi
(2,780,400 sq km)
POPULATION 44,694,000
CAPITAL Buenos Aires

ARMENIA

AREA 11,484 sq mi
(29,743 sq km)
POPULATION 3,038,000
CAPITAL Yerevan

AUSTRALIA

AAREA 2,988,901 sq mi
(7,741,220 sq km)
POPULATION 23,470,000
CAPITAL Canberra

AUSTRIA

AREA 32,383 sq mi
(83,871 sq km)
POPULATION 8,793,000
CAPITAL Vienna

AZERBAIJAN

AREA 33,436 sq mi
(86,600 sq km)
POPULATION 10,047,000
CAPITAL Baku

BAHAMAS, THE

AREA 5,359 sq mi
(13,880 sq km)
POPULATION 330,000
CAPITAL Nassau

BAHRAIN

AREA 293 sq mi
(760 sq km)
POPULATION 1,443,000
CAPITAL Manama

BANGLADESH

AREA 57,321 sq mi
(148,460 sq km)
POPULATION 159,453,000
CAPITAL Dhaka

BARBADOS

AREA 166 sq mi
(430 sq km)
POPULATION 293,000
CAPITAL Bridgetown

BELARUS

AREA 80,155 sq mi
(207,600 sq km)
POPULATION 9,528,000
CAPITAL Minsk

BELGIUM

AREA 11,787 sq mi
(30,528 sq km)
POPULATION 11,571,000
CAPITAL Brussels

BELIZE

AREA 8,867 sq mi
(22,966 sq km)
POPULATION 386,000
CAPITAL Belmopan

BENIN

AREA 43,484 sq mi
(112,622 sq km)
POPULATION 11,341,000
CAPITALS Porto-Novo (official capital),
Cotonou (administrative)

BHUTAN

AREA 14,824 sq mi
(38,394 sq km)
POPULATION 766,000
CAPITAL Thimphu

BOLIVIA

AREA 424,164 sq mi
(1,098,581 sq km)
POPULATION 11,138,000
CAPITALS La Paz (administrative),
Sucre (constitutional)

BOSNIA AND HERZEGOVINA

AREA 19,767 sq mi
(51,197 sq km)
POPULATION 3,850,000
CAPITAL Sarajevo

BOTSWANA

AREA 224,607 sq mi
(581,730 sq km)
POPULATION 2,215,000
CAPITAL Gaborone

BRAZIL

AREA 3,287,956 sq mi
(8,515,770 sq km)
POPULATION 208,847,000
CAPITAL Brasília

BRUNEI

AREA 2,226 sq mi
(5,765 sq km)
POPULATION 451,000
CAPITAL Bandar Seri Begawan

> " **PRIDE AND INDUSTRY.**"
>
> **—NATIONAL MOTTO OF BARBADOS**

ALL POPULATIONS ROUNDED TO THE NEAREST THOUSAND

BULGARIA

AREA 42,811 sq mi
(110,879 sq km)
POPULATION 7,058,000
CAPITAL Sofia

BURKINA FASO

AREA 105,869 sq mi
(274,200 sq km)
POPULATION 19,743,000
CAPITAL Ouagadougou

BURUNDI

AREA 10,745 sq mi
(27,830 sq km)
POPULATION 11,845,000
CAPITALS Gitega (official), Bujumbura (comm.)

CABO VERDE

AREA 1,557 sq mi
(4,033 sq km)
POPULATION 568,000
CAPITAL Praia

CAMBODIA

AREA 69,898 sq mi
(181,035 sq km)
POPULATION 16,450,000
CAPITAL Phnom Penh

CAMEROON

AREA 183,568 sq mi
(475,440 sq km)
POPULATION 25,641,000
CAPITAL Yaoundé

CANADA

AREA 3,855,101 sq mi
(9,984,670 sq km)
POPULATION 35,882,000
CAPITAL Ottawa

CENTRAL AFRICAN REPUBLIC

AREA 240,535 sq mi
(622,984 sq km)
POPULATION 5,745,000
CAPITAL Bangui

CHAD

AREA 495,755 sq mi
(1,284,000 sq km)
POPULATION 15,833,000
CAPITAL N'Djamena

CHILE

AREA 291,932 sq mi
(756,102 sq km)
POPULATION 17,925,000
CAPITAL Santiago

CHINA

AREA 3,705,407 sq mi
(9,596,960 sq km)
POPULATION 1,384,689,000
CAPITAL Beijing

COLOMBIA

AREA 439,735 sq mi
(1,138,910 sq km)
POPULATION 48,169,000
CAPITAL Bogotá

COMOROS

AREA 863 sq mi
(2,235 sq km)
POPULATION 821,000
CAPITAL Moroni

CONGO

AREA 132,047 sq mi
(342,000 sq km)
POPULATION 5,062,000
CAPITAL Brazzaville

CONGO, DEMOCRATIC REPUBLIC OF THE

AREA 905,354 sq mi
(2,344,858 sq km)
POPULATION 85,281,000
CAPITAL Kinshasa

COSTA RICA

AREA 19,730 sq mi
(51,100 sq km)
POPULATION 4,987,000
CAPITAL San José

CÔTE D'IVOIRE

AREA 124,504 sq mi
(322,463 sq km)
POPULATION 26,261,000
CAPITALS Abidjan (administrative),
Yamoussoukro (legislative)

CROATIA

AREA 21,851 sq mi
(56,594 sq km)
POPULATION 4,270,000
CAPITAL Zagreb

CUBA

AREA 42,803 sq mi
(110,860 sq km)
POPULATION 11,116,000
CAPITAL Havana

CYPRUS

AREA 3,572 sq mi
(9,251 sq km)
POPULATION 1,237,000
CAPITAL Nicosia

CZECHIA (CZECH REPUBLIC)

AREA 30,451 sq mi
(78,867 sq km)
POPULATION 10,686,000
CAPITAL Prague

DENMARK

AREA 16,639 sq mi
(43,094 sq km)
POPULATION 5,810,000
CAPITAL Copenhagen

DJIBOUTI

AREA 8,958 sq mi
(23,200 sq km)
POPULATION 884,000
CAPITAL Djibouti

DOMINICA

AREA 290 sq mi
(751 sq km)
POPULATION 74,000
CAPITAL Roseau

DOMINICAN REPUBLIC

AREA 18,792 sq mi
(48,670 sq km)
POPULATION 10,299,000
CAPITAL Santo Domingo

ECUADOR

AREA 109,483 sq mi
(283,561 sq km)
POPULATION 16,499,000
CAPITAL Quito

EGYPT

AREA 386,662 sq mi
(1,001,450 sq km)
POPULATION 99,413,000
CAPITAL Cairo

EL SALVADOR

AREA 8,124 sq mi
(21,041 sq km)
POPULATION 6,187,000
CAPITAL San Salvador

EQUATORIAL GUINEA

AREA 10,831 sq mi
(28,051 sq km)
POPULATION 797,000
CAPITAL Malabo

ERITREA

AREA 45,406 sq mi
(117,600 sq km)
POPULATION 5,971,000
CAPITAL Asmara

ESTONIA

AREA 17,463 sq mi
(45,228 sq km)
POPULATION 1,244,000
CAPITAL Tallinn

ESWATINI

AREA 6,704 sq mi
(17,364 sq km)
POPULATION 1,087,000
CAPITALS Mbabane (administrative),
Lobamba (legislative and royal)

ETHIOPIA

AREA 426,372 sq mi
(1,104,300 sq km)
POPULATION 108,386,000
CAPITAL Addis Ababa

FIJI

AREA 7,056 sq mi
(18,274 sq km)
POPULATION 926,000
CAPITAL Suva

FINLAND

AREA 130,558 sq mi
(338,145 sq km)
POPULATION 5,537,000
CAPITAL Helsinki

FRANCE

AREA 248,573 sq mi
(643,801 sq km)
POPULATION 67,364,000
CAPITAL Paris

GABON

AREA 103,347 sq mi
(267,667 sq km)
POPULATION 2,119,000
CAPITAL Libreville

GAMBIA, THE

AREA 4,363 sq mi
(11,300 sq km)
POPULATION 2,093,000
CAPITAL Banjul

GEORGIA

AREA 26,911 sq mi
(69,700 sq km)
POPULATION 4,926,000
CAPITAL Tbilisi

GERMANY

AREA 137,847 sq mi
(357,022 sq km)
POPULATION 80,458,000
CAPITAL Berlin

GHANA

AREA 92,098 sq mi
(238,533 sq km)
POPULATION 28,102,000
CAPITAL Accra

GREECE

AREA 50,949 sq mi
(131,957 sq km)
POPULATION 10,762,000
CAPITAL Athens

GRENADA

AREA 133 sq mi
(344 sq km)
POPULATION 112,000
CAPITAL St. George's

GUATEMALA

AREA 42,042 sq mi
(108,889 sq km)
POPULATION 16,581,000
CAPITAL Guatemala City

GUINEA

AREA 94,926 sq mi
(245,857 sq km)
POPULATION 11,855,000
CAPITAL Conakry

GUINEA-BISSAU

AREA 13,948 sq mi
(36,125 sq km)
POPULATION 1,833,000
CAPITAL Bissau

GUYANA

AREA 83,000 sq mi
(214,969 sq km)
POPULATION 741,000
CAPITAL Georgetown

HAITI

AREA 10,714 sq mi
(27,750 sq km)
POPULATION 10,788,000
CAPITAL Port-au-Prince

HONDURAS

AREA 43,278 sq mi
(112,090 sq km)
POPULATION 9,183,000
CAPITAL Tegucigalpa

HUNGARY

AREA 35,918 sq mi
(93,028 sq km)
POPULATION 9,826,000
CAPITAL Budapest

ICELAND

AREA 39,769 sq mi
(103,000 sq km)
POPULATION 344,000
CAPITAL Reykjavík

INDIA

AREA 1,269,219 sq mi
(3,287,263 sq km)
POPULATION 1,296,834,000
CAPITAL New Delhi

INDONESIA

AREA 735,358 sq mi
(1,904,569 sq km)
POPULATION 262,787,000
CAPITAL Jakarta

IRAN

AREA 636,371 sq mi
(1,648,195 sq km)
POPULATION 83,025,000
CAPITAL Tehran

IRAQ

AREA 169,235 sq mi
(438,317 sq km)
POPULATION 40,194,000
CAPITAL Baghdad

IRELAND

AREA 27,133 sq mi
(70,273 sq km)
POPULATION 5,068,000
CAPITAL Dublin

ISRAEL

AREA 8,019 sq mi
(20,770 sq km)
POPULATION 8,425,000
CAPITAL Jerusalem

ITALY

AREA 116,348 sq mi
(301,340 sq km)
POPULATION 62,247,000
CAPITAL Rome

JAMAICA

AREA 4,244 sq mi
(10,991 sq km)
POPULATION 2,812,000
CAPITAL Kingston

JAPAN

AREA 145,914 sq mi
(377,915 sq km)
POPULATION 126,168,000
CAPITAL Tokyo

JORDAN

AREA 34,495 sq mi
(89,342 sq km)
POPULATION 10,458,000
CAPITAL Amman

KAZAKHSTAN

AREA 1,052,089 sq mi
(2,724,900 sq km)
POPULATION 18,745,000
CAPITAL Nur-Sultan (Astana)

KENYA

AREA 224,081 sq mi
(580,367 sq km)
POPULATION 48,398,000
CAPITAL Nairobi

KIRIBATI

AREA 313 sq mi
(811 sq km)
POPULATION 109,000
CAPITAL Tarawa

KOSOVO

AREA 4,203 sq mi
(10,887 sq km)
POPULATION 1,908,000
CAPITAL Prishtina

KUWAIT

AREA 6,880 sq mi
(17,818 sq km)
POPULATION 4,438,000
CAPITAL Kuwait City

KYRGYZSTAN

AREA 77,201 sq mi
(199,951 sq km)
POPULATION 5,849,000
CAPITAL Bishkek

LAOS

AREA 91,429 sq mi
(236,800 sq km)
POPULATION 7,234,000
CAPITAL Vientiane

LATVIA

AREA 24,938 sq mi
(64,589 sq km)
POPULATION 1,924,000
CAPITAL Riga

LEBANON

AREA 4,015 sq mi
(10,400 sq km)
POPULATION 6,100,000
CAPITAL Beirut

LESOTHO

AREA 11,720 sq mi
(30,355 sq km)
POPULATION 1,962,000
CAPITAL Maseru

LIBERIA

AREA 43,000 sq mi
(111,369 sq km)
POPULATION 4,810,000
CAPITAL Monrovia

LIBYA

AREA 679,362 sq mi
(1,759,540 sq km)
POPULATION 6,755,000
CAPITAL Tripoli

LIECHTENSTEIN

AREA 62 sq mi
(160 sq km)
POPULATION 39,000
CAPITAL Vaduz

LITHUANIA

AREA 25,212 sq mi
(65,300 sq km)
POPULATION 2,793,000
CAPITAL Vilnius

LUXEMBOURG

AREA 998 sq mi
(2,586 sq km)
POPULATION 606,000
CAPITAL Luxembourg

MADAGASCAR

AREA 226,658 sq mi
(587,041 sq km)
POPULATION 25,684,000
CAPITAL Antananarivo

MALAWI

AREA 45,747 sq mi
(118,484 sq km)
POPULATION 19,843,000
CAPITAL Lilongwe

MALAYSIA

AREA 127,355 sq mi
(329,847 sq km)
POPULATION 31,810,000
CAPITAL Kuala Lumpur

MALDIVES

AREA 115 sq mi
(298 sq km)
POPULATION 392,000
CAPITAL Male

MALI

AREA 478,841 sq mi
(1,240,192 sq km)
POPULATION 18,430,000
CAPITAL Bamako

MALTA

AREA 122 sq mi
(316 sq km)
POPULATION 449,000
CAPITAL Valletta

MARSHALL ISLANDS

AREA 70 sq mi
(181 sq km)
POPULATION 76,000
CAPITAL Majuro

MAURITANIA

AREA 397,955 sq mi
(1,030,700 sq km)
POPULATION 3,840,000
CAPITAL Nouakchott

MAURITIUS

AREA 788 sq mi
(2,040 sq km)
POPULATION 1,364,000
CAPITAL Port Louis

MEXICO

AREA 758,449 sq mi
(1,964,375 sq km)
POPULATION 125,959,000
CAPITAL Mexico City

MICRONESIA

AREA 271 sq mi
(702 sq km)
POPULATION 104,000
CAPITAL Palikir

MOLDOVA

AREA 13,070 sq mi
(33,851 sq km)
POPULATION 3,438,000
CAPITAL Chisinau

MONACO

AREA 1 sq mi
(2.0 sq km)
POPULATION 38,000
CAPITAL Monaco

MONGOLIA

AREA 603,908 sq mi
(1,564,116 sq km)
POPULATION 3,103,000
CAPITAL Ulaanbaatar

MONTENEGRO

AREA 5,333 sq mi
(13,812 sq km)
POPULATION 614,000
CAPITAL Podgorica

MOROCCO

AREA 172,414 sq mi
(446,550 sq km)
POPULATION 34,314,000
CAPITAL Rabat

MOZAMBIQUE

AREA 308,642 sq mi
(799,380 sq km)
POPULATION 27,234,000
CAPITAL Maputo

MYANMAR (BURMA)

AREA 261,228 sq mi
(676,578 sq km)
POPULATION 55,623,000
CAPITAL Nay Pyi Taw (admin.), Yangon (comm.)

NAMIBIA

AREA 318,261 sq mi
(824,292 sq km)
POPULATION 2,533,000
CAPITAL Windhoek

NAURU

AREA 8 sq mi
(21 sq km)
POPULATION 10,000
CAPITAL No official capital; government offices in Yaren District

NEPAL

AREA 56,827 sq mi
(147,181 sq km)
POPULATION 29,718,000
CAPITAL Kathmandu

NETHERLANDS

AREA 16,040 sq mi
(41,543 sq km)
POPULATION 17,151,000
CAPITAL Amsterdam

NEW ZEALAND

AREA 103,799 sq mi
(268,838 sq km)
POPULATION 4,546,000
CAPITAL Wellington

NICARAGUA

AREA 50,336 sq mi
(130,370 sq km)
POPULATION 6,085,000
CAPITAL Managua

NIGER

AREA 489,191 sq mi
(1,267,000 sq km)
POPULATION 19,866,000
CAPITAL Niamey

NIGERIA

AREA 356,669 sq mi
(923,768 sq km)
POPULATION 203,453,000
CAPITAL Abuja

NORTH KOREA

AREA 46,540 sq mi
(120,538 sq km)
POPULATION 25,381,000
CAPITAL Pyongyang

NORTH MACEDONIA

AREA 9,928 sq mi
(25,713 sq km)
POPULATION 2,119,000
CAPITAL Skopje

NORWAY

AREA 125,021 sq mi
(323,802 sq km)
POPULATION 5,372,000
CAPITAL Oslo

OMAN

AREA 119,499 sq mi
(309,500 sq km)
POPULATION 4,613,000
CAPITAL Muscat

PAKISTAN

AREA 307,374 sq mi
(796,095 sq km)
POPULATION 207,863,000
CAPITAL Islamabad

PALAU

AREA 177 sq mi
(459 sq km)
POPULATION 22,000
CAPITAL Ngerulmud

PANAMA

AREA 29,120 sq mi
(75,420 sq km)
POPULATION 3,801,000
CAPITAL Panama City

PAPUA NEW GUINEA

AREA 178,703 sq mi
(462,840 sq km)
POPULATION 7,027,000
CAPITAL Port Moresby

PARAGUAY

AREA 157,048 sq mi
(406,752 sq km)
POPULATION 7,026,000
CAPITAL Asunción

PERU

AREA 496,224 sq mi
(1,285,216 sq km)
POPULATION 31,331,000
CAPITAL Lima

PHILIPPINES

AREA 115,831 sq mi
(300,000 sq km)
POPULATION 105,893,000
CAPITAL Manila

POLAND

AREA 120,728 sq mi
(312,685 sq km)
POPULATION 38,421,000
CAPITAL Warsaw

PORTUGAL

AREA 35,556 sq mi
(92,090 sq km)
POPULATION 10,355,000
CAPITAL Lisbon

QATAR

AREA 4,473 sq mi
(11,586 sq km)
POPULATION 2,364,000
CAPITAL Doha

ROMANIA

AREA 92,043 sq mi
(238,391 sq km)
POPULATION 21,457,000
CAPITAL Bucharest

RUSSIA

AREA 6,601,665 sq mi
(17,098,242 sq km)
POPULATION 142,123,000
CAPITAL Moscow

RWANDA

AREA 10,169 sq mi
(26,338 sq km)
POPULATION 12,187,000
CAPITAL Kigali

SAINT KITTS AND NEVIS

AREA 101 sq mi
(261 sq km)
POPULATION 53,000
CAPITAL Basseterre

SAINT LUCIA

AREA 238 sq mi
(616 sq km)
POPULATION 166,000
CAPITAL Castries

SAINT VINCENT AND GRENADINES

AREA 150 sq mi
(389 sq km)
POPULATION 102,000
CAPITAL Kingstown

SAMOA

AREA 1,093 sq mi
(2,831 sq km)
POPULATION 201,000
CAPITAL Apia

SAN MARINO

AREA 24 sq mi
(61 sq km)
POPULATION 34,000
CAPITAL San Marino

SÃO TOMÉ AND PRINCIPE

AREA 372 sq mi
(964 sq km)
POPULATION 204,000
CAPITAL São Tomé

SAUDI ARABIA

AREA 830,000 sq mi
(2,149,690 sq km)
POPULATION 33,091,000
CAPITAL Riyadh

SENEGAL

AREA 75,955 sq mi
(196,722 sq km)
POPULATION 15,021,000
CAPITAL Dakar

SERBIA

AREA 29,913 sq mi
(77,474 sq km)
POPULATION 7,078,000
CAPITAL Belgrade

SEYCHELLES

AREA 176 sq mi
(455 sq km)
POPULATION 95,000
CAPITAL Victoria

SIERRA LEONE

AREA 27,699 sq mi
(71,740 sq km)
POPULATION 6,312,000
CAPITAL Freetown

SINGAPORE

AREA 269 sq mi
(697 sq km)
POPULATION 5,996,000
CAPITAL Singapore

SLOVAKIA

AREA 18,933 sq mi
(49,035 km)
POPULATION 5,445,000
CAPITAL Bratislava

SLOVENIA

AREA 7,827 sq mi
(20,273 sq km)
POPULATION 2,102,000
CAPITAL Ljubljana

SOLOMON ISLANDS

AREA 11,157 sq mi
(28,896 sq km)
POPULATION 660,000
CAPITAL Honiara

SOMALIA

AREA 246,201 sq mi
(637,657 sq km)
POPULATION 11,259,000
CAPITAL Mogadishu

SOUTH AFRICA

AREA 470,693 sq mi
(1,219,090 sq km)
POPULATION 55,380,000
CAPITALS Pretoria (Tshwane) (administrative),
Cape Town (legislative), Bloemfontein
(judicial)

SOUTH KOREA

AREA 38,502 sq mi
(99,720 sq km)
POPULATION 51,418,000
CAPITAL Seoul

SOUTH SUDAN

AREA 248,777 sq mi
(644,329 sq km)
POPULATION 10,205,000
CAPITAL Juba

SPAIN

AREA 195,124 sq mi
(505,370 sq km)
POPULATION 49,331,000
CAPITAL Madrid

SRI LANKA

AREA 25,332 sq mi
(65,610 sq km)
POPULATION 22,577,000
CAPITALS Colombo (commercial),
Sri Jayewardenepura Kotte (legislative)

SUDAN

AREA 718,723 sq mi
(1,861,484 sq km)
POPULATION 43,121,000
CAPITAL Khartoum

SURINAME

AREA 63,251 sq mi
(163,820 sq km)
POPULATION 598,000
CAPITAL Paramaribo

SWEDEN

AREA 173,860 sq mi
(450,295 sq km)
POPULATION 10,041,000
CAPITAL Stockholm

SWITZERLAND

AREA 15,937 sq mi
(41,277 sq km)
POPULATION 8,293,000
CAPITAL Bern

SYRIA

AREA 71,498 sq mi
(185,180 sq km)
POPULATION 19,454,000
CAPITAL Damascus

TAJIKISTAN

AREA 55,637 sq mi
(144,100 sq km)
POPULATION 8,605,000
CAPITAL Dushanbe

TANZANIA

AREA 365,754 sq mi
(947,300 sq km)
POPULATION 55,451,000
CAPITAL Dar es Salaam (administrative);
Dodoma (official)

THAILAND

AREA 198,117 sq mi
(513,120 sq km)
POPULATION 68,616,000
CAPITAL Bangkok

TIMOR-LESTE (EAST TIMOR)
AREA 5,743 sq mi
(14,874 sq km)
POPULATION 1,322,000
CAPITAL Díli

TOGO

AREA 21,925 sq mi
(56,785 sq km)
POPULATION 8,176,000
CAPITAL Lomé

TONGA

AREA 288 sq mi
(747 sq km)
POPULATION 106,000
CAPITAL Nuku'alofa

TRINIDAD AND TOBAGO

AREA 1,980 sq mi
(5,128 sq km)
POPULATION 1,216,000
CAPITAL Port of Spain

TUNISIA

AREA 63,170 sq mi
(163,610 sq km)
POPULATION 11,516,000
CAPITAL Tunis

TURKEY

AREA 302,535 sq mi
(783,562 sq km)
POPULATION 81,257,000
CAPITAL Ankara

TURKMENISTAN

AREA 188,456 sq mi
(488,100 sq km)
POPULATION 5,411,000
CAPITAL Ashgabat

TUVALU

AREA 10 sq mi
(26 sq km)
POPULATION 11,000
CAPITAL Funafuti

UGANDA

AREA 93,065 sq mi
(241,038 sq km)
POPULATION 40,854,000
CAPITAL Kampala

UKRAINE

AREA 233,032 sq mi
(603,550 sq km)
POPULATION 43,952,000
CAPITAL Kiev

UNITED ARAB EMIRATES

AREA 32,278 sq mi
(83,600 sq km)
POPULATION 9,701,000
CAPITAL Abu Dhabi

UNITED KINGDOM

AREA 94,058 sq mi
(243,610 sq km)
POPULATION 65,105,000
CAPITAL London

UNITED STATES

AREA 3,796,741 sq mi
(9,833,517 sq km)
POPULATION 329,256,000
CAPITAL Washington, D.C.

URUGUAY

AREA 68,037 sq mi
(176,215 sq km)
POPULATION 3,369,000
CAPITAL Montevideo

UZBEKISTAN

AREA 172,742 sq mi
(447,400 sq km)
POPULATION 30,024,000
CAPITAL Tashkent

VANUATU

AREA 4,706 sq mi
(12,189 sq km)
POPULATION 288,000
CAPITAL Port-Vila

VATICAN CITY (HOLY SEE)

AREA 0.17 sq mi
(0.44 sq km)
POPULATION 1,000
CAPITAL Vatican City

VENEZUELA

AREA 352,144 sq mi
(912,050 sq km)
POPULATION 31,689,000
CAPITAL Caracas

VIETNAM

AREA 127,881 sq mi
(331,210 sq km)
POPULATION 97,040,000
CAPITAL Hanoi

YEMEN

AREA 203,850 sq mi
(527,968 sq km)
POPULATION 28,667,000
CAPITAL Sanaa

ZAMBIA

AREA 290,587 sq mi
(752,618 sq km)
POPULATION 16,445,000
CAPITAL Lusaka

ZIMBABWE

AREA 150,872 sq mi
(390,757 sq km)
POPULATION 14,030,000
CAPITAL Harare

UNITED NATIONS

IN SEARCH OF A PEACEFUL WORLD

The UN works to maintain international peace, develop friendly relations among nations, and achieve international cooperation in solving world problems.

The UN assists and protects 71.4 million people fleeing war, famine, and persecution.

MORE OF THE WORLD

TERRITORIES & DEPENDENCIES AROUND THE GLOBE

A leatherback hatchling on a protected beach in St. Croix, U.S. Virgin Islands

45 LOCATIONS, DISTINCTIVE YET NOT TECHNICALLY COUNTRIES

There are 195 countries, 36 dependencies, and 5 other political units that make up the world today. Of those, 13 are U.K. territories and 14 are U.S. territories, also considered dependencies.

THE WORLD

Dependencies Listed by SOVEREIGNTY

AUSTRALIA
Christmas Island, Cocos (Keeling) Islands, Norfolk Island

DENMARK
Faroe Islands, Greenland (Kalaallit Nunaat)

FRANCE
French Polynesia, New Caledonia, Saint-Barthélemy, Saint Martin, Saint-Pierre and Miquelon, Wallis and Futuna

NETHERLANDS
Aruba, Curaçao, Sint Maarten

NEW ZEALAND
Cook Islands, Niue, Tokelau

UNITED KINGDOM
Anguilla, Bermuda, British Virgin Islands, Cayman Islands, Falkland Islands, Gibraltar, Guernsey, Isle of Man, Jersey, Montserrat, Pitcairn Islands, Saint Helena and Dependencies, Turks and Caicos Islands

UNITED STATES
American Samoa, Baker Island, Guam, Howland Island, Jarvis Island, Johnston Atoll, Kingman Reef, Midway Islands, Navassa Island, Northern Mariana Islands, Palmyra Atoll, Puerto Rico, U.S. Virgin Islands, Wake Island

FUTURE
OF THE PLANET

INCREASE IN EXTREMES

Extreme weather events—hurricanes, droughts, floods, heat waves, tornadoes, and other deadly events—have increased in the 21st century. Vulnerable islands and coastal areas are suffering the most. From 1997 to 2016, the nations most affected by extreme weather were in the developing world, including Honduras, Haiti, and Myanmar.

NORTH AMERICA

SOUTH AMERICA

Extreme Climate Risk
Index, 1997–2016
(average)

- ■ Extreme
- ■ High
- ■ Moderately high
- ■ Medium
- ■ Moderately low
- □ Low
- ▨ No data

MODELS PREDICT AN INCREASE IN CATEGORY 4 AND 5 HURRICANES WITH GREATER RAINFALL OVER THE COURSE OF THE 21ST CENTURY.

ROPE

ASIA

FRICA

AUSTRALIA

FUTURE OF
THE WILD ON EARTH

RECOGNIZING BIODIVERSITY

Despite widespread human development, certain regions are still rich in bio-diversity, supporting many different plant and animal species. Brazil and Colombia have the world's highest levels, in part because their lands range from rainforest to savanna, mountain tundra to seacoast. The natural balance of the whole planet depends on our protecting the intensely biodiverse regions that remain.

Terrestrial Mammals,
Amphibians, and Birds
Species Richness

High

Low

No data

SINCE A 2010 UNITED NATIONS CONFERENCE ON BIOLOGICAL DIVERSITY, 168 COUNTRIES HAVE ESTABLISHED STRATEGIC ACTION PLANS FOR THE CONSERVATION AND SUSTAINABLE USE OF THEIR REGIONS' BIOLOGICAL RESOURCES.

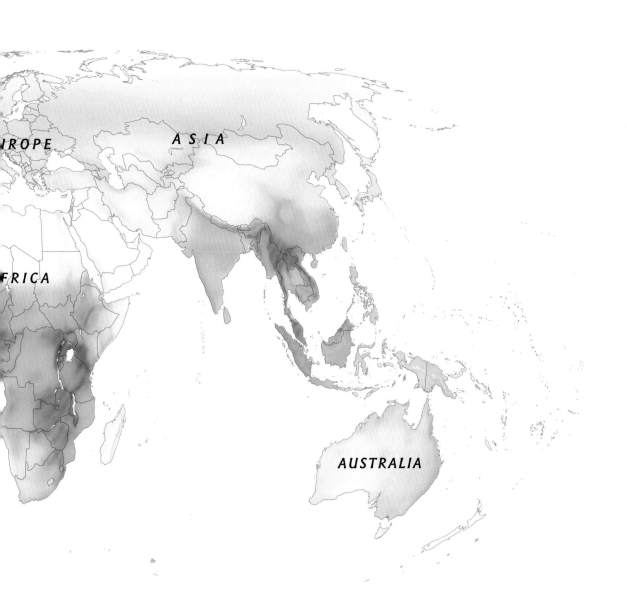

EUROPE

ASIA

AFRICA

AUSTRALIA

FUTURE OF
HUMANS ON EARTH

INTO THE CITY

In the 21st century, people are moving into cities, especially in the continents of Africa and Asia. One-fifth of the world's city residents will live in Africa by 2050. Urbanization can mean access to electricity, sanitation, and clean drinking water—depending on investment in infrastructure and services.

NORTH
AMERICA

SOUTH
AMERICA

Urban Population
Growth, 1950–2020
(in millions)

- More than 100
- 50–100
- 10–49
- Less than 10
- No data

FURTHER

WALKING INTO THE FUTURE

Flowers and greenery provide aerial delights for those using the pedestrians-only Mingzhu Roundabout in Pudong, Shanghai's booming financial district. Shanghai is one of the world's fastest growing cities with a population that may reach 50 million by 2050. With more people come more cars, yet with this roundabout city planners hope to lift people up out of the traffic. The roundabout also reduces pollution as here in Shanghai—and elsewhere around the world—more people are walking to work.

The pedestrian walkway above Shanghai's financial district is part of China's Emerald Cities plan to make fast-growing urban areas more people-friendly

"THE GOALS OF A PEACEFUL WORLD MUST—TODAY AND TOMORROW—SHAPE OUR DECISIONS AND INSPIRE OUR PURPOSES. SO WE ARE ALL IDEALISTS. WE ARE ALL VISIONARIES."

—JOHN F. KENNEDY, U.S. PRESIDENT, 1961–1963

CREDITS

192 (4d – Red Abalone), Illustration © Emily S. Damstra; 193, Paul Nicklen/NG Image Collection; 194-5, David Liittschwager/NG Image Collection; 196 (UP LE), Kenneth Geiger; 196 (UP RT), Anand Varma/NG Image Collection; 196 (LO LE), Tim Laman; 196 (LO RT), Frans Lanting/lanting.com; 197 (UP LE), Ronan Donovan; 197 (UP RT), Jasper Doest; 197 (LO LE), Lucas Foglia; 197 (LO RT), Carlton Ward Jr.; 198 (1a), Diane Pierce; 198 (1b), Diane Pierce; 198 (1c), Peter Burke; 198 (1d), H. Douglas Pratt; 198 (1e), Michael O'Brien; 198 (2a), H. Douglas Pratt; 198 (2b), H. Douglas Pratt; 198 (2c), Diane Pierce; 198 (2d), Michael O'Brien; 198 (2e), David Beadle; 198 (3a), Diane Pierce; 198 (3b), N. John Schmitt; 198 (3c), Donald L. Malick; 198 (3d), H. Douglas Pratt; 198 (3e), H. Douglas Pratt; 198 (4a), H. Douglas Pratt; 198 (4b), Donald L. Malick; 198 (4c), H. Douglas Pratt; 198 (4d), H. Douglas Pratt; 198 (4e), H. Douglas Pratt; 198 (5a-5e), H. Douglas Pratt; 199 (UP), Arterra/Getty Images; 199 (LO), Courtesy of Kevin J. McGowan; 200-201, Monica Serrano, NGM staff; Mesa Schumacher. Art: Vlad Rodriguez; 202 (UP), Sylvain Grandadam/Getty Images; 202 (LO), OGphoto/Getty Images; 203 (LE), Joel Sartore/NG Photo Ark, photographed at El Nispero Zoo, Panama; 203 (RT), David Boughey/Getty Images; 203 (LO), Rick Friedman/Getty Images; 204, Craig Mahaffey; 205, Peter Frank Edwards/Redux; 206, Jared Travnicek; 207 (1a), John Serrao/Science Source; 207 (1b), John Flannery/Flickr (https://creativecommons.org/licenses/by-sa/2.0/legalcode); 207 (1c), J.T. Chapman/Shutterstock; 207 (1d), John Flannery/flickr (https://creativecommons.org/licenses/by-sa/2.0/legalcode); 207 (2a), Steve Byland/Shutterstock; 207 (2b), Arthur V. Evans; 207 (2c), Carolina Birdman/Getty Images; 207 (2d), Steven Russell Smith Photos/Shutterstock; 207 (3a), Claudia Steininger/Getty Images; 207 (3b), Leena Robinson/Shutterstock; 207 (3c), John Flannery/flickr (https://creativecommons.org/licenses/by-sa/2.0/legalcode); 207 (3d), Sari ONeal/Shutterstock; 207 (4a), Paul Reeves Photography/Shutterstock; 207 (4b), Betty Shelton/Shutterstock; 207 (4c), Steven Russell Smith Photos/Shutterstock; 207 (4d), Matt Jeppson/Shutterstock; 208-209, Kees Smans/Getty Images; 210 (UP LE), Farmers at Work, Northern Song Dynasty, 960-1279 (wall painting)/Mogao Caves, Dunhuang, Gansu Province, NW China/Bridgeman Images; 210 (UP CTR LE), Time Life Pictures/Mansell/The LIFE Picture Collection/Getty Images; 210 (UP CTR RT), SuperStock/Getty Images; 210 (UP RT), Bahadir Yeniceri/Shutterstock; 210 (LO LE), Le Do/Shutterstock; 210 (LO CTR LE), andersphoto/Shutterstock; 210 (LO CTR RT), Universal History Archive/Getty Images; 210 (LO RT), emattil/Shutterstock; 210-11, Ralph Lee Hopkins/NG Image Collection; 211 (UP LE), Alfred Eisenstaedt/The LIFE Picture Collection/Getty Images; 211 (UP CTR), TTstudio/Shutterstock; 211 (UP RT), Alex Wong/Getty Images; 211 (LO LE), Clair Dunn/Alamy Stock Photo; 211 (LO CTR LE), Peter Wey/Shutterstock; 211 (LO CTR RT), Jiang Hongyan/Shutterstock; 211 (LO RT), Peangdao/Shutterstock; 212-13, Joel Sartore/NG Photo Ark, photographed at Tierpark Berlin; 213, Doug Gimesy/NG Image Collection; 214-215, Zakir Chowdhury/Barcroft Images/Barcroft Media via Getty Images; 216-17, Paul & Paveena Mckenzie/Getty Images; 218-19, Greg Dunn and Brian Edwards; 220 (TOP), Rebecca Hale, NG Staff; 220 (UP LE), Manoj Kumar/EyeEm/Getty Images; 220 (UP RT), Robert Clark/NG Image Collection; 220 (CTR), Andrii Horulko/Shutterstock; 220 (LO), Ermak Oksana/Shutterstock; 221 (UP LE), stockcreations/Shutterstock; 221 (UP RT), Felipe Tofani/EyeEm/Getty Images; 221 (LO), Zhenyakot/Shutterstock; 222 (UP LE), John Reader/Science Source; 222 (UP RT), Rosa Jay/Shutterstock; 222 (CTR LE), Christian Jégou/Publiphoto/Science Source; 222 (CTR LE CTR), The Venus of Willendorf, Fertility Symbol, prehistoric sculpture, 30,000-25,000 B.C. (front view)/Naturhistorisches Museum, Vienna, Austria/Ali Meyer/Bridgeman Images; 222 (CTR RT CTR), Dja65/Shutterstock; 222 (CTR RT), Cylinder vessel, Guatemala, ca 600-900 (ceramic & paint), Mayan/Collection of the Lowe Art Museum, University of Miami/Anonymous donor/Bridgeman Images; 222 (LO), Temple of Five Terraces, Etzna, Campeche, Mexico (w/c on paper), Hughes, Nigel (b.1940)/Private Collection/Bridgeman Images; 222-3, Michael Melford/NG Image Collection; 223 (UP LE), Science Source; 223 (UP CTR), Science Source; 223 (UP RT), Friedrich Saurer/Science Source; 223 (LO LE), guideline/Shutterstock; 223 (LO RT), Brent Stirton/Getty Images; 224 (UP), © Bone Clones, www.boneclones.com; 224 (CTR), Crazytang/Getty Images; 224 (LO), Richard Nowitz/Science Source; 225 (UP), John R. Foster/Science Source; 225 (CTR), Richard Nowitz/Science Source; 225 (LO), Stefan Fichtel/NG Image Collection; 226, Sculpture by John Gurche, photo by Mark Thiessen, NG Staff; 226-7, Naashon Zalk/The New York Times/Redux; 229, Randy Olson/NG Image Collection; 230, Joe McNally; 231, Map by Charles Berry and Lisa R. Ritter; 232 (UP), R Ramana Reddy Battula/Alamy Stock Photo; 232 (LO), Keren Su/Getty Images; 233 (LE), Ioeskieboom/Getty Images; 233 (RT), Laurent Giraudou/Getty Images; 234-5, Vanderlei Almeida/AFP via Getty Images; 236 (UP LE), Anastasia Taylor-Lind; 236 (UP RT), Mauricio Lima; 236 (LO LE), Lynsey Addario; 236 (LO RT), Nichole Sobecki; 237 (UP LE), Pete K. Muller; 237 (UP RT), Cristina Mittermeier/NG Image Collection; 237 (LO LE), David Alan Harvey; 237 (LO RT), Ed Kashi/VII; 238-239, NG Maps; 240, Wade Davis/Getty Images; 241, Wade Davis; 242-3, NG Maps; 244, Pietro Canali/SIME/eStock Photo; 245, Art: Álvaro Valiño. Source: Sustainable Cities Mobility Index 2017, Planet Sub-Index, Arcadis; 246-7, NG Maps; 248-249, Monica Serrano, NGM Staff; Kelsey Nowakowski. Sources: J.G. Melton, Baylor Univ.; P. Mirecki, D. Stevenson, and S.H. Brody, Univ. of Kansas; B. Collins, Ohio Univ.; S.J. Singh, Sikh Coalition; G. Filson and C. Gaber, Bahá'í Community of Canada; J. Richey, Berea College; National Portal of India; OPM; World Religion Database; 250 (UP LE), Cory Richards; 250 (UP RT), Amy Toensing/NG Image Collection; 250 (LO LE), Sara Hylton; 250 (LO RT), Cristina Mittermeier; 251 (UP LE), Robin Hammond; 251 (UP RT), Diana Markosian; 251 (LO LE), Mike Hettwer; 251 (LO RT), Nora Lorek; 252, Magnus Wennman; 253, Magnus Wennman; 254-5, Graphics by Álvaro Valiño; 256-7, Monica Serrano, NGM Staff; Mesa Schumacher. Sources: Steven Lockley, Brigham and Women's Hospital; Russell Foster, University of Oxford; David Sliney, Johns Hopkins University School of Public Health; Michael Perlis; f.luxometer Project; 258-9, Lynn Johnson/NG Image Collection; 260-61, Jason Treat and Kurt Mutchler, NG Staff. Anthony Schick. Art by Bryan Christie, Photo by Josh L. Morgan, Harvard University, Arthur Wetzel, Pittsburgh Supercomputing Center; 262, Rebecca Hale, NG Staff; 263, Dr. Stephanie Grella; 264 (UP LE), Consultation with an ayurvedic doctor (oil on canvas), Somu, M. (20th-21st century)/Kerala, India/Photo © Luca Tettoni/Bridgeman Images; 264 (UP CTR), Oxford Science Archive/Print Collector/Getty Images; 264 (UP RT), Louis Pasteur (1822-1895) in his Laboratory, 1885 (oil on canvas), Edelfelt, Albert Gustaf Aristides (1854-1905)/Musée d'Orsay, Paris, France/Bridgeman Images; 264 (CTR), Terence Mendoza/Shutterstock; 264 (LO LE), DEA Picture Library/De Agostini/Getty Images; 264 (LO RT), Hill Street Studios/Photolibrary/Getty Images; 264-265, gopixa/Getty Images; 265 (UP LE), © CORBIS/Corbis via Getty Images; 265 (UP CTR LE), Svetlana Voronina/Shutterstock; 265 (UP CTR RT), Living Art Enterprises/Science Source; 265 (UP RT), Neil Harding/Getty Images; 265 (LO LE), Spencer Grant/Science Source/Getty Images; 265 (LO CTR), Africa Studio/Shutterstock; 265 (LO RT), Viktor Drachev/TASS via Getty Images; 266-7, Rebecca Hale, NG Staff (cheeses), Benjamin E. Wolfe (microbes); 268-9, Graphic: Álvaro Valiño. Sources: Natural Resources Defense Council; CDC; USDA; Alliance for the Prudent Use of Antibiotics; National Antimicrobial Resistance Monitoring System; 270-71, Maggie Steber; 272-3, Roger Harris/Science Source; 274 (1a), Dionisvera/Shutterstock; 274 (1b), Karl Allgaeuer/Shutterstock; 274 (1c), Madlen/Shutterstock; 274 (1d), Brian Kinney/Shutterstock; 274 (2a), Swapan Photography/Shutterstock; 274 (2b), Dionisvera/Shutterstock; 274 (2c), Kelvin Wong/Shutterstock; 274 (2d), nednapa/Shutterstock; 274 (3a), Scisetti Alfio/Shutterstock; 274 (3b), Alexander Raths/Shutterstock; 274 (3c), Maks Narodenko/Shutterstock; 274 (3d), Scisetti Alfio/Shutterstock; 274 (4a), givaga/Shutterstock; 274 (4b), Robyn Mackenzie/Shutterstock; 274 (4c), Volosina/Shutterstock; 274 (4d), haraldmuc/Shutterstock; 275 (1a), sherlesi/Shutterstock; 275 (1b), nanka/Shutterstock; 275 (1c), ultimathule/Shutterstock; 275 (1d), Romaset/Dreamstime.com; 275 (2a), Serhiy Shullye/Shutterstock; 275 (2b), bergamont/Shutterstock; 275 (2c), Andrey Starostin/Shutterstock; 275 (2d), Dionisvera/Shutterstock; 275 (3a), Amero/Shutterstock; 275 (3b), ultimathule/Shutterstock; 275 (3c), vladis.studio/Shutterstock; 275 (3d), panda3800/

Shutterstock; 275 (LO), Courtesy Ina Vandebroek; 276-7, Tatiana Kolesnikova/Getty Images; 278-9, Aying Salupan; 280-81, Yaorusheng/Getty Images; 282 (TOP), Rebecca Hale, NG Staff; 282 (UP LE), Nic_Taylor/Getty Images; 282 (UP CTR), Far.screative/Shutterstock; 282 (UP RT), Nick Brundle Photography/Getty Images; 282 (LO LE), igor gratzer/Shutterstock; 282 (LO RT), Timothy Allen/Design Pics/NG Image Collection; 283 (UP LE), Hulton Archive/Stringer/Getty Images; 283 (UP RT), Regien Paassen/Shutterstock; 283 (CTR), Kenneth Garrett/NG Image Collection; 283 (LO), Media24/Gallo Images/Getty Images; 284 (UP LE), Joe McNally; 284 (UP CTR), Seal depicting a mythological animal and pictographic symbols, from Mohenjo-Daro, Indus Valley, Pakistan, 3000-1500 B.C. (stone), Harappan/National Museum of Karachi, Karachi, Pakistan/Bridgeman Images; 284 (UP RT), Aranami/Shutterstock; 284 (CTR LE), anyaivanova/Shutterstock; 284 (CTR RT), Greece: Marble bust of Alexander the Great at the British Museum, London/Pictures from History/Bridgeman Images; 284 (LO LE), Weeding, The Rice Culture in China (color woodblock print), Chinese School, (19th century)/Private Collection/Archives Charmet/Bridgeman Images; 284 (LO CTR LE), DEA/G. DAGLI ORTI/De Agostini/Getty Images; 284 (LO CTR RT), Rodolfo Parulan, Jr./Getty Images; 284 (LO RT), Photos.com/Getty Images; 284-5, Leeuwtje/Getty Images; 285 (UP LE), Boris Vetshev/Shutterstock; 285 (UP CTR LE), Fine Art Images/Heritage Images/Getty Images; 285 (UP CTR RT), Ms FR 22495 f.265v Battle of Damietta in Egypt in 1218-1219, during the fifth crusade (1217-1221) from Historia by Guillaume de Tyr, 1337 (vellum), French School, (14th century)/Bibliothèque Nationale, Paris, France/Tallandier/Bridgeman Images; 285 (UP RT), KHM-Museumsverband, Weltmuseum Vienna; 285 (CTR), Luther as Professor, 1529 (oil on panel), Cranach, Lucas, the Elder (1472-1553)/Schlossmuseum, Weimar, Germany/Bridgeman Images; 285 (LO LE), clu/Getty Images; 285 (LO CTR), rimglow/Getty Images; 285 (LO RT), Pilgrim's "Blue and White" Gourd with Floral Decorations, ca 1403-1424 (ceramic), Chinese School, (15th century)/Musée Guimet, Paris, France/Bridgeman Images; 286-7, Jason Treat, NGM Staff. Art: Sam Falconer. Sources: Sara Graça da Silva, Institute for the Study of Literature and Tradition (IELT), New University of Lisbon, Portugal; Jamie Tehrani, Durham University; 288-9, Fine Art Images/Heritage Image Partnership Ltd/Alamy Stock Photo; 290-91, Album/Art Resource, NY; 292 (UP LE), Asante funerary mask, from Ghana (ceramic), African School/Private Collection/Photo © Boltin Picture Library/Bridgeman Images; 292 (UP RT), Universal History Archive/Getty Images; 292 (CTR LE), Powhatan, Father of Pocahontas, Engraving/Private Collection/J. T. Vintage/Bridgeman Images; 292 (CTR LE CTR), Portrait of Grand Duchess Catherine Alekseevna, future Empress Catherine II the Great, ca 1760 (oil on canvas), Antropov, Alexei Petrovich (1716-1795)/Radishchev State Art Museum, Saratov, Russia/Bridgeman Image; 292 (CTR RT CTR), Portrait of Simon Bolivar; Retrato de Simon Bolivar, ca 1925 (oil on canvas), Colombian School, (19th century)/Private Collection/Photo © Christie's Images/Bridgeman Images; 292 (CTR RT), Photo Researchers/Getty Images; 292 (LO LE), Portrait of King Charles I (1600-1649) (oil on canvas), Dyck, Anthony van (1599-1641) (workshop of)/Private Collection/Photo © Philip Mould Ltd, London/Bridgeman Images; 292 (LO CTR), Cross-section of H.M.S. Endeavour, Captain Cook's ship from his first voyage, (1768-71) (colour litho), Adams, Dennis (1914-2001)/Alecto Historical Editions, London, UK/Bridgeman Images; 292 (LO RT), Queen Victoria, 1877 (oil on panel), Angeli, Heinrich von (1840-1925)/Private Collection/Photo © Christie's Images/Bridgeman Images; 292-3, ArtisticPhoto/Shutterstock; 293 (UP), Keystone/Getty Images; 293 (CTR LE), Soviet poster featuring Lenin (color litho), Russian School, (20th century)/Private Collection/Peter Newark Historical Pictures/Bridgeman Images; 293 (CTR), Hulton Archive/Getty Images; 293 (CTR RT), David Hume Kennerly/Getty Images; 293 (LO LE), Dinodia Photos/Getty Images; 293 (LO CTR LE), swim ink 2/Corbis via Getty Images; 293 (LO CTR RT), Catalina M/Shutterstock; 293 (LO RT), Chris Jackson/Getty Images; 294, Pascal Deloche/Getty Images; 295 (LE), Todd Gipstein/NG Image Collection; 295 (RT), Franck Prevel/Getty Images; 296, Robbie Shone/NG Image Collection; 297, Justin Schneider; 298 (UP LE), Simon Norfolk; 298 (UP RT), Pete McBride; 298 (LO LE), George Steinmetz/NG Image Collection; 298 (LO RT), Michael Yamashita/NG Image Collection; 299 (UP LE), Babak Tafreshi/NG Image Collection; 299 (UP RT), Rena Effendi; 299 (LO LE), Jim Richardson/NG Image Collection; 299 (LO RT), Ira Block; 300-301, Tom Till/Getty Images; 302, Kenneth Garrett/NG Image Collection; 303, Kenneth Garrett/NG Image Collection; 304 (UP LE), Paul Paladin/Shutterstock; 304 (UP CTR LE), asharkyu/Shutterstock; 304 (UP CTR RT), Seated Mastiff, ca 100 (earthenware), Chinese School, Eastern Han Dynasty (25-220)/Indianapolis Museum of Art at Newfields, USA/Eleanor Evans Stout and Margaret Stout Gibbs Memorial Fund/in Memory of Wilbur D. Peat/Bridgeman Images; 304 (UP RT), fotohunter/Shutterstock; 304 (CTR), Agnieszka Skalska/Shutterstock.com; 304 (LO LE), Pecold/Shutterstock; 304 (LO CTR), Marques/Shutterstock; 304 (LO RT), Jan Schneckenhaus/Shutterstock; 304-305, Luis Castaneda Inc./Getty Images; 305 (UP LE), De Agostini Picture Library/Getty Images; 305 (UP CTR LE), SSPL/Getty Images; 305 (UP CTR RT), ullstein bild/ullstein bild via Getty Images; 305 (UP RT), SSPL/Getty Images; 305 (LO LE), Portrait of Benjamin Franklin (Boston, 1706-Philadelphia, 1790), American scientist and politician/De Agostini Picture Library/M. Seemuller/Bridgeman Images; 305 (LO CTR), New York Public Library/Science Source; 305 (LO RT), Nerthuz/Shutterstock; 306-307, Art: Thom Tenery. Source: James Delgado, Search, Inc.; 307, Elias Williams; 308, Fotosearch/Getty Images; 309, New York Times Co./Getty Images; 310 (UP LE), The Arrival of the English in Virginia, from Admiranda Narratio, 1585-88 (colored engraving), Bry, Theodore de (1528-1598)/Service Historique de la Marine, Vincennes, France/Bridgeman Images; 310 (UP RT), Loyalist/Tory, King's American Regt. Officer, 2007 (w/c & gouache on paper), Troiani, Don (b.1949)/Private Collection/Bridgeman Images; 310 (CTR LE), Illustration for the Young Pilgrims, Hardy, Evelyn Stuart (1865-1935)/Private Collection/© Look and Learn/Bridgeman Images; 310 (CTR RT), stoonn/Getty Images; 310 (LO CTR LE), Pontiac (1720-1769) 1763 (oil on canvas), Stanley, John Mix (1814-1872)/Private Collection/Peter Newark American Pictures/Bridgeman Images; 310 (LO CTR RT), Gilbert Stuart/National Gallery of Art, Washington, D.C./Getty Images; 310 (LO), Visions of America/Purestock/Alamy Stock Photo; 310-11, Stock Montage/Getty Images; 311 (UP LE), Harriet Tubman (1820-1913), American Abolitionist, Portrait, ca 1885/Private Collection/J. T. Vintage/Bridgeman Images; 311 (UP CTR LE), John Parrot/Stocktrek Images/Getty Images; 311 (UP CTR RT), U.S. National Archives; 311 (UP RT), AFP/Getty Images; 311 (LO LE), 39th North Carolina flag (textile), American School, (19th century)/Private Collection/Photo © Civil War Archive/Bridgeman Images; 311 (LO CTR LE), GHI/Universal History Archive via Getty Images; 311 (LO CTR RT), NASA/The LIFE Premium Collection/Getty Images; 311 (LO RT), Scott Olson/Getty Images; 312 (UP), Ricky Carioti/The Washington Post via Getty Images; 312 (LO), Women's Suffrage in the USA: Women Voting in the Wyoming Territory after Winning That Right in 1869 (color engraving), American School, (19th century)/Private Collection/Peter Newark American Pictures/Bridgeman Images; 313, FPG/Getty Images; 314-15, Ryan Budhu/Getty Images; 324-5, Nimbus Sankt Peter, 2013, by Berndnaut Smilde, photo by Cassander Eeftinck Schattenkerk; 326-7, NASA/Terry Virts; 328 (TOP), Rebecca Hale, NG Staff; 328 (UP), byvalet/Shutterstock; 328 (CTR LE), Jones/Shimlock-Secret Sea Visions/Getty Images; 328 (CTR RT), Alexander Spatari/Getty Images; 328 (LO LE), Alex Rockheart/Shutterstock; 328 (LO RT), Robin Hammond; 329 (UP LE), Nopparat Promtha/Shutterstock; 329 (UP RT), ETG/Shutterstock; 329 (CTR), Steve McCurry; 329 (LO), Nerthuz/Shutterstock; 334 (UP LE), Enric Sala; 334 (UP RT), David Guttenfelder; 334 (LO LE), Richard Barnes; 334 (LO RT), Michael Christopher Brown; 335 (UP LE), Pete McBride; 335 (UP RT), Frans Lanting/lanting.com; 335 (LO LE), Stephen Wilkes; 335 (LO RT), Daniella Zalcman; 339, Domingo Leiva/Getty Images; 341, Anton Petrus/Getty Images; 343, Nave Orgad/Sime/eStock Photo; 345, Stefano Politi Markovina; 347, Chris Owens; 349, Frans Lanting/NG Image Collection; 351, Frans Lanting/NG Image Collection; 364 (UP LE), Simon Norfolk; 364 (UP RT), Paul Nicklen; 364 (LO LE), Ronan Donovan; 364 (LO RT), Stephen Wilkes; 365 (UP LE), Andy Mann/NG Image Collection; 365 (UP RT), Jimmy Chin; (LO LE), James D. Balog; 365 (LO RT), Ira Block; 372, Osugi/Shutterstock.com; 373, Brian Skerry/NG Image Collection; 380-81, Andrew Moore.

INDEX

Boldface indicates illustrations.

A

A Rocha 246
Abu Dhabi **334**
Aconcagua, Argentina 341
Adad-nirari III, King (Babylon) 289
Adventure travel 46–47, **46–47,**
    84–85, **84–85**
Afghanistan 25, 315, 344, 366,
    366
Africa
    human origins 228, 229
    map and facts 346–347
    urbanization 242–243
African gray parrots 202, 203,
    203
Agriculture 229, 254–255, 342
Ahmad, Magd **77**
Ahmad, Nisrine **77**
Ahmed, Ummey **236**
Aida, Miho 58–59, **58–59**
Akhenaten, Pharaoh 302, 303
Alabama **49, 318**
Alaska 59, 73, **124, 173, 318, 334**
Alatna River, Alaska **124**
Albania 366, **366**
Albatrosses 340, **364**
Aldrin, Edwin "Buzz" 130, **143**
Alex (parrot) 203, **203**
Algeria 98, 347, 366, **366**
Alps, Europe 98
Amazon region, South America 52,
    84, 238
American Samoa **322**
Andaman and Nicobar Islands 358
Andes, South America 98, 109
Andorra 366, **366**
Andromeda galaxy **32**
Anemones **187**
Angel Falls, Venezuela 340
Angola 366, **366**
Animal kingdom 161, **161**
Animal tracks 176, **176**
Anker, Conrad 50, **50**
Anna's hummingbirds **196**
Antarctic Treaty 350

Antarctica
    diving 44–45, **44–45**
    extremes 53
    icebergs **351**
    map and facts 350–351
    @natgeo photos **48, 110, 186, 196**
    oceans 362–363
    travel 71, 89
Anthony, Marek 55
Antibiotic resistance 268–269,
    268–269
Antigua and Barbuda 366, **366**
Apollo missions 130
Apostle Islands National Lakeshore,
    Wisconsin 47, **47**
Arab Spring (2010) 295
Arabian Desert **5**
Archaea 160, **160**
Archaeology, underwater 296–297,
    297, 338
Arctic National Wildlife Refuge,
    Alaska 59
Arctic Ocean 360–361, **365**
Arfvedson, John August 109
Argentina
    Cerro Aconcagua 341
    disappearing languages 238
    flag and facts 366, **366**
    Laguna del Carbón 330, 341
    lithium 108, 109
    @natgeo photos **125**
    Patagonia 42–43, **42–43,** 115, **341**
    travel 66, **66**
Aristotle 294
Arizona 73, **125, 318, 334, 335**
Arkansas 89, **318**
Armenia 366, **366**
Armstrong, Neil 130
Arrigetch Peaks, Alaska **334**
Ashton, Martyn 60, **60**
Asia
    human origins 229
    map and facts 344–345
    urbanization 243
Assal, Lake, Djibouti 347
Asteroid belt 129, 134
Asteroids 134–135, **134–135,** 145
Astronomy see Skywatching; Space

Asylum seekers, map of 24–25
Atacama Desert, Chile 53, **53**
Athens (city-state) 294, **294**
Athens, Greece **77**
Atkinson, Richard 263
Atlantic Ocean 354–355
Atlantic spotted dolphins **186**
Auckland, New Zealand 348
Aurora borealis **146**
Australia
    climate change 99
    dependencies 373
    disappearing languages 239
    exploration and adventure **34–35**
    flag and facts 366, **366**
    Great Barrier Reef 74–75, **74–75**
    human origins 228
    lithium 108
    map and facts 348–349
    travel 65, 74–75, **74–75,** 85, **85**
    wildlife 74–75, 180–181, **180–181,**
        213, 348
Australian king parrots **203**
Australian palm cockatoos 203
Austria 366, **366**
Aviation 308–309, **308–309**
Aymara people 125
Azerbaijan 366, **366**

B

Baboons 182, **182**
Bacon, Sir Francis 20
Bacteria 160, **160,** 266–269, 355
Bagan, Myanmar **299, 345**
Baha'i faith 249, **249**
Bahamas **186,** 235, **326–327,** 338,
    366, **366**
Bahrain 366, **366**
Baikal, Lake, Russia 52
Baker Island 323
Bali, Indonesia 89
Ballard, Robert 309, 355
Ballesta, Laurent 44, **44**
Baluchistan desert, Pakistan **125**
Banff, British Columbia, Canada 89
Banff NP, Canada 17, **17**
Bangalore, India 243

Bangkok, Thailand 243
Bangladesh **21**, 41, **250**, 366, **366**
Banjar, Bali, Indonesia 89
Barbados 332, 366, **366**
Barcelona, Spain **229**, 342
Bears **21**, 174, **175**, 177, **177**
Beck, Maureen 61, **61**
Beef 254, 268
Bees **197**, 208–209, **208–209**
Beijing, China 243
Belarus 366, **366**
Belgium 366, **366**
Belize 366, **366**
Bell, Alexander Graham 9
Bella Coola Valley, British Columbia,
    Canada **124**
Bellamy, Francis 317
Belyaev, Dmitry 179
Benin 366, **366**
BepiColombo spacecraft 126
Beppu, Japan 89
Berg, Pierre 66
Berger, Lee 225, 226, **226–227**
Bhutan 70, **70**, 366, **366**
Bicycling **58**, 58–61, **60, 61**
Big bang theory 140, 141
Big Bend NP, Texas 73
Biking **58**, 58–61, **60, 61**
Biodiversity
    conservation 16
    hot spots 14, 15
    maps 376–377
    new species 17, **17**
    Red List 16
    trends 14–17, **14–17**
    varieties of life 16–17
    wildlife crossings 17, **17**
Birds
    backyard 198–199, **198–199**
    black-browed albatrosses 340
    hummingbirds 200–201, **200–201**
    India 80, **80**
    killed by house cats 179
    @natgeo photos **196–197, 364**
    ornithologists 204–205,
        204–205
    parrots 202–203, **202–203**
    sleep 253
Birds of paradise **196**
Birmingham, England **251**
Bishop, Jack 68, **68**

Black bears **175**, 177, **177**
Black-browed albatrosses 340
Black holes 145
Blacktip reef sharks 75, **186**
Blackwater National Wildlife Refuge,
    Maryland 47
Bligh, William 356
Blizzards **110**
Blue whales 188, **189**, 363
Bobot (language) 239
Bodh Gaya, India 247
Bogotá, Colombia 242
Boivin, Jean-Marc 51
Bolivia 108, 109, 313, 340, 366, **366**
Bolshoi (Grand) Express (train) 65
Bolt, Usain 57
Bonneville Salt Flats, Utah 152,
    152–153
Books, cultural exploration 241
Books, travel 66–67
Bora Bora (island), Tahiti 64, **186, 349**
Borges, Jorge Luis 66
Borneo, Indonesia **17**
Borneo (island), Indonesia 183
Bosnia and Herzegovina 366, **366**
Bosque del Apache National Wildlife
    Refuge, New Mexico **197**
Botswana 71, 346, 366, **366**
Bottlenose dolphins 154, **154–155**
Bounty, as place name 356
Brain, human
    cerebellar folia **218–219**
    memory 262–263, 273
    mindfulness 276–277, **276–277**
    neurons 260–261, **260–261**
    psychobiome 272–273, **272–273**
    sleep and 252–253, 256–257,
        257
Brande, William Thomas 109
Brazil
    Amazon rainforest 84
    Carnival **234–235**, 235
    flag and facts 341, 366, **366**
    greener cities 245
    Nat Geo explorers 40
    @natgeo photos **110, 237**
    wildlife 182, **182**, 340
British Columbia, Canada 84, **84**, 89,
    124, 187
Brooks Range, Alaska **334**
Brunei 366, **366**

Buddhism **240–241**, 246–247, 249,
    249, 298, 299, 344
Buenos Aires, Argentina 66, **66**, 242
Bulgaria 367, **367**
Burgess Shale, Canada **163**
Burkina Faso 367, **367**
Burma *see* Myanmar
Burning Man festival, Nevada **251**
Burrowing owls **197**
Burundi 243, 367, **367**
Butterflies 169, **169**, 206–207,
    206–207
Byers, Alton 41
Byrd Glacier, Antarctica 351

C
Cabo Verde 367, **367**
Cairo, Egypt 243, 245
Calatrava, Santiago 314
California 47, **49**, 53, 64, 73, **318**
Callanish Stones, Scotland **6**
Callisto (Jupiter's moon) 136, **136**
Cambodia 367, **367**
Camels **5**, 347
Cameroon 367, **367**
Canada
    disappearing languages 238
    flag and facts 339, 367, **367**
    fossils **163**, 164
    @natgeo photos **124**
    talking trees 170–171, **170–171**
    travel 70, 84, **84**, 89
    wildlife crossings 17, **17**
Cane toads 180
Cantino, Alberto 291
Cantino Planisphere (map, 1502)
    290–291
Cape ground squirrels **5**
Capestro, Joanne 315
Caribbean region 61, 98, 290
Caribou 59
Carina Nebula **33**
Carnival 234–235, **234–235**
Carriacou (island) 235
Caspian Sea 343, 344
Cassini spacecraft 127
Cassowaries 181
Caterpillars 206, **206**, 254
Catholicism 248, 278, **278–279**, 342
Cats, domesticated 178, 179

Cauliflower coral 75
Caves 53, **53**
Cayman Islands 235
Central African Republic 367, **367**
Central Park, New York City **244**
Cerebellar folia **218–219**
Ceres (dwarf planet) 129
Chaco Canyon, New Mexico 246
Chad 367, **367**
Challenger Deep, Pacific Ocean
    52
Charon (Pluto's moon) 137, **137**
Charote (language) 238
Chechnya, Russia **251**
Cheese 266–267, **266–267**
Chennai, India 243
Cherokee syllabary **49**
Cherrapunji, India 53
Cherry trees **298**
Chesapeake Bay 193
Chicken 254, 268–269, **268–269**
Chile
    Atacama Desert 53, **53**
    disappearing languages 238
    flag and facts 367, **367**
    lithium 108, 109
    marine life **115**
    Patagonia 42–43, **42–43,** 115
    travel 89
Chiller, Tom 268
Chimienti, Giovanni 40
Chimpanzees 183, **183, 184,**
    184–185
China
    climate change 99
    extremes 53
    flag and facts 345, 367, **367**
    Great Wall of China 65, **298**
    greener cities 245
    land claims 344
    lithium 108
    lunar calendar 249
    populous cities 243
    pro-democracy protests 295
    Shanghai 67, **67,** 243, **280–281,**
        380, **380–381**
    space exploration 131
    terra-cotta warriors 300–301,
        300–301
    travel 65, 67, **67**
    water pollution 20, **20,** 21

    as world's most populous coun-
        try 333
Chisholm, Shirley 313
Chocó-Darién forests, South Amer-
    ica 14
Chongqing, China 243
Chouinard, Yvon 43
Christianity 246–249, **249,** 278,
    278–279, 342
Cities 242–245, **244–245**
Clams **4**
Cleisthenes 294
Climate change 98, 99, 189, 229
Climate zones map 98–99
Climbing **34–35, 49,** 50–51, **50–51,**
    61, **61;** see also Trekking
Clinton, Hillary 313
Clotilda (slave ship) 306–307,
    306–307
Clouds 100, **100**
Clownfish 75
Cockatoos 203
Cologne Cathedral, Germany 324–
    325, **324–325**
Colombia 107, 367, **367**
Colonial era 294–295
Colorado 47, 73, 89, **318**
Comets 129, 145
Common ravens **199**
Communication
    animals 188, 203
    trees 166, 170–171, **170–171**
Comoros 346, 367, **367**
Confucianism 249, **249**
Congo, Democratic Republic of the
    346, 367, **367**
Congo, Republic of 367, **367**
Connecticut: state flag **318**
Conservation 210–215
    Arctic National Wildlife Refuge,
        Alaska 59
    biodiversity 16
    birds 204–205
    Patagonia, Argentina-Chile
        42–43, **42–43**
    Photo Ark 212–213, **212–213**
    plastics and 214–215, **214–215**
    time line 210–211, **210–211**
    Wynn-Grant, Rae 174–175,
        174–175
    see also Earth Day every day

Constellations 118–122, **118–122**
Constitution, U.S. 295, **295,** 312,
    323
Continental drift 336
Continents 336–351
    Africa 346–347, **347**
    Antarctica 350–351, **351**
    Asia 344–345, **345**
    Australia & Oceania 348–349,
        349
    Europe 342–343, **343**
    North America 338–339, **339**
    Pangaea 336–337
    South America 340–341, **341**
Coral reefs 74–75, **74–75, 81, 349,**
    354
Coronavirus 26-27, **26-27**
Corvids 199, **199**
Cosmic radiation 146–147, **146–147,**
    151
Costa Rica 367, **367**
Côte d'Ivoire 367, **367**
Countries: flags and facts 366–373
Cranes (birds) **196**
Crater Lake NP, Oregon 73
Crawford Notch State Park, New
    Hampshire 47
Creasman, Pearce Paul 296–297,
    297
Crested black macaques **173**
Crimson-fronted parakeets **203**
Croatia 367, **367**
Crocodiles 75, 340
Crows 199
Cruises 71, **71**
Cuba **364,** 367, **367**
Culture 232–251
    anthropology 240–241, **240–241**
    books 241
    folk tales 286–287, **286–287**
    intangible 232–235, **232–235**
    languages 238–239
    map of immigration worldwide
        24–25
    @natgeo photos 236–237,
        250–251
    urbanization 242–245
    see also Religion
Curaçao **197**
Curiosity (Martian rover) 126
Cyanobacteria 216

Cycling **58,** 58–61, **60, 61**
Cyprus 367, **367**
Czechia 367, **367**

D

Danakil Depression, Africa 53
Dante Alighieri 289
Darius, King (Persia) 298
Dark energy 140–141, **140–141**
Dark matter **140,** 140–141, 150–151, **150–151**
Darwin, Charles 64
Dashi, Dhakti **250**
Dasht-e Lut, Iran **48**
Davis, Wade 240–241, **240–241**
Davy, Sir Humphry 109
De Anda, Guillermo 40
Dead Sea, Israel-Jordan 345
Death Valley NP, California-Nevada 53
Deception Island, Antarctica 89
Declaration of Independence 295
Deer Isle, Maine **364**
Delaware: state flag **318**
Delhi, India 243
Delta Aquarids meteor shower 123
Dementia 252
Democracy 294–295, **294–295**
Democratic Republic of the Congo 346, 367, **367**
Denali NP, Alaska **173**
Denmark 268, 330, 367, **367,** 373
Deserts 98
Dewan, Leslie 40
Dhaka, Bangladesh 243
Día de los Muertos 233, **233**
Diagne, Tomas 40
Dinagyang Festival, Philippines 278, **278–279**
Dinosaurs 162, 164–165, **164–165,** 337
Diodorus Siculus 289
Disabilities, athletes with 60–61, **60–61**
Diving
    Antarctica 44–45, **44–45**
    India 81, **81**
    Kingman Reef **48**
    underwater archaeology 296–297, **297**

underwater art museums 54–55, **54–55**
Djibouti 53, 347, 367, **367**
DNA
    Egyptians 302–303, **302–303**
    human migration 228–229
    Neanderthal 230–231
    track your own ancestry 229, 231
Dogs 178–179, **178–179**
Dolgan (language) 239
Dolphins 154, **154–155, 186,** 253
Domestication 178–179, **178–179**
Dominica 367, **367**
Dominican Republic 235, 367, **367**
Dorje (yak herder) **250**
Douglas fir trees 170–171, **170–171**
Drake Passage 362
Dry Valleys, Antarctica 53
Dubai **76**
Dugongs 75
Dunton, Colorado 89
Dwarf planets 128–129, **128–129**

E

Eagles 75
Earhart, Amelia 308–309, **308–309**
Earth 92–117
    climate zones map 98–99
    clouds 100, **100**
    cosmic radiation 147, **147**
    extremes 52–53, **52–53**
    future 374–375
    hurricanes 104–105, **104–105**
    land surface 331
    lightning 101, **101, 111**
    lithium 108–109
    map of climate zones 98–99
    map of extreme weather events 374–375
    minerals 112–113, **112–113**
    @natgeo photos **110–111, 124–125**
    time line 96–97, **96–97**
    volcanic islands 116–117, **116–117**
    volcanoes 106–107, **106–107**
    wildfires 102, **102–103, 111**
Earth Day every day
    ethnobotany 233

honeybees 209
insects as food 254–255, **254–255**
    light pollution 121
    plastic use 215
    religion 246
East Timor (Timor-Leste) 371, **371**
Easter Island, South Pacific Ocean 357
Eclipses 123
Ecuador **14–15,** 64, **110,** 367, **367**
Egypt
    adventure travel 85
    ancient DNA 302–303, **302–303**
    flag and facts 367, **367**
    Giza Pyramids 64, **299,** 346
    greener cities 245
    primates 182, **182**
Eiffel Tower, Paris, France 67, **67, 236**
El Salvador 367, **367**
El'brus, Mount, Russia 343
Elephants **173,** 346
Emperor penguins **110, 196**
Enceladus (Saturn's moon) 137, **137**
Endangered and threatened species 16
England **251,** 294; *see also* United Kingdom
Equatorial Guinea 367, **367**
Erebus, H.M.S. 338
Eris (dwarf planet) 128
Eritrea 53, 368, **368**
ESA (European Space Agency) 126
Estonia 368, **368**
Eswatini 368, **368**
Ethiopia 53, 224, **224,** 368, **368**
Ethnobotany 233, 275
Eukarya 161, **161**
Eurasian magpies 199
Europa (Jupiter's moon) 136, **136**
Europe
    climate change 98
    human origins 229
    map and facts 342–343
    urbanization 242–243
European Space Agency (ESA) 126
Everest, Mount, China-Nepal 50–51, **50–51,** 53, **250,** 345
Evolution
    human 224–225, **224–225**
    key dates 161, 337

time line 222–223, **222–223**
whales 189
Exoplanets 145, 148–149, **148–149**
Exploration 34–91
    adventure 44–49, **44–49**, 90–91,
      90–91
    classic travel 62–75, **62–75**
    diving Antarctica 44–45, **44–45**
    extremes 50–61, **50–61**
    map 40–41
    Patagonia conservation 42–43,
      42–43
    solar system 126–127, **126–127**
    time line 38–39, **38–39**
    travel trends 76–89, **76–89**
Extremes 50–57, **50–57**
Eyre, Lake, Australia 349

F

Face transplants 270–271, **270–271**
Fagan, Patricia Mary 315
Fairy tales 286–287, **286–287**
Falkland Islands 340, **364**
Farsi language 344
Fazekas, Andrew 119, **119**
Fermented foods 266–267, **266–**
    267, 273
Festivals and holidays
    Carnival 234–235, **234–235**
    Dinagyang Festival, Philippines
      278, **278–279**
    @natgeo photos **250, 251**
    religious holidays **229**, 233, **233**,
      248–249, **248–249**
Fiji 368, **368**
Finland 368, **368**
Fir trees 170–171, **170–171**
Fires 102, **102–103, 111**
Fish 75, 348
Fishing industry 354, 360
Fitz Roy Mountain, Argentina **341**
Flags
    countries of the world **366–372**
    United States 316–317, **316–317**
    U.S. states **318–321**
    U.S. territories 322–323, **322–323**
Flamingos **197**, 216, **216–217**
Flint Hills, Kansas 47
Floods **20–21**, 21, **21**, 111
Florida **2–3**, 47, 54–55, **124**, **197**, 318

Flowers 168, **168**, 169, **169**, 201
Folk tales 286–287, **286–287**
Food
    cheese 266–267, **266–267**
    herbs & spices 274–275, **274–275**
    insects as 254–255, **254–255**
    Italy 68–69, **68–69**
    meat consumption in U.S. 268
    psychobiome and 273
Forests 84, 166, 170–171, **170–171**
Fossils **162–163**, 162–165, 224–225,
    224–225
Foxes 179
France
    asylum-seekers 24
    dependencies 373
    flag and facts 368, **368**
    history of democracy 295
    @natgeo photos **236, 299**
    Paris 67, **67, 236**, 242, **299**
    perfume 233, **233**
Frankfurt, Germany 245
Freedman, Wendy 144, **144**
French Polynesia 64, 71, **186**
Frigatebirds 253
Frill-necked lizards **213**
Frogs **84**
Fuji, Mount, Japan 65, **334**
Fungi 161, **161**, 267
Future
    Earth 374–375
    humans on Earth 378–379
    life on Earth 376–377

G

Gabon 115, 355, 368, **368**
Gachet, Karla **76**
Gaffrey, Justin 55
Gagarin, Yuri 131
Galápagos Islands, South Pacific
    Ocean 64
Galway, Ireland 78–79, **78–79**
Gama, Vasco da 291
Gambia 368, **368**
Ganci, Peter James, Jr. 315
Ganges River, India 52, 247
Ganymede (Jupiter's moon) 136,
    136
Gardens 66, **66**, 201
Gardens of the Queen, Cuba **364**

Gates of the Arctic NP, Alaska **124**
Gaudí, Antoni 342
Geminids meteor shower 123
Gender 258–259, **258–259**
Genetics *see* DNA
Genographic Project 228, 231
Georgia (republic) 368, **368**
Georgia (state) **318**
Geothermal energy 89
Germany 24, 245, 324–325, **324–**
    325, 368, **368**
Geysers **92–93**
Ghana 203, 368, **368**
Giant clams **4**
Giant Magellan Telescope 144
Giant pandas **173**
Giant tortoises **172**
Giza, Egypt 64, **299**, 346
Glaciers **48, 49, 124**
Global warming 360, **365**; *see also*
    Climate change
Goats **172**
Gobi Desert, Mongolia 85, **85**
Golden lion tamarins 182, **182**
Goldilocks zone 148
Gombe Stream NP, Tanzania **184,**
    184–185
Goodall, Jane 184–185, **184–185**
Gorillas 183, **183**
Grand Canyon, Arizona **125, 335**
Gray whales 189
Great Barrier Reef, Australia 74–75,
    74–75
Great Britain *see* United Kingdom
Great frigatebirds 253
Great Ocean Road, Australia 85, **85**
Great Wall of China 65, **298**
Greece 65, **77**, 84, 117, **343**, 368, **368**
Green cities 244–245, **244–245**
Green sea turtles 75
Greenland 330, 338, **365**
Grenada 368, **368**
Grey crowned cranes **196**
Griffith-Joyner, Florence 57
Grimm, Wilhelm and Jacob 286
Grizzly bears 174
Ground squirrels **5**
Gschaar, Robert Joseph 315
Guam **322**, 348
Guangzhou, China 243
Guatemala 368, **368**

Guinea 368, **368**
Guinea-Bissau 368, **368**
Gulf Stream 98
Guyana 368, **368**
Gwich'in Nation 59

H

Hahn, Dave 51
Haida (language) 238
Haiti 235, 368, **368**
Hamadryas baboon 182, **182**
Hamilton, Bethany 60, **60**
Hana Highway, Hawaii 64
Harp seals **187**
Haumea (dwarf planet) 129
Hausa architecture **237**
Havasu Falls, Arizona **335**
Hawaii **49**, 53, 64, **110**, 116–117,
    116–117, 318
Hayabusa spacecraft 135
Hayabusa2 spacecraft 126, 135
Health and medicine
    antibiotic resistance 268–269,
        268–269
    face transplants 270–271,
        270–271
    gender 258–259, **258–259**
    herbs & spices 274–275,
        274–275
    human body, in space 147
    internal clock 256–257, **256–257**
    mindfulness 276–277, **276–277**
    psychobiome 272–273, **272–273**
    sleep 252–253, **252–253**, 256–
        257, **256–257**
    time line 264–265, **264–265**
Heese, Tracey George **250**
Hemis NP, India 81, **81**
Herbs 274–275, **274–275**
Herodotus (historian) 289
Herring, Rachel 55
Herschel, William 137
Hill, Elsie 312
Hillary, Edmund 51
Hinduism **125**, 232, **232**, 246–248,
    248
History 280–325
    democracy 294–295, **294–295**
    DNA from ancient Egypt 302–
        303, **302–303**

exploration time line 38–39,
    38–39
innovations time line 304–305,
    304–305
map (1502) 290–291
@natgeo photos **298–299**
100-meter dash 56–57, **56–57**
prehistory to 1600 time line
    284–285, **284–285**
Sammu-ramat, Queen (Babylon)
    288–289, **288–289**
1600 to recent past time line
    292–293, **292–293**
terra-cotta warriors 300–301,
    300–301
transportation time line 62–63,
    62–63
U.S. history 308–323, **308–323**
U.S. time line 310–311, **310–311**
woman suffrage 312–313, **312–
    313**, 333
world history 286–309, **286–309**
Holidays see Festivals and holidays
Homo naledi 226, **226**
Honduras 368, **368**
Honeybees **197**, 208–209, **208–209**
Honnold, Alex **49**
Hopkinson, Francis 316
Hornbein, Thomas 51
Horsfield's tarsiers **7**
Hot-air balloons **299**
Hot springs 88–89, **88–89, 124**
Hot Springs, Arkansas 89
Howland Island 323
Hubble Space Telescope 30, 32
Huis, Arnold van 254
Human origins
    human ancestors 224–227,
        224–227
    migrations 228–229
    in movies 225
    Neanderthals 230–231, **230–
        231**
    time line 222–223, **222–223**
Humans
    gender 258–259, **258–259**
    map of urban population growth
        378–379
    science of 218–279
    see also Culture; Food; Health
        and medicine

Hummingbirds **196,** 200–201,
    200–201
Humpback whales 75, **188**
Hunga Tonga-Hunga Ha'ipi, Polyne-
    sia 116
Hungary 368, **368**
Hurricanes 98, 104–105, **104–105,**
    338, 365, 375
Hydroelectricity 332
Hydrothermal vents 355
Hyner View State Park, Pennsylva-
    nia 47

I

Ice, Arctic 360, **365**
Ice caps **10–11**
Icebergs **351**
Iceland
    flag and facts 368, **368**
    history of democracy 294
    hot springs 88–89, **88–89**
    @natgeo photos **49**
    urbanization 243
    volcanoes 107, 117
Idaho: state flag **318**
Igbo society 294
Illinois: state flag **319**
Immigration map 24–25
India
    culture 232, **232**
    extremes 52, 53
    flag and facts 368, **368**
    history of democracy 295
    holidays 249
    land claims 344
    Nat Geo explorers 41
    @natgeo photos **77**
    national parks 80–81, **80–81**
    travel 65, 80–81, **80–81**
    urbanization 243
Indian Ocean **187**, 358–359
Indiana: state flag **319**
Indonesia
    Borneo **17**
    disappearing languages
        239
    flag and facts 368, **368**
    hot springs 89
    human ancestors 225, **225**
    Nat Geo explorers 41

number of islands 331
urbanization 243
volcanoes 107, 117
wildlife **7, 17, 173,** 183, **183**
Infectious agents 28-29, **28-29**
Innovations 56–57, **56–57,** 304–305, **304–305**
Insects
butterflies 169, **169,** 206–207, **206–207**
as food 254–255, **254–255**
fossils 162, **162**
honeybees **197**
Intelligence, animal 199, 203
International Union for Conservation of Nature (IUCN) **16**
Io (Jupiter's moon) 136, **136**
Iowa 317, **319**
Iran **48, 298,** 368, **368**
Iraq 368, **368**
Ireland 78–79, **78–79,** 368, **368**
Islam 246–247, 249, **249, 251**
Israel 345, 368, **368**
Istanbul, Turkey 243
Italy
flag and facts 368, **368**
food 68–69, **68–69**
hot springs 89
Nat Geo explorers 40
@natgeo photos **111**
refugee rescues **22–23**
volcanoes 107
IUCN (International Union for Conservation of Nature) **16**
Ivory Coast *see* Côte d'Ivoire

J

Jaguars **14–15**
Jakarta, Indonesia 243
Jamaica 368, **368**
James Webb Space Telescope (JWST) 30–33, **30–33**
Jani, Kila **251**
Japan
flag and facts 368, **368**
@natgeo photos **76, 334**
space exploration 126, 135
travel 65, 89
urbanization 243
volcanoes 107

washi paper 233
World War II 348
Jarvis Island 323
Java Trench, Indian Ocean 359
Jedediah Smith Redwoods State Park, California 47
Jefferson Memorial, Washington, D.C. **298**
Jellyfish 190–191, **190–191**
Jerusalem 247, 291
Jeter, Carmelita 57
John, King (England) 294
Johnson, Robert 286, 287
Johnston Atoll 323
Jones, John Paul 317
Jordan 345, 368, **368**
Joshua Tree NP, California 73
Judaism 246–247, 248, **248,** 249
Jupiter (planet) 123, **126–127,** 136, **136**
JWST (James Webb Space Telescope) 30–33, **30–33**

K

Kalahari Desert, Namibia **5**
Kalema-Zikusoka, Gladys 41
Kami Rita Sherpa 51
Kangaroos 181
Kansas 47, **319**
Karachi, Pakistan 243
Kashmir (region) 344
Katija, Kakani 40
Katmai NP, Alaska 73
Katydids **17**
Kayaking **47,** 84, **84**
Kazakhstan 368, **368**
Kelly, Scott 147, **147**
Kentucky 53, **53, 319**
Kenya **216–217,** 232, **236,** 369, **369**
Keoladeo NP, India 80, **80**
Kepler spacecraft 149
Key, Francis Scott 316
Khonso Im-Heb 303
Kidd, Kenneth 229
Kilauea (volcano), Hawaii 116, **116–117**
Kilimanjaro, Mount, Tanzania 65, 347
Kingman Reef **4, 48,** 323
Kinshasa, Democratic Republic of the Congo 243, 346
Kiribati **193,** 369, **369**

Koalas 181
Kookaburras 181
Kosovo 369, **369**
Krakatau, Indonesia 107, 117
Krill 363
Kuiper belt 128, 129
Kushite culture 296–297, **296–297**
Kuwait 243, 369, **369**
Kyrgyzstan 369, **369**

L

Lagos, Nigeria 242, 346
Laguna del Carbón, Argentina 330, 341
Lahore, Pakistan 243
Lakes 52, **52**
Landscapes, photos **334–335**
Languages 238–239
Lanham, J. Drew 204–205, **204–205**
Lanna, Leonardo 40
Laos 369, **369**
Lashley, Karl 263
Latvia 369, **369**
Laughing kookaburras 181
Leakey, Louis 185
Leatherback turtles 358, **373**
Lebanon 369, **369**
Lemaître, Georges 141
Lemurs **16,** 346
Lesotho 369, **369**
Lesser flamingos 216, **216–217**
Lewis, Isle of, Scotland **6**
Liberia 369, **369**
Libya 369, **369**
Liechtenstein 243, 369, **369**
Life science 154–217
birds 196–205, **196–205**
conservation 210–215, **210–215**
domains of life 160–161, **160–161**
fossils **162–163,** 162–165, 224–225, **224–225**
land animals 172–185, **172–185**
map of future of wildlife 376–377
@natgeo photos **172–173,** 186–**187, 196–197**
plants 166–171, **166–171**
sea life 186–195, **186–195**
time line 158–159, **158–159**
see also Conservation; Health and medicine; Insects; Plants

Light, sleep and 256–257, **256–257**
Light pollution 121
Lightning 101, **101, 111**
Lima, Peru 242
Line Islands **186**
Lions **172**
Lippincott, Donald 56
Lithium 108–109
Lithuania 369, **369**
Livestock 254, 255, 268–269,
    268–269
Lizards **213**
Lohmann, Ulla **34–35**
Lopez, Jennifer W. 142–143, **142–143**
Los Angeles, California 242, 245
Louisiana 21, **319**
Lousios Gorge, Greece 84
Lunar eclipses 123
Luxembourg 369, **369**

M

Ma Jun 20, 21, **21**
Macaques **173**
Macaws 202, **202, 290**
Madagascar **16,** 98, 346, 369, **369**
Magna Carta 294
Magpies 199
Mahatma Gandhi Marine NP, India
    81, **81**
Maine **319, 364**
Majumdar, Onkuri 41
Makemake (dwarf planet) 129, **129**
Malawi 369, **369**
Malaysia 369, **369**
Maldives 345, 369, **369**
Mali 369, **369**
Malraux, André 67
Malta 342, 369, **369**
Mammoth Cave, Kentucky 53, **53**
Manila, Philippines **76**
Manila Philippines 243
Maps
    adventure travel 84–85
    Africa 346
    Antarctic oceans 362–363
    Antarctica 350
    Arctic Ocean 360–361
    Asia 344
    Atlantic Ocean 355
    Australia & Oceania 348

biodiversity 376–377
Cantino Planisphere (1502)
    290–291
climate zones 98–99
disappearing languages 238–239
Europe 342
extreme weather events 374–375
future of wild life 376–377
human migration 228
iconic travel destinations 64–65
Indian Ocean 358–359
lithium 108–109
Nat Geo explorers 40–41
Neanderthal range 231
North America 338
ocean currents 353
ocean trends 354
oceans 352–353
Pacific Ocean 356–357
Pangaea 336–337
physical world 330–331
political world 332–333
religions 246–247
South America 340
urban population growth
    378–379
urbanization 242–243
U.S. national parks 72–73
worldwide immigration 24–25
Maracaibo, Lake, Venezuela 101
Marble 113, **113**
Maremma, Italy 89
Marrakech, Morocco 66, **66**
Mars (planet) 126, **126,** 132–133,
    132–133, 136, **136,** 147
Marshall, Greg 189, **189**
Marshall Islands 369, **369**
Martinique 107, 235
Maryland 47, **319**
Massachusetts: state flag **319**
Massafera, Grazielli **234–235**
Mather, John C. 33, **33**
Maui (island), Hawaii **110**
Mauna Kea, Hawaii 53
Mauritania 369, **369**
Mauritius 369, **369**
Mawsynram, India 53
Maxwell, Gavin 66
Maya 82–83, **82–83**
Mayflower Compact 294
McGowan, Kevin 199, **199**

Meaher, Timothy 306
Mealworms 255
Mecca, Saudi Arabia 247
Medicine *see* Health and medicine
Meditation 276
Meghalaya, India 53
Mekong River, China **20**
Memory 262–263, 273
Mercury (planet) 126, **126**
Messner, Reinhold 51
Meteor showers 123, **123**
Mexico
    culture 233, **233**
    flag and facts 369, **369**
    Mexico City 242, 246
    Nat Geo explorers 40
    @natgeo photos **76, 125**
    Riviera Maya 82–83, **82–83**
    underwater art **54–55**
    wildlife trade 202
Mice 260-261, 263, **263**
Michigan **236, 319**
Microbiome 272–273, **272–273**
Micronesia 369, **369**
Midway Islands 323
Migration, animal 71, **71,** 80, 169, **169,**
    197
Migration, human 22–25, **22–25,**
    228–229
Mijikenda people 232
Mimas (Saturn's moon) 137, **137**
Mindfulness 276–277, **276–277**
Minerals 112–113, **112–113**
Minnesota: state flag **319**
Miranda (Uranus's moon) 137, **137**
Mississippi: state flag **319**
Mississippi River **20–21,** 21
Missouri **20–21,** 317, **320**
Miura, Yuichiro 51
Mohs' scale 112, 113
Moldova 369, **369**
Mollusks 193, **193**
Monaco 369, **369**
Monahans Sandhills State Park,
    Texas 47
Monarch butterflies 169, **169**
Mongolia 85, **85,** 369, **369**
Monkeys 182, **182**
Monsoons 53
Montana: state flag **320**
Montenegro 369, **369**

Monument Valley, Arizona-Utah **335**
Moon 123, 130–131, **130–131,** 136,
   136, 143
Moons 136–137, **136–137**
Moore, Sir Patrick 120
Morocco
   Arab Spring 295
   flag and facts 369, **369**
   Marrakech 66, **66**
   @natgeo photos **365**
   travel along trade routes 70
   trilobites 163
Moscow, Russia 243
Moths **206–207**
Mountain climbing *see* Climbing
Mountain goats **172**
Mountains 53
Movies
   dinosaurs 162, **162**
   Ireland 79
   prehistory 225
   underwater worlds 54
   volcanoes 106, **106**
Mozambique 85, **85,** 369, **369**
Mumbai, India 243
Murray River, Australia 348
Museums 54–55, **54–55,** 87
Music 46, 148
Myanmar 25, **299,** 344, **345,** 369, **369**
Mývatn Nature Baths, Iceland **88–89**

N

Nagarahole NP, India 80, **80**
Namib-Naukluft NP, Namibia 90,
   90–91, 347
Namibia **5,** 90, **90–91,** 347, 369,
   369
Narragansett Bay, Rhode Island 47
Narwhals 361
NASA
   asteroid missions **134–135,** 135
   datanauts 143
   Jupiter missions 136
   Kepler spacecraft 149
   Mars missions 126, 132–133
   moon missions 130–131, 143
   solar system exploration 126–127,
     128
Nashville, Tennessee 64
Nastasen, King (Kush) 297

National Geographic
   explorers, map of 40–41
   Explorers-in-Residence 114–115,
     114–115
   Genographic Project 228, 231
   Photo Ark 212–213, **212–213**
National parks
   India 80–81, **80–81**
   U.S. 72–73
National September 11 Memorial &
   Museum, New York, New York
   314–315, **314–315**
Native Americans 238
Natron, Lake, Tanzania 216
Nauru 349, 370, **370**
Navassa Island 323
Neanderthals 230–231, **230–231**
Nebraska **320**
Nefertiti, Queen (Egypt) 302
Nepal 41, **240–241,** 370, **370**
Neptune (planet) **127,** 137, **137**
Netherlands 64, 370, **370,** 373
Neurons 260–261, **260–261**
Neuroplasticity 276
Neutrinos 147, **147**
Nevada 53, **251,** 320
New Guinea **250**
New Hampshire 47, **320**
New Horizons probe 127, 128
New Jersey **313,** 320
New Mexico **197,** 320, 321
New Year celebrations 249
New York **320**
New York, New York 242, **244,**
   314–315, **314–315,** 339
New Zealand
   cities 348
   dependencies 373
   flag and facts 370, **370**
   travel 70, 89
   voting rights 313, 333
Newton, Isaac 150
Nicaragua 84, **84,** 370, **370**
Niger 370, **370**
Nigeria **237,** 294, 346, 347, 370, **370**
Nile River, Africa 52, **52**
9/11 terrorist attacks 314–315
Nodosaur 164, **164–165**
Noonan, Fred 308, 309
Nordaustlandet, Norway **10–11**
Norgay, Tenzing 51

North America
   human origins 229
   map and facts 338–339
   urbanization 242
North Carolina: state flag **320**
North Dakota: state flag **320**
North Korea 370, **370**
North Macedonia 370, **370**
Northeast NP, Greenland 330
Northern lights **146**
Northern Mariana Islands **322**
Northern Sea Route 360
Northwest Passage 338
Norway **10–11, 187, 276–277,** 342,
   370, **370**
Notre Dame Cathedral, Paris, France
   299
Nubia 296–297, **296–297**
Nurhati, Intan Suci 41
Nuri, Sudan 296–297, **296–297**
Nuuk, Greenland 338

O

Oceania: map and facts 348–349
Oceans 352–363
   Antarctica 362–363
   Arctic Ocean 360–361
   Atlantic Ocean 354–355
   coral reefs, map of 354
   desalination 20, **20,** 21
   fishing industry 354
   Indian Ocean 358–359
   map of currents 353
   @natgeo photos **364–365**
   Pacific Ocean 356–357
   Pristine Seas project 114–115,
     114–115
   as regulators 21
   sea level rise 21
   sea surface temperatures 354
   thermohaline circulation 21
   trends 354
   volcanic islands 116–117, **116–117**
   see also Sea life
O'Connor, Sandra Day 313
Octopuses 194–195, **194–195**
Ohio **111,** 273, **320**
Oia, Santorini, Greece **343**
Okanogan-Wenatchee National
   Forest, Washington 47

Oklahoma **320**
Olympic Games 57
Oman 370, **370**
100-meter dash 56–57, **56–57**
Oort Cloud 129
Orangutans 183, **183**
Oregon 73, **320**
Osaka, Japan 243
Otemanu, Mount, Tahiti **349**
Owens, Jesse 56
Owls **197**
Oysters 193

P

Pacific Coast Highway, California 64
Pacific Ocean
    Challenger Deep 52
    hurricanes **104–105**
    map and facts 356–357
Pakicetus 189
Pakistan 24, **125,** 344, 370, **370**
Palau 370, **370**
Paleontology see Dinosaurs; Fossils
Palmyra Atoll 323
Pamukkale, Turkey 89
Panama 338, 370, **370**
Pandas, giant **173**
Pangaea 336–337
Pantanal, South America 340
Papahānaumokuākea Marine
    National Monument, Hawaii 357
Papua New Guinea **196, 237,** 243,
    349, 370, **370**
Paragliding **48,** 51
Paraguay 238, 332, 340, 370, **370**
Parakeets **203**
Paralympics 61, **61**
Paris, France 67, **67, 236,** 242, **299**
Parrots 202–203, **202–203**
Patagonia, Argentina-Chile 42–43,
    42–43, 115, **341**
Paul, Alice 312
Pelosi, Nancy 313
Penguins **110, 196**
Pennsylvania 47, **320**
Pepperberg, Irene 203, **203**
Performance-enhancing drugs 57
Perfume 233, **233**
Perseids meteor shower 123, **123**
Persepolis (site), Iran **298**

Persian Empire **298**
Persian language 344
Peru
    asylum-seekers 24
    Chinchero **241**
    disappearing languages 238
    flag and facts 370, **370**
    @natgeo photos **237**
    Quechua-speaking people 232,
        232
Pets 178–179, **178–179**
Philippines 16, **16, 76,** 278, **278–279,**
    370, **370**
Phobos (Mars's moon) 136, **136**
Photo Ark 212–213, **212–213**
Photography
    aerial views **124–125**
    birds **196–197**
    Earth **110–111, 124–125**
    history **298–299**
    land life **172–173**
    landscape **334–335**
    ocean **364–365**
    people **250–251**
    sea life **186–187**
    traditions **236–237**
    travel **76–77**
Photosynthesis 167
Pigs 254, 255, 268
Pinwheel Galaxy **150**
Planets 123, 126–129, **126–129;** see
        also specific planets
Plants
    flowers for hummingbirds 201
    fossils 162, **162**
    herbs & spices 274–275, **274–275**
    kingdom 161, **161**
    microscopic view 166–167,
        166–167
    seed vault 342
    talking trees 170–171, **170–171**
    wildflowers 168, **168,** 169, **169**
Plastics 214–215, **214–215**
Platypuses 181
Pledge of Allegiance 317
Pluto (dwarf planet) 128, **128,** 137, **137**
Poland 370, **370**
Polar bears **21**
Pollination 208–209, **208–209**
Pollution 20, 121
Polynesia 64, 71, 116, **186, 193**

Ponta do Ouro Partial Marine
        Reserve, Africa **154–155**
Population
    largest cities 242–243
    world 242
Porcupine Caribou Herd 59
Porgera people **237**
Port Clinton, Ohio **111**
Portugal 370, **370**
Post, Wiley 309
Poultry 268–269
Prehistory time line 284–285, **284–285**
Primate family tree 182–183, **182–183**
Pristine Seas project 114–115, **114–115**
Psychobiome 272–273, **272–273**
Púcon, Chile 89
Pueblo peoples 246
Puerto Rico **322, 365**
Pulsars **146**
Pyramids 64, 296–297, **296–297,**
        299, 346

Q

Qatar 370, **370**
Qin Shi Huang Di, Emperor (China)
        300–301
Quechua-speaking peoples 232,
        232, 237
Quolls 180–181, **180–181**

R

Radiation, space 146–147, **146–147**
Railroads 70, **70**
Rainbows **110, 298**
Rainforests 84
Ramirez, Steve **262,** 262–263
Rankin, Jeannette 313
Ravens 199, **199**
Red kangaroos 181
Reefs see Coral reefs
Reflection Canyon, Utah **6–7**
Refugees **22–23, 251**
    map 24–25
Reilly, Kevin 55
Religion
    holidays 248–249, **248–249**
    India 232, **232**
    Mexico 233, **233**
    mythical birds 199

@natgeo photos **298, 299**
world map 246–247
see also specific religions
Resigaro (language) 238
Rey, H. A. 120
Rhode Island 47, **320**
Ricard, Matthieu **240**
Ring-tailed lemurs **16**
Rio de Janeiro, Brazil **110, 234–235, 237,** 242, 245
Rising Star cave, South Africa 226–227, **226–227**
Rivers 52, **52**
Riviera Maya, Mexico 82–83, **82–83**
Rock climbing *see* Climbing
Rock Island State Park, Tennessee 47
Rocky Mountain NP, Colorado 73
Rocky Mountains, North America 70, 89, 98, 102, **102–103, 172**
Rogers, Lynn 177, **177**
Roman Catholicism 248, 278, **278–279,** 342
Romania 370, **370**
Romero, Jordan 51
Rosemary 166–167, **166–167**
Ross, Betsy 317
Rossini, Gioacchino Antonio 289
Rotorua, New Zealand 89
Running 56–57, **56–57**
Russia
    disappearing languages 239
    flag and facts 343, 370, **370**
    Franz Josef Land 115
    Lake Baikal 52
    @natgeo photos **236, 251**
    space exploration 127
    travel 65, 70
    as world's largest country 333
Rwanda 313, 370, **370**

S

Safaris 71, **71**
La Sagrada Família, Barcelona, Spain 342
Saguaro NP, Arizona 73
Sahara, Africa 331
Saint Kitts and Nevis 339, 370, **370**
Saint Laurent, Yves 66
Saint Lucia 370, **370**

Saint Vincent and Grenadines 370, **370**
Sala, Enric **48,** 114–115, **114–115**
Salar De Arizaro, Argentina **125**
Salas y Gomez, Pacific Ocean 357
Saltwater crocodiles 75
Sammu-ramat, Queen (Babylon) 288–289, **288–289**
Samoa 370, **370**
San Marino 370, **370**
Sanchez, Oz 61, **61**
Sand dunes **5,** 90, **90–91**
Sandhill cranes **197**
Santorini, Greece 117, **343**
São Paulo, Brazil 242
São Tomé and Principe 370, **370**
Sartore, Joel 212–213, **213**
Saturn (planet) 123, 127, **127,** 137, **137**
Saudi Arabia 313, 370, **370**
Scarlet macaws **202**
Schultes, Richard Evans 241
Scotland **6, 299,** 342
Scuba diving *see* Diving
Sculpture, underwater 54–55, **54–55**
Sea anemones **187**
Sea eagles 75
Sea ice 360
Sea kayaking **47**
Sea level rise 21
Sea life 186–195
    coral reefs 74–75, **74–75, 81, 349,** 354
    jellyfish 190–191, **190–191**
    mollusks 193, **193**
    @natgeo photos **186–187**
    octopuses 194–195, **194–195**
    sea shells 192, **192**
    whales 188–189, **188–189**
SEA-ME-WE (submarine cable) 358
Sea squirts 359
Sea surface temperatures 354
Sea turtles 75, 358, **373**
Seals **186, 187**
Seamounts **365**
Semiramis (mythical queen) 288–289, **288–289**
Semon, Richard 263
Senegal 40, 370, **370**
Seoul, South Korea **77**
September 11 terrorist attacks 314–315

Serbia 370, **370**
Serengeti NP, Tanzania 71, **71, 335**
Seychelles **172,** 347, 371, **371**
Shamshi-Adad V, King (Babylon) 289
Shanghai, China 67, **67,** 243, **280–281,** 380, **380–381**
Sharks 75, **186, 187**
Shells 192, **192**
Shenandoah NP, Virginia 73
Shenzhen, China 243, 245
Sherpas 51
Shiffrin, Richard 263
Shinkansen Trans-Siberian Railway 70
Shipwrecks 338
Shooting stars *see* Meteor showers
Siena, Tuscany, Italy **111**
Sierra Leone 371, **371**
Sikhism **229,** 248, **248**
Silva, Sara Graça da 286
Silver foxes 179
Sima Qian (historian) 301
Simard, Suzanne 166, **166,** 170
Simenon, Georges 67
Sinai Peninsula, Egypt 85
Singapore 371, **371**
Skywatching 118–123
    constellations 118–122, **118–122**
    events (2021) 123
    summer sky 120–121, **120–121**
    winter sky 118–119, **118–119**
Slave ships 306–307, **306–307**
Sleep 252–253, **252–253,** 256–257, **256–257**
Slovakia 371, **371**
Slovenia 371, **371**
Smooth cauliflower coral 75
Snow **110, 111**
Solar eclipses 123
Solar system 126–139
    dwarf planets 128–129, **128–129**
    exploration 126–127, **126–127**
    key features 129
    moons beyond ours 136–137, **136–137**
    space science time line 138–139, **138–139**
    see also Moon; *specific planets*
Solomon Islands 371, **371**
Somalia 25, 371, **371**
Sotomayor, Sonia 313

South Africa
    flag and facts 371, **371**
    history of democracy 295
    human ancestors 225, **225,**
        226–227, **226–227**
    @natgeo photos **111**
South America
    map (1502) 290
    map and facts 340–341
    urbanization 242
    wildlife 340
South Carolina 47, **321**
South Dakota 73, **321**
South Korea **77,** 371, **371**
South Sudan 25, 371, **371**
Southern cassowaries 181
Southern Line Islands **186**
Southern Ocean 362
Space
    cosmic radiation 146–147, **146–**
        147, 151
    human body in 147
    time line 138–139, **138–139**
    trends 30–33, **30–33**
    see also Constellations; Moon;
        NASA; specific planets
Space shuttles 131
Space telescopes 30–33, **30–33**
SpaceX 126
Spain **229,** 233, 342, 371, **371**
Spectral tarsiers 182, **182**
Spelman, Lucy 183, **183**
Sperm whales **188, 189**
Spices 274–275, **274–275**
Sports 56–61, **56–61**
Squirrels **5**
Squirts 359
Sri Lanka 371, **371**
St. Croix, U.S. Virgin Islands **373**
St. Lawrence, Gulf of **187**
St. Lucia **71**
Stars 119, 144–145, **144–145, 150;**
        see also Constellations
Steeple Jason, Falkland Islands 340
Stenness, Stones of, Stenness **299**
Steroids 57
Stingrays **186**
Stone, Marc **2–3**
Stones of Stenness, Scotland **299**
Strom, Greg 61
Stubblefield, Katie 270–271, **270–271**

Sudan 24, **52,** 296–297, **296–297,**
        371, **371**
Suffrage 312–313, **312–313,** 333
Sulawesi crested black macaques **173**
Sumatra (island), Indonesia 183
Sumatran tigers **212–213**
Summer Triangle (asterism) 120
Sunflowers **8–9**
Superior, Lake, Canada-U.S. 47, **47,**
        52, 52
Supermoons 123
Supernovae 144–145, **144–145**
Supervolcanoes 106, **106**
Supreme Court, U.S. 313
Surfing **49,** 60, **60**
Suriname 341, 371, **371**
Sustainable living 244–245, **244–**
        245; see also Earth Day every
        day
Suwannee River, Florida **124**
Svalbard, Norway **187**
Svalbard archipelago, Norway **10–11**
Svalbard Global Seed Vault, Norway
        342
Sweden 371, **371**
Switzerland **48,** 70, **70,** 371, **371**
Sydney, Australia 65
Syria 25, 232, 371, **371**

T

Tabei, Junko 51
Taft, William Howard 317
Tahiti 64, **349**
Taj Mahal, Agra, India 65
Tajikistan 371, **371**
Tamarins 182, **182**
Tambora, Mount, Indonesia 107
Tangkoko Nature Reserve, Indonesia
        173
Tanzania
    flag and facts 371, **371**
    flamingos 216
    Gombe Stream NP **184,** 184–185
    human ancestors 225, **225**
    Kilimanjaro 65, 347
    Serengeti NP 71, **71, 335**
Taoism 249, **249**
Tarsiers **7,** 182, **182**
Tasmanian devils 181, 348
Tatum, Vince 55

Tehrani, Jamie 286
Telescopes 30–33, **30–33,** 144
Tennessee 47, 64, **321**
Terra-cotta warriors 300–301,
        300–301
Terror, H.M.S. 338
Terrorism 314–315
Texas 47, 73, **321**
Thailand 371, **371**
Thayore (language) 239
Thermohaline circulation 21
Thiessen, Mark 102, **102**
Thunderstorms 101, **101, 110**
Tianjin, China 243
Tickle, Evelyn 55
Tigers 80, **80, 172, 212–213**
Timor-Leste 371, **371**
Titan (Saturn's moon) 137, **137**
Titanic, R.M.S. 355
Titicaca, Lake, Bolivia 340
Toads 180
Togo 371, **371**
Tokyo, Japan **76,** 86–87, **86–87,** 243,
        334
Tompkins, Doug 42, 43
Tompkins, Kristine McDivitt **42,** 42–43
Tonga 371, **371**
Tortoises **172**
Tourtellot, Jonathan 71, **71**
Track and field 56–57, **56–57**
Trains 70, **70**
Trans-Canada Highway 17, **17**
Trans-Siberian Railroad 70
Transportation time line 62–63,
        62–63
Travel, adventure 46–47, **46–47**
Travel, classic 62–75
    best cities 66–67, **66–67**
    Great Barrier Reef, Australia
        74–75, **74–75**
    greatest expeditions 70–71,
        70–71
    map of iconic destinations 64–65
    map of U.S. national parks 72–73
    taste of Italy 68–69, **68–69**
    transportation time line 62–63,
        62–63
Travel trends 76–89
    Galway, Ireland 78–79, **78–79**
    Iceland's hot springs 88–89,
        88–89

India's national parks 80–81, **80–81**
map of adventure travel 84–85
Maya marvels 82–83, **82–83**
@natgeo photos **76–77**
Tokyo, Japan 86–87, **86–87**
Trees 98, 166, 170–171, **170–171, 347**
Trekking 70, **70,** 90, **90–91;** *see also* Climbing
Trilobites 163, **163**
Trinidad and Tobago 235, 371, **371**
Tristan da Cunha Islands 117
Triton (Neptune's moon) 137, **137**
Trolltunga rock formation, Norway **276–277**
Tulips 64
Tulum (site), Mexico **82–83,** 83
Tunisia **77,** 295, **295,** 371, **371**
Turkey (country) 24, 89, 371, **371**
Turkey (food) 268
Turkmenistan 371, **371**
Turtles 75, 358, **373**
Tuscany, Italy **111**
Tutankhamun, Pharaoh 302, **302,** 303
Tuvalu 371, **371**
Twins **251**

U

Uganda 24, 41, **251,** 255, 371, **371**
Ukraine 371, **371**
Underwater archaeology 296–297, **297,** 338
Underwater art 54–55, **54–55**
United Arab Emirates 372, **372**
United Kingdom **251,** 294, **299,** 372, **372,** 373
United Nations 313, 372, **372**
United States
    asylum-seekers 24
    colonial era 294–295
    Constitution 295, **295,** 323
    flag and facts 316–317, **316–317,** 339, 372, **372**
    greener cities 245
    history 310–323
    history of democracy 294–295
    holidays 249
    Nat Geo explorers 40
    state flags **318–321**

territories, flags of 322–323, **322–323**
travel 64, 72–73, 89
women in Congress 313
Universe 140–151
    birth of 140–141, **140–141**
    dark matter **140,** 140–141, 150–151, **150–151**
    distances 145
    exoplanets 148–149, **148–149**
    Lopez, Jennifer W. 142–143, **142–143**
    space radiation 146–147, **146–147**
    star explosions 144–145, **144–145**
    time line 138–139, **138–139**
Unsoeld, Willi 51
Uranus (planet) **127,** 137, **137**
Urbanization 242–245, **244–245,** 378–379
Uruguay 243, 372, **372**
U.S. Virgin Islands **322, 373**
Utah
    Bonneville Salt Flats 152, **152–153**
    flag and facts **321**
    @natgeo photos **334, 335**
    Reflection Canyon **6–7**
Uzbekistan 372, **372**

V

Valle de la Luna, Chile **53**
Valletta, Malta 342
Van Lawick, Hugo 185
Vandebroek, Ina 275, **275**
Vanuatu 372, **372**
Vaquita 189
Vatican City 343, 372, **372**
Venezuela 101, 340, 372, **372**
Venice, Italy 291
Venus (planet) **126**
Vermilion Cliffs National Monument, Arizona-Utah **334**
Vermont: state flag **321**
Vesuvius, Mount, Italy 107
Victoria Falls, Zambia-Zimbabwe 71
Vietnam 372, **372**
Vilankulo, Mozambique 85, **85**
Vinson, Carl G. 350
Vinson Massif, Antarctica 350, 351
Vinther, Jakob 164

Virgin Islands, U.S. **322, 373**
Virginia 73, **321**
Vogelkop superb bird-of-paradise **196**
Volcanoes 106–107, **106–107,** 116–117, **116–117, 125, 335**
Voltaire 289
Vostok Station, Antarctica 53
Voting rights 312–313, **312–313,** 333

W

Wake Island 323
Walkerton, Ohio 273
Walruses **187**
Wasfia, Nazreen 41
Washington (state) 47, **321**
Washington, D.C. **298,** 323, **323**
Watanabe, Tamae 51
Water
    desalination 20, **20,** 21
    pollution 20, **20,** 21
    rethinking resources 20–21, **20–21**
    sea level rise 21
    trends 18–21, **18–21**
    weather trends 18–19, **18–19**
Weather
    clouds 100, **100**
    extremes 53
    lightning 101, **101**
    map of extreme events 374–375
    @natgeo photos **110–111**
    water trends 20–21, **20–21**
Webb, James 31
Weddell seals **186**
Wee, Darryl Jingwen 86, **86**
Wendover, Peter 316
West Virginia: state flag **321**
Whale sharks **187**
Whales 75, 188–189, **188–189,** 361, 363
White-bellied sea eagles 75
Wickey, Allison 55
Wildebeests **71**
Wildfires 102, **102–103, 111**
Wildflowers 168, **168,** 169, **169**
Wildlife trade 202, 203
Wilhelm, Mount, Papua New Guinea 349
Wilson, Woodrow 317

Wind Cave NP, South Dakota 73
Wisconsin 47, **47, 321**
Wolfe, Benjamin 266
Wolves **173,** 178, **178**
Women
    political firsts 313
    suffrage 312–313, **312–313,** 333
Woods, Lorna Gail 307, **307**
World Trade Center, New York, New
    York 314–315
World War II 348
Wynn-Grant, Rae 174–175, **174–175**
Wyoming **92–93,** 312, **321**

X
Xi'an, China 300–301, **300–301**
Xinjiang, China 53

Y
Yangtze River, China 20
Yasuni NP, Ecuador **14–15**
Yellowstone NP, U.S. **92–93,** 106, **124**
Yemen **364,** 372, **372**
Yoho NP, Canada 84, **84**
Yucatán Peninsula, Mexico 82–83,
    82–83

Z
Zambezi River, Zambia-Zimbabwe 71
Zambia 71, 372, **372**
Zebras **71**
Zimbabwe 71, 372, **372**
Zwicky, Fritz 150

Since 1888, the National Geographic Society has funded more than 13,000 research, exploration, and preservation projects around the world. National Geographic Partners distributes a portion of the funds it receives from your purchase to National Geographic Society to support programs including the conservation of animals and their habitats.

National Geographic Partners
1145 17th Street NW
Washington, DC 20036-4688 USA

Get closer to National Geographic explorers and photographers, and connect with our global community. Join us today at nationalgeographic .com/join

For rights or permissions inquiries, please contact National Geographic Books Subsidiary Rights: bookrights@natgeo.com

ISBN: 978-1-4262-2155-2

Printed in Italy

20/EV/1

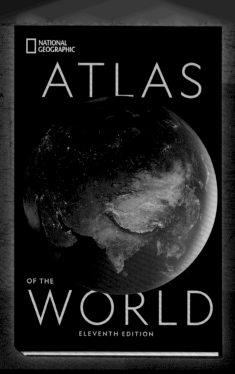

ATLAS OF THE WORLD

ELEVENTH EDITION

YOUR REFERENCE EXPERTS

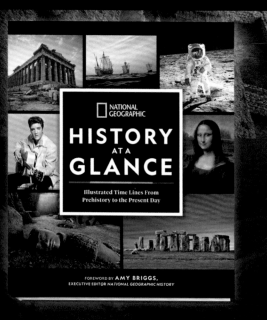

HISTORY AT A GLANCE

Illustrated Time Lines From Prehistory to the Present Day

FOREWORD BY **AMY BRIGGS**, EXECUTIVE EDITOR NATIONAL GEOGRAPHIC HISTORY

AVAILABLE WHEREVER BOOKS AND MAPS ARE SOLD
and at NationalGeographic.com/Books

f NatGeoBooks   **y** @NatGeoBooks

NATIONAL GEOGRAPHIC

© 2020 National Geographic Partners, LLC